Countertransference in Perspective

Dedication

In memory of Malca K. Aleksandrowicz
and Yuad S. Brisker

Countertransference in Perspective

The Double-Edged Sword of the Patient–Therapist Emotional Relationship

Edited by
Dov R. Aleksandrowicz, MD
and Anna O. Aleksandrowicz

SUSSEX
ACADEMIC
PRESS
Brighton • Chicago • Toronto

2 4 6 8 10 9 7 5 3 1

First published in 2017 by
SUSSEX ACADEMIC PRESS
PO Box 139
Eastbourne BN24 9BP

and in the United States of America by
SUSSEX ACADEMIC PRESS
Independent Publishers Group
814 N. Franklin Street, Chicago, IL 60610

and in Canada by
SUSSEX ACADEMIC PRESS (CANADA)

British Library Cataloguing in Publication Data
A CIP catalogue record for this book is available from the British Library.

Library of Congress Cataloging-in-Publication Data
Names: Aleksandrowicz, Dov R., editor. | Aleksandrowicz, Anna O., editor.
Title: Countertransference in perspective : the double-edged sword of the patient– therapist emotional relationship / edited by Dov R. Aleksandrowicz and Anna O. Aleksandrowicz.
Description: Brighton ; Chicago : Sussex Academic Press, 2017. | Includes bibliographical references and index.
Identifiers: LCCN 2016032687 | ISBN 9781845197919 (pbk : alk. paper)
Subjects: | MESH: Countertransference (Psychology) | Psychotherapy—methods
Classification: LCC RC480 | NLM WM 62 | DDC 616.89/14—dc23
LC record available at https://lccn.loc.gov/2016032687

MIX
Paper from responsible sources
FSC® C013056
FSC www.fsc.org

Typeset and designed by Sussex Academic Press, Brighton & Eastbourne.
Printed by TJ International, Padstow, Cornwall.

Contents

The Contributors

CHAPTER ONE

Dov R. Aleksandrowicz, MD, former Associate Professor of Psychiatry at Ben-Gurion University, Beer Sheva, Israel, was the President of the Israeli Psychoanalytic Society, and is a Training and Supervising analyst at the Israel Institute. He is a member of the American Psychoanalytic Association and the International Psychoanalytic Association, and a recipient of the Gustav Bychowski Prize in Psychoanalysis. A founding member of the International Neuro-Psychoanalysis Society, Prof. Aleksandrowicz is a co-founder of the Israeli Forum of Neuro-Psychoanalysis. He is the author of numerous professional publications, in five languages, including *The Injured Self: The Psychopathology and Psychotherapy of Developmental Deviations* (Karnac Books 2011, with Malca K. Aleksandrowicz, PhD), *Developmental Deviations and Personality: Theoretical Issues and Therapeutic Applications* (Taylor & Francis, US, 1989 with Malca K. Aleksandrowicz, PhD); and *Formation of Personality in Early Childhood* (in Hebrew, Papyrus, University of Tel Aviv, Israel, 1987, with Malca K. Aleksandrowicz, PhD).

Anna O. Aleksandrowicz is a science writer who covers current trends in science, technology, and healthcare. A former managing editor at Opus Communications (Massachusetts, USA), she is the author of numerous books in technology and the editor of the first comprehensive report on healthcare accreditation (1998) as well as journal publications in a wide variety of topics.

CHAPTER TWO

Tali R. Marron is a child and educational clinical psychologist. She is currently a PhD student in psychology and brain science at Bar-Ilan University, Israel. Her PhD specializes in the field of Neuro-psychoanalysis. Ms. Marron uses fMRI brain scanning to test psychoanalytic tools and theories. She is an active member of the Israeli Forum of Neuro-Psychoanalysis and has a background in film studies.

CHAPTER THREE

Gustaw Sikora MD, PhD, is a psychoanalyst and psychiatrist, a member of the British Psycho-Analytic Society and the Institute of Psychoanalysis in London; trained in psychiatry and psychotherapy in Poland, he worked as a consultant at Jagiellonian University Hospital in Krakow and held a teaching post at the Psychotherapy Department at Jagiellonian University as a lead at the Psychoanalytic Unit. A founder and the first director of the Personality Disorder Unit at Babinski Memorial Hospital at Krakow, he later trained as a psychoanalyst at BPAS in London.

Dr. Sikora currently works in private practice and as a consultant at the London Clinic of Psychoanalysis. He is a member of the London Philosophy and Psychoanalysis Group and the interdisciplinary project New Imago Forum, which gathers academics and psychoanalysts at Jesus College, Oxford University annually.

Dr. Sikora is also a founding member of the International Neuro-Psychoanalytic Association. He has published several papers and book chapters, and regularly presents papers to conferences and congresses. His most recent papers presented are: "Some notes on repetition compulsion", Psychotherapy Congress in Krakow 2014; and "Some notes on conservatism of drives", Annual Neuro-Psychoanalytic Congress in Amsterdam 2015.

CHAPTER FOUR

Yael Lahav, PhD, is a practicing clinical psychologist, and is presently a research fellow in the I-Core Research Center for Mass Trauma at Tel Aviv University, and a postdoctoral fellow at the University of Southern Denmark. Dr. Lahav received her PhD from Tel Aviv University (2015).

As a clinical psychologist, Dr. Lahav specializes in the treatment of patients suffering from personality disorders and adult survivors of trauma. She completed her clinical internship in two Israeli health establishments: the Mental Health Clinic at the Sourasky Medical Centre in Tel Aviv (2007–2010), and the Kaplan Hospital in Rehovot (2006). During and after her internship (2009–2012) she also held a clinical psychologist position at the Lotem Center at the Sourasky Medical Centre, Tel Aviv, Israel.

Dr. Lahav's research focuses on traumatic stress and particularly on the psychological sequelae of war captivity and sexual abuse. More specifically, Dr. Lahav is investigating the implications of continuous exposure to trauma on the somatic and interpersonal domains. In addition, in her recent studies Dr. Lahav has assessed the consequences of ostensible positive effects of trauma (i.e., post-traumatic growth) among trauma survivors. Her observations and findings have raised questions regarding the essence of post-traumatic growth, thus suggesting that it may have a defensive as well as illusory quality.

Zivya Seligman, PhD, is a supervising clinical psychologist. She is the founding director of the Lotem outpatient clinic for adult survivors of childhood sexual abuse suffering from complex post-traumatic stress disorder, dissociative disorders, and related disorders at the Tel Aviv Souraski Medical Center. She was the founder and the academic director of the Bar Ilan University's postgraduate program for training therapists in the treatment of sexual trauma. She is currently a clinical lecturer at the Center for Trauma Studies and Tel Aviv University. Since 2005, she is the clinical consultant to the "Theater of Testimony," a project for Holocaust survivors. Dr. Seligman co-edited, together with Professor Zahava Solomon, *Critical and Clinical Perspectives on Incest* (2004). Dr. Seligman also co-edited, together with Dr. Ofra Eshel, *Shadows of Sexual Abuse in Psychotherapy* (in press).

Zahava Solomon, PhD, is a Professor of Psychiatric Epidemiology and Social Work at Tel Aviv University and director of the center of excellence for the study of mass trauma. She received both her BA (1973) and MA (1976) from the University of Haifa, Israel and her PhD in Psychiatric Epidemiology from the University of Pittsburgh, (1980).

Prof. Solomon joined the IDF (Israeli Defense Force) in 1981 and served as head of the Research Branch in the Medical Corps between the years 1981–1992. Her military rank is Lt. Colonel.

In 1990, Prof. Solomon joined Tel Aviv University, where she has served as Dean of the Bob Shapell Social Work School, Dean of Special Programs at Tel Aviv University, and as the head of the Adler Center for the Study of Child Welfare and Protection.

CHAPTER FIVE

Major (Res.) **Moshe Z. Abramowitz** MD, MHA, is a former acting commander of the Israel Defense Forces (IDF) Mental Health Department Research Branch, Dr. Abramowitz is Clinical Senior Lecturer of Psychiatry at the Hebrew University Medical School, and a senior Psychiatrist at Madan Group Mental Health Division, Israel.

Col. (Res.) **Haim Y. Knobler**, MD, MPA, is a former commander of the IDF Mental Health Department, Dr. Knobler is a Clinical Associate Professor at the Hebrew University Medical School and Peres Academic Center; a psychiatric advisor to the IDF Disabled Veterans Organization; and the Head of the Madan Group Mental Health Division, Israel.

Lt. Col. (Res.) **Yoram Ben Yehuda**, is a Senior (specialist-instructor)

Clinical and Medical Psychologist; a former commander of the Combat PTSD Unit, IDF Mental Health Department; and the director of the "Ways" ("Drachim") Psychological Institute.

Dov Aleksandrowicz, MD (see Chapter 1)

CHAPTER SIX

Katarzyna Prot-Klinger, MD, is a psychiatrist and psychotherapist, investigating the problems of psychological consequences of trauma for many years now. She conducts individual and group psychotherapy of Holocaust survivors and is the author of many publications on this subject based on her clinical experience and scientific research.

She is the author of the book *Życie po Zagładzie. Skutki traumy u ocalałych z Holocaustu – świadectwa z Polski i Rumunii* (Life after Holocaust: Effects of trauma among the survivors. Testimony documentation from Poland and Romania).

Dr. Prot-Klinger worked for many years in community psychiatry as a head of the Mental Health Center at the Institute of Psychiatry and Neurology in Warsaw. Since 2012, she has held the position of a professor in the Faculty of Psychology at the Maria Grzegorzewska Academy of Special Education, Warsaw, Poland.

CHAPTER SEVEN

Katarzyna Prot-Klinger, MD (see chapter 6).

Krzysztof Szwajca, MD, PhD, is a psychiatrist and psychotherapist. A researcher at the Department of Child and Adolescent in the Psychiatry Department of the Jagiellonian University, Dr. Szwajca is a student of the late Prof. Maria Orwid and a member of her team, which works with the chronic trauma of war, including the children of the Holocaust, second generation Holocaust survivors, and the Roma victims of the Holocaust.

The subject of his PhD dissertation was transgenerational transmission of trauma in the descendants of Holocaust survivors. Dr. Szwajca is the author of about 150 scientific publications and presentations.

Łukasz Biedka, MA, is a psychologist and psychotherapist from Warsaw. Since 1996, he has been a member of the therapeutic team of Prof. Maria Orwid, providing psychological support to Holocaust survivors and their adult children.

Kazimierz Bierzyński, MA, is a clinical psychologist, psychotherapist and supervisor of the Polish Psychiatric Association and the Polish Psychological Association. Mr. Bierzyński is a lecturer at Jagiellonian University, and editor-in-chief of the Polish scientific journal *Psychotherapy.*

Author and co-author of many publications on psychotherapy and research on the process of psychotherapy and psychotherapy of survivors of the Holocaust, Mr. Bierzyński's main area of interest is relations in psychotherapy. In the psychotherapeutic program developed for the survivors of the Holocaust, he acted as the supervisor of psychotherapy processes. After the death of Prof. Orwid, he led the psychotherapy of the group previously led by Prof. Orwid.

Ewa Domagalska-Kurdziel, MA, is a teacher and psychotherapist, now in private practice. She participated in the research program: "Psychosocial consequences of the Holocaust survivors in people and in the second generation of Holocaust survivors in Poland.", carried out under the direction of Prof. Maria Orwid. Today, Ms. Domagalska-Kurdziel is an active member of the therapeutic program for Holocaust survivors and second-generation survivors.

Ryszard Izdebski, MA, is a clinical psychologist and psychotherapist. Head of the Home Hospitalization Unit for Children and Adolescents at the Jagielonian University Hospital in Krakow, Mr. Izdebski is vice-president of the Siemacha Association. He is the winner of the Alina Margolis-Edelman Prize for Particular Merit for his activities in helping abused children. Mr. Izdebski is a long-time collaborator of the late Prof. Maria Orwid, and leads the group therapy program of the Children of the Holocaust.

Marta Agata Szwajca, MA, is a psychologist specializing clinical psychology. She completed a five-year course "Psychotherapy: Systemic–Psychodynamic model" organized by the Department of Family Therapy of the Jagiellonian University in Krakow.

Ms. Szwajca is a graduate of the Observation Seminary "Early Parent–Child Relationship," carried out by Alejandra Perez through the Anna Freud Centre for Children and Families in London. She works as a researcher in the Department of Psychiatry, Jagiellonian University, Krakow.

CHAPTER EIGHT

Elisabeth Brainin, MD, lives and works in Vienna. She is a psychiatrist, psychoanalyst, child analyst in private practice, and a training analyst with the Vienna Psychoanalytic Society (WPV/IPA). Until 2002, Dr. Brainin was the medical director of the Child Guidance Clinics in Vienna.

She has contributed to publications on child analysis, trauma, anti-Semitism, history of psychoanalysis, and the after-effects of persecution. She is on the editorial board of the journal *Kinderanalyse* and is a member of SEPEA (Société Européenne pour la Psychanalyse de l'Enfant et de l'Adolescent).

Samy Teicher has a diploma in psychology and is a psychoanalyst and child psychoanalyst, member of the Vienna Psychoanalytic Society (WPV/IPA), training analyst for psychoanalytic psychotherapy (WPA/WPV) and a training group analyst (ÖAGG – Austrian Study Group on Group Therapy) with coaching and supervision in private practice in Vienna. He is a member of SEPEA (Société Européenne pour la Psychanalyse de l'Enfant et de l'Adolescent). He has contributed to publications on trauma and its after-effects, child analysis, anti-Semitism, and the history of psychoanalysis.

His latest publication is *Dream and Fantasy in Child Analysis*, Editors: Samy Teicher and Michael Gunter (London: Karnac, 2015).

CHAPTER NINE

Friedemann Pfäfflin, MD, is a psychiatrist, psychotherapist, and university teacher, who gained public attention in the field of forensic psychiatry and gender identity. From 1978 to 1992, Dr. Pfäfflin worked in the Department of Sexual Research in Mental Health and Psychiatric Clinic at University Medical Center Hamburg-Eppendorf. In 1992 he was appointed to a professorship for psychotherapy in Forensic Psychotherapy at the Clinic for Psychosomatic Medicine and Psychotherapy at the University Hospital of Ulm, where he worked until his retirement in 2010.

From 1995 to 1997 he was president of the Harry Benjamin International Gender Dysphoria Association, Inc. In 1997, together with Eli Coleman, he founded the journal *The International Journal of Transgenderism*.

His publications include *Gender reassignment: Essays on transsexuality* (Schattauer, Stuttgart, 1992) and *Transsexualism: Contributions to psychopathology, psychodynamics and history* (Enke: Stuttgart, 1993).

CHAPTER TEN

Aviva Edelman, MA, is a rehabilitation psychologist and neuropsychologist, who has worked at the Loewenstein Rehabilitation Hospital in Ra'anana, Israel for the last 25 years as part of the multidisciplinary team. She also conducts psychotherapy sessions in her private clinic.

Ms. Edelman specializes in traumatic brain injury as well as in other neurological problems, including stroke, spinal cord injuries and orthopedic problems. In addition, and often in relation to the physical injury, she treats patients with Post Concussion Syndrome (PCS) and Post-Traumatic Stress Disorder (PTSD).

Ms. Edelman also works with the hospital's Intensive Care Unit staff and with the families of patients suffering from low consciousness levels, accompanying them through the process of awakening from unconscious states, and investigating means of communication with the patients.

In addition to conventional psychotherapy, Ms. Edelman also uses non-verbal techniques, such as plastic art and somatosensory tools.

CHAPTER ELEVEN

Inbal Ben-Ami Bartal, PhD, is a post-doctoral Miller Fellow at the Integrative Biology Department, University of California, Berkeley, where she studies empathy and pro-social behavior. Dr. Bartal uses an integrative approach that combines physiological, cellular, and behavioral techniques to describe the neural mechanisms that give rise to helping behavior in rodents.

She holds a PhD and MA in Integrative Neuroscience from the University of Chicago, and an MSc in Biopsychology from Tel Aviv University, where she was part of the Adi Lautman Interdisciplinary Program for Outstanding Students.

Dr. Ben-Ami Bartal's work has been featured in the global media including *Time Magazine*, *Scientific American*, and *National Geographic,* and on PBS.

Anat Perry, PhD, is a postdoctoral researcher at the Helen Wills Neuroscience Institute, University of California, Berkeley, and will join the Department of Psychology, Hebrew University of Jerusalem, as a faculty member in 2017. She studies interpersonal interactions and social behavior using physiological (EEG and Dual EEG) and behavioral measures in healthy adults and in clinical populations.

Dr. Perry holds a PhD in Psychology from the Hebrew University of Jerusalem, an MA in Clinical Psychology from the Hebrew University of Jerusalem, and a BA in English Linguistics and Cognitive Sciences from the Hebrew University of Jerusalem, Israel.

Dr. Perry's publications have appeared in leading journals in her field, such as *Social Cognitive and Affective Neuroscience*; *Cognitive, Affective and Behavioral Neuroscience*; *NeuroImage* and *Psychoneuroendocrinology.*

Dr. Perry received among other prizes, the Marie Curie Postdoctoral Global Fellowship (GF), the Hebrew University's post-doctoral scholarship for outstanding women doctorate students, the Rothschild postdoctoral fellowship, the Alex Berger Prize for PhD Excellence, the Wolf Foundation Excellence Scholarship, and the Hoffman Leadership and Responsibility scholarship.

CHAPTER TWELVE

Anat Perry and **Inbal Ben-Ami Bartal** (see Chaper 11).

CHAPTER THIRTEEN
Dov Aleksandrowicz, MD (see Chapter 1).

CHAPTER FOURTEEN
Eric Leake, PhD., is an assistant professor of English at Texas State University. His areas of research include empathy, nonrational rhetorics, and writing pedagogy.

CHAPTER FIFTEEN
Dov Aleksandrowicz, MD (see Chapter 1).

Acknowledgements

The editors wish to thank all of the authors for their insightful contributions. We would also like to thank the following people for their invaluable assistance in the completion of this volume:

Karen Marron
Dr. Orley K. Marron
Alex Singer Lavi

The Editors and Publisher gratefully acknowledge the Israel Psychiatric Association, Archives of Psychiatry and Psychotherapy and The Israel Psychological Associationt for permission to use material in this volume from previously published works.

Part I

The History of Countertransference

Part I of this book, "The History of Countertransference", deals with the general aspects of the topic, including this introduction and a chapter by Tali Marron on the history of the concept of countertransference (Chapter Two). The chapter is a review of the concept's development from its early restrictive meaning, as coined by Freud (in "Observations on Transference-Love") through its expansion, mainly in the mid-century, and finally to its present use as a comprehensive term describing the complex emotions of a therapist in relation to the patient and to the therapeutic situation.

Marron argues that such an evolution reflects not only the progress in our understanding of the psychoanalytic process but also the deep cultural changes that occurred in Western societies during the last century, and are still going on, in our "post-modern" culture. One such change is the "transparency" fostered by the "social media culture". An example of such cultural influence on psychoanalytical thinking is the relationist school of psychoanalysis.

CHAPTER
ONE

Introduction to Countertransference: The Double-edged Sword

DOV R. ALEKSANDROWICZ AND
ANNA O. ALEKSANDROWICZ

> "(Compassion) is a double-edged tool. If you don't know how to handle it you had better not touch it, and above all you must steel your heart against it".
>
> STEFAN ZWEIG, *Impatience of the Heart*[1]

In psychoanalysis the term "countertransference", coined by Freud, describes the complex emotional relation between therapist and patient. The term is used, nowadays, in a broad sense, referring to the entire range of emotions experienced by the therapist/analyst covering many types of therapeutic process. Today's mental-health practitioners are called upon to deal with a wide variety of challenges, some of them highly emotionally-charged, such as child abuse, gender identity or catastrophic loss, and a therapist's countertransference reflects also his or her attitude to the issue which brought the patient into therapy.

This introduction chapter provides an overview of the countertransference concept, and describes the four parts of the volume, which cover the history of countertransference; a range of clinical challenges, analyzed by contributor colleagues with extensive experience in these and similar issues; recent findings regarding the biological roots that have implications for the understanding of countertransference; and a summary to the volume, which presents the overall conclusions to the findings presented in the three parts as well as potential implications for the future role of empathy in cosmopolitanism.

Introduction

We humans, like all mammals and probably all the more developed animals, are creatures of emotions. Affects drive our actions, our decisions and our relationships to a degree that science is demonstrating more and more extensively. Therefore, it is only to be expected that the emotional relationship between the patient and the psychoanalyst, and, to some extent, any healer, be a critical factor in the healing process (Balint, 1957).The term "countertransference", in its narrow meaning, i.e. the therapist's reaction to the patient's transference, is too restrictive to describe all that we know today about the therapist-patient emotional relationship, but it has been entrenched by custom, and we follow that tradition. In similar vein, we use the term "psychoanalysis" for simplicity's sake, referring equally to psychoanalysis and psychoanalytic psychotherapy.

A therapist's emotional state, especially the repressed or split-off parts of his or her personality can, and often are, a critical factor in the progress of an intervention. Far from being (supposedly) an objective healer, a "psychological surgeon" (Freud 1912), the therapist employs not a scalpel, but a truly "double-edged sword", whose power to both benefit – and injure – cannot be overestimated.

This book is intended for practitioners and students of mental health. It is a study of the emotional ambience in which the process of psychoanalysis (or any other intensive therapy) takes place. The name of this book, therefore, is a paraphrase of a quote from a novel by Stefan Zweig, *Impatience of the Heart*, (published in English under the name *Beware of Pity*[2]), which aptly describes the power and the antithetical nature of the transference-countertransference paradigm.

The capacity of countertransference to produce as well as its ability to resolve a therapeutic impasse, as well as its potential to harm the patient, the therapist or both, is illustrated by an example, which was recounted to us by a psychologist colleague (and is herein referred to as Kristie). She told me that a few years earlier she was seeing a patient with a serious personality disorder, manifested by self-destructive, reckless behavior, apathy and moodiness. The patient's family life and his work situation were in shambles and he did nothing to deal with it. He rationalized his troubles or blamed them on others and sometimes seemed to relish his recklessness. Kristie felt irritated by the patient's stubborn clinging to his symptoms and his seeming indifference; occasionally, she also experienced unexplained anxiety. She felt the treatment was not progressing and contemplated suggesting termination. She was tempted to do so, but was deterred by the knowledge that the patient would experience the termination as a rejection and a traumatic loss (something she herself had experienced in a therapeutic situation in the past). She then recalled that the patient had lost a sibling; during the initial consultation, the patient had mentioned that his sister died of a disease at the age of three, when he was six years old. According to Kristie, the patient had reported this detail unemotionally and added callously: "I must have been pleased because I was intensely jealous of the attention she was getting".

Kristie was so concerned about her emotional difficulties that she brought the subject up during her training analysis. She recalled that her grandmother had lost a child during the war, a fact that seemed to have little emotional significance for her grandmother. Kristie asked her own mother about the child's death, and learned to her surprise that in addition to the child that died in the war, there was also secret in her family, a secret supposedly kept from her. [We know that attempts to keep a secret in the family are often futile; children usually realize that something is being hidden from them and that the topic is "taboo".] Kristie's mother had lost a baby shortly before her pregnancy with Kristie. When considering this "secret", and as far as Kristie could reconstruct from her past, her infancy was permeated by grief and "interminable" mourning and now she could appreciate the impact of it on her personality.

At that point, it occurred to Kristie that she might have been avoiding the subject of her patient's loss, as much as he did. She decided that the patient's ostensible aloofness in regard to that early loss was the result of denial and brought up the topic with the patient. The result, after his initial reluctance, was a gradual unfolding of the story of his childhood memories; he not only resented his sister, he also loved her and was heartbroken by her death. The patient recalled a touching memory of hugging his dying sister and telling her: "Do not be afraid, everything will be alright".

As her patient was discovering his unacknowledged grief and the ensuing guilt, his life changed slowly but dramatically. Gone was the callousness, the emotional dullness and, eventually, the self-destructiveness. The patient and the therapist realized that the patient's self-destructiveness was an attempt to punish himself for his "evil" thoughts about his sister and to atone for his "survivor guilt", i.e., his guilt at being spared his sister's fate. Ostensibly, the psychotherapist's ability to deal with her own past and apply her insight into its role in her countertransference, were a crucial factor in overcoming the therapeutic impasse. Thus, the fact that the therapist is irritated with a patient and wishes to "get rid" of him or her, may be indicative of a parallel "split-off" psychic content, which the therapist wishes to "expel" by discharging the patient.

Such experiences made us think of a quote from one psychologist who said that "You can only lead the patient as far as you yourself are prepared to go" (J.C.L.: unpublished lecture). The quote also echoes an apt metaphor in Dante's *Divine Comedy;* after rendering a blood-curdling account of the horrors awaiting an unwary traveler to the Netherworld, the Poet (Virgil) invites Dante to join him on the way to Hell, with himself leading the way.

> *"Therefore I think and judge it for thy best*
> *thou follow me, and I will be thy guide;*
> *and lead thee hence through the eternal place;*
> *where thou shalt hear the desperate lamentations."*

Dante's encounter with Virgil is an apt, if unintentional, metaphor for psychotherapy. Dante is frightened by the "Beast" guarding the entrance to "*The Unknown*". The Poet tells him, in effect that "there are, indeed, horrible sights inside, but you need not fear them; follow my lead", implying that he, the leader, knows his way around *The Unknown*. Dante, however, tells us little about why The Poet is taking upon himself this unusual task, implying, perhaps, that Virgil saw in Dante a fellow poet in need.

During the planning of this book, it became evident to us that we wanted to incorporate not only intriguing cases of how the authors(therapists) handled the intricacies of countertransference with their patients, but also to show the extent to which countertransference is prevalent in the complex relationship between the therapist and patient. In fact, as the chapters that follow will show, therapists may encounter situations of countertransference in nearly every possible patient-therapist relationship, given that both the therapist and the patient bring their own 'baggage' to the treatment session. Moreover, both are also rooted in their subjective social fabric, which embodies values, stereotypes and contested issues. Such factors, while external to the therapeutic setting, are often deeply involved in the problem that brings the patient to ask for help, and may exert a powerful influence on the relationship. While most of the existing psychoanalytic literature on countertransference deals with a "couch and armchair" setting, the mental health practitioner of today is asked to deal with a very broad range of challenges and settings. With this understanding, we employed a methodology that would enable us to paint a broad canvas, incorporating diverse cases studies, backgrounds, fields of expertise, geographic locations, and therapeutic approaches. We also included several chapters on the biology of empathy, which is the foundation of countertransference.

For the case study chapters, we decided to approach therapists that we knew had specialized in treating specific types of patients (such as second-generation Holocaust survivors or siblings of fallen soldiers) or who had shared with us specific situations of countertransference with their patients.

In Chapter Two, Tal Marron examines how attitudes towards countertransference arising in the therapist during psychotherapy have evolved in the past century, reflecting cultural changes in Western society, as reflected in both philosophy and the arts. She begins with Freud, who regarded countertransference as a 'disturbance in treatment', and progresses to today's approach to the patient-therapist relationship, in which the relationship is characterized by equality, and, in some intersubjective therapies, by mutual disclosure. This chapter is critical to the reader's understanding of how the patient-therapist relationship has evolved, in the context of how we view countertransference within this relationship.

The third chapter, by Gustaw Sikora, deals with the cultural dimension of the patient-therapist relationship in our multicultural society. Using fragments of the analysis of a patient, he discusses the problem of understanding subtler nuances of communication and the feelings of impotence when the patient uses such a misunderstanding to devalue the therapist. Moreover, cultural stereotypes of an ethnic group in the eyes of the other may affect the emotional relationship on both sides.

In Chapter Four, Yael Lahav, Zivya Seligman, and Zahava Solomon describe the therapy of an adult victim of incest from the perspective of "post-traumatic growth" as a result of traumatic exposure in therapy. They analyze the therapist's countertransference in regard to the patient's reports of gains or positive changes. The countertransference progressed from the position of the dissociated child, the blind parent, the aggressor and the rescuer. These countertransference reactions reflect the re-enactment of the trauma that must be worked-through in therapy.

In Chapter Five, Moshe Z. Abramowitz, Haim Knobler, Yoram Ben Yehuda, and Dov Aleksandrowicz discuss countertransference problems that arise in the therapy of siblings of fallen soldiers, with particular reference to Israeli society and present clinical examples of to illustrate the issue. In this context, is it important to explain that Israeli society not only reveres its veterans; it actively supports the efforts of bereaved family to idealize the fallen soldier. This environment, however, may interfere with therapist's need to identify with the sibling's natural ambivalence and feelings of neglect.

Chapter Six, by Katarzyna Prot-Klinger, describes her experience as a second-generation Holocaust survivor in Poland, treating first- and second-generation survivors. Prot-Klinger shares with the reader her own struggle with her countertransference feelings in both situations, reflecting her own relationships with her survivor-parents and her Jewish identity.

In Chapter Seven, Prot-Klinger, Łukasz Biedka, Kazimierz Bierzyński, Ewa Domagalska, Ryszard Izdebski, and Marta Szwajca, describe a unique therapeutic experiment, namely a group therapy of Holocaust survivors in Poland, initiated *by* a Holocaust survivor, and continued as a group of second-generation survivors, which is currently conducted jointly by second-generation survivor and non-Jewish therapists. They discuss the countertransference aspects of that group as well as the complex situation of Jewish survivors in post-war Poland and its effects on the countertransference.

In Chapter Eight, Elizabeth Brainin and SamyTeicher report on their survey of survivors of the Nazi extermination of disabled children (called the T-4 program). The survivors came from *Spiegelgrund*, which was, ostensibly, a psychiatric center but in reality was a transition and selection center for extermination. In this chapter, the authors describe the difficult countertransference feelings experienced by the interviewers, namely their painful identification with the traumatized children and indignation at the laxity of the post-war authorities. The interviewers' feelings are compounded by the concurrent trial of the medical director of the children's ward, who until then had enjoyed wide degree of impunity and a prominent status in the Austrian psychiatric community.

Chapter Nine, by Friedemann Pfäfflin, deals with countertransference issues in the therapy of transgenic patients. Addressing a highly-volatile topic that has received recent international attention, including in popular culture and film, he describes the gradual evolution of his own attitude and therapeutic approach to transgender patients, as well as his experience as a supervisor. Pfäfflin also presents clinical examples, including his first encounter in the 1970s with a patient displaying transsexual symptoms, through recent cases, where most patients have already lived for some time in their desired genders.

Chapter Ten provides the reader with a unique view of countertransference towards a patient with a severe brain injury. In this chapter, Aviva Edelman reports on the case of a patient with total short-term memory loss caused by brain injury, and her year-long struggle with these handicaps in the therapy under such circumstances. Unlike the likable protagonist of the 2004 movie "First Fifty Dates", Edelman's patient not only suffered from short-term memory loss, but was also aware of it, which further complicated his treatment and required the therapist to suppress her own reactions to his lashing out.

Chapter Eleven, by Dov Aleksandrowicz, looks at the biological roots of compassion, derived from the mammalian "parenting response" and the implications for the understanding of countertransference.

Chapter Twelve, by Inbal Ben-Ami Bartal and Anat Perry, analyzes the biological roots of pro-social behavior. The authors show that animals, and humans among them, are equally capable of acting aggressively or pro-socially, depending on the social context. The authors believe that understanding this construct can contribute to our ability to facilitate pro-social behavior between groups, reduce conflict and treat anti-social behavior. Ben-Ami Bartal and Perry also trace the biological roots of pro-social behavior to maternal care, later evolving to include a broader social group, and illustrate their thesis by describing rat-facilitation behavior experiments and other findings relating to animal pro-sociality.

Chapter Thirteen, also by Perry and Ben-Ami Bartal, is a review of findings from neuroscience, developmental and social psychology, which reveal the neural architecture, neuropeptides and systemic activity involved in the empathic response, as well as the biological mechanisms by which social context, personality traits, or pre-existing knowledge interact with empathy.

Chapter Fourteen, by Eric Leake examines the role of empathy in cosmopolitanism, the understanding that, in spite of the multiple differences and deep divisions, we all belong to the community of mankind. Cosmopolitanism entails the ability to relate to other people whoever they may be. Leake argues that education, especially the teaching of humanities, can inspire empathy and is the most effective tool to foster cosmopolitanism.

Finally, Chapter Fifteen, by Aleksandrowicz, is a concluding summary of the findings presented by the contributing authors and the implications for our understanding of the vicissitudes of countertransference.

Notes

1 Zweig, S. (2011), *Impatience of the Heart*, London, Pushkin, p. 241.

2 The translator used the term "pity", but in our opinion "compassion" better renders the German "*Mitleid*", literally "suffering together".

References

Alighieri, D. (2009). Inferno. In *The Divine Comedy)*, Vol. I, Canto 1. Trans. H.W. Longfellow, Project Gutenberg. (Original work published circ. 1308–21).

Balint, M. (1957). *The Doctor, his Patient and the Illness*. Oxford: International Universities Press.

Freud, S. (1955). Recommendations to physicians practising psycho-analysis. In J. Strachey (Ed. and Trans.), *Standard edition of the Complete Psychological Works of Sigmund Freud* (Vol. 12). London: Hogarth Press. (Original work published in 1912).

J.C.L.: unpublished lecture

Zweig, S. (1946). *Beware of Pity*, Berlin: S. Fischer Verlag. (Original work published in 1939).

CHAPTER
TWO

History of a Concept: Countertransference – A Socio-philosophical Review

Tali R. Marron

Edited by Karen Marron

Over the past 100 years western society has undergone significant transformations. The rise of postmodernity in the face of modern ideology brought about vast changes in society, science, and art as well as in the conceptualization of human nature. The fields of psychology and psychotherapy have been highly influenced by these changes as well, including the definition of goals of therapy and patient-therapist relations. This chapter examines how attitudes towards countertransference, the feelings and thoughts arising in the therapist during psychotherapy, have evolved in the past century, reflecting changes in philosophy and society.

The author categorizes the main attitudes towards countertransference into three general groups of practitioners and theoreticians. The first group (1910–1950), of which Freud is the main representative, perceives countertransference as an impediment to treatment, something to be overcome in order to focus on the patients' narrative and unveil their unconscious truth (which is objective and unchanging). The second group (1950s–1970s), which includes Paula Heimann (1950) and Donald Winnicott (1949), considers countertransference to be an important tool that can assist in the psychoanalytic process. The third group (1970s–present day), influenced by postmodern ideology, adopts an entirely different approach to countertransference. In line with the idea that there is no single truth or master narrative, this group believes not only that the feelings and thoughts of the therapist are helpful for understanding the patient, but that there can be no therapy without them. As described and demonstrated by theorists such as Ogden and Davies, the patients' (and the therapists') self and narrative are constructed in every moment and in every interaction between them. Patient–therapist relationships are characterized by equality and in some intersubjective therapies by mutual disclosure with a common goal to create a new reality and perspective through the space created between the two.

Introduction

Freud first identified the phenomenon of countertransference in 1910, defining it as unconscious feelings that analysts experience towards their patients, and, specifically, as an unwanted byproduct of the analytic situation (Freud, 1910). In the decades since, attitudes towards countertransference in psychodynamic theory and practice have undergone dramatic shifts (Orr, 1954). Several good reviews have been published on the history of the concept of countertransference (Bernstein, 1999; Etchegoyen, 2005; Hinshelwood, 1999; Jacobs, 1999; Orr, 1954; Young, 1994). The current chapter seeks to provide a clear outline of the evolution of the concept and, in particular, a deeper understanding of the socio-cultural environment and the philosophical influences that contributed to the development of each stage in the process.

It is possible to categorize the main attitudes towards countertransference according to three general groups of practitioners and theoreticians, which correspond to different periods of the twentieth century (Laplanche & Pontalis, 1973). The first group, of which Freud is the main representative, believed that countertransference is elicited in the analyst by the patient, and that these unconscious feelings harm the analytic process. Accordingly, the analyst must overcome countertransference, through self-analysis (Freud, 1910/1957). The second group, which includes Paula Heimann (1950) and Donald Winnicott (1949), considered countertransference to be an important tool that can assist in the psychoanalytic process. This group subscribed to the idea that the countertransferential feelings and thoughts that arise in the analyst result from the patient's internal conflicts, and that understanding these feelings can assist in understanding the patient. Most members of this group agreed that insights obtained through countertransference should usually be used to interpret the patient's transference, and that the analyst should not disclose these feelings (Heimann, 1950). The third group, which includes Ogden (1977), Aron (1991), and Davies (1994), recognizes that countertransference, like the analytic process in general, consists of feelings that the patient and analyst elicit in each other, as well as new feelings and experiences that they create together. These feelings have a crucial role in the therapeutic process, beyond their potential to assist the analyst in understanding the patient: they are part of the therapeutic change, and must be brought to the foreground of therapy. Some analysts might disclose these feelings in a direct manner, whereas others allow them to remain in unconscious interactions.

The consecutive development of these groups represents the gradual evolution of the concept of countertransference over the course of the twentieth century. It should be noted, however, that firm believers in the theories of the first group still exist, and forerunners of the third group were already present at the inception of the concept of countertransference.

First group (1910–1950s): Countertransference as an obstacle to analysis

Freud's first official reference to the concept of countertransference was in his article "The future prospects of psycho-analytic therapy" (1910/1957), in which he referred to "the unconscious feelings of the physician through the influence of the patient", and stated that "we advise that the physician should recognize and overcome this countertransference in himself. . . . ". In other words, Freud viewed countertransference as feelings that the patient elicits in the therapist. Irrational feelings on the part of the analyst can harm the precise analysis of the patient, and it is therefore the therapist's duty to recognize these feelings and overcome them " . . . with a self-analysis which he should steadily deepen as he gains experience from his patients" (1910/1957).

Freud's point of view reflects the somewhat contradictory characteristics of the society in which he lived and worked, namely, Vienna in the late nineteenth- and early twentieth-centuries. After a series of wars, Austria had stabilized itself politically against the German-Prussian-Italian fronts by creating a dual monarchy with Hungary, which lasted from 1867 to 1918. As a result of being part of a monarchy, under an emperor who ruled in God's name, Austrian society was hierarchical, patriarchal and authoritative. Yet, at the same time, Vienna was becoming increasingly modern, liberal and permissive in many ways (Ticho & Ticho, 1972). Viennese society during this so-called "Modern Age" put an emphasis on the individual and what drives him or her, and made room for new types of artistic expression and scientific advances (Ackerl, 1999). It was also characterized by a movement towards rationalism and positivism, a belief in the existence of an objective truth, and in the idea that empirical science was the only way to discover it (Ackerl, 1999; Psillos, 2008). In this period, physicians represented the patriarchy, yet also embodied modernity: Society considered them to be god-like in terms of authority, ridding patients of disease as if exorcising the devil. However, the tools used to fight disease were rational, based on scientific experiments (Kaba & Sooriakumaran, 2007).

Freud, too, was a complex mix of authority and modernity, and both elements are inherent in his attitude towards countertransference. His ideas regarding the role of the therapist were in line with general perceptions of medical professionals as figures of authority. The analyst is doctor of the psyche – he is in charge, and owns the power of knowledge (Mayer, 1996). Freud's personal attitudes were similarly patriarchal (Moi, 1981); in fact, he has even been quoted as saying, "I am also too patriarchal to be a good analyst" (Kardiner, 1957, p. 52). On the other hand, his methods were based in modern theories of biology and evolution (Hacker, 1957), and he liberated people (mostly women) by emphasizing feelings and drives as an important part of the human experience (Erikson, 1970). According to Freud, the analyst's mission is to reveal the truth, the patient's unconscious conflicts, by carefully, scientifically, analyzing all aspects of his or her free associations and transference, in a manner similar to a surgical procedure (Freud, 1912/1955a). The purpose of this approach is to rid the patient of neurotic disease. Only the patient's feelings are to be addressed and analyzed; the analyst's feelings have no role in the process.

As noted above, Freud attributed those feelings that do arise in the analyst to the influence of the patient (Freud, 1910/1957), instead of acknowledging that they might stem from within the analyst. This idea may have been inspired, in part, by the fact that, in the early days of psychoanalysis, most analysts were male, and most patients were female. The feelings arising in the therapist were commonly feelings of attraction, and it may have been easier to assign blame to the women for eliciting these irrational feelings, rather than to suggest that the doctor himself is responsible for having them (Moi, 1981). This proposition is further strengthened by the fact that Freud's first unofficial reference to countertransference was in a 1909 letter to Jung, in which Freud provided advice regarding Jung's love affair with his patient Sabina Spielrein (1885–1941):

> " . . . *Such experiences, though painful, are necessary and hard to avoid . . . I myself have never been taken in quite so badly, but I have come very close to it a number of times and had a narrow escape . . . They help us to develop the thick skin we need and to dominate 'countertransference,' which is after all a permanent problem for us; they teach us to displace our own affects to best advantage. They are a 'blessing in disguise.' . . . The way these women manage to charm us with every conceivable psychic perfection until they have attained their purpose is one of nature's greatest spectacles.*" (Freud, 1974, p. 230)

Most of the psychoanalysts of Freud's time adopted his attitude, though they continued to develop the understanding of countertransference. With therapeutic experience, many of these followers grew to understand that countertransference cannot be defined merely as feelings that the patient elicits in the therapist, but is composed of aspects of the therapist's personal feelings, his or her own unconscious and repressed material, and transference towards the patient (e.g., Glover, 1927). Freud's followers did not abandon the idea, however, that countertransference is something that should be gotten rid of through self-analysis, in order to prevent it from influencing the course of analysis (Glover,1927; Orr, 1954). As English and Pearson (1937) sum up, these psychoanalysts subscribed to the belief that "the good psychotherapist . . . is able and willing to conceal any feelings he may have beyond desire to help the patient" (quoted in Orr, 1954, p. 662).

This attitude persisted into the next era of the evolution of countertransference (e.g., Annie Reich, 1951). Melanie Klein, for example, who was active until her death in 1960, can be classified as a member of this first group, in that she did not believe that significant benefits could be gleaned from countertransference. Like Freud, she emphasized the patient's feelings rather than the analyst's (although, unlike Freud, she suggested that the analyst's feelings are not likely to pose a problem for analysis, unless the analyst is deficient). Accordingly, she did not think that the analyst's feelings regarding a patient could provide information that would be of use in the analytic process. In fact, Klein thought that incorporation of these feelings into analysis might encourage analysts to blame their own deficiencies on their patients (Spillius, 1992). Interestingly, despite Klein's dismissal of the value of countertransference, her theories on projective identification – the patient's projection of unbearable parts of his or her psyche into the analyst – broadened the understanding of transference and countertransference and deeply influenced the group of theorists who led the second group, discussed in the following section (e.g., Heimann, 1950; Hinshelwood, 1999; Winnicott, 1949).

Freud's direct followers Jung and Ferenczi shared some of Freud's views with regard to countertransference, and can thus also be considered as members of the first group. Jung agreed with Freud that the "counter-transference phenomenon is one of the chief occupational hazards of psychotherapy", and, consistent with his time, he saw neurosis as a "demon of sickness" to be rid of (1929/1966). Ferenczi, like Freud, subscribed to the Modern positivistic approach, according to which there is one objective psychic truth that can be uncovered through analysis (Aron, 1998). Likewise, he saw countertransference as being primarily a hindrance to analysis: "The narcissism of the analyst seems suited to create a particularly fruitful source of mistakes; among others the development of a kind of narcissistic countertransference which provokes the person being analyzed into pushing into the foreground certain things which flatter the analyst and, on the other hand, into suppressing remarks and associations of an unpleasant nature in relation to him" (Ferenczi & Rank, 1925/1988, p. 33).

Yet, certain elements of the theories and practice of Jung and Ferenczi can be seen as forerunners of the second and third approaches to countertransference, respectively. Ferenczi was ahead of his time in that, in stark contrast to Freud, who asserted that a patient's truth stems from internal experiences and intrapsychic dynamics, Ferenczi believed that the patient's truth is rooted in relationships and can be revealed through an understanding of the nature of the patient's interpersonal experiences (Aron, 1998). Specifically, in terms of his attitude towards the authoritative, hierarchical approach characterizing the medical profession at the time, Ferenczi broke all norms to an extreme. In his later years he experimented with mutual analysis; he would analyze the patient for an hour, and then, in order to overcome and explore countertransferential issues, he would let the patient analyze him (Aron, 1998; Szecsödy, 2007). He was a postmodernist in that he blurred the boundaries between analyst and patient, healthy and sick, and male and female (Harris & Aron, 1997). In this sense he was a forerunner of the latest attitude towards countertransference, the relational post-modern approach (see the section on the "third group" below for a detailed discussion of these ideas).

Similarly, Jung wove into his papers ideas that represent a more mutual and less authoritative approach than Freud's: "By no device can the treatment be anything but the product of mutual influence, in which the whole being of the doctor as well as that of his patient plays its part. It is futile for the doctor to shield himself from the influence of the patient and to surround himself with a smoke-screen of fatherly and professional authority. By so doing he only denies himself the use of a highly important organ of information" (1929/1966). Although Jung did not fully develop these ideas, he was a forerunner of the second stage of the evolution of countertransference, which will be discussed in the next section. Some scholars suggest that the mutual and egalitarian tendencies espoused by Jung and Ferenczi, which diverged from the authoritative approach that was common at the time, may have reflected these analysts' craving for a less authoritative and more mutual relationship with Freud, their teacher and mentor (Aron, 1998; Boschan, 2011).

Second group (1950–1970s): Countertransference as a tool in psychoanalysis

Countertransference as a reflection of the projected psyche of the patient

The second stage in the evolution of countertransference involved recognition of countertransference as a critical tool in psychoanalysis. The theoreticians who were active during this stage viewed the analyst as a necessary object (or environment) into which the patient projects unconscious conflicts and unbearable parts of the self. These projections elicit certain feelings (countertransference) in the analyst, who, by understanding these feelings, can assist the patient in understanding his or her unconscious, regressive state and psychic truth. As discussed above, seeds of this idea could be found among Freud's earliest followers, as in the case of Jung, who referred to the influence of a patient as an "important organ of information" (see above; 1929/1966). Nevertheless, the major shift in attitude was led by the subsequent generation of psychoanalysts, such as Racker (1953), and primarily by second-generation Kleinians such as Winnicott (1949) and Heimann (1950) – British Independents who were members of the object relations group. The shift became apparent later also in the US, for example, in the works of Kernberg (1965) and Kohut (1971).

Winnicott defines two main types of countertransference: The first, which corresponds to Freud's definition (i.e., the first stage in the evolution of the concept), comprises neurotic, abnormal reactions to the patient that evolve from "set relationships and identifications that are under repression in the analyst". In relation to these reactions Winnicott advises the analyst to undergo analysis (1949, p. 69). However, Winnicott distinguishes this form of countertransference from a second type, "the truly objective countertransference . . . .the analyst's love and hate in reaction to the actual personality and behavior of the patient, based on objective observation" (1949, p. 70). He explains that feeling hate is natural in relationships, as even a mother can hate her newborn child. In psychotherapy, an analyst is bound to have feelings of hatred towards the patient. In treating neurotics the analyst may find it easy to restrain and hide such feelings. When analyzing psychotics or antisocial patients, however, the analyst may find it more difficult to restrain hate feelings and " . . . in these cases the counter-transference phenomena will at all times be the important things in the analysis" (1949, p. 70). Winnicott's recommendation is first and foremost not to deny hate feelings, but to acknowledge and become aware of them. If the analyst does not stay in contact with feelings of hate, while simultaneously containing them, the patient will be unable to do the same – and the analysis will fail (Young, 1994). Regarding interpretation, Winnicott advises that the analyst should not disclose hate feelings towards the patient. In some cases, however, the analysis might eventually reach a stage at which it will become possible to reflect on past feelings (1949).

Paula Heimann (1950) further developed the concept of countertransferential feelings as an important element of psychotherapy in her pioneering lecture "On counter-transference". She defined countertransference as "all the feelings which the analyst experiences towards his patient," and she expressed disagreement with Freud's "demand that the analyst must 'recognize and master' his counter-transference" (Heimann, 1950, p. 83). Rather, Heimann states that the analyst "must use his emotional response as a key to the patient's unconscious. This will protect him from entering as a co-actor on the scene which the patient re-enacts in the analytic relationship and from exploiting it for his own needs" (Heimann, 1950, p. 83). Importantly, though, Heimann believes that the therapist should not communicate these feelings to the patient: "In my view such honesty is more in the nature of a confession and a burden to the patient. In any case it leads away from the analysis. The emotions roused in the analyst will be of value to his patient, if used as one more source of insight into the patient's unconscious conflicts and defenses; and when these are interpreted and worked through" (Heimann, 1950, p. 83).

Margaret Little, who underwent analysis with Winnicott, also supported the view that countertransference could be used as a tool. In her seminal paper "Counter-transference and the patient's response to it" (1951), she elaborated on the importance of using countertransference as a means of progressing therapy. Unlike Winnicott and Heimann, however, she emphasized that countertransference does not necessarily consist solely of "objective" feelings, i.e., feelings that the analyst experiences as a direct result of the patient projecting his or her conflicts onto the analyst. Rather, countertransferential feelings can arise from the subjectivity of the analyst and his or her own unique personality. Little states that "transference and counter-transference are not only syntheses by the patient and analyst acting separately, but, like the analytic work as a whole, are the result of a joint effort . . . transference and counter-transference are still further syntheses in that they are products of the combined unconscious work of patient and analyst. They depend on conditions which are partly internal and partly external to the analytic relationship, and vary from week to week, day to day, and even moment to moment with the rapid intra- and extra-psychic changes" (Little, 1951, p. 37). In this approach she foresaw Christopher Bollas (1983), as well as analysts from the third stage in the evolution of the concept of countertransference, who recognize the relational and intersubjective aspects of the analytic situation (see the following section).

Margaret Little's approach was especially revolutionary in its acceptance of the analyst as a human being, who cannot be expected to be flawless and to be constantly aware of his or her unconscious countertransference. Rather, Little advises that it is sometimes beneficial to address and disclose countertransferential feelings directly. Moreover, the analyst should be humble enough to admit when his mistakes arise from countertransference: "We often hear of the mirror which the analyst holds up to the patient, but the patient holds one up to the analyst too, and there is a whole series of reflections in each, repetitive in kind, and subject to continual modification". Little emphasizes that countertransferential feelings and their corresponding interpretations should not be disclosed to the patient in an overly detailed, "confessional" manner. Rather, it is necessary simply for the existence of these feelings, and the need for the analyst to analyze them, to be "recognized by both analyst and patient" (Little, 1951, p. 37).

The following example, provided by Little, shows the difference between Little's approach of directly acknowledging the psychoanalyst's feelings, and the more "typical" second-stage approach of Heimann and Winnicott, in which these feelings are not disclosed to the patient. Both approaches seek to utilize countertransference and the patient's reaction to it in psychotherapy. Consider a patient who responds to his perception of unconscious anger in the analyst. Heimann and Winnicott would use this reaction in the following manner to analyze transference: "You feel that I am angry, as your mother was when . . . " Little, in contrast, would say more directly,

"I'm not angry as far as I know, but I'll have to find out about it and, if I am, to know why, for there's no real reason for me to be" (Little, 1951, p. 39).

Kernberg (1965) also shared the view that countertransference is an important diagnostic tool. He suggested that countertransferential feelings carry valuable clinical implications; for example, they can assist the analyst in evaluating the degree of regression in the patient. Specifically, intense and quickly-changing feelings on the part of the therapist are likely to reflect severe regression in the patient (Kernberg, 1965). Additionally, according to Kernberg (1965), countertransference can shed light on the emotional position of the patient towards the analyst. For example, "the analyst may identify with a superego function connected with a stern, prohibitive father image, feeling critical and tempted to control the patient in some particular way, while the patient may be experiencing fear, submission, or rebelliousness connected with his relationship to his father" (p. 49). Kernberg, like many of his time, advises not to disclose countertransferential feelings, but to use this information for interpretation of the transference. He also explains in detail problems that can occur as a result of countertransference. Money-Kyrle (1956), whose general approach to countertransference was similar to Kernberg's, emphasized the problematic situation in which the analyst cannot distinguish between feelings of countertransference, elicited by the patient, from "real" feelings that he or she experiences regardless of the patient. For example, a psychotherapist might feel "small", and that he or she is a poor therapist, and the source of these feelings might be unclear.

In sum, we can see that most theoreticians of the second group – which, in addition to the analysts mentioned above, includes Kohut (1971) and Sandler (1976) (Sandler used the term "role responsiveness" to refer to the beneficial aspects of countertransference) – believed that the analyst's role is to be a receptive environment for projections and transference. Countertransference is caused by these projections, and thus recognizing and understanding it can assist the analyst in understanding the patient's unconscious psychic truth. Problems with countertransference occur when the analyst cannot separate his or her personal feelings from those elicited by the patient. In these cases the analyst must analyze and separate these feelings in order to progress in therapy. Most theorists in this group (with the exception of Little) do not advise disclosure of countertransferential feelings, but rather suggest that these feelings should be used in order to understand and interpret the patient's inner state.

Factors influencing the transition between the first and second stages

What brought about the transition between the first and second stages in the evolution of the concept of countertransference? First, the field of psychoanalysis was continuing to develop and grow, and as analysts gained experience, it became increasingly clear that emotional reactions to one's patients were a reality of the profession that could not simply be ignored (Hinshelwood, 1999). These reactions became increasingly salient in the wake of World War II, as analysts became exposed to a wider variety of mental conditions, particularly those resulting from trauma. In their work with such patients (e.g., borderline and psychotic), who exhibited primitive affects such as blatant sexuality and raw aggression, analysts often experienced powerful emotions, which they had to contend with (Jacobs, 1999). Concurrently, in the middle of the twentieth century, researchers and psychoanalysts began to take a growing interest in infants and their relationships with their mothers (Bowlby, 1951). The mother was viewed as an environment for the infant, receiving the infant's projections as a means of communication. Acceptance of the feelings arising in mothers in relation to their infants led to the recognition of the importance and legitimacy of these feelings in the analyst as "mother" (e.g., Pick, 1985).

Moreover, the two World Wars that had taken place had profound effects on society in general, and on the field of medicine in particular. Scientists began to devote substantial attention to the idea of aggression (Freud, 1920/1955b). The wars, and particularly World War II, had revealed not only that one's enemy may have the capacity for horrific aggression, but also that, in order to protect oneself, one might have to engage in similar aggressive behavior. Consequently, aggression and other complex feelings were increasingly being accepted as an inherent part of the psyche. Studies in science, and specifically in biology, supported this idea, finding aggression to be an important aspect of all living things, necessary for survival (Lorenz, 1966). The understanding that we contain "bad" as well as "good" also began to be reflected in approaches to medical practice. Harsh symptoms were no longer "bad demons" that needed to be expelled, but were a result of the body trying to overcome a problem, and could provide physicians with important information (Magner, 2005). This attitude also influenced the field of psychoanalysis, as in the case of Anna Freud, who no longer saw resistance as something negative to be rid of, but as a means for the psyche to protect itself, and an important source of information that should be analyzed (A. Freud, 1992). These developments were likely to have had a role in the shifting attitudes towards countertransference, which began to favor greater acceptance of the feelings that arise in the analyst during therapy, and to search for a way to utilize these feelings.

Wilfred Bion and the seeds of transition to the third group

The work of Wilfred Bion, a Kleinian psychoanalyst who was active during the years 1940–1979, can be seen as an important stepping stone between the shifting conceptualizations of countertransference. Interestingly, at different stages, his ideas regarding countertransference were compatible with the approaches of both the first and second groups, and included aspects that subsequently developed into the third group's view. In his early writings Bion explicitly states that "countertransference has to play an important part in analysis of the schizophrenic" and that "evidence for interpretations has to be sought in the counter-transference" (Bion, 1954, p. 113). Although this statement sounds like a classic "second group" view, he changed this outlook in later writings and lectures and made claims that are more typical of the "first group". He defined countertransference as transference towards the patient that results from the analyst's repressed conflicts, and considered action driven by countertransference to be harmful (Walters, 2009). Specifically, he believed that the analyst "cannot use his counter-transference. There is only one thing to do with counter-transference and that is to have it analyzed" (Bion, 1990, p. 122).

But Bion did not reprehend all feelings on the part of the analyst. He recognized that feelings such as hate, love, and the desire to seek knowledge arise in the analyst, as well as in the patient, and are necessary for therapy; he just gave these feelings a different name: "passion" (Bion, 1984, p. 12). The analyst's passion, according to Bion, entails acknowledging, containing, and synthesizing ambivalent feelings while simultaneously linking with the mind of the patient. Bion believed that this passion, in contrast to countertransference, can be conscious and utilized, and can serve in processes that organize meaning in analysis (Billow, 2000). This approach positions Bion as a member of the second group, which considers feelings and emotions – albeit only those that do not derive from the analyst's repressed conflicts – as a critical tool. He writes: "passion is evidence that two minds are linked and that there cannot possibly be fewer than two minds if passion is present" (Bion, 1984, p. 13).

Bion viewed therapy as a process in which the patient projects "unthinkable" thoughts into the analyst's "reverie", an intrapsychic space in which the analyst can think (or dream) the unthinkable thoughts. In creating this "reverie" the analyst should abandon "memory and desire" (Ogden, 1998, p. 133); only by being fully receptive can the analyst enable real psychic truth to arise. This approach, in which the analyst is seen as a receptive container, is very typical of the "second group." Moreover, in line with the philosophical approaches of the first and second groups, Bion was a strong believer in the existence of an objective truth, and saw humanity as driven by the need to know this truth (Ogden, 2009). The need for truth is what causes humans to think genuinely about reality and allows them to learn from their emotional experiences.

In analysis, according to Bion, the analyst helps the patient think ("dream") his truth until he can do it himself. This can only happen in a relational context. In other words, although "passion" is an intrasubjective process, it can only take place in an intersubjective context (Billow, 2000). In emphasizing relational importance, and recognizing the analyst as a subject with passion, and not merely an object, Bion essentially foresaw the third group of countertransference, which was based on intersubjective ideas – discussed below.

Finally, Bion was a pioneer in that he adopted postmodern perspectives, which are also a hallmark of the third group: He spoke about the psychotic aspects of normal people and normal aspects of psychotic people, closing the dissociation between the two. He wrote about the "need for employing a technique of constantly changing points of view" (1961, p. 86) (e.g., conscious and the unconscious mind paranoid-schizoid, and the depressive positions; Ogden, 2009). And he emphasized the value of not knowing, which he referred to as "negative capability" – a term first used by the poet Keats to refer to the state of "being in uncertainties, mysteries, doubts, without any irritable reaching after fact and reason" (quoted by Bion, 1970, p. 125). Specifically, although Bion believed in an objective truth, he attributed importance to being in stages of not knowing it, and being able to tolerate the harsh feelings that might arise from this situation: "Genuine thinking, though driven by the need to know what is true, is at the same time characterized by a firm recognition that conclusions are always inconclusive, endings are always beginnings" (Ogden, 2009, p. 96). Bion's postmodern views might have been a product of the influence of the postmodern writer Samuel Beckett, who was one of Bion's first patients (Anzieu, 1989).

Third group (late 1970s–present day): Intersubjectivity and postmodernism

Shifts in worldview: (Inter)subjectivity and the blurring of boundaries

Bion's (and Little's) recognition of the relational aspect of the feelings that arise in both the patient and the analyst was influenced by changes in psychoanalysis and society, and this aspect ultimately became the guiding principle of the contemporary view on countertransference, which has been widely accepted for the past 40 years or so. This view can be summarized as acceptance of the analyst as a profound subject and creator of meaning in the analysis, in the sense that she or he is not merely a container, an environment for the transference and the projected parts of the patient. The analyst's subjective aspects of countertransference are crucial for mutually creating new meanings in the therapeutic process. Thus, the transition to the third stage of the evolution of countertransference reflects a shift in perceptions of the nature of psychoanalysis: from a process whose goal is to uncover the patient's (objective) psychic truth, to an understanding that truth is created in therapy in the "here and now", by the subjective experiences of the patient and analyst of each other, and by new experiences that they create together.

This significant shift occurred in the late 1970s in North America (Jacobs, 1999). Until then, psychoanalysis in North America was dominated by Freud's followers, who had immigrated to America after World War II. Their view on countertransference was very much in line with that of the "first group" (the Freudian group) – despite the "second-stage" developments in the concept described above (and particularly the works of Heimann, Winnicot, and Little, in Britain). Yet, as time passed, the influence of the older European analysts began to fade. American analysts became increasingly exposed to new ideas outside of classic psychoanalytic theory, including the work of Racker, the English object-relations school, and the Kleinians. They began to take interest in the analyst's subjectivity and in the idea that it can reflect aspects of the patient's inner world. Likewise, following increasing exposure to the interpersonal and cultural schools (Sullivan, 1953; Thompson, 1964; Fromm-Reichmann, 1950; Horney, 1939), analysts began to take interest in the relational and intersubjective aspects of analysis, largely ignored by Freudian canon. As the stronghold of this canon began to diminish, analysts felt freer to acknowledge their countertransference reactions and to discuss them with colleagues – as well as to explore the potential role of these emotional responses in psychotherapy (Jacobs, 1999).

These shifts in the analytic climate occurred on the backdrop of (and, in turn, had an influence on) the renewed popularity of post-modern Nietzschean philosophy, which was dominating various aspects of society, including the sciences, the arts, medical practice, and the political scene. These ideas included deconstruction of the assumption of a single objective truth or narrative of self, and an understanding of the existence of multiple truths and a self-comprising multiple identities (Nietzsche, 1954). The prevalent line of thinking was that formulations of "truth" and "reality" are dependent on and embedded in the systems of language in which we live. Similarly, meaning is a social construct, generated through communication between people, and is a product of the social, political, and historical context in which it arises. These notions challenge the traditional dichotomy of doctor-patient, analyst-analysand (and the superiority assigned to the doctor over his patient), focusing instead on the relational system in which the two parties participate (Harris & Aron, 1997).

The subjectivity of reality is also a key principle in theories of quantum physics. Such theories began to emerge in the 1920s, but became more widely recognized by people outside the field of physics in the 1970s, around the time when Heisenberg (the "creator" of quantum mechanics, for which he received the Nobel Prize) gave a lecture at Harvard (1973) . Until then, the scientific world had been dominated by the positivistic approach, which is based on the assumption that the laws of science are absolute, deterministic and based on cause and effect. The researcher believes that she or he is independent of the research and thus is purely objective. This view coincides with empiricism, the idea that the world and knowledge about it are external and objective, and that the purpose of scientific research is to discover empirically how the world works, by observing what can be seen or measured (Psillos, 2008). Quantum theory, in contrast, posits that there is no absolute objective truth that can measured or discovered. The researcher affects the object of research, and "true knowledge" is created only when the observer observes. This is the idea behind Schrodinger's famous thought experiment: If a cat is placed in a box with poison that may or may not be released (depending on the state of a subatomic particle), the cat is both dead and alive, until someone opens the box; that is, two oppositions can exist together. The most prominent interpretation of this thought experiment – the Copenhagen interpretation – is that the observation is what finally causes the cat to be either alive or dead (Faye, 2014).

The medical profession, too, was profoundly influenced by the movement towards deconstruction of dichotomies and the blurring of boundaries. As noted above, in the post-World War II era (corresponding to the second stage in the evolution of the concept of countertransference), doctors were already beginning to move away from the idea that disease is a devil to be exorcised, and instead to relate to disease and symptoms as a way for the body to convey important information. In the third stage, the very distinction between disease and health was called into question, as scientists and doctors realized that disease initiators such as bacteria can also be crucial for the function of the body (e.g., Finegold, 1969). Additionally, the doctor-patient relationship rapidly shifted; whereas the doctor had previously been the sole authority in this relationship, patients began to take more control, participating actively and autonomously in their own treatment (Kaba & Sooriakumaran, 2007). This shift was influenced, among other factors, by the increasingly personal nature of relations in the field of psychotherapy (Kaba & Sooriakumaran, 2007). Likewise, patients were gaining more access to medical knowledge, as medical research began to be translated and disseminated globally, particularly in the last decade of the twentieth century, with the advent of the Internet (Hardey, 1999). More generally, the empowerment of the patient – as reflected in the deconstruction of the doctor's authority as a holder of "sacred" knowledge – may be considered as a manifestation of the trend towards empowerment of the "common" individual, which had begun to take hold more than a century earlier with the rise of communism in Russia, and with the rise of Jacksonian democracy in the US (Eaton, 1963). Possibly as the center of psychoanalytic activity shifted from Western European monarchies to the US, the notion that the patient holds power in the therapeutic process became increasingly salient.

The shifts in worldview described above were mirrored in shifts in the prevailing thinking regarding countertransference. The analyst was no longer seen as the sole possessor of knowledge about the patient's psychology, which he conveys through interpretation. Rather, the patient was increasingly viewed as a partner in the analytic journey, with valuable insights and intuitions of his own (Mayer, 1996). As discussed above, in the first and second stages of the development of the concept of countertransference people believed that there was an objective truth about the mechanisms of the patient's psyche and narrative, and that the goal of analysis is to uncover this truth. Now, in the third stage, the positivistic view that the patient's experiences and psyche are fixed, objective entities was deconstructed. Instead, the truth was viewed as being relative, ever-changing and in motion. The analyst's reactions and feelings are subjective, and they shape and influence the patient's unconscious as well. Together, both patient and analyst are co-creators of a new truth and narrative that exists in the here and now (Jacobs, 1999). Thomas Ogden, one of the central theorists of this group, sums up these principles:

> *Heisenberg brought this to our attention in the realm of quantum physics. It is equally true in psychoanalysis and the arts that in interpreting or sculpting or making music, we are not simply unveiling what has been present all along in latent form; rather, in the very act of giving humanly sensible form to what is true to an emotional experience, we are altering that truth.* (Ogden, 2005, p. 65)

As noted by McLaughlin (1981), the idea of the analyst as subject challenges the distinction between transference and countertransference – a distinction that, he claims, is an arbitrary hierarchical construct, which serves to "protect the analyst from having to recognize that he or she has no greater claim to objectivity, reality, or truth than does the patient" (Mayer, 1996, p. 161). These views belong to a movement called intersubjectivism. As discussed above, although this school of thought gained prominence only in the latter half of the twentieth century, the ideas on which it is based were already present in the relational theories and practice of earlier analysts such as Bion and Ferenczi.

Recognition of the role of the analyst as a subject was also affected by developments in feminist thought and infant studies (Aron, 1991). In initial studies of the mother-child relationship, studies that affected the second group, the mother was portrayed as the object of the infant's drives, and the fulfiller of the baby's needs (Aron, 1991). Now, the mother was increasingly acknowledged as another subject in this relationship, who influences and is influenced by her child (see Aron, 1991 for a review; Benjamin 1988).

Ogden (1977) described psychoanalysis as a "dialectical movement of subjectivity and intersubjectivity" (p. 62), in which "opposing elements each create, preserve, and negate the other" (p. 14). Ogden used the term "intersubjective analytic third" to refer to the product that is generated when the separate subjectivities of analyst and analysand meet within the analytic setting, creating a new subjectivity (Ogden, 1977, p. 64). These theories diverge from the ideas of Bion, which correspond more to the second stage of the development of countertransference: Bion considered the analyst's experience, including thoughts and feelings, to be a product of the patient's projections. The analyst and patient were two separate entities. Even Bion's reverie is the environment of the analyst's own experience as affected by the patient. Ogden, in contrast, emphasizes that the analyst's experience is influenced by his or her own unconscious together with the patient's – and, more importantly, that it is the product of a third element, the intersubjective experience created by analyst and patient (Ogden, 1977). This intersubjective experience is always changing; "truth" is created in the present, through the mutual experience of patient and analyst, as new thoughts and feelings arise.

Ogden believed that these processes occur through unconscious dialogue between the analyst and patient, and that the analyst should not reveal all of the thoughts that arise in the reverie. The analyst should examine his or her countertransference from outside the analytic third, in an undefended manner; such self-consciousness might pose a challenge and cause discomfort. This is the only way for the analyst to acquire "access to the nature of the states of being, comprising the matrix of the patient's internal world" (Ogden, 1977, p. 164). The analyst should not speak about his own thoughts, but should speak through the experience of the reverie or through the intersubjective experience created in the room.

Other important analysts belonging to the intersubjective movement include Emmanuel Ghent (see Ghent, 1995 for a beautiful example of mutually creating meaning in a session), in addition to McLaughlin (1981); Stolorow *et al.*, (1983); Renik (1993), and others.

Perspectives regarding disclosure of countertransferential feelings

As noted above, during the third stage, the notion of the doctor as a figure of absolute authority had begun to change. This shift was reflected in the establishment of rules that doctors must disclose all information regarding diagnosis and treatment to their patients (Kaba & Sooriakumaran, 2007). The emphasis on disclosure was becoming a general trend in society, which seems to have reached a peak in recent years, with the emergence of mass social networks and the overall diminishment of privacy and secrecy (Zheleva & Getoor, 2009; Johannesen & Zucman, 2014).

Similar changes took place in the psychoanalytic situation: The more symmetrical/mutual nature of the relationship between the analyst and the analysand began to be reflected in a growing tendency for analysts to disclose their countertransferential feelings. Ogden, as noted above, did not believe that such feelings should be disclosed; rather, he attempted to speak from the newly-created experience of the analytic third (Ogden, 1977). Yet, many other intersubjective analysts have found that different degrees of disclosure can be beneficial to therapy.

Aron, like Ogden, strongly believes that the analyst's experience is not only reactive to the patient's behavior, but also "subjective, emanating from the center of the analyst's psychic self" (1991, p. 33). He also believes that patient and analyst influence each other mutually, albeit not symmetrically. Aron is more in favor of self-disclosure than Ogden, provided that such disclosure is appropriately timed, and is left open to being resolved within the context of the unique psychoanalytic situation at hand. He also emphasizes the importance of "the analysis of the patient's experience of the analyst's subjectivity. The very expression by patients of their perceptions of the analyst leads to the establishment of the analyst as a separate subject in the mind of the patient" (Aron, 1991, p. 43).

Jody Messler Davies is an extreme example of using direct self-disclosure when more indirect methods have failed. In her opinion such disclosure promotes the creation of meaning in the session. Davies cited herself telling a patient that she and the patient "sometimes hate each other" (Davies, 2004, p. 716) after the patient accused Davies of hating her, and told another patient that she has sexual fantasies about him (Davies, 1994). Other analysts who find self-disclosure valuable include Gerson (1996), Marcus (1998), and Searles (1979).

Notably, self-disclosure is a controversial issue. Many prominent psychoanalysts and theoreticians today still share the second-stage perspective that the analyst's feelings should not be disclosed to the patient. According to this view, such disclosure can easily disrupt the expression of transference by switching the focus to the real relationship between the analyst and the patient, thus distorting the therapeutic alliance (e.g., Fisher, 2004; Meissner, 2002).

Christopher Bollas (1983) presents an important perspective on self-disclosure. In line with theoreticians and analysts of the second group, he views the analyst as an object in relation to the patient. The patient uses the analyst's open receptiveness as a place to create an environment into which the patient projects and relives with the analyst parts of himself or herself that are split off, unbearable or in need of cure. Bollas strongly believes that an important part of analysis is the analyst's free associations, including his or her feelings, emotions and internal states. He views the analyst's free association as an extension of the patient's free associations, the free associations that the patient cannot be in touch with due to his illness. In line with second-stage views, Bollas believes that it is still the patient's subjective truth that is unconsciously passed on to the analyst's experience; however, in line with more modern views, Bollas recommends that the analyst should utilize his or her subjectivity by releasing "countertransference states for elaboration, and [that] in so doing, he makes certain split off elements of the patient available for knowing through analyzing. As so much of that which is nowadays experienced is within the analyst, one of our emerging technical difficulties is how to give back to the patient either what he has lost, or bring those parts of himself to his attention that he may never have known" (Bollas, 1983, p. 8). The idea of respecting the patient and giving him what "belongs to him" is a tenet of modern medicine, as discussed above.

Bollas emphasizes that the analyst must exercise caution regarding both the timing and the frequency of countertransferential disclosure, stating that "any disclosure on the analyst's part of how he feels must be experienced by the patient as a legitimate and natural part of the analytic process" (Bollas, 1983 p. 12). Likewise, according to Bollas, the analyst must express his feelings in a humble manner, making sure not to present them as absolute truth but instead using phrases such as: "what occurs to me", or "I am thinking that", or "I have a hunch about something" "now I don't think you are going to like what occurs to me but . . . " (Bollas, 1983, p. 8). Aron (1991) summarizes these concerns as stemming from the fact that in "any approach that focuses on analysts' subjectivity . . . analysts may insist on asserting their own subjectivity . . . thus forcing the patient to assume the role of object" (p. 42).

Summary and conclusions

Psychoanalysts' view of countertransference and how to handle it has changed greatly over the past century, a process that has been influenced by changes in society and philosophy. This process can be divided into three main stages, or groups of analysts and theoreticians. The first and second groups – corresponding approximately to the years 1910–1950, and 1950–1970, respectively – subscribed to the idea of a single objective truth: The first group, influenced by the hierarchical, authoritative structure of society and medicine, considered countertransference to be feelings that are elicited in the analyst by the patient, and that these feelings may obstruct discovery of the truth about the patient, and thus must be gotten rid of. Experience in psychoanalysis, acceptance of complex emotions as inherent in human nature, and researchers' increasing interest in infant development caused a shift in the view of countertransference, towards the object-relational second group. The concept grew to include more feelings and thoughts of the analyst, but such feelings were still considered to originate in projected parts of the patient as well as in transference. Acceptance of countertransferential feelings enabled analysts to use them as a tool to understand the patient and uncover his or her truth, mostly by using them to interpret transference, but here and there also through self-disclosure.

Deconstruction of the concept of a single objective truth, of authority, of the doctor as sole possessor of knowledge – which was driven, in part, by technological developments, globalization, and advances within the field of psychoanalysis (including infant studies) – shifted the patient-analyst relationship to one characterized by more equality, comprising two subjects rather than an object and a subject. These changes led to a perception of countertransference as a critical tool of analysis. Not only the patient's feelings but also those of the analyst are critical for creating meaning and change. This view was accompanied by a heightened tendency to disclose countertransferential feelings, although this is still a controversial matter.

What does the future hold for perspectives on countertransference and its use in therapy? It seems that most therapists today acknowledge the importance of countertransference for understanding unconscious processes. However, it seems possible that the misuse of disclosure – exacerbated by the current culture of sharing extensive personal information on social media – might cause a regression in the abstinence and space between patient and analyst.

References

Ackerl, I. (1999). *Vienna Modernism: 1890–1910.* Vienna: Federal Press Service.

Anzieu, D. (1989). Beckett and Bion. *International Review of Psychoanalysis, 16*, 163–169.

Aron, L. (1991). The patient's experience of the analyst's subjectivity. *Psychoanalytic Dialogues, 1*(1), 29–51.

Aron, L. (1998). "Yours, thirsty for honesty, Ferenczi": Some background to Sándor Ferenczi's pursuit of mutuality. *The American Journal of Psychoanalysis, 58*(1), 5–20.

Benjamin, J. (1988). *The Bonds of Love: Psychoanalysis, feminism, and the problem of domination.* New York, NY: Pantheon.

Bernstein, J. W. (1999). Countertransference: Our new royal road to the unconscious?. *Psychoanalytic Dialogues, 9*(3), 275–299.

Billow, R. M. (2000). Bion's "passion"; the analyst's pain. *Contemporary Psychoanalysis, 36*(3), 411–426.

Bion, W. R. (1954). Notes on the theory of schizophrenia. *International Journal of Psychoanalysis, 35*, 113–118.

Bion, W. R. (1961). *Experiences in Groups and Other Papers*. London: Tavistock.
Bion, W. R. (1970). *Attention and interpretation: A scientific approach to insight in psycho-analysis and groups*. London: Tavistock.
Bion, W. R. (1984). *Elements of Psychoanalysis*. London: Karnac Books.
Bion, W. R. (1990).1973, São Paulo; 1974, Rio de Janeiro/São Paulo. London: Karnac Books.
Bollas, C. (1983). Expressive uses of the countertransference: Notes to the patient from oneself. *Contemporary Psychoanalysis*, *19*(1), 1–34.
Boschan, P. J. (2011). Transference and countertransference in Sándor Ferenczi's clinical diary. *The American Journal of Psychoanalysis*, *71*(4), 309–320.
Bowlby, J. (1951). *Maternal Care and Mental Health*. Geneva: WHO.
Davies, J. M. (1994). Love in the afternoon: A relational reconsideration of desire and dread in the countertransference. *Psychoanalytic Dialogues*, *4*(2), 153–170.
Davies, J. M. (2004). Whose bad objects are we anyway? Repetition and our elusive love affair with evil. *Psychoanalytic Dialogues*, *14*(6), 711–732.
Eaton, C. (1963). *The Leaven of Democracy: The growth of the democratic spirit in the time of Jackson*. New York, NY: G. Braziller.
English, O. S., & Pearson, G. H. J. (1937). *Common Neuroses of Children and Adults*. New York, NY: W. W. Norton & Co.
Erikson, E. H. (1970). Autobiographic notes on the identity crisis. *Daedalus*, *99*(4), 730–759.
Etchegoyen, R. H. (2005). *The Fundamentals of Psychoanalytic Technique*. London: Karnac Books.
Faye, J. (2014). Copenhagen interpretation of quantum mechanics. In E. Zalta (Ed.), *The Stanford Encyclopedia of Philosophy* (Fall 2014 Edition). Retrieved from http://plato.stanford.edu/archives/fall2014/entries/qm-copenhagen/.
Ferenczi, S., & Rank, O. (1988). The development of psychoanalysis: A historical critical retrospect. In B. Wolstein (Ed.), *Essential Papers on Countertransference* (pp. 25–35). New York, NY: New York University Press. (Original work published in 1925).
Finegold, S. M. (1969). Intestinal bacteria – The role they play in normal physiology, pathologic physiology, and infection. *California Medicine*, *110*(6), 455.
Fisher, C. D. (2004). Ethical issues in therapy: Therapist self-disclosure of sexual feelings. *Ethics & Behavior*, *14*(2), 105–121.
Freud, A. (1992). *The Ego and the Mechanisms of Defence*. London: Karnac Books.
Freud, S. (1955a). Recommendations to physicians practising psycho-analysis. In J. Strachey (Ed. and Trans.), *Standard Edition of the Complete Psychological Works of Sigmund Freud* (Vol. 12, pp. 1911–1913). London: Hogarth Press. (Original work published in 1912).
Freud, S. (1955b). Beyond the pleasure principle. In J. Strachey (Ed. and

Trans.), *Standard Edition of the Complete Psychological Works of Sigmund Freud* (Vol. 18, pp. 7–23). London: Hogarth Press. (Original work published in 1920).

Freud, S. (1957). The future prospects of psycho-analytic therapy. In J. Strachey (Ed. and Trans.), *Standard Edition of the Complete Psychological Works of Sigmund Freud* (Vol. 11, pp. 139–151). London: Hogarth Press. (Original work published in 1910).

Freud, S. (1974). Letter from Sigmund Freud to C. G. Jung, June 7, 1909. In W. McGuire (Ed.) & R. F. C. Hull (Trans.), *The Freud/Jung Letters: The correspondence between Sigmund Freud and C. G. Jung* (pp. 230–232). Princeton, NJ: Princeton University Press.

Fromm-Reichmann, F. (1950). *Principles of Intensive Psychotherapy.* Chicago, IL: University of Chicago Press.

Gerson, S. (1996). Neutrality, resistance, and self disclosure in an intersubjective psychoanalysis. *Psychoanalytic Dialogues*, *6*(5), 623–645.

Ghent, E. (1995). Interaction in the psychoanalytic situation. *Psychoanalytic Dialogues*, *5*(3), 479–491.

Glover, E. (1927). Lectures on technique in psycho-analysis. *International Journal of Psychoanalysis*, *8*, 486.

Hacker, F. J. (1957). Freud, Marx, and Kierkegaard. In B. Nelson (Ed.), *Freud and the Twentieth Century* (pp. 125–142). Cleveland, OH: World Publishing Company.

Hardey, M. (1999). Doctor in the house: The Internet as a source of lay health knowledge and the challenge to expertise. *Sociology of Health & Illness*, *21*(6), 820–835.

Harris, A., & Aron, L. (1997). Ferenczi's semiotic theory: Previews of postmodernism. *Psychoanalytic Inquiry*, *17*(4), 522–534.

Heimann, P. (1950). On counter-transference. *International Journal of Psychoanalysis*, *31*, 81–84.

Heisenberg, W. (1973). Development of concepts in the history of quantum theory. In J. Mehra (Ed.), *The Physicist's Conception of Nature.* Dordrecht: Springer Netherlands.

Hinshelwood, R. D. (1999). Countertransference. *International Journal of Psychoanalysis*, *80*(4), 797.

Horney, K. (1939). *New Ways in Psychoanalysis.* New York, NY: Norton.

Jacobs, T. J. (1999). Countertransference past and present: A review of the concept. *International Journal of Psychoanalysis*, *80*(3), 575.

Johannesen, N., & Zucman, G. (2014). The end of bank secrecy? An evaluation of the G20 tax haven crackdown. *American Economic Journal: Economic Policy*, *6*(1), 65–91.

Jung, C. (1966). Problems of modern psychotherapy. In G. Adler (Ed.) & R. F. C. Hull (Trans.), *The Collected Works of C. J. Jung, Bollingen Series XX* (2nd ed., Vol. 16, pp. 53–75). Princeton, NJ: Princeton University Press. (Original work published in 1929).

Kaba, R., & Sooriakumaran, P. (2007). The evolution of the doctor-patient relationship. *International Journal of Surgery*, *5*(1), 57–65.

Kardiner, A. (1957). Freud – The man I knew, the scientist, and his influence. In B. Nelson (Ed.), *Freud and the Twentieth Century* (pp. 46–58). Cleveland, OH: World Publishing Company.

Kernberg, O. (1965). Notes on countertransference. *Journal of the American Psychoanalytic Association*, *13*(1), 38–56.

Kohut, H. (1971). *The Analysis of the Self*. New York, NY: International Universities Press.

Laplanche, J., & Pontalis, J. B. (1973). *The Language of Psycho-analysis*. (D. Nicholson-Smith, Trans.). London: Hogarth Press.

Little, M. (1951). Counter-transference and the patient's response to it. *International Journal of Psychoanalysis, 32*, 32–40.

Lorenz, K. (1966). *On Aggression*. (M. Latzke, Trans.). London: Methuen.

Magner, L. N. (2005). *A history of Medicine*. New York, NY: Informa Healthcare.

Marcus, D. M. (1998). Self disclosure: The wrong issue. *Psychoanalytic Inquiry*, *18*(4), 566–579.

Mayer, E. L. (1996). Changes in science and changing ideas about knowledge and authority in psychoanalysis. *The Psychoanalytic Quarterly*, *65*, 158–200.

McLaughlin, J. T. (1981). Transference, psychic reality, and countertransference. *The Psychoanalytic Quarterly*, *50*(4), 639–664.

Meissner, W. W. (2002). The problem of self-disclosure in psychoanalysis. *Journal of the American Psychoanalytic Association*, *50*(3), 827–867.

Moi, T. (1981). Representation of patriarchy: sexuality and epistemology in Freud's "Dora." *Feminist Review*, *9*(1), 60–74.

Money-Kyrle, R. E. (1956). Normal counter-transference and some of its derivations. *International Journal of Psychoanalysis*, *37*, 360.

Nietzsche, F. (1954). On truth and lie in an extra-moral sense. In W. Kaufmann (Ed. and Trans.), *The Portable Nietzsche* (pp. 46–47). New York, NY: Penguin.

Ogden, T. H. (1977). *Subjects of Analysis*. Lanham, MD: Jason Aronson.

Ogden, T. H. (1998). *Reverie and Interpretation*. Lanham, MD: Jason Aronson.

Ogden, T. H. (2005). *Dreaming Undreamt Dreams and Interrupted Cries*. London: Routledge.

Ogden, T. H. (2009). Bion's four principles of mental functioning. In *Rediscovering Psychoanalysis: Thinking and dreaming, learning and forgetting* (pp. 90–113). East Sussex: Routledge.

Orr, D. W. (1954). Transference and countertransference: a historical survey. *Journal of the American Psychoanalytic Association*, *2*(4), 621–670.

Pick, I. B. (1985). Working through in the countertransference. *International Journal of Psychoanalysis*, *66*, 157–166.

Psillos, S. (2008). Philosophy of science. In D. Moran (Ed.), *The Routledge Companion to Twentieth-Century Philosophy* (pp. 618–658). London: Routledge.

Racker, H. (1953). A contribution to the problem of counter-transference. *International Journal of Psychoanalysis*, *34*, 313.
Reich, A. (1951). On counter-transference. In R. Langs (Ed.), *Classics in Psychoanalytic Technique* (pp. 153–159). Lanham, MD: Jason Aronson.
Renik, O. (1993). Analytic interaction: Conceptualizing technique in light of the analyst's irreducible subjectivity. *Psychoanalytic Quarterly*, *62*(4), 553–571.
Sandler, J. (1976). Countertransference and role-responsiveness. *International Review of Psychoanalysis*, *3*, 43–47.
Searles, H. F. (1979). *Countertransference and Related Subjects: Selected papers*. New York, NY: International Universities Press.
Spillius, E. (1992). Clinical experiences of projective identification. In R. Anderson (Ed.), *Clinical Lectures on Klein and Bion* (pp. 59–73). London: Routledge.
Stolorow, R. D., Brandchaft, B., & Atwood, G. E. (1983). Intersubjectivity in psychoanalytic treatment: With special reference to archaic states. *Bulletin of the Menninger Clinic*, *47*(2), 117.
Sullivan, H. S. (1953). *The Interpersonal Theory of Psychiatry.* New York, NY: Norton. Szecsödy, I. (2007).
Sándor Ferenczi–The first intersubjectivist. *The Scandinavian Psychoanalytic Review*, *30*(1), 31–41.
Thompson, C. (1964). *Interpersonal Psychoanalysis: The selected papers of Clara M. Thompson*. M. Green (Ed.). New York, NY: Basic Books.
Ticho, E. A., & Ticho, G. R. (1972). Freud and the Viennese. *The International Journal of Psycho-analysis*, *53*, 301.
Walters, D. A. (2009). Transference and countertransference as existential themes in the psychoanalytic theory of W. R. Bion. *Psychodynamic Practice*, *15*(2), 161–172.
Winnicott, D. W. (1949). Hate in the counter-transference. *The International Journal of Psycho-Analysis*, *30*, 69.
Young, R. M. (1994). *Mental Space*. London: Process Press.
Zheleva, E., & Getoor, L. (2009). To join or not to join: The illusion of privacy in social networks with mixed public and private user profiles. In *Proceedings of the 18th International Conference on World Wide Web* (pp. 531–540). New York, NY: ACM.

PART II

The Clinical Challenge

Some clinical situations settings carry a greater than usual risk of counter-transference difficulties. Such is, for instance, the case of patients with more severe psychiatric disorder, such as schizophrenia or borderline personality, and these problems have been amply discussed in the literature.

There are cases, however, in which countertransference difficulties are related not so much to the severity of the patient's pathology, as to issues outside the therapeutic situation. The patient and the therapist belong, each of them, to social groups. Social entities have their own stereotypes, values and divisive issues. Most of these issues, especially the divisive ones, carry considerable emotional charge. Such issues may invade the therapeutic setting and stir up countertransference problems. The problem may be even more critical when the emotionally charged social issue is itself the reason for the patient seeking help (or being referred by an outside agency, as the case may be).

Today's mental health practitioner is often called to deal with a wide range of challenges, from counselling law-enforcement authorities in cases of child abuse, to rehabilitation of victims of genocide. In such cases it may be more difficult for the analyst to assume that "dispassionate compassion" that is the essence of the therapeutic contract. These issues may or may not involve of the therapist's unresolved personal conflicts, and, therefore, may not have surfaced in his or her training analysis or therapy.

Part II of the book, therefore, contains contributions by clinicians with in-depth personal experience of therapy in such cases of heightened counter-transference risk.

CHAPTER

THREE

"Why do we have to remain so different?" Some Notes on Working with a Racially Abused Patient whose Skin Color Differs from that of the Analyst

GUSTAV SIKORA

"We do not see things as they are. We see things as we are."
ANAIS NIN, "Seduction of the Minotaur."

The concept of countertransference is complex issue that has undergone a significant transformation, from being viewed as a misperception caused by the analyst's pathology to an important instrument of research of the patient's unconscious. One of the important discussions on this topic was initiated by Money-Kyrle, who addressed the issue of "normal" versus defensive countertransference (Money-Kyrle, 1978). Brenman-Pick also added that "these [two separates types of counter-transference] do not operate in pure culture; rather, it is a question of to what extent the one or the other is in the ascendance" (Brenman-Pick, 2012). In this context, it appears that when working with traumatized patients, the complexity of transference-counter-transference become even more difficult to understand.

This chapter focuses on a particular aspect of countertransference, namely the limitations of the analyst's imagination and this limitation's influence on empathy and understanding. This chapter also addresses the further complication caused by overlapping between transference and the actual social and political situation experienced by the patient.

The author presents a case where the resulting conflicting feelings in the countertransference process were unavoidable. On the one hand, the analyst found himself being made to feel useless and meaningless by the patient; on the other hand, being urged to contain those feeling, feeling sorry for the patient, and wanting to relieve the patient's suffering, and, sometimes, even feeling guilty at the helplessness he experienced in witnessing the patient's suffering.

Eric Brenman wrote "Possibly the most challenging of all narcissistic problems for the analyst is . . . where the analyst is made to feel meaningless . . . " (Brenman, 2006); I would add that in this type of situation, the pressure from the analyst's superego also plays an important role. Bearing in mind the patient's history of trauma(s), the fact that the patient was a victim of abuse, and the analyst's own relatively "better life and situation" causes the analyst to feel both helpless and often guilty (as though an "insufficient parent" mixed with "liberal guilt"). The analytic situation becomes even more complex when the abuse and traumatizing factors continue to some extent.

This problem will be illustrated by a clinical vignette – working with a racially- and sexually-abused woman, who, at in certain stage of her analysis, began accusing her analyst of a lack of understanding caused by his race and sex (gender), implying an accusation of racism and sexism. Using this case as a basis, this chapter will endeavor to show some of the difficulties in working through the countertransference and its impact on the therapeutic technique. To clarify the complexity of this situation, the author briefly discusses multiple meanings of an understanding in analysis and of the patient's complaint regarding the lack of understanding on part of the analyst. Additionally, he discussed the links between understanding and empathy, considering different aspects of the latter, including biology and the role of imagination.

Using clinical materials, the author shows how the patient struggled with this situation and her effort to sort it out, although the main focus of the chapter is on how the analyst's worked through his countertransference.

Finally the author discusses the role of truth in the analytic process, which includes the acceptance of limitations and differences by both the patient and analyst alike.

In the conclusion, the author focuses on the ongoing internal process that takes place in the analyst's mind and the role of this internal process in the analytic process as a whole.

Introduction

This chapter focuses on the complex connection between facts encountered and their meaning to us, through the lens of certain elements of my work with a traumatized patient. The patient described in this case was a black woman, born in eastern Africa, who had lived since adolescence in continental Europe, but who had moved as an adult to England; whereas I, the analyst, am a white man who was born in Poland and moved to England as an adult. Although both of us were living and working outside our countries of birth and using a language (English) that was not our mother tongue, only the patient was an ongoing target of repetitive, continuous. and often severe white-on-black racial abuse. Here, I will focus on describing countertransference reactions that occurred during therapy. This dimension of analytic work confronted me with some particular problems. These problems, and my reflections on them, seem to be worth sharing with a wider audience.

This chapter presents observations from one analytic treatment. Its specificity lies not only in the role of trauma in the development of the patient's psychic structure, but also in the presence of traumatic experience at the time of analysis. Later in the text, I will give a more detailed account of it. This chapter does not aim to establish any general rules, but to serve as an observation of one analytic treatment.

Hans-Georg Gadamer, in his essay on "Philosophy and practical medicine," suggests that the physician must find what is most appropriate for a sole specific case, whereas science provides him with knowledge of general rules, mechanisms, and principles (Gadamer, 1996). Therefore it is obvious that the physician faces a completely new challenge with the specific case. In other words, any treatment is a hermeneutic process informed by our theory and knowledge. This is even truer when the treatment is psychoanalytic. Schafer describes psychoanalysis simply as "a process of construing meaning and constructing influential ways of telling it to others"; he also notes that others/analysands are ambivalent about being understood, something therapists are well-acquainted with in clinical practice (Schafer, 2003).

One of the most crucial tools used for the tasks of both understanding and formulating an interpretation, is the analysis of countertransference reactions. There is rich and vast literature on countertransference and I am not going to fully review it. However, I will try to point out, from a theoretical perspective, those aspects of working with countertransference that played an important role in the clinical work with my patient.

Empathy and countertransference

Racker, in his classic book *Transference and Countertransference*, makes a crucial distinction between concordant and complementary identifications (Racker, 1968). Specifically, concordance involves the analyst identifying with the analysand's self-state, whereas complementarity involves the analyst identifying with what the analysand disowns (see also Carveth, 2012). Racker regards the former as empathy, and claims that the term countertransference applies only to the latter, although he also notes that the two are closely connected. He suggests that complementary identifications develop when an analyst fails to establish concordant ones. Although we know that the process is far more complicated, in my opinion, Racker correctly captures interconnections between empathy, countertransference, and the analyst's defenses against what he or she encounters.

Money-Kyrle adds another dimension to our thinking on countertransference (Money-Kyrle, 1978). He differentiates "normal" versus defensive countertransference reactions, regarding the first as helpful for understanding a patient, whereas the latter poses a risk of subsequent harm to the patient. Brenman-Pick extends this discussion, saying that these two reactions never operate in a pure culture, and it is rather a question of which one is in the ascendance (Brenman-Pick, 2012). I would go even further and say that, in a clinical situation, the analyst's experience always contains a mixture of concordant and complementary identifications.

Schafer states that "What we know is not the fact of the matter plain and simple; rather, it is our interpretation of whatever is the case" (Schafer, 2003). Theory and clinical practice suggest that this understanding applies to what we know about our patients as well as about ourselves, since, during the process of analyzing the countertransference, the analyst interprets his or her own unconscious reactions, which come to some extent from his or her own unconscious phantasies. The definition of unconscious phantasy in 'The new dictionary of Kleinian thought' reads "unconscious phantasies underlie every mental process and accompany all mental activity . . . phantasy is the mental expression of both libidinal and aggressive impulses and also of defence mechanisms against those impulses . . . [they are] . . . underlying and shaping thought, dreams, symptoms and patterns of defence" (Spillius *et al.*, 2011). I think we can say that what Schafer describes as interpretations are, to a degree, driven by our phantasies. Segal explains that phantasies are unconscious hypotheses of the internal and external world (Segal, 1964). We can say that all our perception and experiences are, to some extent, shaped and limited by our phantasies, which are complex dynamic entities containing, among other elements, our previous experiences. When we try to understand our reactions, including empathy and countertransference (in Racker's narrow sense, as complementary identification), our interpretations have to take into account our phantasies; however we must be aware of that these interpretations are, to some extent, shaped by those same phantasies.

This view receives strong support from neuro-scientific findings. One of the leading researchers on biological understanding of empathy, Keysers, explains that a human brain reacts to what happens to another human being or to the other's actions by replicating the other's bodily experience via its "mirror neurons" (Keysers, 2011). Such an input is then interpreted by higher structures of the brain/mind. If we put this together with the theory of unconscious phantasy, whose origins are a " . . . mental representation of somatic events in the body . . . physical sensations interpreted as relationships with objects that cause those sensations"; we could assume that our empathy as analysts is an interpretation of what the patient is experiencing, but through our own experiences, embedded in our unconscious phantasies. Furthermore, Keysers claims that because the mirror system develops through Hebbian learning, we can only empathize with experiences/states that fit our prior experiences (Keysers, 2011). We, of course, know from clinical experience how important the analyst's broad life experience is. However, my point here is that because we always operate with approximate interpretations, sometimes we have to rely on imagination rather than on experience to make those interpretations. Furthermore, our imagination is limited by our experience.

To place this in a different frame of reference: the neuroscientist Friston developed a functional model of the brain as a hierarchically constructed "probability machine" (Friston, 2003)) and convincingly matched it with Freud's metapsychology. Others tried to develop it further by creating links to Bion's theory of thinking, drives, and ego functions (Hopkins, 2012). According to Friston, one dimension of this complex theory is that the entire process of perception involves the verification of a prior hypothesis that the brain has produced. These prior hypotheses have a hierarchical structure. When the reality (internal or external) differs from the hypotheses, "free energy" (which is a measure of surprise in this model) is released. Free energy can be bound by correcting the hypotheses or by action to change the reality or its perception; the latter includes ego functions of misrecognition (in Lacan's term, *meconnaissance*). Therefore, we can say that we are prone to interpret "what we see" in a way that is as close as possible to our prior experiences.

In spite of these causations and constraints, empathy and countertransference remain invaluable sources of knowledge about patients.

Role responsiveness

Sandler adds the dimension of role responsiveness to the discussion on countertransference, stating that "the interaction between the patient and the analyst . . . is in large part determined by the intrapsychic role-relationship that each party tries to impose on the other" and " . . . the role-relationship of the patient in analysis at any particular time consists of a role in which he casts himself and a complementary role in which he casts the analyst at that particular time" (Sandler, 1976). Later, he says " . . . in the analyst's overt reactions to the patient as well as in his thoughts and feelings what can be called his 'role responsiveness' shows itself, not only his feelings but also his attitudes and behavior, as a crucial element in his 'useful' countertransference". He further suggests that "very often the irrational response of the analyst, which his professional conscience leads him to see entirely as a blind spot of his own, may sometimes be usefully regarded as a compromise-formation between his own tendencies and his reflexive acceptance of the role which the patients is forcing on him". The analyst's efforts to distinguish and to analyze the patient's and his own contributions to his (the analyst's) reactions, are one of most important and most difficult tasks in an analytic session. Otherwise, using Segal's words, countertransference, instead of being the best servant becomes the worst master (Segal, 1981). I would emphasize that this process is very dynamic and is never fully completed. Therefore, we operate with approximations and what we call "truth" is rather estimation.

What the analyst must say; what the analyst can say

Freud placed priority on the search for truth (Freud, 1927). An analyst's efforts to understand his or her countertransference reactions is undertaken to glean some truth about the patient and use it in the interpretation, although it is well known that making an interpretation is a much more complex process than simply sharing the truth with the patient. There is always a risk that interpretation may become something that Steiner terms 'interpretative enactment' (Steiner, 2006).

Sedlak gives a very clear account of the importance of the analyst containing countertransference and suggests that proper containment not only prevents enactments but is also sensed by the patient and contributes to his or her development (Sedlak, 2015). O'Shaughnessy adds an interesting aspect to this discussion in her paper "What is a clinical fact?" in which she presents very vivid clinical illustrations of when an interpretation, even if containing a truth, may disturb the patient by actualizing his or her anxiety (O'Shaughnessy, 1994). She contrasts this with the situation in which the analyst interprets correctly by taking into account the patient's state of mind and his or her capacity to make use of this interpretation.

Doubts

Finally, before proceeding to the case study itself, I would like to draw attention to the analyst's doubts and convictions during the therapy session. In spite of all the constraints and problems that arise in the process of working through countertransference, the analyst must attain a certain degree of conviction. Of course, analysts are usually aware that they are not omniscient and they also have a large body of knowledge upon which to draw to verify the accuracy of their interpretations. However, analysts should always be cautious and try to evaluate whether their interpretation contains insight or rather an overvalued idea. Britton and Steiner suggest that analysts need to sustain doubts and be aware of their own defensive needs, excitement of discovery, and sense of achievement (Britton & Steiner, 1994). All this may constrain their ability to examine and evaluate their understanding. They go further, claiming that certain losses of conviction, doubt, guilt, and other depressive feelings are an inevitable part of the analyst's work in continuously monitoring the effect of the interpretation, which is a main tool by which to evaluate it. To this, Feldman adds the proposal that analysts should consider their doubts and convictions in terms of "to what extent they reflect processes within the analyst and to what extent they derive from the patient's pressures or projections, how these elements interact and their possible effect on the movement in the session" (Feldman, 2009).

Understanding

All the above dealt with the process of understanding, including the difficulties the analyst faces and ways of overcoming them. The need to work through countertransference is simply one cost of understanding the patient's mind, which is a main task of the analyst.

Usually, patients seek psychoanalysis because they want to be understood. However, as Schafer notes, they are ambivalent about understanding (Schafer, 2003). The meeting between the analyst who wants to understand and the patient who wants to be understood is never straightforward. Many patients say that they seek understanding of what's going on in their lives and minds when they come for consultation, yet unconsciously they are looking for something else or something more. What could understanding mean for them? "Understand me" may mean "love me" – the common teenager complaint of "you don't understand me" often means "you don't love me enough". Other times, "understand me" means "accept me" as I am; in spite of my problems, my aggression or any other perceived blemish. Until the patient cannot accept him or herself as he or she is, then understanding for the patient may mean not talking about what we really managed to understand in the process of analysis.

In fact, there is no contradiction between 'psychoanalytic' understanding and love and acceptance; on the contrary, proper understanding is very difficult or even impossible without love and acceptance. Early suggestions that the analyst should be emotionally neutral seem to have been widely abandoned. Hanna Segal used to say that the analyst who is emotionless is not neutral but neutered (Segal, private communication).

In the paragraphs above, I described some of the internal difficulties an analyst faces in the process of attaining understanding of the patient. Now, we can say that there are two important problems: Firstly, the patient is ambivalent about being understood psychoanalytically; the patient is often anxious about or hostile towards the analyst's understanding. Secondly, the patient and the analyst have different experiences and histories; therefore, they have different ways of understanding or even seeing things. This causes inevitable tension, which is, I believe, an important part of what Bion described as a 'storm', which inevitably appears when two personalities encounter each other (Bion, 1979).

Work with traumatized patient brings an additional dimension to the analysis. Obviously, the trauma shapes the patient's needs, expectations, and also defenses, and sometimes the entire functioning of the mind. However, the patient's trauma also has an enormous impact on the analyst's responses to the patient.

Racially abused patients

In this clinical material, I will try to illustrate elements of the process of working through countertransference in the analysis of a significantly traumatized patient. The additional specificity of this particular process stems from the repetitive and continuous character of the trauma.

A racial difference between an analyst and a patient adds an additional dimension to a psychoanalytic encounter. Within the growing body of psychoanalytic writing on race, one may find very different approaches; it is hard to say which approach is the most productive. Davids in his book "Internal Racism" claims that racism should be seen as a universal feature of the human mind and, as such, racial difference must be part of psychoanalytic investigation in a similar way that we investigate the gender divide (Davids, 2011). I found his approach convincing and clinically helpful. Here, I present a clinical situation which, in my opinion, illustrates this in detail and shows some problems specifically linked with racial difference and a trauma brought by racial stereotypes.

Analyzing Ms. C. was a very complex task for various reasons. However, the racism aspect was present from the first encounter. Initially, I thought that my gaining an understanding of her experience of the ethnic differences between us, and then working through its meaning and role in the analytic process, was a necessary task to establish the usual working patient–analyst relationship, one that contains, understands, and leaves enough air for interpretations to be acceptable, rather than persecutory. However, it quickly became clear that the trauma of racial abuse was a crucial aspect of Ms. C's mental functioning and shaped her defensive system and internal object relationships. This created a particular clinical reality in which we had very limited room for analysis. Room for analysis was restricted, on the one hand, by a risk that my fear of the inequality between us would disable my ability to interpret and, on the other hand, by a risk that the trauma would be re-enacted through a sense of submission on her part towards me. The dynamic of a dilemma of inequality is common in therapeutic work, but has special meaning in work with traumatized patients. Racial abuse brings further particularity to it.

A crucial dimension of the abuse was that it was located in the unchangeable features of the individuals involved. Thus, the different race of the analyst signifies otherness but also, and more importantly, is directly associated with an abuser. Race operates on a semantic level through linguistic, historic, and social narratives implanted in personal experience as well as at the semiotic level, in Bronstein's understanding of semiotic aspects of unconscious phantasy (Bronstein, 2013). The latter means that features, such as the color of the skin and eyes, or of other features that are normally even unnoticeable, can activate particular affective states.

Being of different races makes the actual experience of race division very difficult to match. Empathy, in this situation, is based on imagination rather than real experience. There is a risk that one may try to empathize too strongly either by denying reality or by covering feelings of guilt and threat stemming from the knowledge of the racial difference. Davids states that a victim of racial abuse is, in fact, utterly alone (Davids, 2011). I found his argument convincing; particularly in the consulting room with a patient seeking empathy from an analyst who had not had such an experience and even embodied the injustice experienced by the patient to some degree.

Finally, racial abuse is often a repetitive and ongoing experience, and this was certainly the case for this patient. The very first sentence of Davids' book reads 'to be black in a white world is an agony'; it is not possible to argue with this. It places the white analyst in a position where, alongside the usual analytic work, he or she witnesses repetitive trauma. The actual powerlessness and helplessness of the analyst is exposed, and this brings another dimension to the analytic situation at every level; the actual human relationship, transference, and countertransference. Shame, anger, sadness, and a whole range of feelings raised by those situations on both sides have to be digested. It is not always possible to locate these feeling within the psychic structure of the patient or, very often, within the mind of the analyst.

The patient

Ms. C. was a middle-aged black woman. She came to the analysis with difficulties in completing some academic work, which was bound up with her sense of identity. She had two fairly separated parts that were continuously present in her external appearance, the language she used, the level of her mental functioning, and my countertransference reactions. Sometimes, I could see a stylish, intelligent woman, very keen to talk about sophisticated matters, and at other times I saw a shattered child who could not find the words to express what she felt. Equally, I could feel one moment downgraded, insufficient, and attacked, and the next regarded as a fairly idealized man, who was able to rescue her life. Both these states very clearly were saturated with an element of racial and class tension.

As very often happens, that first encounter was very significant. At first, during a preliminary meeting, Ms. C. said she had hoped that her analyst would be a black woman who would be able to speak her native language; she suggested clearly that a person like me could never understand her. In the middle of the meeting, she expressed her fear that she could not express herself because she had no language at all and felt lost. Eventually, at the end, she said she had hoped to improve her English during her analysis by being analyzed by a well-spoken English intellectual, and she seemed to be very disappointed with me (with my Polish origin, I clearly have a foreign accent).

This first encounter enabled a brief glimpse into the world of her internal objects, whose detailed meaning would unfold later in analysis. The first object was black women, whom she consciously *wished* to identify with, yet unconsciously felt *obliged* to identify with and actually despised while feeling superior to. An unshaped object also emerged – this object could contain, understand and put in words what it was experiencing but was unnamed. Also apparent was a white privileged intellectual object that she wished to be; an object she would admire, fear, and hate at the same time.

The clinical situation of such a moment, however, was more complicated. On the patient's part, she experienced disappointment, fear of possible abuse, a sense of helplessness and worst of all – a sense of actualization of a past scenario in which she had to depend on a person who might treat her with superiority. On the analyst's side, I faced various disturbing feelings. On the one hand, I was somehow, I was trapped between the pressure of avoiding overly defending my analytic stance, which could easily lead to enactment of my "superiority" (by using psychoanalysis, which "belongs to white people" in her view); on the other hand I was trapped by my own sense of meaninglessness, which is accurately described by Eric Brenman as "possibly the most challenging of all narcissistic problems for the analyst" (Brenman, 2006). At the same time, I needed to deal with a risk of feeling guilty for having "a better life and situation" that approached the so-called "liberal guilt" and was coupled with helplessness as a witness of abuse. All of these had their sources in both the transference–countertransference, and in real, external situations, and it was often difficult to distinguish between the two.

Ms. C. was born in circumstances that she found degrading to the social status of her family. Her family's status was low in every respect: financially, socially, and even their house was located on the outskirts of the town. Class and racial divisions were ever-present. The value judgement based on skin color was so embedded in her life that even between siblings, there was a hierarchy based on the color of their skin.

Ms. C.'s mother seemed to be unable to maintain any long-term relationship, and was presented as a very disappointed, desperate woman. She was able to meet only the very basic needs of her children, and probably had some problems with impulse control: both sexual and aggressive. Ms. C. was a victim of her mother's violent behavior – she had a violent temper. As a teenager, Ms. C. very often felt she had to look after her mother. She said that her relationship with her mother had improved since the mother developed dementia. Since childhood, Ms. C. was a victim of sexual abuse, including from a teacher in her primary school.

When Ms. C. was 16 years old, she was sent to her mother's family in Europe, which she said was the dream of every child in her country at the time to be sent to Europe. In Europe, however, things were far different from what she had expected; once again, she found herself the victim of sexual abuse, which this time included her brother-in-law as the perpetrator. After a year, her grandmother and uncle decided to send her back to her mother; this was planned secretly to punish Ms. C. When she accidentally found out about their plan, she ran away from home and, following her friend's advice, provoked the police so that they would place her under state care. She spent three years in a state institution, but her life was continuously turbulent. She said that in that European country, racism was so common that it was a norm in her view. Later on, she tried to settle down and eventually she started a relatively stable relationship. Unfortunately, her partner ended it abruptly after several months; she believes he was persuaded to do so by his family. After the split, she was devastated and soon after moved to London. She completed an undergraduate university degree and then a Master's degree while working for a living.

During her last year at university, she began a relationship with a black man, and they had two children. She describes the relationship as an abusive one. She believes her partner suffered from the same problems she did – they were both from a similar background and they accused each other of selfishness, lack of confidence, and lack of support – but he always took advantage of being male, which seemed natural to her at the time. This relationship lasted for nine years, until Ms. C. decided to end it. Soon after, she started a new relationship with a white "old friend", who, in her estimation, was a permanent underachiever, weak, and childish, but their relationship functioned, they received some financial support from his parents.

Positioning and seduction

From the very beginning of her analysis, Ms. C. presented two different sides of herself, which meant that there was a form of superiority/inferiority between us. For instance, she was sensitive and black; I was white and did not understand racism. At other times, I was a brilliant analyst whom she did not deserve. Sometimes she was the sophisticated intellectual giving lectures on analysis to a Polish plumber (a derogatory English stereotype for Polish immigrants) who was pretending to be an analyst, whereas at other times she could experience me as a person who truly wanted to understand her difficulties, integrate her very varied experiences, and help her find her identity. These aspects interchanged very often and very fast.

In many ways, she settled into analysis well, bringing a lot of material from her past and current problems. She benefited from certain insights and started making some changes in her life. However, at the same time, a very omnipotent, narcissistic part of her personality believed that she had seduced me. This part considered us an ideal couple, with no limitations and absolutely free from any negative aspects of real life. An important dimension of this phantasy was her sense of control over the analyst, which could minimize her fear of sexual and racial abuse. This gave her a sense of super power and retreat from external and internal problems, yet also caused anxiety about a possible catastrophe – for example, that her analysis would end when a sexual relationship began – and was also accompanied by signs of terrible guilt. It was very rare at this stage of the analysis for Ms. C. to use race to undermine my analytic position directly. At that time, she would say that I simply could not understand her because I was white, or that I had learned a lesson from Fannon and I was deluded into thinking that I understood something. However, the racial aspect of our relationship seemed to remain relatively silent, controlled and almost "removed" by seduction. Over time, it gradually began to unfold through acting out, certain somatic reactions, and eventually in dreams and words.

Direct attacks, although rare, were always difficult and demanded serious internal work on the analyst's part to avoid defending myself (internally) that "I was not racist" and not respond to the attack; at the same time, it was important to not lose faith in my ability to understand her, while, remembering that I really understood very little about being a black victim of racial abuse. A "silent sense of racial division" was at least equally difficult. There was a sense that the inevitable asymmetry between the patient and the analyst activated a phantasy saturated with racial inequality, and that abuse might easily be enacted either by the patient's submission or in rebellion against the analyst's "domination".

We are the same

When her narcissistic defenses abated slightly, we gained more access to her traumatic experiences. Ms. C. started to talk about her experiences of racial abuse from the past and the present in a different way; there was a strong sense that the transference was saturated with seeking help and understanding, rather than with accusation and aggression. Despite this, there were clear signs of her internal struggle with accepting the racial difference between us. Thus, for example, when I appeared in her dreams, I was black, and in the subsequent session, she praised British psychoanalysts in contrast to a well-known foreign female psychoanalyst whose racial outburst she had witnessed; it was very hard to link it with the transference.

One day, Ms. C. reported a horrible incident. The previous day, her daughter had been refused tenancy of a flat on clearly racial grounds. She was understandably moved, angry and sad. I struggled with what I could say at such a moment. I wondered how to express my empathy without going too far. Davids vividly describes a possible outcome of going too far: "they [white friends] seem to be trying too hard to empathize with you, to establish common ground, to show that they too know what it is like to come up against blind prejudice. But do they? Is their tone now a little too condemnatory? Does it cover up guilt over the fact that the police [landlord, in our case] would not treat them like that, which threatens to expose the fact that you and they do not make we? That you are on different sides of the black–white divide?" (Davids, 2011).

Suddenly, Ms. C. said "I know you understand me. In that respect we are the same; Poles are treated equally badly here". It seemed she really believed that. I knew it was not true and I could not let a false sense of unity develop between us. On the other hand, I felt she really wanted me to be with her in this horrible moment. I replied, rather instinctively, that I didn't think that we could ever have the same experience in that respect, but I tried to imagine how horrible it is to be in such a situation and that my sympathy came from something other than having shared the same experience. Ms. C. was silent for considerable time. I was left uncertain as to whether I had addressed her denial of difference between us correctly, which was part of an idealized transference, or whether I had left the analytic position and stabbed her in back, and taken away the comfort she badly needed.

Eventually, she said that she knew that and appreciated that I had said it aloud. She was very sad but was able to think about what had happened.

Re-emerging and fear

In the following sessions there was clear sense of relief and a feeling that we could discuss her experience of being black openly. Ms. C. began bringing material involving racial issues to the therapy sessions on a regular basis. Sometimes this material was painful, such as when she intervened when she saw a black teenager being treated unfairly by police. Other times she needed to explain to me how it was to be the only black person at the concert hall, or why she thought that a certain film, which had garnered awards and been widely praised, cemented racist stereotypes. She was able to question and reconsolidate her identity to the degree that she became freer from self-victimization. Importantly, it became possible to see such material in terms of transference without excessive fear.

Additionally, as an analyst I could feel freer, as the risk of enactment was reduced. Even when she was angry and the old pattern of racial stereotypes came to the fore, Ms. C. was able to reflect on it. Gradually this reflection enabled us to gain a better understanding of other aspects of her mental functioning, such as unconscious guilt at being undeservedly better off in comparison with her siblings, or a feeling of omnipotent control that was covered by racial and gender stereotypes. All this helped Ms. C. to start using analysis to build a sense of her identity.

"Betrayal", guilt and mourning

Later on, when it became possible in analysis to look more closely at her identifications and objects, we could both see again how important the racial aspect has been. Ms. C. began searching for answers to questions such as "what does it mean to be in a loving relationship with her white partner?" and "what does it mean to be grateful to the white analyst?" She had to reconsider the meaning of her using psychoanalysis, which in her initial view belonged to white culture. She asked how she could be angry with me, and yet not feel overwhelmed by racial stereotypes. All this hard work confronted her with a sense of betrayal, guilt, and a sense of loss or mourning. Simultaneously with her own internal work, Ms. C. was confronted with accusations and doubtfulness by some of her friends and relatives. There was a sense that working through the racial aspect could create not only a sense of internal loss but also some real difficulties in actual relationships

These stages were accompanied by ongoing efforts on my part to work through countertransference issues, including checking the existence of my own racial stereotypes and defenses against them. The risk of being blind towards her aggressive impulses or, by contrast, of interpreting them in a persecutory or defensive way, was present all the time. Very often I had to learn about things whose existence I had not been aware of and then to integrate them and search for their meaning, for my patient as well as for myself.

Concluding remarks

The same principles and rules apply to analytic work with a traumatized patient as to any analytic treatment. As always, the patient and the analyst have to accept a painful reality. As always, the psychoanalytic process is largely a process of the search for meaning and understanding. Although the two sides start from very different positions and are equipped, sometimes, with very different experiences, we seek to find common ground in all these meanings and, for the sake of achieving this, we must acknowledge and accept our separateness and the differences between us. Nothing is new in this.

What I want to emphasize is one dimension of this process that lies completely on the analyst's side. Accepting one's own limitations is always hard; we have to deal with the difficult job of understanding the patient's experience when we are not equipped to do so out of our own personal experience. This makes empathy, complementary identifications, and our defenses more entangled than usual. Furthermore, in the case of patients traumatized by racism, the analyst is confronted with a real external situation that is unacceptable, and which inevitably evokes feelings of powerlessness, helplessness, anger, and guilt in the analyst. The analyst must deal with these feeling while under pressure from his or her superego to be a good analyst who is capable of understanding the patient, an empathizing human being, and a responsible member of the society. The analyst's ability to negotiate with his or her own superego is sometimes a crucial aspect of working through such complicated countertransference reactions.

References

Bion, W. R. (1979). Making the best of a bad job. *Bulletin of the British Psychoanalytic Society*, 10:15.

Brenman, E. (2006). The recovery of the good object relationship: The conflict with the superego. In G. Fornari Spoto (Ed.) *Recovery of the Lost Good Object*. London: Routledge.

Brenman-Pick, I. (2012). Working through in the counter transference – second thoughts, *Bulletin of the British Psychoanalytic Society*, 48: 3–9.

Britton, R., & Steiner, J. (1994). Interpretation: Selected fact or overvalued idea? *International Journal of Psychoanalysis*, 75: 1069–1078.

Bronstein, C. (2013). Finding unconscious phantasy in the session: Recognizing form. *Bulletin of the British Psychoanalytic Society*, 49, 14–21.

Carveth, D.L. (2012). Concordant and complementary countertransference: A clarification. *Canadian Journal of Psychoanalysis*, 20, 70–84.

Davids, F. (2011). *Internal Racism: A psychoanalytic approach to race and difference*. Basingstoke (UK): Palgrave Macmillan.

Feldman, M. (2009). The problem with conviction in the session. In B. Joseph (Ed.), *Doubt, Conviction and the Analytic Process*. London: Routledge.

Freud, S. (1959). *Postscript to the Question of Lay Analysis* (*Standard Edition*, vol. 20). London: Hogarth Press. (Original work published in 1927).

Friston, K. (2003). Learning and inference in the brain. *Neural Networks*, 16, 1325–1352.

Gadamer, H. G. (1996). Philosophy and practical medicine. In *The Enigma of Health*. Stanford, CT: Stanford University Press.

Hopkins. J. (2012). Psychoanalysis, representation, and neuroscience. In A. Fotopoulu, D. Pfaff, & M. Conway (Eds.). *From the Couch to the Lab*. Oxford, UK: Oxford University Press.

Keysers, C. (2011). *The Empathic Brain*. Amsterdam: Social Brain Press (Independent Publisher).

Money-Kyrle, R. E. (1978). Normal countertransference and of its deviation. In D. Meltzer & E. O'Shaughnessy (Eds.). *Collected Papers of Money-Kyrle*. Starthtay, Pertshire (UK): Clunie Press. (Original work published in 1956).

O'Shaughnessy, E. (1994). What is clinical fact? *International Journal of Psychoanalysis*, 75, 939–947.

Racker, H. (1968). *Transference and Cuntertransference*. London: The Hogarth Press.

Sandler, J. (1976). Countertransference and role-responsiveness. *International Review of Psychoanalysis*, 3, 43–47.

Schafer, R. (2003). *Insight and Interpretation*. London: Karnac.

Sedlak, V. (2015). The development of the psychoanalyst – the role of the superego. *Bulletin of the British Psychoanalytic Society*, 51:3–14.

Segal, H. (1981). Countertransference. In *The Work of Hanna Segal*. London: Jason Aronson.

Segal, H., *Private Communication.*

Segal, H. (1964). Symposium on phantasy–fantazy and other mental processes. *International Journal of Psychoanalysis*, 45, 191–194.

Spillius, E., Milton, J., Garvey, P., Couve, C., & Steiner D. (2011). Unconscious phantasy. In *The New Dictionary of Kleinian Thoughts.* London: Routledge.

Steiner, J. (2006). Interpretative enactments and analytic setting. *International Journal of Psychoanalysis*, 87, 315–320.

CHAPTER

FOUR

Countertransference in the Face of Growth: Reenactment of the Trauma

Yael Lahav, Ziya Seligman and Zahava Solomon

Treatment of survivors of childhood sexual abuse (CSA) poses difficult challenges for therapists, namely because of the wide array of powerful countertransference reactions. A vast amount of literature exists that describes these patterns; however, discussion until now has focused predominantly on the reaction of therapists to the negative effects of the trauma.

The present chapter addresses an aspect of countertransference that, to the best of the authors' knowledge, has yet to receive any attention in the literature on trauma: countertransference in response to reports of gains or positive changes after trauma. This has been defined in the literature as post-traumatic growth (PTG). Exploring countertransferential reactions to PTG and the mutual effects that occur between the two will provide further insight into the phenomenon of PTG. It will also assist therapists in assuming responsibility for their part in the appearance of PTG and the ways in which PTG unfolds in therapy. Five distinct positions of countertransference will be presented: dissociated therapist; therapist as perpetrator; therapist as neglectful parent; therapist as rescuer; and mourning therapist. The authors argue that these positions should be considered as reenactments of dissociated self-states and relational dynamics, rooted in the original trauma, that must be worked through in psychotherapy in order to foster integration and healing.

Introduction

Treatment of survivors of childhood sexual abuse (CSA) poses difficult challenges for therapists, due to of the wide array of powerful countertransference reactions. While the literature on this topic is vast and describes these patterns, the discussion until now has predominantly focused on the reaction of therapists to the negative effects of trauma, while overlooking their reactions to patients' reports on the positive effects of trauma.

The present chapter, therefore, addresses countertransference that develops in response to patients' reports of gains or positive changes after the trauma, defined in the literature as post-traumatic growth (PTG). Exploring countertransferential reactions to PTG and the mutual effects that occur between the two will provide further insight into the phenomenon of PTG. It will also assist therapists in assuming responsibility for their part in the very appearance of PTG and the ways in which it unfolds in therapy.

The present chapter will first discuss the psychological process and long term ramifications of CSA. Second, the concept of PTG will be presented together with a clinical vignette. Following this, the controversy regarding the nature of PTG will be discussed. Third, the role of transference and countertransference dynamics within the treatment of CSA will be presented, with a particular focus on the reenactments of dissociated self-states and relational dynamics through transference-countertransference. Fourth, in regards to the patients' reports of PTG, five countertransference positions will be offered. Lastly, the significance of the therapist's reflective stance will be discussed.

The trauma of childhood sexual abuse

The World Health Organization (WHO) defines childhood sexual abuse as:

> *. . . the involvement of a child in sexual activity that he or she does not fully comprehend, is unable to give informed consent to, or for which the child is not developmentally prepared and cannot give consent, or that violates the laws or social taboos of society. Child sexual abuse is evidenced by this activity between a child and an adult or another child who by age or development is in a relationship of responsibility, trust or power, the activity being intended to gratify or satisfy the needs of the other person.* (World Health Organization, 1999, p. 75)

CSA is considered incest when the sexual act is performed by a parent, family member, as well as relatives or people who function in family roles.

CSA is one of the most malevolent traumas occurring within the interpersonal realm. The abused child is subjected to exploitation, use of force, betrayal and fiduciary breaches at the hands of the perpetrator, who uses the child for sexual gratification while invalidating the child's needs. Denial and abandonment by other adult figures who overlook the abuse are also part of the abused child's experience, as they minimize or justify the abuse and thus enable its continuation.

Moreover, unlike other forms of interpersonal violence, sexual abuse of children, particularly when committed by someone emotionally close to the child, who the child knows and trusts, constitutes an intolerable combination of exploitation, injury and intrusion. Although such an act invalidates the child's needs, he or she may interpret this as an expression of love and affection by the perpetrator who uses the child's need for tenderness as a way to satisfy his or her needs. Thus, the child experiences unbearable conflict, since any kind of recognition regarding the abuse may impede the child's perceived ability to preserve close emotional connections, which are essential for normal development (Seligman, 2004). Different psychological mechanisms, dissociation in particular, help the child avoid the unbearable knowledge concerning the abuse and preserve the bonds with the abusive perpetrator (Ferenczi, 1932).

A wide variety of long-term effects have been associated with childhood sexual abuse (e.g., Briere & Elliott, 2003). A meta-analysis, including thirty-seven studies published between 1981 and 1995, indicated that adults who were sexually victimized during their childhood appeared to be at an increased risk for developing a variety of symptoms, such as post-traumatic stress disorder (PTSD), depression, suicidality, sexual promiscuity and sexual perpetration (Paolucci, Genuis, & Violato, 2001).

Furthermore, according to various researchers and clinicians (e.g., Herman, 1992; Herman & van der Kolk, 1987), exposure to a protracted pernicious interpersonal trauma, such as CSA, could result in a complex form of post-traumatic stress disorder (PTSD), or disorders of extreme stress not otherwise specified (DESNOS) (van der Kolk, Roth, Pelcovitz, Sunday, & Spinazzola, 2005). This disorder includes deep and long-lasting difficulties in a variety of domains in one's life, and reflects damage to the basic elements of the survivor's personality. Alterations in the regulation of affective impulses, attention and consciousness, self-perception and relationships with others, as well as somatization and changes in systems of meaning, may be a part of this syndrome (Herman, 1992; Herman & van der Kolk, 1987). Although the main focus of clinical and empirical studies have been on the long term negative effects of CSA, the post-traumatic experience is often more complex, as the present vignette demonstrates:

Tal, a woman in her thirties, sought help for emotional distress resulting from incest trauma. During the intake, she reported that she was eight years old when her father sexually assaulted her for the first time. These sexual assaults lasted for five years. She described feelings of contamination and shame and constant vigilance towards others. She reported that she found it hard to trust her partner, and when he touched her without warning, she felt as though she might burst, or alternatively, she experienced dissociation and detachment. However, before ending our session, she smiled, and commented that she felt that the abuse was not in vain and that it made her stronger. As a result of the incest, she now knew that she "could handle anything" and she "believed in herself and in her abilities". She reported that her relationships with those close to her were stronger, as she learned to appreciate others and to be honest with the people in her life.

CSA survivors' perceptions regarding their traumatic past may be multifaceted. Notwithstanding the reports of the trauma's negative ramifications, survivors may also attribute positive effects to their traumatic past, as was demonstrated in the vignette, a phenomenon which is most commonly known as *post-traumatic growth* (PTG).

How can one understand reports of PTG among survivors of severe and harsh trauma, such as CSA? What challenges might it raise during psychotherapy, and how do therapists react to such reports of PTG, and what are their common countertransferential reactions? While the former question has gained much attention within the trauma literature, the latter remains largely uninvestigated. Hence, this chapter explores therapists' countertransference reactions in response to their patients' reports of PTG.

Post-traumatic growth (PTG) – Definition and prevalence

Post-traumatic growth (e.g., Calhoun & Tedeschi, 2006; Calhoun, Tedeschi, & Tedeschi, 1999) –also known as *perceived benefits, positive aspects,* and *transformation of trauma* (Bloom, 1998; Calhoun & Tedeschi, 1990; Tedeschi & Calhoun, 1988) – is defined as positive psychological changes resulting from a struggle with a past traumatic experience (Calhoun & Tedeschi, 2006).

PTG refers to the individual's report of personal development that, at least in some areas, has surpassed what was perceived by the person as being present before the traumatic event. Hence, trauma survivors who report PTG have not only survived or recovered from the trauma, returning back to their level of pre-trauma functioning, but they have also undergone positive changes that surpass their previous status quo. Post-traumatic growth, then, has been conceptualized as a phenomenon that has the quality of transformation, or a qualitative change in functioning, unlike the seemingly similar concepts of resilience, sense of coherence, optimism, and hardiness (Tedeschi & Calhoun, 1995).

It is important to underline that, according to Tedeschi and Calhoun (2004), PTG and traditional measures of psychological adjustment are thought to be independent, because domains of growth are conceptually distinct from general emotional adjustment. PTG is not the same as an increase in well-being or a decrease in distress (Tedeschi & Calhoun, 2004). Therefore, as was demonstrated in the vignette, PTG and emotional distress may very well coexist.

Many stressful or traumatic events have produced reports of post-traumatic growth, at least in some form, including bereavement (e.g., Calhoun & Tedeschi, 1989–1990), disease (e.g., Tennen, Affleck, Urrows, Higgins, & Mendola, 1992), combat (e.g., Sledge, Boydstun, & Rabe, 1980), terror (e.g., Levine, Laufer, Hamama Raz, Stein, & Solomon, 2008) and war captivity (e.g., Feder *et al.*, 2008; Lahav, Bellin, & Solomon, In Press). PTG has also been documented among sexual assault survivors (Burt & Katz, 1987; Frazier, Conlon, & Glaser, 2001; Veronen & Kilpatrick, 1983), as well as among CSA survivors (Draucker, 1992; McMillen, Zuravin, & Rideout, 1995; Silver, Boon, & Stones, 1983).

According to Tedeschi and Calhoun (2004), PTG is exhibited in three domains: elevated positive self-perception, improved interpersonal relationships, and a more optimistic world view. An increased appreciation for life is a major element of trauma survivors' reports of PTG, with a possible report of a major revision of how they approach and experience their daily lives. They might also report a change in life priorities with an increase in the importance of aspects that might have previously been considered insignificant, and a recognition of the importance of not taking things for granted. Growth in this domain might also manifest in an engagement with or strengthened belief regarding spiritual and existential matters.

A general sense or recognition of increased personal strength is another domain of post-traumatic growth. According to Tedeschi and Calhoun (2004), while coming to grips with surviving the trauma, individuals may gain insight into the sense of possessing more strengths and powers than they ever imagined. This experience of enhanced competency could enable more active, assertive and effective coping with difficulties in the future. Moreover, the need to develop new interests during the trauma as a way to improve coping may expose individuals to new possibilities for one's life. This may lead to taking a new and more fulfilling path in life.

Lastly, PTG might be indicated in the interpersonal domain (Calhoun *et al.*, 1999). Closer, more intimate, and more meaningful relationships are also reported as part of the individual's experience of post-traumatic growth. A greater connection to others can also be manifested by experiencing an increased sense of compassion, particularly for others who may share the same difficult fate.

The nature of PTG – Genuine transformation or illusory defenses

Although PTG has been repeatedly reported in numerous psychosocial studies, there remains a controversy regarding its nature and long-term implications. On the one hand, PTG is viewed as a genuine transformation in basic beliefs about the self and the world, resulting from struggles with the effects of trauma (e.g., Calhoun & Tedeschi, 2006; Schaefer & Moos, 1998). On the other hand, PTG is contested as a phenomenon that reflects, at least in part, illusory defenses that may be maladaptive and that may hinder coping in the long-term (e.g., Davis & McKearney, 2003; Hobfoll *et al.*, 2007; Maercker & Zoellner, 2004; McFarland & Alvaro, 2000). This view suggests that individuals facing threatening events may respond with positive illusory perceptions of themselves, of personal control, as well as unrealistic optimism (e.g., Taylor, 1989). These positive illusory perceptions might serve as a cognitive avoidance strategy in the face of trauma, strengthening efforts to avoid acknowledging the traumatic event and the multiple losses it entails. However, such perceptions may have deleterious effects on adjustment in the long run (e.g., Maercker & Zoellner, 2004).

Maercker and Zoellner's (2004) *Janus Face Model of PTG* suggests that PTG includes both a constructive aspect and an illusory aspect. While the constructive component of PTG is purportedly associated with functional cognitive restructuring and adjustment, the implications of the self-deceptive illusory component is inconclusive, depending on its function as well as the time when it is applied.

According to Maercker and Zoellner (2004), in the short run, the illusory component of PTG does not necessarily represent denial or efforts to avoid thinking about the traumatic material. On the contrary, this aspect of PTG might coexist with deliberate thinking about the trauma and reflect an acute coping mechanism that fosters self-enhancement cognitions while under threat, in order to reduce stress. Hence, use of this mechanism might lead to short-term palliative results, with neither positive nor negative effects. However, if this illusory element is linked to avoidance efforts, fostering the evasion of thinking about the trauma in the long run, then it could act as a way to deny and repress traumatic memories, having long-term negative effects on adjustment (Maercker & Zoellner, 2004).

The contested discourse regarding the nature of post-traumatic growth and its implications is further accentuated by findings that imply the potential illusory function of PTG. For example, McFarland and Alvaro (2000) investigated the impact of self-enhancement motivation on the temporal comparisons of survivors of stressful life events. Their results, based on experimental approaches, revealed that survivors were more likely than their acquaintances to describe greater improvement in their personal qualities after traumatic life events than after mild negative life events. Moreover, the findings revealed that while there were no differences between the two groups (i.e., severe-event survivors and mild-event survivors) regarding their current assessment of personal capabilities, the recalled pre-event ratings by those who endured severe events were significantly more negative in comparison. Thus, it seems that survivors of severe events appeared to have perceived improvement by devaluing their previous attributes rather than by elevating their current traits. In addition, findings showed that threats to feelings of self-worth played a causal role in prompting self-enhancing temporal comparisons; as such participants who experienced negative feelings had a tendency for negative pre-event ratings, compared to participants who, during the experiment, were induced to experience more pleasant feelings. Altogether, the findings of these studies support the view that perceptions of personal improvements reflect, at least at some level, motivated illusions (McFarland & Alvaro, 2000).

Mixed empirical findings regarding the relationship between PTG and well-being among survivors of various traumatic events also deepens the debate concerning the nature of PTG. For example, considering the relation between PTG and psychological distress, studies varied, as did the findings, which indicated positive, negative, and no relation between the two (Helgeson, Reynolds, & Tomich, 2006; Linley & Joseph, 2004; Zoellner & Maercker, 2006). The meta-analytic review by Helgeson *et al.*, (2006), found PTG to be related to lower depression but greater avoidance and intrusive thoughts. Notwithstanding, the studies in the review that used well-established measures indicated that PTG was related to more global distress and intrusive-avoidant thoughts.

A similar trend of mixed findings has been found regarding the association between PTG and PTSD symptoms (e.g., Helgeson *et al.*, 2006; Linley & Joseph, 2004). While some studies have revealed a negative association between the two (e.g., Frazier *et al.*, 2001), with lower levels of distress associated with greater growth, others have found the opposite (e.g., Dekel, Ein-Dor, & Solomon, 2012; Greene, Lahav, Kanat-Maymon, & Solomon, 2015), with higher posttraumatic symptoms associated with greater growth. Others still have uncovered a curvilinear relationship between trauma and PTG (Levine *et al.*, 2008).

Thus, the discourse concerning the essence of PTG implies that PTG may be a complex multifaceted phenomenon that holds various meanings for CSA survivors. This may have important implications that are not limited to the theoretical realm but which are also concerned with the clinical realm.

The following sections look at the therapist's responses, as reflected in countertransference reactions, when facing their patient's reports of PTG. First, the definition of countertransference and its particular role in the treatment of trauma survivors is presented. We will then discuss our understanding of the countertransference relations as a reflection of the patient's unsymbolized and dissociated representations of the self as well as internalized relational systems. From this perspective, and based on Ferenczi's trauma theory, we will then suggest five variations of countertransference reactions in regards to the patient's reports of PTG.

Countertransference reaction in the face of PTG

The concept of countertransference has gone through major transformations over the years. The view of the analyst as a blank screen upon which the patient projects feelings and wishes has shifted to that of two co-participants involved in a process of discovery and co-construction centered upon the evolving patient's sense of self (Aron, 1996). The intersubjective perspective, which is adopted by the authors, views countertransference as "the analyst's experience of and contribution to the transference-countertransference . . . [which] refers to an unconscious intersubjective construction generated by the analytic pair" (Ogden, 1998, p.25). [See Marron, Chapter Two of this volume for a full discussion of this transformation.]

In psychoanalytic treatment, transference and countertransference relationships are considered to be central to understanding the patient's self-transformative process. This emphasis is especially critical when it comes to treating trauma survivors (Herman, 1992). This is because profound trauma, such as CSA, cannot be registered symbolically or verbally (Ferenczi, 1932). Often, the traumatic experience remains unorganized and unsymbolized, and, therefore, cannot be contained, apprehended, articulated, represented, or narrated, nor can it be recalled (Laub, 1992). Survivors are often entrapped in their trauma, "not truly in touch either with the core of his traumatic reality or with the fatedness of its reenactments, and thereby remains entrapped in both" (Laub, 1992, p. 69). In treatment, these unsymbolized memories begin to emerge as formless affects and body sensations, frequently taking the form of unexpected reactions to external stimuli, particularly in relation to the therapist. In these moments, there is an activation of the past, or a collapsing of the past and present via transference-countertransference enactments.

Countertransferential reactions are often an expression of dissociated aspects of the traumatic past. The therapist's countertransference may unfold the patient's dissociated self-states, which are unavailable to consciousness and highly disintegrated (Bromberg, 2011). Furthermore, the patient's split-off representations of irreconcilable aspects of the traumatic relations may be reenacted through the countertransference relationship (Davies & Frawley, 1992, 1994). It is, therefore, critical that the therapist be ready to attend to his or her countertransferential responses, since they are the map that should guide the therapist through the hidden banks of the transference and the patient's dissociation. Working through the transference-countertransference dynamics is clearly the foundation that enables the healing process to take place, as the therapist helps the patient name, form, and symbolize these dissociated, unformulated aspects of trauma and integrate them.

The trauma literature has indeed paid extensive attention to countertransference and documented various reactions experienced by the therapist treating CSA survivors (Davies & Frawley, 1994; Neumann & Gamble, 1995). However, these accounts describe the countertransference patterns only in relation to the *negative* ramifications of the trauma. The therapist's CT, in the face of the patient's positive reports of PTG, has yet to be explored, and will be investigated within the present chapter for the first time.

Based on Ferenczi's (1932, 1949) theory concerning psychological adaptation to child abuse, and the authors' clinical experience in therapy and during clinical supervision, the authors have identified five different types of countertransference reactions to reports of PTG during the treatment of CSA survivors. As will be demonstrated, these countertransference patterns may reflect reenactments of the patient's dissociated self-states and dissociated relational dynamics. These types of countertransference include the dissociated therapist, the therapist as perpetrator, the therapist as neglectful parent, the therapist as rescuer, and the mourning therapist.

The fragmentation of the patient's self-object world, as resulting from the original trauma, is reflected in the countertransference reactions of the therapist. Two general polarities can be identified within the presented countertransference positions: on the one hand, the therapist's embrace of the patient's reports of PTG, as reflected in the first three positions; and, on the other hand, the therapist's complete negation of the patient's reports of PTG, as indicated in the last two positions.

Position I – The dissociated therapist

The countertransference position of the dissociated therapist develops as a form of identification with the dissociated child. The sexually abused child reacts to the overwhelming, unbearable, and dangerous attacks at the hands of the perpetrator by dissociating the self from these experiences. Dissociation, which constitutes splitting off from the immediate perception of the experience, enables the abused child to escape from the pain and suffering temporarily, an ability that is crucial for their survival (e.g., Davies & Frawley, 1994; Putnam, 1993). According to Ferenczi, in stressful situations the "partial negation and distortion of reality is its replacement by a dream" (1932, p. 180). In more extreme circumstances, dissociation is manifested by the "total negation of reality" (Ferenczi, 1932, p. 180). As a result, the child feels invulnerable to pain or to being hurt, as if the traumatic event is happening to someone else. Moreover, the dissociated child may even show "a manic feeling of pleasure, as if [he or she] had succeeded in withdrawing completely from the painful situation" (1932, p. 6), while in fact trying to survive the abuse.

The extreme gap between the split-off suffering and the trauma survivor's appearance of intactness and even pleasure from the abuse, which commonly appears as part of dissociation, may be the key for understanding the reports of PTG by CSA survivors. Reports of gains and benefits as a result of the trauma, as indicated in PTG, could reflect the negation of the traumatic reality and its replacement by an alternate dissociative narrative (Lahav *et al.*, In Press). This narrative is detached from the intolerable pain of the abuse and constitutes a substitute reality where the abuse was not in vain, and where the self not only survived the trauma but was also strengthened by it.

While the dissociated beliefs of PTG may be essential for the child's survival during the trauma, it might pose impediments when experienced after the trauma is over. Similar to other dissociated experiences, PTG may entail significant mental maneuvering (Braude, 2000), including disavowal and even temporal or complete amnesia of the traumatic and painful experiences. These are often re-experienced in the form of dreams, flashbacks, and flooding of the original feelings and sensations (Chu & Dill, 1990). Moreover, this fragmentation prevents working through the trauma and inhibits the healing process (Davies & Frawley, 1994).

In psychotherapy with CSA survivors, the self-state of the dissociated child that holds on to the PTG narrative might be reenacted by and with the therapist. The therapist who experiences this form of countertransference tends to embrace, in excessive fashion, the patient's reports of post-traumatic growth, over emphasizing it and even viewing it as a reflection of the patient's strengths and capabilities. This trend goes hand-in-hand with emotional detachment and avoidance of traumatic content by the therapist, who feels compelled to keep the patient's hope and faith in the benevolence of the world and to protect the patient from emotional pain.

The therapist who identifies and reenacts the dissociated child through this form of countertransference cannot bear the pain and sense of helplessness associated with CSA. As a result, the therapist splits these feelings off from his or her consciousness. Instead of experiencing the intolerable agony, horror, and helplessness, of learning about such acts of sadism, cruelty, deception and betrayal, alternate narratives about the 'positive' aspects of the trauma, as manifested in PTG reports, become dominant.

While at the beginning of the therapeutic process this position might serve as a source of comfort for both the patient and the therapist, encouraging hope, in the long run it might hinder the healing. As the therapy progresses, this countertransference position will possibly impede the reflection and processing of those parts of the patient's experience that deviate from the narrative of growth. The patient's painful traumatic experiences, as well as other dissociated self-states that relive the traumatic past and suffer desperation and pain, do not have the opportunity to be expressed in therapy and thus remain unspoken and overlooked. These self-states would likely be expressed outside therapy in untreated dissociated symptoms, such as self-injury or re-victimization. In this way, the original dissociation is repeated in the present, as the fragmentation of the self only deepens.

Position II – The therapist as perpetrator

The countertransference position of the therapist as perpetrator develops when the therapist comes to embody the patient's representation of the abuser, a representation that was previously internalized to protect him or herself during the abuse. This belongs to the process known as identification with the aggressor, as described by Ferenczi (1932, 1933).[1]

According to Ferenczi, the sexually abused child who experiences both repeated invalidation of his or her basic needs, as well as protracted sadistic attacks, must identify with the perpetrator in order to protect the self. Subordinating themselves to the perpetrator, abused children replace their own experience and agency with that of the perpetrator (Ferenczi, 1932, 1949; Frankel, 2002). The child's self has been demolished by terror, leaving him or her with "no emotions of [his or her] own – living somebody else's life . . . instead of one's own life" (1932, p. 171; see also 1933, p. 163).

The child who identifies with the perpetrator subordinates him or herself to the perpetrator as a way of coping with the abuse. Consequently, the child then seeks to enter into the perpetrator's mind in order to know what the perpetrator wants. In this way, the child can anticipate the abuse and minimize the hazards. Lastly, in order to ensure survival, the child submits and complies (Ferenczi, 1932, 1949; Frankel, 2002).

The abused child, who identifies with the perpetrator, is no longer resistant or hateful, but feels for and understands the perpetrator. The child in this position feels the way the perpetrator expects him or her to feel. This also includes experiencing what the perpetrator feels. This form of identification may also include denial of the abuse. This identification creates confusion, leading the child to doubt his or her own perception of reality (Ferenczi, 1932). The child might even experience the pleasure the perpetrator derives from the abuse and "become so sensitive to the emotional impulses of the person he fears that he feels the passion of the aggressor as his own". (Ferenczi, 1932, p. 91)

According to Ferenczi (1932) the split part of the personality that identifies with the perpetrator is able to escape from the cruel reality. This occurs through premature progression, which includes rapid sexual, emotional and intellectual maturity manifested in precocious abilities, hypersensitivities, superintelligences and even clairvoyance (Frankel, 1998). This precocious development enhances survival by enabling the child to assess the environment and to satisfy the perpetrator's needs (Ferenczi, 1932).

The defensive process of early maturity may lead to excessive achievement and the compulsive tendency to take on "superhuman tasks" (Ferenczi, 1932, p. 80). However, this part of the child's self is lacking feelings of its own, since this might hinder efficient performance. In addition, this dissociated self-state remains vulnerable due to a continuing wish to regress (Ferenczi, 1932), and not to take on any responsibilities, to make an effort and work hard (Ferenczi, 1949). As an adult, this self-state allows the survivor to preserve relationships with the abuser and to keep the experiences of the abuse at bay.

We would like to suggest that the survivor's perceptions regarding the salutogenic effects of the trauma, manifested in the reporting of PTG, might be rooted in this process of identification with the perpetrator. Adopting the perpetrator's denial regarding the prolonged pernicious ramifications of the abuse and embracing the perpetrator's distorted beliefs concerning the gains and advantages of the abuse for the victim, may lead to reports of positive change and growth. Moreover, CSA survivors' reports of PTG may reflect their inappropriate, over-matured presentation, which were defensive reactions in the face of the abuse.

In psychotherapy, the traumatic relational matrix between the perpetrator and the abused child who identifies with the perpetrator, is often relived and reenacted (Davies & Frawley, 1994). The therapist in this countertransference position takes on the role of the perpetrator who ignores the child's needs and exploits the child's trust for the therapist's own sake. Similar to the former countertransference position (the dissociated therapist), the therapist in this position overemphasizes and validates the patient's reporting of PTG and takes it at face value. Unlike the retreated and detached approach that characterizes the preceding countertransference position, the current position of the therapist reflects aggression and sadism towards the patient. The therapist who reenacts the role of the perpetrator unconsciously uses the patient's reporting of PTG as a legitimate excuse to doubt the harshness of the patient's trauma, to invalidate the distress, and to expose the patient to excessive pain in an unregulated manner during therapy.

Furthermore, the therapist in this position could use the patient's reports of PTG as a way of overlooking the social responsibility regarding the abuse. Similar to other voices often heard within the social discourse, the therapist also perceives the patient as responsible for the abuse, as though the patient initiated the abuse and even benefited from it.

The patient, on the other hand, may reenact the self-state of the abused child who identifies with the perpetrator and relive the traumatic dyadic relational system. As in the original abusive dynamics, the patient subordinates to the therapist and adopts the therapist's stances, feelings and perceptions. Therefore, the patient gives special emphasis to the "good parts" of the traumatic past – the advantages and the positive changes accompanying the abuse. Moreover, the overmatured self-state of the patient may become dominant in therapy, demonstrating impressive abilities and achievements, thus strengthening the therapist's stance regarding the patient's growth.

However, in instances when the patient's split-off part of the injured child arises and expresses distress, the therapist may express his or her disappointment and accuse the patient of being 'spoiled'. The therapist may even misuse prior reports of PTG in order to dismiss the patient's protests. Lastly, if the patient abandons the narrative of PTG, the therapist might experience this as a personal attack against him or her or the therapy and use clinical concepts, such as resistance or negative therapeutic reaction, as a means to justify emotional abandonment of the patient.

Position III – The therapist as neglectful parent

The countertransference position of the therapist as neglectful parent develops when the therapist identifies with the patient's internal representation of the neglectful parent. The trauma of CSA often exposes the child not only to the betrayal of the abuser, who is often someone who is bound to the child emotionally, but also to the neglect and betrayal of the non-abusive parent(s). This neglect is manifested by the denial of the abuse and disavowal of the child, signaling that something wrong is going on. The neglectful parent minimizes the severity of the abuse and degrades the child's perceptions of and reactions to it (Davies & Frawley, 1994; Ferenczi, 1932). As a result, the child cannot find help or support within the relationship with the parent and is left profoundly and unbearably alone (Ferenczi, 1949).

Although emotions such as disappointment and rage towards the neglectful parent do exist, the parent was often also loved and needed by the child. Therefore, the relational constellation of the neglected child with the neglectful parent is split off from consciousness, and instead, the patient preserves a conscious image of either a loving and available parent, or of a weak and helpless parent (Davies & Frawley, 1994).

The CSA survivor's report of PTG might, therefore, reflect the abused child's attempts to please the neglectful parent. By minimizing the harsh ramifications of the abuse and pointing to the positive benefits of the trauma, the CSA survivor can preserve their attachment to the neglectful parent and keep other parts of the self at bay, those that cry out for help and experience rage against the parent's neglect.

In psychotherapy, the abused child – neglectful parent relational matrix is reenacted in the transference-countertransference relationship regarding the patient's reporting of PTG. As such, the therapist who reenacts the role of the neglectful parent may over-embrace the patient's reports of PTG, while ignoring its potential defensive qualities, as well as overlook the patient's needs and distress. Invalidating the severity of the abuse and over-relying on the reports of PTG, the therapist may experience an exaggerated confidence concerning the patient's mental condition, as if the patient can cope with the traumatic memories without any help. Moreover, the therapist in this position may be occupied with his or her own narcissistic needs and use the patient's positive reports as a way of enhancing their professional self-image. As in the original traumatic interaction, the therapist's attitude towards the patient may be characterized by hypocrisy (Ferenczi, 1931). Specifically, while on the surface the therapist expresses caring concern, the therapist actually remains uninvolved and even denies the patient's adversity.

On the other hand, the patient who reenacts the role of the neglected child in therapy may try to live up to the therapist's expectations. Thus, the patient may report PTG excessively or emphasize the positive aspects of the trauma, while underestimating the negative effects. The patient may present optimistic points of view and portray himself or herself as a well-functioning adult who enjoys life. It is as if the patient is saying to the therapist, "I am fine. You should not worry about me. The thing that happened to me was not so bad and even has a positive side, so you do not have to care for me".

Although the patient tries to please the therapist by emphasizing alleged growth, he or she may often use alternative paths to communicate the things that are left unspoken, such as distress, unbearable pain, and suffering, as well as anger towards the neglectful therapist. Similar to the abused child, who disperses clues in a desperate effort to get the parent's attention and save the self, the patient uses the symptomatic language or somatization as a way to express adversity. As long as the transference-countertransference dynamics remain unelaborated, the patient's distress could be manifested outside the therapy by various symptoms such as self-injury or re-victimization. More so, as time passes, the patient might express rage towards the therapist for overlooking his or her needs, directly as well as indirectly, through the exacerbating symptoms.

Position IV – The therapist as rescuer

This countertransference position of the therapist as rescuer develops when the therapist enacts the role of an omnipotent, all-giving rescuer in reaction to the patient's helplessness and suffering. Even though the abused child often develops compensatory self-states in order to survive the abuse, there are other dissociated states that perpetuate the experience of the defenseless and helpless child, who remain defenseless and helpless, constantly reliving the trauma. Desperately dependent, this part of the self-state cries out for help and rescue (Ferenczi, 1932).

In psychotherapy, this patient's self-state of the helpless victim, which yearns to be rescued, may elicit strong rescuing responses from the therapist (Herman, 1992; Saakvitne, 1990). This dynamic leads to the development of the omnipotent rescuer-helplessness victim dyad, which then creates a position of countertransference expressed by negative attitudes towards the patient's reports of PTG.

The therapist who enacts the omnipotent rescuer perceives the patient as a helpless child who must be saved. This comes at the expense of other aspects of the patient's condition that deviate from the victim role, effectively obscuring the patient's strengths. In this state, moreover, the therapist is unable to tolerate reports of positive feelings on the part of the patient regarding either the abuse or the perpetrator, considering them to be distorted.

Thus, when the patient reports PTG, the therapist who enacts the role of the rescuer responds to the patient with negation and dismissal. The therapist ignores the patient's reports of positive transformations resulting from the abuse or, at other times, minimizes these reports and emphasizes the negative effects of the trauma. The therapist may even adopt a didactic approach that could be manifested by pointing out the "distortions" or biases accompanying PTG beliefs and encouraging the patient to acknowledge the "true" effects of the trauma.

Meanwhile, the patient might try to gratify the therapist's needs by intensifying the victim role. The patient may appear to be a defenseless and powerless victim who cannot take responsibility for their own healing process or help themselves in any way. Feeling lost and weak, the patient becomes extremely dependent on the therapist and expects the therapist to rescue him/her and even to undo the abuse. It is as if the patient says to the therapist, "Rescue me, save me! I know nothing, you have the knowledge and the power to help me, and without your help I will be lost".

At the same time, however, the patient conceals conflicting feelings and perceptions. As such, experiences of being potent and powerful, dissociative states of the self that negate the abuse and/or identify with the perpetrator, are all eradicated from the therapy discourse. This dynamic leaves the PTG beliefs silenced and censored. Moreover, the patient may feel great guilt and shame for holding PTG beliefs, as if they indicate that as a child he or she in fact enjoyed or wanted the abuse or that he or she is in a state of denial. Thus, these split-off parts of the self are left untouchable and unelaborated, and instead reenacted outside of therapy, perpetuating fragmentation of the self.

Position V – The mourning therapist

The countertransference position of the mourning therapist develops when the therapist identifies with the patient's experience of profound loss. Thus, the therapist views the CSA survivor has having been robbed of his or her childhood. The abused child loses (and sometimes never had) his or her sense of safety, innocence, and playfulness of childhood, which are replaced by experiences of danger, terror, pain, isolation, and confinement. These negative experiences are not integrated into the self and are registered separately in split-off self-states that reflect painful loss as well as a sense of deadness. Ferenczi (1932) described this self-state, which performs like a "body divested of its soul," as reflecting "the ashes of earlier mental sufferings" (pp. 9, 10).

In psychotherapy, the therapist's identification with the patient's experience of loss and despair leads to the development of the countertransference position of the mourning therapist (Herman, 1992; Saakvitne, 1990). The therapist in this countertransference position feels deep agony and grief, mourning over the abused child. Sinking into despair and losing hope, the therapist may view the abuse as a malignant wound that cannot be overcome and perceive him or herself as helpless and incapable of assisting the patient. The therapist's faith in the therapeutic process is, thus, impeded dramatically.

Flooded with anguish, the therapist in this position cannot discern other self-states of the patient that may hold the experience of enduring the abuse, competence, and even growth. Therefore, the therapist might ignore the patient's reports of PTG or even negate it offhand without reflecting or investigating its meaning. At other times, the therapist may refer to the patient's reports of PTG as an echo from the past – as the child's desperate clinging onto comfort or hope that no longer exists.

The patient might hold different perceptions regarding the abuse that are reflected in PTG. Alternatively, the patient might unconsciously resonate with the therapist's countertransference by only bringing to therapy the self-state of the lost, emotionally dead child. Frozen, numb and detached from emotions, the patient may appear in therapy as lifeless. This "emotionally dead" self-state has already given up on the possibility of salvation and thus does not express resistance, distress or pain.

As a result, other split-off self-states of the patient, which remain alive and even experience growth and self-enhancement, are excluded from therapy. From time to time the patient may attempt to bring up these types of experiences and discuss them with the therapist. Nevertheless, as long as the therapist is immersed in grief, these efforts are doomed to fail and the healing process is in jeopardy.

Discussion

For the first time in the trauma literature, this chapter presents five possible countertransference positions that develop in relation to reports of PTG by patients who are survivors of CSA. We suggested that these countertransference positions should not be studied in isolation but in the context of the patient's reports, and that they should be understood as reenactments of dissociated self-states or traumatic relational dynamics that are split off from the patient's consciousness. As such, the countertransference reaction of dissociation may be viewed as an expression of the therapist's identification with the dissociated abused child. The countertransference position of the perpetrator may be understood as an embodiment of the patient's internal representation of the abuser. Likewise, the other positions are also reflections of the traumatic representations.

The reenactments of the dissociated traumatic representations are inevitable and essential to the therapeutic process in the treatment of CSA survivors. Such therapeutic stances constitute the main avenue for expressing the unthinkable traumatic experiences and uncovering dissociated elements (Davies & Frawley, 1992, 1994). This eventually allows the patient to identify, mentalize, and integrate the dissociated elements of his or her inner world. However, at the same time, these reenactments, when manifested in countertransference reactions, may pose a threat to the healing process and run a risk of re-traumatization, as they constitute repetition of the original trauma.

Therefore, it is crucial for the therapist to attend to his or her emotional responses towards the patient and to use them as a way of learning more about the patient's own experience. Moreover, the therapist should take responsibility for his or her reactions and consequent behavior, and avoid "blaming" the patient's past. Although the emotional responses of the therapist might originate from the patient's internal world, the therapist reacts, and by doing so he or she has a responsibility for the resulting consequences. Furthermore, the therapist's countertransference stems not only from the survivor's internal world, but also from the therapist's internal world and dissociated material, as well as from the interplay between the two.

The current analysis of the countertransference reactions in relation to the patient's reports of PTG further illuminates the phenomenon of PTG. PTG appears to be a multidimensional phenomenon constituting multiple meanings for CSA survivors, reflecting *repetition* of the traumatic past, rather than its resolution. Reports of PTG often represent enactments of dissociated self-states or dissociated relational dynamics that originated in the trauma. Therefore, even when the patient reports PTG, he or she can, at the same time, hold other perceptions, which are equally valid, regarding the trauma and its implications. The dissociative structure of the survivor's personality can elucidate the often documented, co-existence of reports of PTG and emotional distress. These contradicting reports may reflect dissociated and disintegrated aspects regarding the past trauma.

As the current chapter has illustrated, the patient's initial reports of PTG can elicit a variety of countertransference reactions from the therapist during treatment, which in turn can affect the patient's future reports of PTG. While some countertransference reactions enhance the patient's reports of PTG, others contribute to minimizing and obscuring PTG within therapy. Thus, similar to the polarized dissociated states, split-off extremities regarding PTG might be reenacted during treatment, leading to over-embracement versus complete negation of reports of PTG. This could constitute a repetition of the original trauma, as parts of the survivor's experience are, again, invalidated and split-off from consciousness. Thus, working through these reenactments is essential and could enable the extrapolation of the dichotomous polarities, while taking into account other aspects of the traumatic experience, thus allowing gradual integration and healing.

Note

1 Ferenczi's concept was originally named "identification with the aggressor". The authors will refer to "identification with the perpetrator" based on Ferenczi's concept. Ferenczi's concept of identification with the aggressor is very different from Anna Freud's (1936) later use of the term, by which she describes that by impersonating the aggressor, assuming his attributes or imitating his aggression, the child transforms himself from the threatened person into the person who makes the threat. While Ferenczi denotes a pervasive change in the abused child's perceptual

world, Anna Freud describes a more limited event of behaving like the perpetrator and taking on his attributes (Frenkel, 2002).

References

Aron, L. (1996). *A Meeting of Minds: Mutuality in psychoanalysis*: Hillsdale, NJ: The Analytic Press.

Bloom, S. L. (1998). By the crowd they have been broken, by the crowd they shall be healed: The social transformation of trauma. In R. G. Tedeschi, C. L. Park & L. G. Calhoun (Eds.). *Posttraumatic Growth: Positive changes in the aftermath of crisis* (pp. 179–213). Mahwah (NJ): Lawrence Erlbaum Associates, Publishers.

Braude, S. E. (2000). Dissociation and latent abilities: The strange case of Patience Worth. *Journal of Trauma & Dissociation,* 1(2), 13–48.

Briere, J., & Elliott, D. M. (2003). Prevalence and psychological sequelae of self-reported childhood physical and sexual abuse in a general population sample of men and women. *Child Abuse & Neglect, 27*(10), 1205–1222.

Bromberg, P. M. (2011). *The Shadow of the Tsunami: And the growth of the relational mind.* New York, NY: Routledge.

Burt, M. R., & Katz, B. L. (1987). Dimensions of recovery from rape focus on growth outcomes. *Journal of Interpersonal Violence, 2*(1), 57–81.

Calhoun, L. G., & Tedeschi, R. G. (1989–1990). Positive aspects of critical life problems: Recollections of grief. *Omega – Journal of Death and Dying, 20*(4), 265–272.

Calhoun, L. G., & Tedeschi, R. G. (1990). Positive aspects of critical life problems: Recollections of grief. *Omega – Journal of Death and Dying, 20*(4), 265–272.

Calhoun, L. G., & Tedeschi, R. G. (2006). *Handbook of Posttraumatic Growth: Research and practice.* New York, NY: Routledge.

Calhoun, L. G., Tedeschi, R. G., & Tedeschi, R. G. (1999). *Facilitating Posttraumatic Growth: A clinician's guide.* New York, NY: Routledge.

Chu, J. A., & Dill, D. L. (1990). Dissociative symptoms in relation to childhood physical and sexual abuse. *The American Journal of Psychiatry, 147*(7), 887–892.

Davies, J. M., & Frawley, M. G. (1992). Dissociative processes and transference countertransference paradigms in the psychoanalytically oriented treatment of adult survivors of childhood sexual abuse. *Psychoanalytic Dialogues,* 2(1), 5–36.

Davies, J. M., & Frawley, M. G. (1994). *Treating the Adult Survivor of Childhood Sexual Abuse: A psychoanalytic perspective.* New York (NY): Basic Books.

Davis, C. G., & McKearney, J. M. (2003). How do people grow from their experience with trauma or loss?. *Journal of Social and Clinical Psychology, 22*(5), 477–492.

Dekel, S., Ein-Dor, T., & Solomon, Z. (2012). Posttraumatic growth and posttraumatic distress: A longitudinal study. *Psychological Trauma: Theory, Research, Practice, and Policy, 4*(1), 94–101.

Draucker, C. B. (1992). Construing benefit from a negative experience of incest. *Western Journal of Nursing Research, 14*(3), 343–353.

Feder, A., Southwick, S. M., Goetz, R. R., Wang, Y., Alonso, A., Smith, B. W., *et al.*, (2008). Posttraumatic growth in former Vietnam prisoners of war. *Psychiatry, 71*, 359–370.

Ferenczi, S. (1931). Child-analysis in the analysis of adults. *International Journal of Psychoanalysis, 12*, 468–482.

Ferenczi, S. (1932). *The Cinical Diary of Sandor Ferenczi* (M. Balint & N. Z. Jackson, Trans.). Cambridge, MA: Harvard University Press.

Ferenczi, S. (1949). Confusion of the tongues between the adults and the child – (the language of tenderness and of passion). *International Journal of Psycho-Analysis, 30*, 225–230.

Frankel, J. B. (1998). Ferenczi's trauma theory. *The American Journal of Psychoanalysis, 58*(1), 41–61.

Frankel, J. B. (2002). Exploring Ferenczi's concept of identification with the aggressor: Its role in trauma, everyday life, and the therapeutic relationship. *Psychoanalytic Dialogues, 12*(1), 101–139.

Frazier, P., Conlon, A., & Glaser, T. (2001). Positive and negative life changes following sexual assault. *Journal of Consulting and Clinical Psychology, 69*, 1048–1055.

Greene, T., Lahav, Y., Kanat-Maymon, Y., & Solomon, Z. (2015). A longitudinal study of secondary posttraumatic growth in wives of ex-POWs. *Psychiatry: Interpersonal and Biological Processes, 78*, 186–197.

Helgeson, V. S., Reynolds, K. A., & Tomich, P. L. (2006). A meta-analytic review of benefit finding and growth. *Journal of Consulting and Clinical Psychology, 74*, 797–816.

Herman, J. L. (1992). *Trauma and Recovery*. New York, NY: Basic Books.

Herman, J. L., & van der Kolk, B. A. (1987). Traumatic antecedents of borderline personality disorder. In B. A. van der Kolk (Ed.), *Psychological Trauma* (pp. 111–126). Washington, DC: American Psychiatric Publishing, Inc.

Hobfoll, S. E., Hall, B. J., Canetti Nisim, D., Galea, S., Johnson, R. J., & Palmieri, P. A. (2007). Refining our understanding of traumatic growth in the face of terrorism: moving from meaning cognitions to doing what is meaningful. *Applied Psychology, 56*, 345–366.

Lahav, Y., Bellin, E., & Solomon, Z. (In Press). Posttraumatic growth and shattered world assumptions among ex-POWs: The role of dissociation. *Psychiatry: Interpersonal and Biological Processes.*

Laub, D. (1992). Bearing witness, or the vicissitudes of listening. In S. Felman & D. Laub (Eds.). *Testimony: Crisis of witnessing in literature, psychoanalysis, and history* (pp. 57–74). New York, NY: Routledge.

Levine, S. Z., Laufer, A., Hamama Raz, Y., Stein, E., & Solomon, Z. (2008). Posttraumatic growth in adolescence: Examining its components and relationship with PTSD. *Journal of Traumatic Stress, 21*, 492–496.

Linley, P. A., & Joseph, S. (2004). Positive change following trauma and adversity: A review. *Journal of Traumatic Stress, 17*(1), 11–21.

Maercker, A., & Zoellner, T. (2004). The Janus face of self-perceived growth: Towards a two-component model of posttraumatic growth. *Psychological Inquiry, 15*, 41–48.

McFarland, C., & Alvaro, C. (2000). The impact of motivation on temporal comparisons: Coping with traumatic events by perceiving personal growth. *Journal of Personality and Social Psychology, 79*, 327–343.

McMillen, C., Zuravin, S., & Rideout, G. (1995). Perceived benefit from child sexual abuse. *Journal of Consulting and Clinical Psychology, 63*(6), 1037–1043.

Neumann, D. A., & Gamble, S. J. (1995). Issues in the professional development of psychotherapists: countertransference and vicarious traumatization in the new trauma therapist. *Psychotherapy: Theory, Research, Practice, Training, 32*(2), 341–347.

Ogden, T. H. (1998). *Reverie and Interpretation*: Northvale, NJ: Jason Aronson.

Organization, W. H. (1999). Report of the consultation on child abuse prevention, 29–31 March 1999, WHO, Geneva. Geneva: Author.

Paolucci, E. O., Genuis, M. L., & Violato, C. (2001). A meta-analysis of the published research on the effects of child sexual abuse. *The Journal of Psychology, 135*(1), 17–36.

Putnam, F. W. (1993). Dissociative disorders in children: behavioral profiles and problems. *Child Abuse & Neglect, 17*(1), 39–45.

Saakvitne, K. W. (1990). *Psychoanalytic Psychotherapy with Incest Survivors: Transference and countertransference paradigms*. Paper presented at the Annual Convention of the American Psychological Association Boston, MA.

Schaefer, J. A., & Moos, R. H. (1998). The context for posttraumatic growth: life crises, individual and social resources, and coping. In R. G. Tedeschi, C. L. Park, & L. G. Calhoun (Eds.). *Posttraumatic Growth: Positive changes in the aftermath of crisis* (pp. 99–125). New Jersey: Lawrence Erlbaum Associates.

Seligman, Z. (2004). Introduction to incest. In Z. Seligman & Z. Solomon (Eds.). *Critical and Clinical Perspectives on Incest*. Tel Aviv: Tel Aviv University & Hakibbutz Hameuchad.

Silver, R. L., Boon, C., & Stones, M. H. (1983). Searching for meaning in misfortune: making sense of incest. *Journal of Social Issues, 39*(2), 81–101.

Sledge, W. H., Boydstun, J. A., & Rabe, A. J. (1980). Self-concept changes related to war captivity. *Archives of General Psychiatry, 37*, 430–443.

Taylor, S. E. (1989). *Positive Illusions: Creative self-deception and the healthy mind*. New York, NY: Basic Books.

Tedeschi, R. G., & Calhoun, L. G. (1988). *Perceived Benefits in Coping with Physical Handicaps*. Paper presented at the Annual meeting of the American Psychological Association Atlanta, GA.

Tedeschi, R. G., & Calhoun, L. G. (1995). *Trauma and Transformation:*

Growing in the aftermath of suffering. Thousand Oaks, CA: Sage Publications.

Tedeschi, R. G., & Calhoun, L. G. (2004). Posttraumatic growth: Conceptual foundations and empirical evidence. *Psychological Inquiry, 15*(1), 1–18.

Tennen, H., Affleck, G., Urrows, S., Higgins, P., & Mendola, R. (1992). Perceiving control, construing benefits, and daily processes in rheumatoid arthritis. *Canadian Journal of Behavioural Science/Revue Canadienne des Sciences du Comportement, 24*(2), 186–203.

van der Kolk, B. A., Roth, S., Pelcovitz, D., Sunday, S., & Spinazzola, J. (2005). Disorders of extreme stress: the empirical foundation of a complex adaptation to trauma. *Journal of Traumatic Stress, 18*(5), 389–399.

Veronen, L. J., & Kilpatrick, D. G. (1983). Rape: a precursor of change. In E. J. Callahan & K. A. McCluskey (Eds.). *Life Span Development Psychology: Non-normative events* (pp. 167–191). New York, NY: Academic Press.

Zoellner, T., & Maercker, A. (2006). Posttraumatic growth in clinical psychology – a critical review and introduction of a two component model. *Clinical Psychology Review, 26*(5), 626–653.

CHAPTER
FIVE

Countertransference in the Treatment of Siblings of Fallen Israel Defense Forces (IDF) Soldiers

MAJOR (RES.) MOSHE Z. ABRAMOWITZ,
COL. (RES.) HAIM Y. KNOBLER,
LT. COL. (RES.) YORAM BEN YEHUDA AND
DOV R. ALEKSANDROWICZ

Psychotherapy of bereaved family members of fallen Israeli soldiers involves complex countertransferential issues, and countertransference in the treatment of bereaved siblings of fallen soldiers is a unique example.

Since 1948, the bereaved parents and spouses of the fallen soldiers have been at the center of public attention. While they are called the "families of bereavement", the term "family" included, in fact only, some of the family, the parents, and where relevant, spouses. Consequently, the soldiers' bereaved brothers and sisters were overlooked, and were often told that their responsibility was mainly to take care of their parents – the "real" bereaving in the families of bereavement.

Over the last decades, the importance of treating the bereaved siblings was revealed, and multi-faceted countertransference issued in these treatments, which should be explored. These countertransferences may be divided into three major areas: Socially-derived countertransference, which is based on the therapists' values and opinions; Siblings-derived countertransference, based on the therapists' inner representations of their own siblings; and parents/others-derived countertransference, which may include, the therapists' attitude to the way in which the patients relate to their bereaved parents.

All types of countertransference may be beneficial for the therapeutic alliance, but may cause over-protection or a negative attitude towards the patients.

Another interesting topic is the part the bereaved parents take in their children's' treatment; when bereaved parents take an active role in helped their distressed children, this may be crucial to the treatment's success.

Different cases representing such types of countertransference will be presented, and the importance of understanding countertransference for the success of the treatments will be discussed.

Background: Israeli society and the concept of the "family of the bereaved"

Since Israel's War of Independence in 1948 – which took place only three years after the end of the Holocaust – the families of Israel's fallen soldiers have "have been assigned the special status of "families of the bereaved". Israel considers itself morally bound to care for such families, an imperative first articulated by David Ben-Gurion, the founding prime minister of Israel, who stated that "the welfare of IDF [Israel Defense Forces] casualties is an inseparable part of national security" (Department of Family and Commemoration publication).

More than 6,000 Israelis were killed in the 1948 war, most of them soldiers, and the first Israeli Independence Day in 1949 was also marked as a day of commemoration for the fallen. Two years later, Israel instated a separate national Memorial Day to honor the fallen, taking place annually on the day before Independence Day. The term "family of the bereaved" was coined during this period. Since that time, Israeli society has handled the families of the IDF's fallen soldiers differently than the families of civilians whose lives were tragically cut short (such as road accident fatalities), and in the young Israeli state, it was a belief taken for granted that these "families of the bereaved" deserved preferential treatment.

Until recently, the Israeli term "family of the bereaved" excluded the siblings of the fallen, and focused almost exclusively on the parents and spouses of the deceased. Thus, siblings had to bear a double injury: the loss of a brother or sister, and the fact that they were excluded from the special treatment given to grief-stricken families. Furthermore, siblings were told to be "strong" for their parents' sake. These types of attitudes created the belief that only the parents' grief was in fact true grief.

Over the past decade, and perhaps because of the therapy that the siblings of the fallen have undergone, Israelis' attitudes towards sibling grief have changed. In 2007, a group of bereaved siblings established an association called "Forever My Brother" ("La'nezach Achi"), to raise awareness in Israel society and among Israeli authorities regarding the existence and the plight of bereaved siblings of fallen soldiers, and to encourage action on their behalf. While the foundation does not provide counseling to its members, it encourages them to seek therapy and support, and refers grieving siblings to therapists who specialize in caring for bereaved families.

Psychotherapy of Israel's "families of the bereaved" – and bereaved siblings in particular – has given rise to unique questions involving countertransference. Examples of treatment issues that must be identified and addressed include guilt felt by therapists over the lack of recognition of sibling grief in Israeli society; and coping with the anger felt by siblings towards their parents, particularly in situations in which the therapist identifies with the bereaved parents. In some cases, the therapist must deal with a bereaved sibling who falls into a special category, such as those who are also children of Holocaust survivors, or siblings of IDF soldiers who committed suicide or did not die on the battlefield, for example, soldiers who died in training accidents, roadside fatalities (while active members of the IDF or during reserve duty), and even soldiers who died of illness, sudden or otherwise.

In what follows, we first present a clinical vignette that demonstrates the complex dynamics within the family of a fallen soldier. Next, we engage in a more detailed discussion of transference and countertransference issues that arise during psychotherapy of bereaved siblings. All names in this chapter have been changed to preserve anonymity.

Case vignette[1]

Rachel S., a twelve-year-old girl, was referred to psychiatric consultation after being admitted to the hospital because of an attempted suicide. A few hours before that, she had swallowed several tablets of a tranquilizer, used by her mother because of "nervousness". The girl was only mildly somnolent on admission, but the pediatricians realized that she had seriously intended to kill herself and requested a consultation.

Rachel, a bright, vivacious, well-developed girl, was sullen and diffident during the initial interview, but it was possible to establish a modicum of cooperation. She admitted being very angry at her mother, though she preferred to complain of minor grudges, such as interfering with plans for a Bat-Mitzvah party, and was vague and evasive about the family's deeply disturbed situation.

Rachel was the youngest of four children. Her father, an uneducated, but intelligent and energetic man, was a self-made prosperous businessman, and her mother was a housewife. Jonathan, the eldest son, had always been his mother's favorite; a friendly boy, liked by his peers, a good student and a considerate son and brother, Jonathan was particularly fond of his youngest sister, Rachel, whom he used to read stories to and play with. The mother was always very anxious about Jonathan and reluctant to separate from him. When he was drafted, she begged him not to volunteer for any of the commando units; he gave in to his mother's pressure and was sent to a non-commissioned officers' (N.C.O.) training course. When the Yom Kippur War broke out in 1973, his unit was sent to an assignment on the front lines, and he was killed in action.

Rachel's mother, Ms. S., in her own words, "stopped living" when Jonathan was killed. She became indifferent to the rest of the family, refused to meet friends or relatives, and, for a while, was in psychiatric treatment after trying to commit suicide by an overdose of medication. She stopped treatment after several months, no longer suicidal, but resigned herself to merely waiting for death and for the reunion with her son. To her family's reproaches about neglect she would reply angrily: "What do you want? I cook and keep the house, our needs are provided for. Leave me alone!" She imposed a strict regime of mourning; since Jonathan (the fallen son) had loved music, no music was allowed in the house. Family members could watch television, but only with the sound turned off. Since Mr. S. refused to give up news bulletins, Ms. S. would retire to her room at that time; otherwise she made no concessions to the family.

After many futile attempts to involve Ms. S. in family life again, each member of the family coped with the loss in his or her own way. The second son essentially left home, coming to the house only to sleep and to eat. The other daughter, four years older than Rachel, spent most of her time with friends, began dating, and assumed an indifferent, defiant attitude. Mr. S. tried to hold the family together and took care of Rachel as much as his busy schedule allowed, but otherwise permitted his wife to impose her way of mourning on the family.

Rachel was a model child during the first years of mourning and appeared to show no signs of being affected by the devastating loss of her idolized brother. In the year preceding her suicide attempt, however, she had become more willful and demanding, confrontational towards her siblings, and defiant to her parents. The attempted suicide followed a disappointment at school and a quarrel with her mother.

Following the initial evaluation, the psychiatrist conducted a series of family meetings with Rachel and both parents, intended as a crisis intervention. The topic that dominated these meetings was the depth of Ms. S.'s grief and her profound estrangement from the rest of the family. It appeared as if she had been carrying the pain of the entire family on her shoulders. The other family members' expressions of grief were muted, as if silenced by the mother's implied exclusiveness of suffering. The meeting revealed hints that the rest of the family felt resentment towards Ms. S.; beyond their open criticism of her emotional estrangement, it seemed they felt she belittled the others' right to suffer and to grieve the loss.

During the course of the sessions, it became apparent that Rachel's attempted suicide served several purposes:

- A conscious attempt to punish the parents, especially the mother, for ignoring her needs, and an unconscious attack on the introjected "bad object";
- A conscious wish to rejoin her beloved brother (Rachel revealed that she had been reading articles about parapsychology and reincarnation);
- A preconscious wish to regain the love of her mother by competing with her brother: "Since Mother loves the dead let me be dead, too".

In the last interview, we discussed the parents' disagreement about how to treat the girl. It became apparent that Ms. S. was overwhelmed by guilt and fear of Rachel's possible suicide to the extent that the girl now had the mother firmly under her control. Although she resented the mother's clinging and nagging, Rachel cherished her new power and used it to put an end to some of the mother's impositions: the TV was allowed now, as well as visits by friends.

From the beginning, Ms. S. was a reluctant participant in the family sessions; her resistance increased when we discussed her grief and when Rachel and her father expressed their feelings of being rejected and neglected. The therapist tried to help her to express affection towards the husband and surviving children, but that seemed to increase her hostility. The family left for a vacation (another concession to Rachel), and they later sent a message that "everything was alright" and no further treatment was needed.

The therapist discussed the case extensively with his supervisor. In retrospect, it appeared that the change that had taken place was more a result of the girl's suicidal attempt than of psychotherapeutic intervention. The main issue the therapist expressed was his failure to engage Ms. S. in the process beyond her formal cooperation. The therapist seemed not to have realized that his intention to help Ms. S. to "terminate" her "interminable mourning" was perceived by the mother as an attempt to deprive her of her last, desperate hold onto the beloved object. The supervisor also pointed out that the therapist's empathy was "asymmetrical"; he identified with the child's feelings of rejection deeply, but the empathy he felt towards the mother's catastrophic loss seemed more in the nature of understanding rather than intuitive identification. The therapist was initially skeptical about that interpretation, but later realized that it was correct and had to do with some of his own life-experience, which made him ambivalent about the "idealization of the fallen", particularly prominent in Israeli society.

Understanding the role of the "family of the bereaved"

The characteristic bereavement of the parents of fallen soldiers has been described in several studies. Simon S. Rubin, for example, compared parents who had lost young children to parents who had lost sons to war (Rubin, 1990). Although all parents demonstrated pronounced mourning, parents of fallen soldiers were particularly affected by the loss in the initial year, and as much as ten years after the loss.

Israel's special treatment of bereaved families in the first few years after the birth of the nation may have been driven, in part, by the difficulty of Israeli society to confront the overwhelming trauma of the Holocaust and its aftermath, which was then still raw and prominent. It might be supposed that the grief and guilt over the Jewish victims of the Nazis in Europe was displaced to the fallen soldiers; the extreme nature of this act of displacement is reflected in the fact that the *civilian* casualties of the War of Independence (estimated at up to 20 percent of the total fallen) to this day are not formally commemorated by the state.

Over the years, many brothers and sisters of fallen IDF soldiers felt excluded. Often, they were required to take on a special role in the grief-stricken family, such as the one who can be depended on, or the scapegoat. Grief and mourning were mostly reserved for the parents or spouse. Indeed, the name given to the organization commemorating the fallen soldiers was "Yad La'banim" or "Memorial for Our Sons", underlining the parents' loss, not the loss of the family as a whole. Until recently, the siblings of fallen soldiers received special consideration only in specific contexts; for example, assignment of a bereaved sibling to a combat unit was contingent upon his or her parents' written consent, resulting in tensions and lasting resentment on both sides. Much later, special loans, student loans, and grants began to be offered to siblings of fallen soldiers. In the 1950s the Ministry of Defense set up the Department of Rehabilitation to act on behalf of bereaved families' welfare, and to provide them with professional and readily-available services (in 2005 the Ministry established the Department of Families and Commemoration, which took over these duties)[5]. However, only many years later were siblings formally recognized as part of the families' tragic situation. Nowadays, siblings are eligible for individual psychotherapy sessions, with a treatment period of up to three years. However, most of the siblings receive (and seek) treatment at public or private clinics, not through the assistance of the Department of Families and Commemoration. Similarly, in recent years Israeli authorities have become increasingly aware of the need to treat siblings of victims of terror attacks; these victims are also commemorated during Memorial Day, albeit in separate ceremonies from those commemorating fallen soldiers, and their families are considered "families of the bereaved" (Moss & Raz, 2001).

Transference and countertransference

The psychotherapy of the brothers and sisters of fallen soldiers raises special issues of transference and countertransference. The countertransference process is unique in Israel, where many of the siblings of the fallen are also the children of Holocaust survivors (as are many of the therapists themselves; see *Chapter 5: Countertransference in the Treatment of Holocaust Survivors by a Second Generation Therapist* for a detailed discussion). We now want to focus on the countertransference processes in the treatment of the siblings, with special attention given to the psychotherapy of siblings who have served in the military. (In Israel, all Jewish, Druze and Circassian citizens are required to serve in the military, unless they meet specific criteria for exemption.) The added mental/psychological burden these siblings bear, while forging their own paths in the army, warrants a discussion on the dynamics of the therapy. It is important to note that the countertransference we describe does not negate other, more common aspects of therapist-patient dynamics shared by many different groups.

As members of Israeli society, Israeli psychotherapists tend to view bereaved parents as those who maintain the memory or heritage of the IDF's fallen soldiers for the rest of the population, and as such, they treat these parents with respect, gratitude and compassion, and sometimes, with awe.

Siblings of the fallen may take on the collective role of being part of the "family of the bereaved", or may see their parents as needing their protection and support. However, we have also experienced another type of reaction, of anger towards the parents who have focused all their attention on the fallen brother or sister while they, the siblings who remain, feel discounted (Aleksandrowicz, 1980). In any event, all of these types of emotions are likely to play out in therapy. Accordingly, the patient may exhibit displaced anger towards the therapist instead of aiming at the grieving parents, who have not licensed anyone else to mourn the family loss. A "remaining survivor" sibling may even exhibit rivalry with a therapist's other patients, reenacting a similar dynamic towards the deceased sibling that predates the tragic loss.

Similarly, countertransference can manifest in various ways. In particular, the therapist may feel resentment that the patient is overprotective of his or her parents, despite the fact that the parents are oblivious to the patient's own needs. Moreover, the therapist may feel the need to protect the patient, to try to fill the emotional void caused by the parents' distraction with their own pain. Indeed, the therapist may find it very difficult to treat the surviving soldier-sibling, a "lost-child" who has no one looking out for him or her. This can lead to a fantasy on the part of the therapist, who sees himself as a replacement for the natural parent as a nurturing and caring surrogate concerned with the survival of the living sibling.

In other cases, when the patient is angry at his/her parents, the therapist might identify with a parent, feeling uncomfortable that the treatment does not acknowledge the legitimacy of the parents' own genuine grief.

Case I – The therapist as the patriarch Jacob

Guy, 22, was a second son, two years younger than his older brother, Roni, who was killed in action, leaving Guy an only child. Barely a year after the tragic loss, Guy asked his parents for their written consent to enable him to volunteer for an elite paratroopers' unit. His parents, observant Jews, who were still reciting *Kaddish* (the traditional prayer for the dead) for their beloved Roni, were asked to do the unthinkable – to play an active role in putting their surviving son in harm's way.

For the first two years of his conscription, Guy did everything in his power to stay alive and healthy. He was terrified of the thought that if anything happened to him, his parents would be devastated. These thoughts led him to freeze up even under combat conditions. Taking into consideration every contingency, he would plan the least dangerous path and go through a personal protocol to prevent injury from the enemy (i.e., terrorists) as well as from friendly fire. He avoided hitchhiking, which was very common among soldiers, never slept on bus rides, and was always on the alert for "something bad" just waiting to strike him. Towards the end of his tour, he found himself in the midst of an ambush, bullets whistling around him, paralyzed between his fear of getting in harm's way and his sense of duty to his comrades and to his mission. Finally, after what seemed to him like an eternity, with a sudden burst of energy, he attacked the enemy with a frontal charge and overcame the assault.

Guy came for treatment half a year later after completing his military service. He came to the treatment frustrated, wanting to trek in the Far East, to experience what the world had to offer, to live dangerously, but still feeling that he could not afford to be that reckless. The psychotherapy was extensive and not easy for the therapist.

The therapist came to realize that what Guy was asking of him, the therapist, was permission to live – which was tantamount to granting him a license to die. Guy's transference was evident; he displaced his anger from his parents towards the therapist, and wanted the therapist to "set him free", something his parents were incapable of doing. Conversely, the therapist had to resolve an unconscious wish to take on the parents' role as Guy's protector, and his anxiety at Guy's wish "to have it all, and experience it all". In encouraging Guy to live his own life, the therapist, in the countertransference, felt like a parent who was sending his son to his death in battle.

At times the therapist felt like the biblical Jacob, bidden by his son Judah to set free, at his peril, the youngest surviving son (Benjamin) of his mother, Rachel. Guy's Orthodox parents, similar to the vanquished patriarch Jacob, relinquished their hold on their remaining boy against their own better judgment. The therapist too felt an overwhelming burden and responsibility of an almost biblical nature. Only when cognizant of this burden could the therapist approach the therapy with less guilt, and less of a need to contain the patient's conflict between compliance and self-realization.

At the end of the therapy, Guy felt more capable of understanding his feelings towards his injured parents, balancing his need for personal growth and individuality against his fantasy to protect his parents from his own death. No less important, Guy also realized that he would require additional therapy to confront his own grief over his brother's death.

Countertransference related to the dead

As members of Israeli society, therapists often regard fallen soldiers as heroes, objects of admiration and respect. However, siblings of these soldiers may regard them in a somewhat different manner, feeling that the fallen have been over-idealized, and their faults forgotten, and that those who remain are required to suppress any negative memories of those who have been tragically lost. Siblings may experience anger towards the deceased for not staying alive, and for suddenly abandoning them. Idealizing feelings are evident as part of the transference phenomena in therapy. Less evident are the negative feelings, where identification of countertransference processes may be an instrument for improvement.

Case II – The therapist as the frustrated parent

Dina was only 12 when her brother was killed in battle. She and her family lived on a kibbutz where everyone was encouraged to serve in the IDF. Much attention was paid to the communal bereavement of the fallen brother, but there was no acknowledgement of the surviving sister's emotional needs.

Dina continued her studies at school and in the children's group in the kibbutz without any true mourning period. She later refused any psychological help, did not want to be comforted, and tried to be an excellent student, as was her deceased brother. To her surprise, even though she did get the highest grades in her class, this did not make her parents happy. Despite every effort, she felt that there was nothing she could do to compete with her brother's memory, and felt her parents were impatient towards her and her attempts to gain their favor. Regardless of how hard she strived, it appeared, to Dina, that her parents continued to prefer her dead brother. Dina herself was never satisfied by her own achievements, and at the age of 42, having accomplished academic successes, she came to therapy feeling empty and with a sense of failure. These feelings were in contrast to Dina's conscious recognition of her success in building a family and landing a prestigious job.

During the therapy, Dina felt the therapist less and less empathetic towards her fear of failure. He had little patience for Dina's preoccupation and comparisons with her dead brother. The therapist related that, at times, he found himself exasperated with Dina and her inability to enjoy her successes. Understanding this exasperation led the therapist to the realization that he, similarly to Dina's parents, was not giving enough attention to Dina's positive achievements.

Only when the therapist connected this transferential and countertransferential process to Dina's relationship with her parents, and to her deeply-rooted feelings that her parents did not "see" her, was Dina able to begin talking about her brother and the consequences of his tragic death for the family. Dina slowly realized her mixed feelings towards her brother and parents and was able to feel the repressed anger at her brother for winning their parents' love even after his death.

Countertransference connected to the exclusion of the bereaved sibling from the bereavement process

The therapist often finds him or herself identifying with a patient's feeling of resentment. Many times, this countertransferential attitude towards the family underlies a sense of resentment that the patient/sibling has not been included in the "family of the bereaved." As stated previously, this special status has, in the past, been applied nearly exclusively to the parents and spouses of fallen soldiers.

Case III – The therapist at a dead end

Yossi was 13 years old when his older brother was killed in combat. Six years later, while serving as a young soldier, Yossi was admitted to a psychiatric hospital in an acute state of anxiety and depression. His parents stressed to the therapist that their extended family did not have any psychiatric problems, and that they hoped Yossi would recover soon and return to his army duties. The parents emphasized that they did not connect their loss – the death of Yossi's brother in battle – with the hospitalization, and appeared most worried about the possibility that Yossi would not be able to continue his military service and would be discharged.

During the first three weeks of his therapy (as part of his hospitalization), Yossi was reluctant to talk about his brother, and became annoyed whenever asked about his loss. The therapist felt a similarity between his own frustration dealing with Yossi's parents, in their insistence not to go into the topic of the tragedy, and Yossi's own unwillingness to talk about his feelings.

The therapist felt as if he was "walking into a wall"; with every turn he would take, the same obstacle stood in his path. The therapist was able to use this insight to be more empathetic to Yossi's predicament and his sense of being "walled-in" by his family's defensive posture. Moreover, this understanding enabled the therapist to explore, together with Yossi, his (Yossi's) fear of touching his own pain and his fear of causing the family to collapse once the grief was finally communicated.

After his acute state resolved, Yossi was determined to return to his home-front army unit, where he felt most comfortable. He became more verbal, and talked about the grieving process that he, his parents, and his sister had begun to work through six years earlier. During supervision, the therapist revealed his countertransferential attitude towards Yossi's family, and his sense of resentment that the family had not extended their "family of the bereaved" status to include their son Yossi.

Countertransference in the treatment of siblings of soldiers who committed suicide

The rate of suicide during service in the IDF has decreased significantly during the last decade, due to improvements in diagnosis, treatment, and commanders' awareness, as well as specific restrictions such as reducing access to firearms when indicated (Lubin *et al.*, 2010). Yet, because all soldiers are screened extensively for psychopathology prior to conscription, suicide during military service comes most often unexpectedly and without any prior indication, only intensifying the trauma for the families (Apter *et al.*, 1993).

Guilt feelings of the bereaved family are predictably prevalent in these situations, characterized by statements such as – "How could I have missed the signs?" "Could I have given more support?" – and they sometimes manifest as displaced anger towards the dead soldiers' commanders. Some families sue the IDF in court, in an attempt to find someone to be held responsible, and "to pay for their child's death".

Therapy of the siblings in such cases may be complicated by their anger towards the army, towards the dead sibling, or towards their parents. In addition, the therapist often finds him or herself in the position of "doing" or acting on behalf of the patient. This is especially true in cases of mental health professionals working within the framework of the Ministry of Defense or the IDF. Similar situations of identification with the families (and even anger against the military establishment) were observed among mental health professionals during the Vietnam War (Camp, 1993).

Case IV – The therapist as the mirror of angry feelings

Avi's brother committed suicide while serving in a unit on Israel's northern border. His suicide came as a traumatic surprise to his family, as there were no signs or "red flags" before the suicide. Avi, 17, and his family were treated by the Department of Families and Commemoration, a division of the Ministry of Defense. The program included family therapy for about two years.

When Avi was called up for his military service, he asked to serve in his late brother's unit. The family therapist who was treating the family believed this to be a positive development, and supported Avi's wish. He even helped Avi be assigned to the exact post in which his brother had served. Shortly after beginning his service, Avi began to experience various symptoms; he could not sleep and became anxious, and disputed or procrastinated when given orders. He was then moved to a different post in the same unit, where, following a severe run-in with a staff sergeant, he was sent for a psychological evaluation.

Avi told the evaluating mental health officer that he had lost his temper repeatedly since arriving at the post, something that was uncharacteristic of him. During his therapy sessions, he talked about his parents' persistent attempts to gain access to the army's commission of inquiry's report regarding his brother's death.

The mental health officer, a clinical psychologist, found himself identifying with Avi. He became increasingly outraged at the army's decision to send Avi to his dead brother's unit, even though Avi had requested this assignment with the support of the family therapist.

After the therapist shared his thoughts with Avi, Avi began to realize the level of anger he felt towards his brother's unit for not having done their best to prevent the suicide.

As a result of the therapy sessions, the therapist and patient both came to the conclusion that Avi should be transferred to a different unit in a different part of the country, and continue therapy. Avi was transferred eventually, continued therapy for a few months, and finished his military duty successfully. In supervision, it was suggested that the countertransference was helpful in identifying the negative feelings Avi harbored against the army despite his previous expressed desire to serve in the same unit as his brother. Being able to talk directly and openly about the circumstances surrounding his brother's death enabled the patient to express his feelings of helplessness, insecurity and anger.

Discussion

The transference-countertransference dynamics faced by Israeli therapists who treat siblings of soldiers who were killed in military action (or as a result of their military service) are closely related to the bereavement and traumatic loss that are so common in a state like Israel. In Israel, experiences of bereavement and traumatic loss are commonly shaped by several influences, including religion, the ethos of the Israeli state, and the struggle to reestablish the Jewish people in its homeland (Witztum *et al.*, 2001).

Part of the attitude of Israeli society towards the "family of the bereaved", which now includes bereaved siblings, may have begun as a displacement of the attitude towards the much larger group of Holocaust survivors. Three years after the Holocaust, and following the death of 6,000,000 Jews, the grief expressed over the 6,000 soldiers killed during the Israeli Independence War became as pronounced in the young Israeli state as the grief for the Holocaust victims. We now know that despite the overwhelming grief and trauma caused by the Holocaust, its survivors were not regarded as individuals who needed special treatment. Israeli society's attitude towards the "family of the bereaved" may have started as displaced guilt regarding their treatment of the much larger group of Holocaust survivors, alongside displaced grief for the victims, which was projected onto fallen soldiers and their families, who serve as the keepers of their fallen children's memory (Knobler *et al.*, 2015). Recently, many initiatives have begun encouraging young college students to visit the graves of the Holocaust survivor casualties of the 1948 war, those who came to the country directly from the horrors of Europe and died as soldiers for the young state, but who had no one to grieve for them. This and similar social phenomena demonstrate the intensity of the sense of loss and perhaps the collective guilt felt towards the survivors who tragically met their deaths only a short time after coming to the newborn state. In fact, at the time of the birth of the state, these survivors were not even regarded as post-traumatic individuals.

Conclusion

In Israel, where the notion of the "family of the bereaved" is a powerful force in society, the psychotherapy of bereaved siblings of soldiers who have fallen in battle – or who died under other circumstances – has given rise to unique questions involving countertransference. We have addressed some examples of those questions herein. In some cases, the therapist's countertransference reflects underlying guilt caused by Israel's failure to sufficiently recognize sibling grief. Alternatively, the therapist may identify with the bereaved parents, or with the anger the sibling feels towards his or her parents.

Given recent – albeit subtle – changes in Israeli attitudes towards the siblings of fallen soldiers, it is important to bear in mind that the perception that sibling grief is undervalued may lead to an exaggerated assumption that all siblings are routinely neglected by Israeli society (and by their grieving parents). Needless to say, not all of the mental difficulty experienced by the siblings of the fallen is connected to their bereavement, nor are all of the parents' problems related to their bereavement.

Additionally, in some situations, the therapist must also deal with special sub-groups of siblings, such as those who are also children of Holocaust-survivors, or siblings of IDF soldiers who committed suicide, or those who did not meet their death on the battlefield (road accidents, misdiagnosed medical deaths, etc.) or whose deaths resulted from "friendly fire" (in the latter case, whereas in the past the military did not reveal the exact circumstances of a soldier's death in these cases, now it is impossible to avoid this issue, particularly in the therapy room).

In light of the violent conflict that continues in the region, the dynamics and consequences of therapy for bereaved families – including the siblings of fallen soldiers as full members of these families, deserving of the same compassion and treatment – warrant further investigation.

Note

1 This case was adapted from Aleksandrowicz, D. R. (1978). Interminable mourning as a family process. *Israel Annals of Psychiatry & Related Disciplines*, Vol. 16(2), June 1978, 161–169, by kind permission of the Israeli Psychiatric Association.

References

Aleksandrowicz, D. R. (1978). Interminable mourning as a family process. *Israel Annals of Psychiatry & Related Disciplines*, 16(2), 161–169.

Aleksandrowicz, D. R. (1980). Family split as a result of mourning. *Interaction*, 3(2), 85–91.

Apter A., Bleich, A., King, R. A., Kron, S., Fluch, A., Kotler, M., Cohen, D. J. (1993). Death without warning? A clinical postmortem study of suicide in 43 Israeli adolescent males. *Archives of General Psychiatry*, Feb.; 50(2), 138–42.

Camp, N. (1993). The Vietnam War and the ethics of combat psychiatry. *The American Journal of Psychiatry,* Vol. 150 (7), 1000–1010.

Israel Ministry of Defense, Department of Family and Commemoration publication, https://www.mishpahot-hantzaha.mod.gov.il.

Knobler, H. Y., Haber, L., Brutin, B., Zemishlany, Z. (2015). Myth and reality:

on "future generations" of the Holocaust. In N. Davidovitch & D. Soen (Eds.) *Shoa and Experience – A Journey in Time*. Boston, MA: Academic Studies Press.

Lubin, G., Werbeloff, N., Halperin, D., Shmushkevitch, M., Weiser, M., Knobler, H. Y. (2010). Decrease in suicide rates after a change of policy reducing access to firearms in adolescents: A naturalistic epidemiological study. *Suicide and Life-Threatening Behavior*, 40, 421–424.

Moss, E., & Raz, A. (2001). The ones left behind: A siblings' bereavement group. *Group Analysis*, 34, 395–407.

Rubin, S. (1990). Death of the future? An outcome study of bereaved parents in Israel. *Journal of Death and Dying*, 20, 323–339.

Witztum, E., Malkinson, R., Rubin, S. (2001). Death, bereavement and traumatic loss in Israel: A historical and cultural perspective. *Israel Journal of Psychiatry and Related Sciences*, 38, 157–170.

CHAPTER
SIX

Countertransference in the Treatment of Holocaust Survivors by a Second Generation Therapist

KATARZYNA PROT-KLINGER

> Counter-transference is the best of servants but the worst of masters.
>
> SEGAL, 1986

Therapy of severely traumatized patients, such as Holocaust (or Shoah) victims or their descendants, present a counter-transference challenge. The countertransference will be shaped by the therapist's life experience as well as by the attitudes and conflicts dominating the society in which the therapy takes place. The chapter analyses the different countertransference reactions of the second generation therapist, who often recognized in the patients' accounts their own childhood experiences with a Shoah survivor parent.

The aim of this chapter is to show how the therapist's personal history affects his or her relationship with a patient who shares membership of the same small and traumatized social group. The author adopts the relational/constructivist perspective of the countertransference. Some clinical examples illustrate the process.

Introduction

Treatment of the traumatic consequences of the Holocaust (*Shoah*) was launched in Poland in 1990, as a belated continuation of an earlier programme provided by the Kraków clinic to former concentration camp prisoners with post-concentration camp syndrome (Ryn, 2005).

The subsequent programme, which focused on the impact of the Holocaust on the survivors and their children, originated from research by the Kraków team (Orwid, *et al.*, 1995; Orwid *et al.*, 1995b), which was headed by Maria Orwid (a Polish psychiatrist and one of the pioneers of the psychiatry of children and family in Poland).

In 1995, a group of therapists began first individual and then group therapy (continuing to the present) for the Holocaust survivors, as initiated by Professor Orwid. The therapy participants are a specific group, as far as their social identification is concerned. They usually come from assimilated Jewish families, and owe their survival to contacts their families had with non-Jewish Polish people. It is this double Polish–Jewish identity that prevented them from emigrating after World War II or during the 1968 wave of emigration. As they are often the only survivors in their families, they seek contacts with people who have similar experiences, and it is due to this particular need that the "Children of the Holocaust" Association was established in 1991. The "Children of the Holocaust" members are people of Jewish origin who, as children, lived through at least a part of World War II in areas in which the Holocaust took place.

A considerable number of the current therapy participants were very young children during the war who experienced trauma in the very early stages of life. They have fragmentary memories of their traumatic experiences, while some participants have no wartime memories at all.

Countertransference in the treatment of Holocaust survivors

Numerous publications deal with the problem of countertransference specificity in work with a traumatized person. The emotional responses of the therapist to the person suffering from trauma range between two extremes: from excessive helping and empathic tendencies to complete withdrawal and distancing (Wilson & Lindy, 1994). Such phenomena are emphasized as identification with the drama participants (i.e., the victim, perpetrator, or bystander) versus succumbing to hopelessness or chaos (Herman, 1997; Dalenberg, 2007). People who suffered trauma in childhood frequently manifest borderline personality traits that exert multiple effects on therapeutic work and countertransference specificity – the therapist feels that his/her thoughts are attacked and boundaries are trespassed

(Gabbard & Wilkinson, 1994). The pathological countertransferential reactions of therapists who work with traumatized persons are referred to as vicarious (secondary) victimisation (McCann & Pearlman, 1990; McCann & Coletti, 1994; Jankoski, 2010; Newell *et al.*, 2016).

Holocaust survivor psychotherapy, similarly to the psychotherapy of other patients with massive trauma, confronts the therapist with feelings of helplessness. A challenge arises concerning the possibilities and limits of psychotherapy. To what extent do we treat our clients and to what extent do we accompany them in their mourning? Wardi (Wardi, 1999) poses a question as to whether the sense of restriction in survivor psychotherapy is a clinical observation or whether it is related to collective countertransference where the Holocaust is perceived as a powerful aggressive entity, while the therapist feels him or herself to be a powerless impotent victim.

Danieli (Danieli, 1980) describes countertransference reactions in the psychotherapy of Holocaust survivors as involving bystander's guilt, rage, dread, shame, viewing the survivor as a victim or hero, considering oneself also a survivor, conflicts over Jewish identity, stressing the deaths rather than murder of lost relatives, and feeling like a privileged voyeur. Some of these reactions occur also in working with other victims of trauma. For example, the position of "privileged voyeur" may be particularly difficult in work with victims of sexual abuse (Dolan, 1991). According to Danieli (Danieli, 1994), in reaction to the Holocaust, these feelings of the therapist are displaced onto survivors instead of being his/her direct reaction to the patient; this is referred to as "event countertransference". Tauber (Tauber, 1998; Tauber, 2003), describing this phenomenon, coined the term "a *priori* countertransference", where the therapist's emotions are related not to the individual patient, but rather to the traumatic event itself. That concept was also critically discussed (Smith *et al.*, 2007; Hafkenscheid, 2005).

According to Hafkenscheid (Hafkenscheid, 2005), the event countertransference and vicarious traumatization perspectives could be used to cover up the therapists failures. Hoppe (Hoppe, 1984) points to the danger of over-identification in work with survivors. Over-identification includes being overwhelmed by pity and one's own guilt feelings.

An important issue that emerges in countertransference studies seems to be whether there is a similarity between the therapist's and the patient's life courses (Dasberg, 1993; Fogelman, 1998; Tauber &, van der Hal, 1998). What happens if the therapist's life history is similar to that of his patient? And what if they have a similar family history? In the context of work with Holocaust survivors, Marcus outlined the difficulties therapists with a Jewish background have helping survivors confront Jewish identity, given that they have often not adequately dealt with these issues in their own lives (Marcus, 1984).

The aim of this chapter is to show how the therapist's personal history affects his or her relationship with a patient who shares membership of the same small social group. These considerations seem important because of changes currently taking place in Europe. As Europe becomes more and more multicultural, a question arises as to whether the therapist and the patient should belong to the same (frequently traumatized) group, and if so, how this situation affects psychotherapy.

Psychological problems specific to Holocaust survivors in Poland

The psychological problems of survivors as encountered in therapeutic work are consistent with those described by researchers and therapists dealing with the psychological consequences of the Holocaust (Kellermann, 2009). Complaints reported in individual and group therapy include loneliness, a sense of isolation, and difficulty in interpersonal contacts. Traumatic memories are activated by losses that naturally occur in the survivors' age group (such as the death of a close person, retirement, ill health, and disability).

Important issues in Poland are the secret of the survivors' Jewish background and the secret of the Holocaust (Schneiderman & Budziszewska, 2012). Almost all therapy participants had hidden their Jewish ancestry from their children until the latter reached the "right" age (survivors believed the right age to be one when they judged their child capable of "hiding" him or herself). The parents were afraid their child might feel "different" – humiliated and rejected. Their own fears and apprehension were sometimes projected in an extreme form related to their wartime experiences. At the beginning of their therapy, some participants continued to hide their Jewish ancestry from their already adult children. Other families, when talking among themselves about their Jewish roots, still maintained silence as regards the survivors' experiences during World War II. These families and their functioning can be classified using the Danieli (Danieli, 1981; Danieli, 2015) typology as "victim families," where the family atmosphere is characterized by depression, worrying, distrustfulness, and fear of the external world, as well as a symbiotic attachment to the family. In the course of therapy, a majority of the participants decided to "come out" within the family forum at least.

My family history

I would like to present my family history to exemplify the specificity of mixed families, typical of our patients. This will enable me to analyse specific countertransferential phenomena in what follows.

I am the only child of a Polish mother and a Jewish father. Both of my parents emerged from the war as traumatized 15-year-olds. My father with the trauma of continually hiding on the "Aryan side", outside the ghetto walls, during the war; he had so-called false "Aryan papers" testifying to his non-Jewish origin and was hidden by Poles, but at the same time was afraid of being denounced by neighbors.

My mother was taken to Germany as a slave worker when she was still a child. Her mother (my maternal grandmother) died there. Both parental traumas were concealed at home. There was no mention either of my Polish grandmother and the circumstances of her death or of my father's aunts, uncles and cousins. The war trauma, and my father's Jewish "roots," had been likewise kept secret until 1968 (I was nine years old) when my father's sister immigrated to the US and my father told me that we were of "Jewish origin." It was quite clear to me that I was to tell no-one about this.

I remember just one "Jewish" episode from my early childhood. I came home from school and told my father that I would not like to be called a "Jew". My father asked me why and I, amazed that he was so naïve, said that would be equivalent to calling someone a "pig". My father asked me whether I would recognise a Jew if I saw one. I remember my growing impatience with his ignorance. "Of course I would," I replied, "Jews are black, like the Holy Virgin in the picture, aren't they?" Then he surprised me. He said they weren't black at all, and that my beloved paediatrician was a Jewess. I remember every word of this interchange but I think that much more happened at the nonverbal level.

As I grew up, I increasingly revolted against this secretiveness and when I finally went to university I came out of hiding. This did not mean, however, that I was able to answer the question "Who am I?" – Polish? Jewish? A Pole with Jewish origins? Gradually my father also began to come out of hiding. He would take photographs of my children to work: "These are my grandchildren, Jakub and Sara". Say no more. If I were to describe my family using Danieli's (Danieli, 2015) categories, I would say that it had most of the attributes of the "victim family" group. Somatization was a frequent mode of communicating because illness was viewed as a catastrophe, separation was forbidden, and expression of anger was unthinkable. Even today my parents recall that I was a "good child".

At home there was no mention of either my mother's Polish trauma or my father's Jewish trauma. In that silence, my parents transmitted "the wounds but not the memories" (Gampel, 1998). Neither did we talk about pre-war events. My paternal grandmother never mentioned her siblings who perished in the Holocaust, until she was on her deathbed, when she unconsciously shouted their names. My mother never reminisced about her pre-war home either. When I asked her to tell Sara (my daughter) about her great-grandmother, I was told that it was still "too early".

In 1993, when I was gravitating towards my Jewish part, I met Maria Orwid, who was studying second generation survivors at the time, at a psychiatric congress. "Who do you feel you are?" she asked me. "Nobody," I replied. I had no idea who I was in the Polish-Jewish context.

When she finished her research, Orwid suggested that I join a therapeutic program addressed to members of "Children of the Holocaust". I had mixed feelings. This touched upon everything that was difficult for me – "Jewishness", trauma, my fears and anxieties, particularly with respect to my children. On the other hand, this could help me to deal with my sense of obligation in a reasonable manner. Working in a heterogeneous group would be a good opportunity not only to solve the problems that emerge in therapy, but also to alleviate my anxiety related to opening Pandora's Box (Durst, 2003).

My experience in working with survivors: Therapy and research

As a therapist, I have worked with survivors in three different settings:

1. **Group therapy** with a slow-open group, from 1997 to the present,
2. **Individual psychotherapy** of survivors, from 1995 to the present
3. **Individual interviews** with survivors in Poland and Romania, for research purposes, in the years 2002–2007.

Each of these situations created different therapeutic problems, which I shall now try to present.

Group therapy

Group therapy is conducted in a marathon mode: three-day marathon workshops offering six hours of therapy daily, held outside of hospital settings twice a year (Prot *et al.*, 2011). Initially, about 80 people received this form of therapy, with 50 to 60 attending every meeting, working in four different groups. No preliminary assessment was necessary to enter therapy. When the first groups were formed, the chairman of the "Children of the Holocaust" at the time thought that every association member was entitled to participate in psychotherapy, and the idea was supported by Orwid. Any selection procedure or exclusion of anyone who had experienced the horrors of war seemed unthinkable. This had an impact on the way that the groups are organized, since of the people attended the group nearly all of the time, but there have also been new regular participants.

With respect to dysfunction level, the participants represent a full spectrum: from psychotic, through borderline (frequently encountered in traumatized persons) to neurotic disorders. The participants drop out of therapy for various reasons, and some have died of old age. Over the 14 years of group therapy, one therapist quit the team, and three new therapists have joined. Orwid died in 2009, and her group was taken over by the psychotherapist who had supervised the team.

"Children of the Holocaust" frequently share feelings of abandonment, loneliness, and being insufficiently cared for. Therapists are often perceived as idealized objects onto which survivors' regressive fantasies about fusion, harmony, and safety are projected. Thus, the therapist may easily become a 'bad object' that cannot protect the patients from being hurt in either in-group or out-group conflict situations. In the "enchantment phase," the group is perceived as a family until the participants' loss of hope for symbiosis leads to "disappointment and despair" (Agazarian & Peters, 1981). Although idealization and devaluation processes take place in every therapeutic group, a distinguishing characteristic of survivor groups is their oscillating between the symbolism and metaphor of group work and the real situation, what Herzog (Herzog, 1982) calls the work "beyond metaphor." The group feels like a family, and fantasizes about possible blood connections, but in survivor associations, finding a blood relation many years after the war does, in fact, occur.

One of the major goals of the group psychotherapy is to overcome the survivors' sense of isolation, which is one of the sources of the so-called *survivor syndrome* (Bettelheim, 1979). During the first phase of group psychotherapy, participants shared their war-time experiences. This phase was accompanied by very intense emotions. Participants often said: "I've never talked about it that way before"; "It is the first time I'm telling my whole history." The main task of both the therapist and the group in this phase was to contain emotions. I worked single-handed with the group at that time and this was a very difficult, but also a very important, experience for me. At first, the group had a largely "narrative" character and, as in the groups described by Dasberg and colleagues (Dasberg *et al.*, 2001), regression was not encouraged. Even so, working with this group was associated with powerful emotions that can be described in psychodynamic terms.

It is not clear to me to what extent the sense of participation often accompanying me in my relations with the group resulted from my need to discover my family's concealed experience and to what extent it was caused by the group's need to "make me a member of the family". Group members certainly often view me as a member of their own rather than their children's generation. This became very evident in co-therapy, where group members see my co-therapist as a second-generation representative and approach him about issues concerning their children, whereas they repress the fact that both of us belong to their children's generation.

Perhaps due to my single-handed work in the first stage of therapy, when the participants needed to have a caring object that they had all lacked in early life, the group tended to cast me in a "parental" role. On the other hand, the introduction of the co-therapist coincided with a shift of group members' interest towards transgenerational issues. Thus, their casting the new therapist as a "child" was need-appropriate. Acceptance of the therapists as "family members" might also serve to protect the group members against their own anger or distrust to the therapists, since all of the group members had experienced abandonment by their nearest in early life. These aggressive feelings are often very intense in survivor groups (Haans, 1988).

Changes in patients' perceptions of the therapists may be regarded as positive developments: the overwhelming feeling among the group participants was initially that their suffering was totally incomprehensible to people who had never shared their experiences. However, a new belief emerged with time; that also those with different past life experiences may be helpful and empathic.

The group as a whole and individual members evoke my protective feelings as a countertransference reaction. A question arises as to what extent this is determined by problems specific to the group, and to what extent by the "second generation's" tendency to play a caring role in various situations (Rapoport, 2011). It is no coincidence that my family delegated me to care for and accompany my dying paternal grandmother, a Holocaust survivor. I have noticed that in my therapeutic work with other groups or individual patients, I need to be careful and moderate my overprotective tendencies so as not to become over-controlling.

Case report 1

This clinical example comes from the survivor group I worked with, initially single-handedly, and then for many years with my co-therapist. As noted earlier, we conduct three-day marathon workshops. On one occasion I hurt my foot severely while closing our gate after the first day. I had to go to the emergency department where my wound was stitched. Despite the doctor's orders to stay in bed, the next day I "heroically" attended further therapy sessions, looking evidently sick – limping and using a walking stick. Nevertheless, I felt I could not leave my "children", which I hoped they would appreciate. Clearly, I lived in a different time zone, where nothing could justify my abandoning the group. The participants were not particularly interested in my obviously poor condition, but instead heatedly discussed the indifference that the therapists showed when listening to their war-time stories. There were such comments as: "They have to do so, they are doctors" or "They cannot die together with their patient every time". After our mostly transposing and reflective interventions, which evidenced our ability to survive the attack, the group participants began talking about their mothers "destroyed" by the war, who had been incapable of protecting their children during the war and who, if they survived, had to be taken care of themselves. For the first time it was possible for the survivors to express anger towards their parents, who, from the child's perspective "had consented to be destroyed," and were unable to protect either themselves or their children.

This situation exemplifies the typical relationship between the first and second generations. The second generation members take on a "parenting" role regarding their parents, with fantasies about possibly regaining their own lost childhood (Kestenberg, 1989). The survivor group participants, who never experienced good care, are angry not only about being exposed to the sight of an "impaired" parent, but also about their guilt feelings related to that.

Individual therapy

I usually see my individual patients once a week. Their problems are similar to those discussed in group therapy, but the transference and countertransference reactions are more powerful in a one-on-one setting, which lacks the opportunities for dispersal provided by the presence of a co-therapist and other group members.

Countertransference is manifested mainly by my overprotective tendencies and feeling guilty that I cannot satisfy the patients' needs fully. This is particularly pronounced in my work with patients with a history of early separation.

People who have experienced such massive losses view therapy as an ideal relationship that will never end. This makes it very difficult for the therapist to end the therapy for fear that the patient will experience this as yet another abandonment (Klein, 1968). In an administratively enforced change of therapy settings, I discovered that at least some of my fears had more to do with countertransference than with the real situation. Indeed, I took great care to ensure that the patients would be able to continue therapy under the most favourable conditions possible, at my own inconvenience. Under the circumstances, I felt guilty for not having protected them against the trauma of change. This feeling had been so powerful and obvious that I was surprised and bewildered to hear during my supervision that the patients should be grateful for my efforts.

Discontinuation of therapy is difficult for survivors, but also for the therapist. It is particularly difficult for second generation therapists who have received from their families the message that separation is equal to a complete and final loss (Danieli, 1981; Shoshan, 1989). Thus, it is crucial that therapists distinguish between the patient's separation anxiety and their own fears and difficulties (Seritan *et al.* 2006).

The specific feature distinguishing patients who experienced early separation from others is that the former desperately need to know that, although their therapy has ended, they can be readmitted "if necessary". This does not pertain to all patients, but some patients must make sure from time to time that the object has not disappeared.

Case report 2

Lidia was rescued from the Warsaw ghetto as an infant under six months of age. She never learned who her parents were. She was quite explicit about her experiencing me as her lost mother. When telling me about Almodavar's film "Volver" (Almodavar, 2006) in which a mother is given up for dead, she said she would like her mother to be found, but that she should not be as old as the mother in the film – she would like her to be my age. She herself was surprised with her casting me in the role of her mother although I could have been her daughter, but here again reality was mixed with transference. We may say that the therapist becomes a transference object whatever his or her age. However, it is also true that at the time of separation, the patient's mother had not been even my age, but actually much younger, therefore the patient's needs were related to *that* mother.

Since the patient had been deprived at a very young age, her needs (now directed towards me) were hard for her to experience and for me to contain. In therapy, the patient became a little girl, idealizing her mother and longing to be intimately, bodily close to her. At first, the patient was very uncomfortable with these massive, directly expressed transference feelings that in countertransference turned out to be equally disturbing to me because of their erotic character. Once the patient saw these feelings in the mother–child context, she was willing to discuss her therapy-related feelings that she had formerly concealed because she had been ashamed of them.

Interviews

One can wonder why I decided not only to conduct therapy but also to interview people who had experienced the *Shoah*. This may have something to do with the need for a sense of both collective and family identity (Wardi, 1999). The need for collective identity is also expressed in the typical second-generation involvement in the maintenance of the memory of the Holocaust in the familial and social dimensions.

I suppose my need to interview people might be related to the problem of family silence and the opportunity the interviews presented to ask somebody else whether it was linked with the feeling that "we were lucky", as my family tradition has it. This can be said to be typical "survivor guilt" – "we were lucky because we survived". However, my interviews with survivors suggest that "survivor guilt", a frequent phenomenon, is often associated with a particular situation, such as guilt at the feelings of joy experienced when leaving the ghetto to start a new life (Prot, 2009; Prot, 2011) or guilt at feeling relief after being sent to the side of the living in Auschwitz (Fried, 1996). These are sometimes extreme situations, as in, for example, when survivors committed acts viewed as immoral in order to survive. In my family transmission, such a "situation" had been their pre-war choice of assimilation, which enabled my grandmother and her two children, with "bad looks" but speaking fluent Polish and proficient in the Catechism of the Catholic Church, to survive the war, avoiding both the ghetto and the concentration camp. I know from my grandmother that during the war her siblings had sent her from the Płaszów ghetto with a request for help in procuring documents, but she was unable to do so. They all died. I share my family's feelings of guilt and shame for considering themselves "lucky" because they had severed their Jewish roots.

I included the interviews to exemplify a therapeutic intervention evoking powerful emotions in both the interviewee and the "researcher", where the maintenance of "scientific objectivity" is often difficult. This applies not only to the situation where traumatic past events are discussed. Even simple administrative questions may elicit intense emotions, as in the case of an interviewee whom I asked what her first name had been before the war. At our next session she produced a letter in which she accused me of questioning her parents' right to give her a Christian name.

I think that my choosing the interview format for my research is not without significance. This format is most similar to the therapeutic situation and, in my opinion, allows survivors to remain subjects rather than objects, engaging not only the interviewee but also the interviewer.

Summary

In this specific situation where the therapist belongs to the second generation, he or she must cope with countertransference in both the roles of the child and the parent. As children, we were helpless in our efforts to cope with our parents' trauma, and in survivor psychotherapy we encounter feelings similar to those of a helpless child. Even in our "parental" role as therapists, we feel unable to satisfy our patients' parental deprivations (Tauber & van der Hal, 1998). To what extent can we integrate these traumatic experiences?

From my point of view, one of the major issues in the therapy of survivors, particularly younger "Children of the Holocaust", by a second-generation therapist, is the dangerous similarity of problems regarding identity, fears about children, and relationship difficulties due to being reared by traumatized parents. In other words, not everything can be explained in terms of projective identification. Irrespective of the therapy they conduct, therapists are confronted with these problems of their own. I am not sure whether it is an overstatement to say that I am recovering with my patients, but it would be probably fair to conclude that along with my patients, I seem to cope with these problems more successfully.

We are not only changing together, but also getting older together with our patients. More and more frequently, survivors bring up the problem of aging and fears of incapacity and death. Since the Holocaust lurks in the shadow, death is not viewed as a natural part of the life cycle, but as a brutal separation.

I feel that in psychotherapy with survivors, the therapist is confronted with existential problems in a unique way – having lost their world, our patients were given a possibility of living on with the certainty that they will yet depart from this new world that they regained with such effort. My understanding of countertransference is close to that of the Kleinian theory (Hinshelwood, 1989), namely, it is a specific response to the patient, a phenomenon in which the therapist acts as a container for the experiences the patient is unable to withstand. Containment of these unbearable experiences allows the patient and therapist to translate them into words. Pathological countertransference is the failure of a psychotherapist who is unable to understand a patient who begins to resemble some aspect of the therapist.

When analysing countertransference in our work with trauma, it is also important to adopt the relational/constructivist perspective (Rubenfeld, 2005), which views countertransference as normalised and de-pathologised. Rubenfeld wrote, in the context of working with trauma that we and our group members travel together on the same road. I think that this clearly defines my own situation in the therapy of Holocaust survivors.

References

Segal, H. (1986). Countertransference. In H. Segal (Ed.). *The Work of Hanna Segal*. London: Free Association Books & Maresfield Library. 81–87.

Ryn, Z. (2005). Auschwitz survivors: Clinical-psychiatric studies. In *Medical Review-Auschwitz*. Kraków: Przegląd Lekarski (Medical Review), in cooperation with the Auschwitz-Birkenau State Museum in Oświęcim.

Orwid, M., Domagalska-Kurdziel, E., Pietruszewski, K., Czaplak, E., Izdebski, R., Kamińska, M. (1995). Psychosocial effects of the Holocaust on survivors and the second generation in Poland: Preliminary report. In J. Lemberger (Ed.). *A Global Perspective on Working with Holocaust Survivors and the Second Generation*. Jerusalem: JDC. 205–242.

Orwid, M., Domagalska-Kurdziel, E., Pietruszewski, K., Czaplak, E., Izdebski, R., Kamińska, M. (1995a). The psychosocial effects of the holocaust on Jewish survivors living in Poland. *Psychiatria Polska*, 293(suppl.): 29–48. http://www.holocaustechoes.com/5orwid.html

Wilson, J. P., & Lindy, J. D. (1994). Empathic strain and countertransference. In J. P. Wilson & J. D. Lindy (Eds.). *Countertransference in the Treatment of PTSD*. New York, NY: Guilford Press. 5–30.

Herman, J. (1997). *Trauma and Recovery*. New York, NY: Basic Books.

Dalenberg, C. (2000). *Countertransference and the Treatment of Trauma*. Washington, DC: American Psychological Association.

Gabbard, G.O., & Wilkinson, S.M. (1994). *Management of Countertransference with Borderline Patients*. Washington, DC: American Psychiatric Press.

McCann, L., & Pearlman, L.A. (1990). Vicarious traumatization: A framework for understanding the psychological effects of working with victims. *Journal of Traumatic Stress*, 1:131–149.

McCann, L., & Coletti, I. (1994). The dance of empathy. In J. P. Wilson & J. D. Lindy (Eds.). *Countertransference in the Treatment of PTSD*. New York, NY: Guilford Press. 87–121.

Jankoski, J. A. (2010). Is vicarious trauma the culprit? A study of child welfare professionals. *Child Welfare*, 89: 105–120.

Newell, J. M., Nelson-Gardell, D., MacNeil, G. (2016). Clinician responses to client traumas: A chronological review of constructs and terminology. *Trauma, Violence & Abuse (Trauma Violence Abuse)*, 17:306–313.

Wardi, D. (1999). Therapists' responses in Holocaust survivors and second generation psychotherapy. *Croatian Medical Journal*, 40: 479–485.

Danieli, Y. (1980). Countertransference in the treatment and study of Nazi Holocaust survivors and their children. *Victimology*, 5: 355–367.

Dolan, Y. (1991). *Resolving sexual abuse: Solution focused therapy and Ericksonian hypnosis for adult survivors*. London: Norton.

Danieli, Y. (1994). Countertransference, trauma and training. In J. P. Wilson & J. D. Lindy (Eds.). *Countertransference in the Treatment of PTSD*. New York, NY: Guilford Press. 368–388.

Tauber, Y. (1998). *In the Other Chair: Holocaust survivors and the second generation as therapists and clients*. Hewlett, NY: Gefen Publishing House.

Tauber, Y. (2003). We're listening, but can we hear? Psychotherapy with Holocaust survivors and the second generation in Israel, under (threat of) conditions of armed conflict. *Journal of Trauma Practice*, 2:17–46.

Smith, A. J., Kleijn, W. C., Trijsburg, R. W., Hutschemaekers, G. J. (2007). How therapists cope with clients' traumatic experiences. *Torture*, 17: 203–15

Hafkenscheid, A. (2005). Event countertransference and vicarious traumatization: theoretically valid and clinically useful concepts? *European Journal of Psychotherapy, Counselling and Health*, 7: 159–168.

Hoppe, K. D. (1984). Severed ties. In S. A. Luel & P. Marcus (Eds.). *Psychoanalytic Reflections on the Holocaust: Selected essays*. New York, NY: KATV Publishing House. 94–111.

Dasberg, H. (1993). How psychotherapists cope with their patients' trauma. In S. Robinson (Ed.). *Echoes of the Holocaust: Bulletin of the Jerusalem Center for Research into the Late Effects of the Holocaust*. Jerusalem: Talbieh Mental Health Center. 31–45.

Fogelman, E. (1998). Group belonging and mourning as factors in resilience in second generation of Holocaust survivors. *Psychoanalytic Review*, 85; 537–549.

Tauber, Y., & van der Hal, E. (1998). Countertransference and life-and-death issues in group psychotherapy with child Holocaust survivors. *American Journal of Psychotherapy*, 52: 301–312.

Marcus, P. (1984). Jewish consciousness after the Holocaust. In S. A. Luel & P. Marcus (Eds.). *Psychoanalytic Reflections on the Holocaust: Selected essays*. New York, NY: KATV Publishing House. 179–195.

Kellermann, N. P. (2009). *Holocaust Trauma: Psychological effects and treatment*. New York, Bloomington: iUniverse.

Schneiderman, G., & Budziszewska, M. (2012). Sixty-five years after World War II: A family secret. *Psychiatric Times*. http://www.psychiatrictimes.com/ptsd/sixty-five-years-after-world-war-ii-family-secret.

Danieli, Y. (1981). Differing adaptation styles in families of survivors of the Nazi Holocaust. *Child Today*, 10: 6–10.

Danieli, Y. (2015). The Danieli inventory of multigenerational legacies of trauma, Part I: Survivors' posttrauma adaptational styles in their children's eyes. *Journal of Psychiatric Research*, 68:167–175.

Gampel, Y. (1998). Reflections on countertransference in psychoanalytic work with child survivors of the *Shoah*. *Journal of American Academy of Psychoanalysis*, 26: 343–368.

Durst, N. (2003). Child survivors of the Holocaust: Age specific traumatization and the consequences for therapy. *American Journal of Psychotherapy*, 57: 499–518.

Prot, K., Szwajca, K., Biedka, Ł., Bierzyński, K., Domagalska, E., Izdebski, R.(2011). Psychotherapy of Holocaust survivors – group process analysis. *Archives of Psychiatry and Psychotherapy*, 1:21–33. Agazarian, I., & Peters, R. (1981). *The Visible and Invisible group*. London: Routledge & Kegan.

Herzog, J. (1982). World beyond metaphor. Thoughts of the transmission of trauma. In M. S. Bergmann & M. E. Jucovy (Eds.). *Generations of the Holocaust*, New York, NY: Basic Books. pp. 103–119.

Bettelheim, B. (1979). *Surviving and Other Essays*. London: Thames and Hudson.

Dasberg, H., Bartura, J., Amit, Y. (2001). Narrative group therapy with ageing child survivors of the Holocaust. *Israel Journal of Psychiatry and Related Sciences*, 38: 27–35.

Haans, T. (1988). Group psychotherapy with survivors of World War II persecution. *Group Analysis*, 21: 267–280.

Rapoport, E. R. (2011). Growing up in the shadow of the Holocaust: A psychoanalyst addresses intergenerational transmission of trauma in her family. *Isssues In Psychoanalytic Psychology*, 33: 43–50.

Kestenberg, J. S. (1989). Transposition revisited: clinical, therapeutic and developmental consideration. In P. Marcus & I. A. Rosenberg (Eds.). *Healing their Wounds: Psychotherapy with Holocaust survivors and their families*.Westport, CT: Praeger. pp. 67–82.

Klein, H. (1968). Problems in the psychotherapeutic treatment of Israeli survivors of the Holocaust. In H. Krystal (Ed.). *Massive Psychic Trauma*. New York, NY: International Universities Press, Inc. pp. 233–248.

Danieli, Y. (1981). Differing adaptation styles in families of survivors of the Nazi Holocaust. *Child Today*, 10: 6–10.

Shoshan, T. (1989). Mourning and longing from generation to generation. *American Journal of Psychotherapy*, 43: 193–207.

Seritan, A. L., Gabbard, G. O., Benjamin, L. (2006). War and peace:

Psychotherapy with a Holocaust survivor. *American Journal of Psychiatry*, 163: 1705–1709.

Almodavar, P. (Dir.) (2006). *Volver*. Spain.

Wardi, D. (1999). Therapists' responses in Holocaust survivors and second generation psychotherapy. *Croatian Medical Journal*, 40: 479–485.

Prot, K., (2009). *Życie po Zagładzie: Skutki traumy u ocalałych z Holocaustu. Świadectwa z Polski i Rumunii (Life after Holocaust: Effects of trauma among the survivors. Testimony documentation from Poland and Romania)*. Warsaw: Institute of Psychiatry and Neurology.

Prot, K. (2011). Le sentiment de culpabilité et de honte chez les survivants de l'Holocauste (Guilt and shame in Holocaust survivors). *L'évolution psychiatrique*, 76: 201–217.

Fried, H. (1996). *The Road to Auschwitz: Fragments of a life*. Lincoln, NE, University of Nebraska Press.

Tauber, Y., & van der Hal, E. (1998). Countertransference and life-and-death issues in group psychotherapy with child Holocaust survivors. *American Journal of Psychotherapy*, 52: 301–312.

Hinshelwood, R. D. (1989). *A Dictionary of Kleinian Thought*. London: Free Association Books.

Rubenfeld, S. (2005). Relational perspectives regarding countertransference in groups and trauma. *International Journal of Group Psychotherapy*, 55:115–135.

CHAPTER

SEVEN

A Therapy Group for the Children of Holocaust Survivors in Poland Faces Loss, Bereavement and Problems of Countertransference

Katarzyna Prot-Klinger, Krzysztof Szwajca, Łukasz Biedka, Kazimierz Bierzyński, Ewa Domagalska-Kurdziel, Ryszard Izdebski, and Marta Szwajca

Transmission of the Holocaust trauma has been widely discussed in the psychoanalytic literature in terms of the transposition phenomenon, or projective identification, where children contain their parents' uncontainable feelings of bereavement and aggression. The child begins to think, feel and act in accordance with this projection, and "returns" these feelings in an attempt to compensate for the parental losses through avoiding rebellion and giving up separation. The children feel they cannot leave their family home without a total loss of the object – since separation denotes death, both symbolically and literally. The Holocaust trauma is transmitted with a devastating effect onto the child, mostly because the parents are unable to support the separation.

Specificity of the Polish "second generation" consists in their living in families being a fraction of the extremely small and dispersed Jewish community, in generational families with a double taboo of not only the Holocaust, but also of their Jewish origin. The silence surrounding

the Holocaust leads to terrifying fantasies about parental experiences, making the separation process even more difficult.

In this context, the authors describe a group process in the therapeutic group for "the second generation" conducted by therapists differentiated with regard to their relationship to "Jewishness" and the Holocaust what released various countertransferential reactions. They describe the process of crucial importance to the Survivors' children – of separation from their parents and therapists in the parental role through establishing an organization of "The Second Generation" aimed at preserving memory and building up Jewish identity. The authors assume that enabling "the second generation" children to complete the process of separation gives them a chance build the history of Holocaust into the family history, to perceive the Holocaust as a myth, and to focus on living their lives and not only dwelling upon death. The myth of the Holocaust becomes a part of their identity, influencing both their way of perceiving life and their philosophy of life.

Introduction

Transmission of the Holocaust trauma has been widely discussed in the psychoanalytic literature in terms of the transposition phenomenon (Kestenberg, 1982), or projective identification (Klein, 1946), in which children contain their parents' uncontainable feelings of bereavement and aggression. The child begins to think, feel, and act in accordance with this projection, and "returns" these feelings in an attempt to compensate for the parental losses through avoiding rebellion and giving up separation. The child feels unable to leave the family home without a total loss of the object (e.g., mother, father, other family members), since separation denotes death, both symbolically and literally (Kestenberg & Gampel, 1983). The Holocaust trauma is transmitted with a devastating effect onto the child, mostly because the parents are unable to support separation.

The frequency and severity of difficulties experienced by the Second Generation, as reported in the psychoanalytic literature, are a subject of considerable controversy. Increasingly popular is the view that Holocaust survivors' descendants essentially do not differ from the general population, and differences, if any, are relatively subtle, such as a latent vulnerability to distress manifested after their own traumatic injury (Kellerman, 2001; Levav *et al.*, 2007). Moreover, evidently impaired functioning of the second generation is regarded as the exception rather than the rule (Helmreich, 1996; Giladi & Bell,

2013). More recent studies (Weinberg & Cummins, 2013; Fossion *et al.*, 2015), in which participants were second generation descendants living either in Israel or in the USA, describe them as relatively well-adjusted populations in which the "transgenerational effect" becomes less and less discernible. Against this background, the small and relatively isolated group of second generation members living in Poland seems particularly interesting and distinctive. We consider transgenerational transmission of trauma more salient in this group than in other samples studied, as we explain in the following sections.

The second generation in Poland

The estimated number of Jews in Poland ranges from a few to several thousand (Potel, 2010). In 1968 an eruption of anti-Semitism was followed by the last Jewish migration from Poland. Among the almost 13,000 Jews who left during 1968–1972 were very large numbers of scientists, engineers, doctors, artists, musicians, and journalists (Eisler, 2006; Stola, 2000). The small, traumatized, decimated Jewish community that remained in Poland kept apart until 1989, when new Jewish organizations began to emerge.

Most of the survivors who remained in Poland came from Jewish families that had assimilated before World War II. Due to their parents' and their own experiences, they had identity problems. A vast majority had survived the Holocaust "on Aryan papers" (i.e., by hiding their Jewishness) and some of them continued this strategy after the war. After the Holocaust people quite often purposefully cut themselves off from Jewishness, sought identities other than ethnic, merged into the Polish community, and married Christian partners. The second generation children were often brought up in families with a "double taboo" (Orwid *et al.*, 1994) covering not only the Holocaust, but also the Jewish background of their parent(s). One study found that this situation was reported by 59 percent of second generation respondents interviewed (Szwajca, 2009).

The second generation members of the therapy group lived for a long time in a country where not only a collective memory of the Holocaust was lacking, but also their parents' traumatic experiences were contrary to the predominating social narrations about the war. Furthermore, the Holocaust survivors who remained in Poland after World War II and 1968 were generally those who had been younger during the Holocaust than those who emigrated. Experiencing trauma at a younger age increases the risk of developing symptoms of post-traumatic stress disorder (Yehuda *et al.*, 2001), and parental post-traumatic stress is positively associated with transmission of trauma to the next generation (Yehuda, 2008; Brand, 2011).

Their children (the second generation) were born later, thus their identity formation took place in the difficult period between the year 1968 and the late 1980s, when Jewish issues were absent from the public discourse, it was difficult to acquire knowledge about Jewishness, and the Jewish community was destroyed. Due to all these factors, transgenerational phenomena remain very salient and meaningful, even nowadays, among the children of Holocaust survivors living in Poland, and separation problems are so important.

History of the group

In this context, we describe a group process in a therapeutic group for "the second generation". Following the first meeting in late 1998, we met every two to three months for an approximately six-hour session. In the initial stage, the group was entirely open, but from 2007 until its closure in 2014, and following a discussion within the group, we changed our rules to become a "slow open" group. The initial rules seem to have resulted from the need to create a non-exclusionary climate among a group of people that frequently experiences a sense of exclusion. However, as group work proceeded to a deeper level, a need for security prevailed and limits were set. At first, as many as five therapists acted as group leaders. This was due to the original idea of establishing many smaller groups. However, the original idea was never implemented for organizational and financial reasons.

The program was created and led by a Polish psychiatrist and one of the pioneers of the psychiatry of children and family in Poland, Maria Orwid (a Polish psychiatrist and one of the pioneers of the psychiatry of children and family in Poland), a Holocaust survivor herself, who invited younger therapists (two Jewish and two non-Jewish) to collaborate. The program grew out of studies of post-traumatic problems among the second generation that had been conducted by Professor Orwid together with a group of young Cracovian psychiatrists as early as 1959 (Orwid, 1962; Orwid, 1964). During these studies, the team interviewed over a hundred former prisoners of the Auschwitz concentration camp (Leśniak *et al.*, 1961; Leśniak, 1964; Szymusik, 1964; Teutsch, 1962). These studies were the first in Poland and among the first worldwide to investigate delayed consequences of trauma. The Cracovian studies were ahead of their time, being more holistic, atheoretical, interested in context, and less biological than contemporary research projects. For years, those studies were a rare (if not the only) example of research conducted entirely irrespective of insurance claims and reparations to Holocaust survivors.

Professor Orwid investigated the functioning of former concentration camp prisoners in various spheres (in the family, community, at the workplace), as well as their value systems. Her research revealed loneliness and silence among prisoners of Auschwitz, their seeking a reference group, the importance of social support, the complex combination of their strength, fragility, and not always effective psychological defenses. In addition, their satisfaction with work and family life was assessed. Thirty years later phenomena described in her research were incorporated into diagnostic classifications as enduring personality change after catastrophic experience (World Health Organization, 1992).

In Professor Orwid's early studies, no Jewish subgroup was distinguished among prisoners of the Auschwitz concentration camp. Jewish issues only emerged in Professor Orwid's research in the years 1989–1992, that is, during a period of radical sociopolitical changes in Poland during which the taboos of the Holocaust and Jewishness were lifted. Together with a team of collaborators, she then examined twenty Holocaust survivors and an equal number of second generation respondents (Orwid *et al.*, 1994; Orwid *et al.*, 1994a; Orwid *et al.*, 1997). This study revealed a traumatized population of persons struggling with loneliness, with questions concerning their identity, and with their suboptimal functioning in family life. Owing to energetic efforts undertaken by Professor Orwid, a therapeutic program was launched in 1997.

Since 1992, Professor Orwid, in collaboration with her team, has published about 70 papers, articles, and conference presentations concerning delayed consequences of the Holocaust trauma. Most of the publications were related to the therapeutic program conducted by the team. The program, called the Children of the Holocaust, continues through to the present day. Moreover, in the years 1998–2014, a second generation group operated. Here, we describe the group process within the second generation group in the context of two traumatic events: a therapist leaving the group in 2006, and the death of Professor Orwid in 2009.

Defining the "second generation"

Traditionally a "second generation" representative was assumed to have at least one parent of Jewish background who had survived the

Holocaust in German-occupied Europe. This definition quickly proved to be inadequate in our "second generation" group. Some participants who regarded themselves as natural members of the group had parents who had either escaped or been deported with their families from areas affected by the Holocaust to the Soviet Union (these were the so-called "Siberians"). In the initial stages of the group's establishment, this issue was heatedly discussed among the therapists. One of the therapists belonged to the strictly defined second generation, in that her father had survived the war within the territory of Poland, while the mother of another therapist had survived the war in the Soviet Union.

At first, Professor Orwid was against the participation of the children of Siberians, assuming that their parents' lives had been entirely different from hers and from those of other Holocaust survivors. With time, the group participants' life histories turned out to be very similar, particularly as regards the aspect of "hiding oneself" and living with a traumatized parent (even if the trauma had been experienced under different circumstances). Therefore, we decided that anyone having a Jewish parent who had survived the war, irrespective of where, was entitled to join the group.

We also refer to this discussion because of a difference of opinion between two Jewish therapists. One of the therapists belonged to the strictly defined second generation (her father had survived the war on the territory of Poland), while the mother of another therapist had survived the war in the Soviet Union. This difference between the therapists helped us to better understand the differentiation within the group. The different personal histories of the therapeutic team members helped us to better understand the differentiation within the group. "Absence", unresolved mourning, a lack of graves and/or a lack of Jewish relatives did not differentiate between the group members, since the parent-survivors from the Soviet Union had usually also lost almost all their families, murdered by the Nazis. However, their personal experiences of survival had been different: being a Jew in the Nazi-occupied territories was a death warrant, and to survive people had to hide their Jewishness and experienced extreme loneliness.

By contrast, Jews who had escaped or been deported to the Soviet Union experienced a collective trauma – they suffered and were at risk of death the same as others, as "non-Jews". Theoretically, this should have led to less severe problems with Jewish identity for themselves and their children. In practice, in this respect, the children of Siberian survivors did not differ from the second generation children of Holocaust survivors who remained within Nazi-occupied Europe, who predominated in the group. Namely, in the Siberian families there was the same secrecy about the parents' ethnic background, and the children had the same identity problems.

Diversity in the therapist group

Various psychotherapeutic approaches were represented in the therapeutic team: psychodynamic, systemic and group-analytic. The therapists' Holocaust-related experiences were also different: both parents of two female therapists were non-Jewish Poles, while the parents of two male and one female therapist were in mixed Polish–Jewish marriages and these therapists identified, at least partly, as Jewish. The presence of both non-Jewish and Jewish therapists in a team headed and created by a Holocaust survivor seems to be particularly valuable.

The second generation group (similarly to any homogeneous group) was at risk of projecting anger and "bad objects" onto the outside, beyond themselves, such that the "others", the "Poles", would become the persecutors. The presence of non-Jewish Polish therapists not only prevented the group from closing up, or focusing entirely on Jewish specificity, but also enabled its members to keep situations, attitudes, and choices in a more universal and objective perspective. These therapists' activity added a dimension of non-specificity to any problem under consideration, bringing a part of the outside world into the group. Moreover, they represented a Polish side of the identity of the group as a whole and of each individual group member. Almost all the group participants came from ethnically mixed families, and for all of them Polish culture was the first and dominating one. When the group was working hard on "Jewish" issues, the "Polish" therapists felt like a "minority", taking the role of the "Other". This can be interpreted also as a projective identification of the group members, who experienced being a social "minority" in their own lives.

The leaving of therapist M

The fact that a therapist left the group initially triggered the group to attack the therapists. This was associated with the group members' fantasy of their own omnipotence; the group fantasized that they would bring the therapist back, and resorted to acting out this fantasy by contacting her outside the group. During a session confronting their fantasies with reality, group members perceived the therapist's leaving as her having been expelled by the bad mother, namely, by the group leader, Professor Orwid. She became a constant object of idealizing and hostile projections. The therapist's leaving was followed by an evident crisis in the group, manifested by absences, questioning of the purposefulness of the group's existence, and by acting-out ideas, such as to establish the Association of the Second Generation. This idea, which occasionally recurred in the group, had a number of functions. On the one hand, it was a mature attempt to create a forum for meetings between survivors' children beyond the therapeutic group, and on the other hand it seemed to be the acting-out answer to the frustrations experienced in the group.

We may also wonder to what extent the quitting of the therapist, who was identified with "Polishness", aroused group members' anxiety about the condition of their own "Polishness".

Under threat of a therapist's death: The reactivation of themes concerning relations with Holocaust survivor parents

In January 2009, the group was informed that Professor Orwid was critically ill. As mentioned, Professor Orwid had formed the group and led it from its inception. Furthermore, she perceived herself and was perceived by the group's members as a mother figure. Since the group members' attitude towards their "Jewish" part, represented by "Jewish" therapists and "Jewish mothers", was very ambivalent, her severe illness raised many issues, as illustrated by the following excerpts from a group session.

> DANKA: *Fifteen years ago I did not make it to say the last goodbye to my Mom; she had been in a coma for almost four weeks. My Mom used to live with a constant sense of threat, feeling that people were against her, and she kept transferring it to me. I was an insensitive child. I cannot forgive myself for that. Her doctor told me her condition was stable, so I went home and kept calling him up every hour. He never told me, not until the morning. I have a realistic dream – my Mom is alive, I have not visited her, I do not contact her, I have to go to her, but don't know where. This dream has been recurring over the past three weeks, recently every night. Recently, that Mom is comatose, I go to her hospital and cannot find her. The feeling that I failed to fix all that, I did not call her up, Mom is waiting. Our conflicts keep coming back – we could not live without each other, but mother held grudges against me all the time. I feel guilty I could not be a substitute for her of the world she had lost. She suffered from mental illness all her life, she had spent three years in a ghetto cellar. I know from Mother's stories that I was expected to replace her family. I*

wanted to escape, cut off, and that is why I married so early. At that time, I practically interrupted all my life activities, as a matter of fact, kept sitting at her bedside.

IGOR: *I would not be normal if I submitted myself to my mother. She is apodictic. I have fought all my life for dignity, and have won it. If I had not fought, she would have crushed me. I am a father myself, and don't know how to bring up my children. I told myself – my children would not be reared the way my mother was rearing me.*

MAGDA: *When I was 30, I realized my mother was mortal, and I decided to teach her how to cuddle me and my children. I had more time – God had taken from you, Danka, the 15 years He gave to me. I understand my mother was an extremely apodictic person. I had no chance to be the best daughter, I was fed up with the idea that everybody around us was mean and horrible, and that a disaster was lurking everywhere.*

THERAPIST Ł.: *Magda is talking about the other side – her disappointment and grudges against her Mom.*

MAGDA: *Yes, I had a similar mother. I cannot cope with my guilt feelings and my grudges against her. I was expected to be a substitute for the whole world for her. I tried to bugger off as fast as I could. I didn't know for years why this burden. I have learned rather late that my Mom was a Jew. . I felt for a long time she did not love me, that I was unimportant to her, but she could not behave otherwise. I feel guilty I could not, that I failed to cope with that. My Mom was dying for over a year, I had a year to sit at her bedside and hold her hand. It was unusual, since I earlier used to tell myself "I won't give her anything when she is in need". I was the child my mother had hung her life on.*

IWONA: *My father was very difficult towards my mother – she revived after his death. Since we were little kids we were brought up knowing that our father had survived in a cellar. I did not know what that meant because it was the daily bread – as if everyone had been hiding in a cellar and survived the war. It is not the reason to pick on our mother, on us, or to be permanently right. My brother had understood it earlier and wrote a letter to our father telling him that it would take a hero to survive and rescue one's parents. I understood it later that it was not quite so normal. I am not sure whether I understand it now. I don't even know whether I would be capable of saying the last goodbye to my father, I don't know if I would have anything to say to him today.*

In this material, difficult relations can be seen between the Holocaust survivors and their children, as well as the specific characteristics of families of survivors who stayed in Poland after the Holocaust. One such feature is a "conspiracy of silence" (Danieli, 1981) regarding not only the Holocaust, but also the participants' Jewish origins. This is evidenced by Magda's narrative *("I didn't know for a long time my mother was a Jew".)*, as well as by Iwona's story, where children were told only that their father had survived in a cellar.

The second generation members are sensitive to their parents' need to maintain silence. The parents do not tell, the children do not ask questions, but they cannot understand their parent's emotional inaccessibility. The survivors, engrossed in the past, hardly contain their children's fears. The children perceive this parental state as lack of love (Magda). Moreover, low parental reactivity could violently turn into extreme hyper-reactivity, when survivors responded in an over-excitable way to minor events (Iwona). Their children express empathetic tenderness towards the "changed" parent, and are sensitive to his/her needs, but in consequence, their own losses are minimized and neglected as unimportant. The children feel responsible for their parent(s) and that they must care for them, as if they were themselves the parents of their parents (Dorota, Magda).

This type of intergenerational transmission of trauma consists of a role reversal, where the parental role is described as "defensive caregiving", "narcissistic parenthood", "entanglement", "over-involvement", or "blurring of the parent–child roles" (Hass, 1990). By the same token of "invisible loyalties" (Boszormenyi-Nagy & Spark, 1973), the children feel responsible for their parents, undertaking the role of a "parental" child (Perel & Saul, 1989). In descriptions of these phenomena, the transmission of trauma is considered in terms of non-specific problems related to the traumatized patents' lack of caregiving skills and their "holding" (Winnicott, 1965). The uniqueness of this relationship is due to the children's inability to express their anger at the parents who, in consequence of their tragic experiences, have not developed empathy; thus a vicious circle of anger and anger-related guilt feelings arises.

The group's bereavement after their therapist's death

The subsequent group session took place after Professor Orwid's death. The session began with deciding the date of the next meeting and optimistic comments about coping after Orwid's passing away. Then Magda said: *"I actually believed this would not go to pieces. I mean I am not sure whether I was really certain of that. I wanted us not to be a reminiscing group, but to continue being therapeutic. Because for me it is a therapeutic group."* Then she proceeded to describe her sense of exclusion during the funeral ceremony for Professor Orwid.

> THERAPIST K. : *I feel we have started optimistically, that at first we established the date and were talking about how we tried to cope with Maria death, and now you Magda are telling us about your feeling of having failed to come to terms with it. Perhaps other people in the group also can find such a part in themselves that failed to cope with this death.*
> OLGIERD: *There is one more thing that lies heavy on my mind. I feel M. [the female therapist who had quit] is missing, I and Stasia feel she is missing.*
> THERAPIST K.: *I have a feeling that there is a wish in the group for the birth of a new person, since M. would be a new person in this group, and that it is easier to talk about somebody joining the group than about bereavement after the loss of Maria .*
> STASIA: *For me it would be a good moment for someone joining us, because for me this group is not what it used to be. I feel this very clearly today. Madam Professor is really missing in everything today. It will not be the same group. I feel the moments when Madam Professor would say something. For me it would be a good moment if someone was to join, something has been closed and re-opened, we begin from scratch, it would do me good, because I do not feel well. I did not want to come, that's true. Even now I would like to go home.*
> IGOR: *I feel Madam Professor would wish the group to stay, but I think no reanimation by force is needed, it must go the natural way. If the group remains, then it remains, but if it starts to fall apart, there is no need to stimulate by force. I would like the group to remain, although it will be different.*
> ALA: *I am looking around, we are here and all of us speak, so the group is necessary, if we spend this beautiful spring day here. I would like to return to the issue of M., too.*
> THERAPIST E.: *We are talking about whether there is readiness to go on being in the group without Maria.*
> MAGDA: *I would like the therapeutic team to stay and the group to remain, we have all benefitted from the presence of MariaI do not think the competences of the therapeutic team have markedly decreased, because there is a thing called continuation.*
> EWA: *When I heard this term "intergenerational transmission of trauma" I did not know for a long time what it was about, and then I thought that it might be about me, and then I thought it might be about the transmission between therapists. The first one was Kępiński, then Professor Orwid, and now you are therapists and the*

former generation has given something to you. I need this group extremely. I need people to whom the term "mother in a cupboard" means something.
THERAPIST E.: *I have heard Magda's anxiety that the group would fall apart, and Stasia's difficulties with coming here because the group that used to be does not exist anymore. Kasia was talking about individual ways of experiencing bereavement and about things that people cannot cope with, then the issue of introducing a new person cropped up. Isn't it an attempt to avoid the experience of bereavement, an attempt at replacing bereavement with somebody else, something new?*
THERAPIST Ł.: *There was such a natural readiness in me that we would go on meeting and continuing, and I needed to hear what you have said, that it was defensive on my part and it was my problem with experiencing bereavement. It is only you who told me that this group would not be the same group.*
IGOR: *I have a question: have you had a good co-operation with M.?*
THERAPIST Ł. : *This does not belong to the therapeutic subject matter under consideration, since we are dealing with what is going on between us here.*
IGOR: *I thought there might be something between you as colleagues, that is why I asked, but of course my question is inappropriate.*
THERAPIST K.: *When Maria was with us, you perceived us as a team, a family, there were no such questions asked whether we quarreled or not. Her death has changed things, you started to look at the team members wondering whether we are in agreement or do we quarrel, and whether this M. was sort of a sister.*
Olgierd and Ala return to the issue of therapist M. (re)joining the group.
EWA: *I am a new one here, I do not know M., but I understand that the therapist for some reason has left the group, and my question is: does she want to come back? Do you have such knowledge? If she wants to come back, so why does this issue return now, when Madam Professor is no longer with us? I understand the decision had been made by Madam Professor, and Madam Professor cannot answer these questions any more. So why now? How do you know the therapist wants to come back to the group? And who is to make the decision? We, the patients? Or the therapists, the group leaders?*
ALA: *I have always been for M.'s coming back, but I wouldn't dare tell this to Madam Professor, she had been obviously against it.*
IWONA: *I feel disgusted that at first we are talking for two hours about how Madam Professor is no longer with us, and how nothing will be the same any more, and then after a while a suggestion crops up to*

do something Madam Professor was clearly against. That is how I see it. I think I probably would not be so disgusted if the issue cropped up some two or three sessions earlier. From outside it looks like that: Madam Professor was against it, but Madam Professor passed away, so the issue can return.

ALA: *I feel hurt by such an opinion, we deserved to be told, I thought we have never been told the whole truth and the matter has not been fully explained to us.*

THERAPIST K. : *I understand it is about anger towards Mariaand anger at us. And I understand it can be difficult to talk about one's anger at a person only just deceased, but death can be accompanied by feelings of anger caused not only by what this person had done, but also by the fact that this person abandoned us.*

OLGIERD: *This is not an issue There is no issue that I waited for Madam Professor to pass away, I raised the subject as soon as M. quitted, my opinion in this matter was well known to Madam Professor, I've never hidden my views. She had her definite opinion, so had I, but she was Madam Professor, and I was a group member, so the problem was resolved the way it was, but this matter was closed by force arguments only for a while, it had to return. Perhaps it would be better if I waited, but although I am bereaved by Madam Professor's death, I decided there was no point in waiting. You know quite well that it is definitely not the matter of substitution, because nobody can be substituted by someone else.*

THERAPIST Ł.: *It has suddenly turned out that from the therapeutic team, stable for years, one person disappears over which you had no influence whatever, and that such a disappearance may make you feel afraid that someone else might disappear anytime, which may be threatening. Besides, your fantasy that you can introduce changes in the team and introduce somebody may also be disturbing.*

EWA: *I was wondering whether the therapeutic team would be able to manage, whether they would wish to continue. And you, Ł. , said that you were a monolith and would continue. It is most important to me that you are prepared to take over this intergenerational baton.*

Magda: I was under the impression that after Maria's death things are difficult for you, too.

EWA: *I was angry about our not meeting sometime in April. I needed our group to meet after the funeral, even if only for 15 minutes. I am angry you failed to do that.*

THERAPIST E. : *It is important what you have just said that you were angry at us. You, Magda, have said we were weakened, and perhaps it is difficult to express one's anger at such weakened therapists who are in bereavement themselves.*

STASIA: *I feel better now. I think we have hammered this matter out and now I am calmer.*
IGOR: *Luckily it was not limited to our talking about the late Madam Professor, what she was like. It is good that some dirty linen was out, because everything is appropriate here. At the beginning I felt disconcerted, now it is a relief.*
ALA: *I am allergic to attempts at glorifying people, I am a person who has her authorities, but they are neither obvious nor imposed from outside. I do not think that questioning somebody's decision or expressing feelings towards someone could be regarded as tarnishing her memory. I respect the team of therapists and I am going to keep my distance. I also feel relieved that some things have been explained, because I used to feel neglected and now I am OK, I respect your decisions, although I believe that M. was unfairly treated then and it is still my opinion.*
EWA: *I wanted either to hear it from someone or to say it myself in the nearest future – what is there between me and my nonexistent family, between me and my nonexistent Mom.*

This extensive excerpt of the group session recording illustrates the work on separation, bereavement and, above all, on the accompanying feelings of anger. In contradistinction to the real parents of most of the group members, the therapists, despite their weakening and their own bereavement, are able to deal with anger-related themes and to set boundaries without retaliating. The participants exhibit a willingness to explore the relationships within the "family" of therapists (motivated perhaps by the group's envy at their closeness with the late therapist), and secondly, their claiming the status of siblings. The group defends itself from feelings of sadness by means of fantasies about a newborn therapist.

The Association of the Second Generation

From the second session after the funeral of Professor Orwid, the most frequently recurring theme became that of the Association of the Second Generation, which some of the group members were trying to establish. In addition, the issue of difficult relations with "parents" was introduced right away: "We do not wish to make the Association of "Children of the Holocaust" think we want to appropriate their territory, or to take their place. So we want to arrange a meeting with their leadership, to let them know there is such an initiative among us and that we are willing to cooperate with them. I have heard they might feel threatened". The participants talked not only of their attempts at understanding their Holocaust survivor parents, but also of the possibility of repairing their relationships with them:

> IGOR: *Madam Professor never wanted to have children, because she had seen how they die. And our mothers decided to have children and undoubtedly loved them so that they would have given their life for them – and with this love they incapacitate us, such a destructive effect of love on the development of sons, above all. I am talking here about myself, and Tadeusz, and Krzysztof. I can see a common denominator here. The umbilical cord has not been cut.*
>
> JOLA: *I was dominated by my mother. I am not saying my Mom wanted to dominate over me, it is only that she has always been most important to me and I loved her, while I respected my father and was afraid of him. And Mother was the entire world to me and I wanted to please her; even if I was not always successful, nevertheless I kept trying as best as I could, and that is why I am under pressure. It has remained like that. When doing a lot of things I thought: what would my Mom say to that, would she like that or not? I would have done or not done many things if it were not for my mother.*
>
> KRZYSZTOF: *I remember my Mom saying this and it is somewhat unpleasant what I am going to say, but she did say so and this is what life is like: she reached adulthood only when she had lost her parents. So I thought that's the normal thing and that it is simply so that sooner or later I will have to reach adulthood.*
>
> EWA: *It is meaningful that the only photo in my new apartment is that of my Mom, and not of my little son whom I miss so much. Never before have I had my Mom's photo standing around. Now suddenly there is enough room for my Mom. I was told by my therapist that when my mother is no longer here, when she becomes a rather virtual person, it will be easier for me to come to terms with her. Indeed, she passed away a few years ago and she is now more present than ever, really. It is a paradox. I begin to get on well with her. Perhaps I have made some room for her in my life. My mother told me once that the real life had been until the war. My mother missed a lot of things. She was so insecure, unable to summon up overprotectiveness, or protectiveness. I blame myself for not understanding my Mom for such a long time. I was cruel to her, nursing grudges against her, I thought she did not love me, she had always seemed to me old and continually angry. I misjudged her feelings – she was worried and unhappy, and aggression and anger were secondary in her case. But it is only nowadays that I am so wise. What a horrible life she must have had. My Mom had lost everything during the war; she was the only one to*

survive, absolutely alone. Then she happened to meet my SOB father and then had a no-good daughter. I had so many grudges against my Mom. I kept asking: Mom, why have you never told me all that? She did not want me to know: I was to be happy in a happy country. She wanted to spare me fear. I have understood what she wanted to protect me from. But anyway she failed. She unconsciously transmitted her fear to me. She was hiding in the cupboard till the end. Few people knew she was Jewish. She said once she was sorry she had not told me. I used to have a grudge against my mother, I thought she did not love me and that I did not love her for many things – for not throwing my father out, not emigrating, not having therapy, not taking care of herself and me. I leveled a number of charges. Finally, I ran away from my constantly dissatisfied, hysterical, unhappy mother. But I could not talk with her. I think my Mom tried to, but she could not do it. I have never got it and could not give it back. But I have done something good. Although I did not like my mother, I always cared for a good relationship between her and my son. And my son loved his Granny and they were friends. I did not transfer to my son my dislike of Granny. I have taught him that Granny is important. They loved each other very much. I like myself for their friendship. And I envied my son that he had his Granny.

Ewa's narrative, cited above, shows the dynamic of individual work in the group and the influence of external events and of the situation within the group on how the participant thinks about her relationship with her mother, where guilt feelings may be counterbalanced by a sense of pride.

The theme of the Association was also directly raised during a group discussion concerning the relationship between the Association and the therapeutic group.

MAGDA: *I do not intend to belong to this Association, because I do not wish to focus my social life on my being the second generation. One can be a cool person without being a representative of the second generation at all.*

IWONA: *This Association was born because people want to talk, even not necessarily about the Holocaust, but about Jewish themes. They have similar experiences and feel a need for such a community of communication, when you start to talk about something [and] there is no need to explain the basic things.*

MAGDA: *I would like to mention here the book entitled "Trauma" by Maria Orwid, I have read it and the trauma relates to various things. I do not want to perceive myself solely in terms of the trauma due to*

being the second generation. I like to think about my traumas of divorce, giving birth, job loss, sociological, and so on. I do not want any of these traumas determining my life.
ALA: *I do not want to resign from the group, since the group is most important to me. The Association cannot replace the group.*
Igor: I do agree. I have given years and years to social life, and now I find it tiresome, that's why I like solitude and this group is important to me.
EWA: *I have never had my Jewish circle for a long time, not until I started coming to Kraków for our group meetings. The Association gives you an opportunity to enter the Jewish community.*

This discussion clearly shows the impact on the group members of their having grown up without Jewish reference points as a result of the decimation of the Polish Jewish community, which did not begin to recover until 1989, by which time the group members were well into adulthood / in late middle-age.

The "second generation" members in Poland live with a feeling of the loneliness and uniqueness of their situation, which lacks reference groups and a generational narrative. They strongly feel that they are only a fraction of the very small and dispersed Jewish community. In this context, the establishment of the Association may be seen as an important step on the way to integration. This is a departure from the formula of a therapeutic group as the only specific forum where the second generation members could meet. Consequently, individuals whose problem was their Jewish identity or, in Iwona's words, those seeking a sense of community, were reduced to the role of patients by the therapeutic group. Moreover, the discussion reveals an acceptance for a differentiation of attitudes within the group, as well as for different choices made by individual members of the group.

At subsequent sessions, the group members reported their work on the Association and in this context reflected on their relationships with their parents:

"I understand why "Children of the Holocaust" bristled so at us when they heard we wanted to establish the Association. Because they so terribly didn't want to hand anything down to us and they are so terribly convinced we are normal and cool, while we have been coming to the therapeutic group in Kraków for years, and then this Association. And why? What do you want? What do you need it for? And finally they told us: "It seems we were perhaps not quite successful".

In February 2011, the first meeting of the Association of the Second Generation was scheduled for the same time as the therapeutic group session. The founders of the Association requested to postpone the group therapy session. We (the therapists) interpreted this as their attempt at resolving feelings of rivalry towards the therapists by excluding them and the group from the Association. Subsequent discussion in the therapy group showed the group members' apprehension that putting this session off may lead to the dissolution of the therapeutic group, whose existence was threatened after Professor Orwid's death. Emotions related to the conflict were discussed, and the group members were allowed to decide whether one group session can be postponed. These developments were perceived as stabilizing the group.

The therapeutic group existed until 2014; the decision to close the group was made as soon as the Association of the Second Generation was established. The Association seems to be a good response to its members' needs for shared community experiences. The Association of the Second Generation organizes discussions, group outings, feasts for Purim, and essay competitions on the subject of identity. The Association of the Second Generation defines a survivor's descendant broadly. The children of people who survived the war in the Soviet Union qualify for membership, while trauma has been rejected as the criterion defining collective identity. At the same time, the second generation in Poland began debating their condition using the language of literature and arts. Their debate turned out to be of universal importance. At least several books on the condition of the second generation in Poland became best-sellers, eagerly read, widely discussed, included in the mainstream media (Kuryluk, 2004; Tuszy ska, 2005; Keff, 2008; Tulli, 2011). The pivotal problems of the second generation, namely marginality, alienation, non-belongingness, being "other", seeking, insecurity, the necessity of making choices, and fluid identity, which are often used by the second generation in self-description, turned out to be translatable into the languages of literature, literary criticism, and the arts. Thus, a worldwide process that took place much earlier, in the 1980s, has recurred here in Poland. The process is quite natural and developmental.

On the other hand, group therapy conducted in the form of marathon sessions held every two to three months was insufficient to contain the more severe problems of some group members. After an interval, they decided to continue their meetings as a support group, but without therapists. Thus, the therapeutic group working in such settings has fulfilled its task after serving for years as the only place where the "second generation" could meet.

The therapists' countertransference reactions

As evidenced by the above report, the group therapy, conducted by therapists so differentiated with regard to their relationship to "Jewishness" and the Holocaust, released various countertransferential reactions. Professor Orwid, perceived by the group as the "mother", used to emphasize that the program of work with the second generation was particularly important to her. In a sense, she seemed to feel like a mother of both the group and the therapists. Non-Jewish "Polish" therapists, besides their sense of exclusion (as discussed earlier), had feelings of anxiety about the extent to which they were accepted. Moreover, they were afraid they might hamper freedom of expression in the group and suspected the group might be overprotective towards them, for example, by avoiding critical comments on anti-Semitism or the role of the Catholic Church. "Jewish" therapists were also in a difficult situation. They faced the risk of "over-identification" (Hoppe, 1984; Fogelman, 1979), because of the similarities between their own family histories and those of the group members, and because of their own identity-related conflicts.

In contacts with the group, the "Jewish" therapists expressed anger more frequently than their "Polish" counterparts. Questions remain as to whether this anger was associated with their stronger identification with the problems of the group members (e.g., enmeshment in family relationships, shared anxiety feelings) or with their stronger identification with the group's favorite defense mechanisms (i.e., projection of hostility to the outside).

Alternatively, perhaps "Polish" therapists did not dare to let themselves express their anger freely, being afraid of identification with the perpetrator.

In 2014, the therapists decided to close the group and discussed their decision with the participants, thus delivering a message about the possibility of separation. It was important for the group members to see that their current situation was different from that at the beginning of their group therapy. Symbolically, they became "parents" themselves through the establishment of the Association, which aimed not only at transmission of memory, but also at mutual support.

Summary

This chapter has attempted to present a fragment of a group process related to separation in the real world (i.e., the leaving of a therapist and the death of the therapist-mother), which activated the participants' unresolved grief over their Holocaust survivor parents. In contrast to their family situation, where trauma was left unspoken, the therapists encouraged the group members to express their feelings related to loss. Moreover, in contradistinction to their parents, the therapists demonstrated that, despite their own grief, they were able to deal with the anger of the group. Working through their anger at the therapists initiated a repair processes directed at parental objects, and in consequence enabled separation and the establishment of the Association. It is significant that the main goals of this "second generation" organization include memory transmission and Jewish identity development. This can be considered as a transition from a "curse" to a "legacy" perception (Kellerman, 2008). Thus, through enabling the process of separation, the participants were given a chance to build the history of the Holocaust into their family history and to start a process of repair.

References

Kestenberg, J. (1982). A metapsychological assessment based on an analysis of a survivor's child. In M. S. Bergmann & M. E. Jucovy (Eds.). *Generations of the Holocaust*. New York, NY: Basic Books.

Klein, M. (1946). Notes on some schizoid mechanisms. *International Journal of Psycho-analysis*, 27: 99–110.

Kestenberg, J., & Gampel, Y. (1983). Growing up in the Holocaust culture. *The Israel Journal of Psychiatry and Related Sciences*, 20:129–146.

Kellerman, N. P. (2001). Psychopathology in children of Holocaust survivors: A review of research literature. *The Israel Journal of Psychiatry and Related Sciences*, 38(1):36–45.

Levav, I., Levinson, D., Radomislensky, I., Shemesh, A., Kohn, R. (2007). Psychopathology and other health dimensions among the offspring of Holocaust survivors: Results from the Israel National Health Survey. *The Israel Journal of Psychiatry and Related Sciences*. 44.2:144–51.

Helmreich, W. B. (1996). *Against All Odds: Holocaust survivors and the successful lives they made in America*. New York, NY: Transaction.

Giladi, L., & Bell, T. S. (2013). Protective factors for intergenerational transmission of trauma among second and third generation Holocaust survivors. *Psychological Trauma: Theory, Research, Practice, and Policy*, 5(4):384.

Weinberg, M. K., & Cummins, R. A. (2013). Intergenerational effects of the Holocaust: Subjective well-being in the offspring of survivors. *Journal of Intergenerational Relationships*, 11(2):148–161.

Fossion, P., Leys, C., Vandeleur, C., Kempenaers, C., Braun, S., Verbanck, P., Linkowski, P. (2015). Transgenerational transmission of trauma in families of Holocaust survivors: The consequences of extreme family functioning on resilience, sense of coherence, anxiety and depression. *Journal of Affective Disorders*, 171: 48–53.

Potel, J. Y. (2010). *Koniec Niewinności. (End of Innocence)*. Kraków: Znak. 275–297.

Eisler, J. (2006). *Polski rok 1968. (Polish Year 1986)*. Warszawa: Instytut Pamięci Narodowej Komisja Ścigania Zbrodni Przeciwko Narodowi Polskiemu.

Stola, D. (2000). *Kampania Antysyjonistyczna w Polsce 1967–1968. (Anti-Zionist Campaign in Poland 1967–1968)*. Warszwa: ISP PAN.

Orwid, M., Domagalska-Kurdziel, E., Pietruszewski, K., Czaplak, E., Izdebski, R. (1994), Kamińska M. Psychospołeczne następstwa Holocaustu w drugim pokoleniu ofiar Holocaustu ocalonych w Polsce. (Psychosocial consequences of the Holocaust in the second generation of Holocaust survivors in Poland). *Psychiatria Polska*, 1:113–130.

Szwajca, K. (2009). *Uwarunkowania Transgeneracyjnego Przekazu Traumy u Potomstwa Osób Ocalałych z Holocaustu. (The Conditionings of Transgenerational Transmission of Trauma in Offspring of Holocaust Survivors)*. (Doctoral dissertation, Jagiellonian University Medical College).

Yehuda, R., Halligan. S. L., Grossman, R. (2001). Childhood trauma and risk for PTSD: Relationship to intergenerational effects of trauma, parental PTSD, and cortisol excretion. *Development and Psychopathology*, 13:733–753.

Yehuda, R., Bell, A., Bierer, L. M., Schmeidler, J. (2008). Maternal, not paternal, PTSD is related to increased risk for PTSD in offspring of Holocaust survivors. *Journal of Psychiatric Research*, 42(13):1104–1111.

Brand, S. R., Schechter, J. C., Hammen, C. L., Brocque, R. L., Brennan, P. A. (2011). Do adolescent offspring of women with PTSD experience higher levels of chronic and episodic stress?. *Journal of Traumatic Stress*, 24(4): 399–404.

Orwid, M. (1962). Uwagi o przystosowaniu do życia poobozowego u byłych więźniów obozu koncentracyjnego w Oświęcimiu. (Remarks on adapting to life after the camp of former prisoners of the Auschwitz concentration camp). *Przegląd Lekarski*, 1:94–97.

Orwid, M. (1964). Socjopsychiatryczne następstwa pobytu w obozie koncentracyjnym Oświęcim-Brzezinka. (Social and psychiatric consequences of staying in the concentration camp of Auschwitz-Birkenau). *Przegląd Lekarski*, 1:17–22.

Leśniak, R., Mitarski, J., Orwid, M., Szymusik, S., Teutsch, A. (1961). Niektóre zagadnienia psychiatryczne obozu w Oświęcimiu w świetle własnych badań. II doniesienie wstępne. (Some issues in the psychiatric camp in Oswiecim in light of their own research. II preliminary report). *Przegląd Lekarski*, 1: 64–73.

Leśniak, R. (1964). Zmiany osobowości u byłych więźniów obozu koncentracyjnego Oświęcim-Brzezinka. Doniesienie wstępne. (Changes of personality in former prisoners of the concentration camp Oswięcim-Birkenau. Preliminary report). *Przegląd Lekarski,* 1: 29–30.

Szymusik, A. (1964). Astenia poobozowa u byłych więźniów obozu koncentracyjnego w Oświęcimiu. (Asthenia after the camp among the former concentration camp prisoners in Oświęcim). *Przegląd Lekarski,* 1:23–29.

Teutsch, A. (1962). Próba analizy procesu przystosowania do warunków obozowych osób osadzonych w czasie II wojny wiatowej w hitlerowskich obozach koncentracyjnych. Doniesienie wstępne. (An attempt to analyze the process of adapting to the conditions of the camp of prisoners during World War II in Nazi concentration camps. Preliminary report). *Przegląd Lekarski,* 1:90–94.

Organization, W. H. (1992). *The ICD-10 Classification of Mental and Behavioural Disorders: Clinical descriptions and diagnostic guidelines.* Geneva: World Health Organization. 208–210.

Orwid, M., Domagalska-Kurdziel, E., Pietruszewski, K., Czaplak, E., Izdebski, R. (1994). Kamińska M. Psychospołeczne następstwa Holocaustu w drugim pokoleniu ofiar Holocaustu ocalonych w Polsce. (Psychosocial consequences of the Holocaust in the second generation of Holocaust survivors in Poland). *Psychiatria Polska,* 1: 113–130.

Orwid, M., Domagalska-Kurdziel, E., Pietruszewski, K. (1994a). Psychospołeczne następstwa Holocaustu u osób ocalonych i żyjących w Polsce (The psychosocial consequences of the Holocaust on survivors and people living in Poland). *Psychiatria Polska,* 1: 91–112.

Orwid, M., Domagalska-Kurdziel, E., Pietruszewski, K., Czaplak, E., Izdebski, R., Kamińska, M. (1997). The psychosocial effects of the Holocaust on Jewish survivors living in Poland. *Psychiatria Polska.* 5: 3–13.

Danieli, Y. (1981). Differing adaptational styles in families of survivors of the Nazi holocaust. *Children Today,* 10(5).

Hass, A. (1990). *In the Shadow of the Holocaust.* New York, NY: Cornell University Press.

Boszormenyi-Nagy, I., & Spark, G. M. (1973). *Invisible Lyalties: Reciprocity in intergenerational family therapy.* Hagerstown, MD: Harper & Row.

Perel, E., & Saul, J. (1989). A family therapy approach to Holocaust survivor families. In P. Marcus & A. Rosenberg (Eds.). *Healing their Wounds: Psychotherapy with Holocaust survivors and their families.* New York, NY: Praeger.135–152.

Winnicott, D. W. (1965). *The Maturational Process and the Facilitating Environment.* London: Hogarth Press.

Kuryluk, E. (2004). *Goldi.* Warszawa: Wydawnictwo Twój Styl.

Tuszyńska, A. (2005). *Rodzinna Historia Lęku. (Family History of Anxiety).* Kraków: Wydawnictwo Literackie.

Keff, B. (2008). *Utwór o Matce i Ojczyźnie. (A Song about Mother and Motherland).* Kraków: Korporacja Halart.

Tulli, M. (2011). *Włoskie szpilki. (Italian high heels).* Warszawa: Wydawnictwo Nisza.

Hoppe, K. D. (1984). Severed ties. In S. A. Luel & P. Marcus (Eds.). *Psychoanalytic Reflections on the Holocaust: Selected essays*. New York, NY: KATV Publishing House. 94–111.

Fogelman, E., & Savran, B. (1979). Therapeutic groups for children of Holocaust survivors. *International Journal of Group Psychotherapy.* 29 (2): 211–235.

Kellerman, N. P. (2008). Transmitted Holocaust trauma: Curse or legacy? The aggravating and mitigating factors of Holocaust transmission. *The Israel Journal of Psychiatry and Related Sciences.* 45(4): 263–70.

CHAPTER
EIGHT

Countertransference Reactions towards Victims: The Traumatization of Children Held as Inmates in Vienna's *Spiegelgrund* Paediatric Psychiatric Hospital

Elisabeth Brainin and Samy Teicher

The purpose of this chapter is to show the countertransference reactions of the members of an interdisciplinary research group dealing with the child-survivors of the Nazi Euthanasia Program in Vienna, called "Spieglegrund"*. The authors presumed that the members' reactions would represent defensive responses towards the victims and survivors, responses that that could be generalized.*

What they came to realize was the countertransference reactions could not be understood solely through the interviews, but must also address the way in which these programs were addressed in Austria more than 40 years after the country's liberation from the Nazi regime. A special emphasis is placed on the feelings of vengeance expressed by the survivors and the reactions of the research group to these feelings.

Background

For several years, we have been working in an interdisciplinary research group on the subject of traumatization caused by social administration institutions under National Socialism. During that period, many hundreds of children were held as inmates in Vienna's *Spiegelgrund* paediatric psychiatric hospital. In practice, the children did not receive any therapeutic treatment at *Spiegelgrund*.

During the National Socialist period, certain diagnoses (including those of mental illness, physical disability, "hereditary" disorder, alcoholism of the parents, rickets, and/or deformities) were tantamount to a death sentence, consistent with the National Socialist ideology of who was deemed "worthy or unworthy of life", In the event of any such diagnosis, the Reich Committee ("*Reichsausschuss*") had to be notified and it formally determined the patient's life or death.[1]

Following Hitler's euthanasia decree of 1939, many hundreds of children classified as "persons who, according to human judgment, are incurable" were "accorded a mercy death" (i.e., murdered) during the Nazi period at *Spiegelgrund* (Kaul, 1979). "Incurable" conditions in children included mental illness, physical disability or deformity (even rickets), and criminality Starvation and torture, including human experimentation, were widespread at the hospital which was led by Ernst Illing; the doctor who was responsible for the children's ward at *Spiegelgrund* was Heinrich Gross (Klee, 2003, p. 203) who would later become the head of a psychiatric department at a the same hospital in Vienna (the Psychiatrisches Krankenhaus am Steinhof, and from 2000 on, called Otto Wagner Krankenhaus) .

Aims, methodology and motivation

We obtained the written records from *Spiegelgrund*'s Youth Welfare Office, including the clinical histories of the "children of *Spiegelgrund*" and internal decision-making documents and compiled them into a compendium for each survivor. Our multidisciplinary group of psychoanalysts and psychiatrists then read and discussed the material in the compendia in preparation for our interviews with ten *Spiegelgrund* survivors. The interviews were loosely structured around the compendium; we asked further questions about particular segments of the survivors' histories or our interlocutors continued to talk without being prompted. It was necessary to follow the order of the written records in order to keep the structure of the Nazi Youth Welfare ("*Nationalsozialistische Jugendwohlfahrt*") in mind, to bring the written information in line with the dialogue, and to be able to follow up on it. It was important to know the mode of admission to *Spiegelgrund*, the "diagnosis", and the institutional decision-making structure to comprehend the reports of the survivors.

From 2000–2003, the psychoanalysts conducted interviews with ten survivors of the *Spiegelgrund* hospital, which were recorded, transcribed, and subsequently discussed by a group of psychoanalysts and psychiatrists (these have been previously in Berger, 2007).

We did not conduct our dialogues in a semi-structured manner. There was a "compendium," which primarily related to each life history, and about which we asked further questions on particular segments, or our interlocutors continued to talk without being prompted. This was necessary in order to keep the structure of the Nazi Youth Welfare ("*Nationalsozialistische Jugendwohlfahrt*") in mind, to bring the written information in line with the dialogue, and to be able to follow up on it. It was important to know the mode of admission to *Spiegelgrund*, the "diagnosis," and the institutional decision-making structure to comprehend the reports of the survivors.

For the current research, we re-examined the interview transcripts to identify countertransference reactions that occurred during our interviews with the child-survivors. These reactions, which will be illustrated by quotes from the interviews, arose in the context of the content of our dialogues with the survivors and of concurrent outside events, specifically, the political handling of *Spiegelgrund*-related matters in Austria more than 40 years after its liberation from the Nazi regime.

In analysing the interviews for countertransference reactions, we adopted the angle of inner-emotional processes. We chose this angle on the basis of our psychoanalytical work with children and adolescents, our theoretical knowledge about developmental processes, and our papers (Brainin & Teicher, 1997, 2008, Brainin & Ligeti, & Teicher, 1989, 1993) on the effects of persecution and trauma. We were interested in both the processing of the survivors' terrible childhood experiences and the reactions of the research group, since we assumed that these would represent generalizable defensive reactions towards victims and survivors.

We have also drawn on the neuroscientific work of Leuzinger-Bohleber, in which she deals with a certain counter-transference constellation that we want to use for others as well.

> *Soon after the war, a young woman just coming back after deportation went to see a psychoanalyst. In the first interview (and there was no other following) she told her some episodes from her camp experiences. The analyst, who listened attentively, without saying a word until the end of the session, asked her: In which bad novel did you read all this?* (pp. 39)[2]

Here, the analyst's intervention cannot to be understood in the sense of counter-transference towards an unbearable, traumatic situation. The reaction can only be understood through the personal history of the analyst, who did not want to know about the Nazi-past, because she herself belonged to a generation of bystanders. She did not want to be confronted with a survivor, with a reality she even denied during the war. Chasseguet speaks about a camouflage of the truth, a denial of reality, which could correspond to an ego-split. She describes the situation as follows: "The irony of this phrase at the end of the session and the rejection, that it indicates, shows . . . how this colleague could avoid until this moment disturbing feelings of shame, guilt and anxiety" (p. 40)[3]. At the end, Chasseguet states: "The duty to remember arises from a collective effort to deconstruct denial" (p. 45).[4]

Chasseguet expresses what we found in our encounters with survivors of Spieglegrund. We had made a conscious decision to throw light on the Nazi past of *Spiegelgrund*. We *believed* the reports of the survivors and wanted to create a condition for treatments that would render denial of the horrible past impossible. Nevertheless, we faced both inner and external impediments to achieving our goal. The inner impediments took the form of emotional reactions and countertransference, whereas the external impediments arose from the political situation in Austria, which is a society that until now has been unable to fulfil its duty to break down the denial.

In our deliberations, we proceeded from the following psychoanalytical questions: How do traumatic childhood experiences manifest themselves? How does a traumatic childhood affect later development? Do psychic symptoms exist in adulthood that can be attributed to the trauma suffered in childhood or adolescence? What elements of the children's terrible experiences can be defined as trauma? The basis for our deliberations included the works of Hans Keilson (1979), and Sophie Dann and Anna Freud (1951).

The *Spiegelgrund* survivors were not suffering from a single traumatic experience that represented a turning point in their lives up until then. Separation from the mother and frequently changing relationships that did not allow the creation of stable inner objects mostly occurred very early on during infancy. The Nazi era, and admission to *Spiegelgrund*, only presented a turning point in the sense that it was only there that most of them became aware that they lived under a death threat. Any "deviation" from prescribed behaviour could have lethal consequences, although these were not really predictable.

We consider Greenacre's considerations regarding trauma, anxiety, and guilt feelings to be the closest applicable to this kind of fate-related experience: "Anxiety in itself carries with it the psychic element of anxious anticipation, which in these cases then becomes expanded into a kind of expectation of doom, as it is amalgamated with guilt feelings", (Greenacre, 1987, p. 183). This was also the only predictable aspect in these children's lives, something they fought against, while everything else was unforeseeable. In the children's case, it is highly likely that fear of punishment was prominent because it can be assumed that their superego only developed under the cruel conditions at the hospital.

From our dialogues with the survivors, we obtained very little information about the symptoms appearing during their forced stay as children at *Spiegelgrund*. However, we learned that it was not only the symptoms themselves that were painful for the children, but also the draconian measures they invoked. For example, the consequences of bedwetting were punitive sanctions with the characteristics of torture that humiliated the children. We also learned from the autobiographical reports that aggression or stubbornness (together with other instinctual manifestations) was punished, that any libidinous relationship between the children was prevented, that the children were sexually abused by their "educators", and subjected to sadistic measures that may equally be considered abuse.

We were able to confirm everything we learned from the autobiographical reports of the survivors through our extensive dialogues with them. The survivors told us about sanctions, punitive measures, and humiliations that they endured then and continue to suffer from until today. Symptoms that today would lead to psychotherapeutic treatment, during the Nazi period provided the reason for mistreatment, sadistic punishments, and murder. Thus, the actual symptoms suffered by the "children of *Spiegelgrund*" at the time faded into the background, as their consequences were far more grave and life-threatening.

Research results from previously published psychoanalytical work with child survivors paint a different picture from that which emerges from our dialogues with the *Spiegelgrund* survivors. The majority of Jewish children who survived concentration camps, ghettos, and hiding places came from intact families that had been destroyed by external forces resulting from National Socialist terror. The trauma of the Jewish children in most cases began with the forceful separation of the children from their parents, and was followed by additional cruel events (see the work of Hans Keilson (1979) for the various sequences of traumatisation). Thus, Jewish child survivors were able to identify with the idealised image of their murdered parents, and built it into their family romance.

By contrast, most of the children at *Spiegelgrund* were not Jewish and were placed under the "care" of the Youth Welfare Office by their parents very soon after birth. From that time, they moved between foster families or children's homes; for the majority this occurred before the Nazis came to power. None of these institutions gave consideration to the developmental needs of these children. Initially, for most of the children, the Nazi period did not bring any drastic changes to their already bad situation. However, over time, the *Spiegelgrund* hospital became a particular place of horror for all of them in which not a single good object typically existed.

The fantasy of a "good object", which is equally significant for the development of object relationships and for psychosexual development, was easier to maintain if a good object had actually once existed in the lives of these children. We presume that children always experience their being handed over to a welfare institution as being abandoned by their parents. In the imagination of the children, their parents quasi handed them over to their tormentors. The further development of the children demonstrates what an important role a "good object" could play in the creation of new object relationships. During puberty, the family romance will be spun around a good object, and one of those is present in every life story. To us, this appears to be a universal prerequisite for human development. The search for new object relationships, and the opportunity to create such relationships, even if this is often merely imagined, we attribute to ego plasticity (resilience). Some of the children were able to win the sympathies of individual caregivers or educators, such as nurses or temporary foster parents. In only two cases did the "*Spiegelgrund* children" place biological parents or family members in their family romance. In both cases, these were a father and an uncle who had opposed the Nazi ideology. In one case, the father died in unresolved circumstances, and in the other the child assumed that the uncle was put to death. Both children had been "rebellious" youths who identified with the imagined father figures while resisting the mistreatments to which they were subjected.

The dialogues with the survivors took place under very specific political circumstances, which had a broad influence on the emotional worlds of the interlocutors. During this period, the court case against Gross, who had been a leading physician (and head of the children's ward) at *Spiegelgrund*, was reopened for about an hour before being suspended on the grounds that the suspect was experiencing dementia.[5] Up until his trial at advanced age, he had been a respected member of the medical community. It was not only the asylum survivors who felt that this was an enormous injustice. While their claims for recognition as victims of National Socialism are still not fully met until today, this physician, who had tortured them for years, continued to practice in his profession, was respected, and even continued to have power and opportunities to decide on the further fate of individual survivors because he worked as a forensic expert.[6] In some cases, the survivors told us that Gross's expert opinions even contributed to the former victims of National Socialism being particularly severely punished in criminal proceedings (Lehmann & Schmidt, 2001). For this purpose, he presented "preliminary expert opinions," some of which originated from the Nazi era. He authored expert opinions with the intent of silencing the *Spiegelgrund* survivors. Gross was not only the busiest court psychiatrist in Austria after 1945; he was chief physician, holder of various awards, and had his own research institute where the body parts of murdered *Spiegelgrund* children were stored and research was conducted upon them. This only became public knowledge during the time of our dialogues (between 2000 and 2003) with the survivors.

In view of this situation, a sense of injustice and powerlessness also spread among the "interviewers." Despite the fact that the National Fund of the Republic of Austria for Victims of National Socialism ("*Nationalfonds der Republik Österreich für die Opfer des Nationalsozialismus*"), established on 27 April 1995, provided quick assistance with minimal bureaucratic impediments, our salvation fantasies and reparation wishes were utterly dashed by the socio-political reality in Austria.

The solemn funeral for the burial of the murdered children's remains and dissected body parts organised by the Republic in 2002 and attended by political state representatives served as late recognition and also rehabilitation for the handful of survivors. Our dialogues offered us the opportunity to discuss their traumatic experiences with them, to understand them, and to delve into the factual material at the same time. The narcissistic offense inflicted on the survivors, not only during the Nazi period but also after the war, and which continues into the present, was meant to be removed in our imagination by our research work (Brainin, 2001).

We all approached the dialogues with "pre-existing information," meaning that every one of us already had some knowledge of the Nazi period, including National Socialist "welfare" policies, euthanasia, and child rearing methods. This pre-existing information coloured expectations about the course of the dialogues and about the people we would be dealing with. Nonetheless, "normal" values and judgments also played a role in the dialogues. During our analysis of the dialogues, we frequently observed denial reactions on the part of the interviewers, who did not want to leave the cruel and frightening stories as they were, or who wanted to promote reconciliation between survivors and their parents, who had left their children under the authority of the Youth Welfare Office for whatever reasons.

In a dialogue, Ms H. has this to say about her feelings towards her mother: " . . . but at the same time I hated her. .". To which the interviewer responded: " . . . although you have written a very nice essay about your mother . . . ". In retrospect, this example strikes us as an attempt by the interviewer to undo or make amends for what had happened because he was unable to bear the misery and suffering of the child, with whom he identified during the dialogue. This aspect, after all, was one of the motives for our entire research programme. For all of us, it coloured our approach to the dialogues with the survivors. We wanted to treat the survivors leniently, not delve into them, and avoid confronting them with the terrors beyond what was necessary, as if we had feared hurting them all over again with those dialogues. This apprehension was further intensified because some interlocutors related that the group of survivors, who met regularly at the initiative of an ESRA psychosocial institution[7] psychiatrist, had begun re-experiencing previously dormant fears and nightmares. Some colleagues in our research group were therefore concerned that dialogues about the past would "agitate" the survivors, and questioned our work and our opportunities to sufficiently support the survivors.

We gained the impression that the "rebellious" children, who at the time were already adolescents, knew perfectly well what the *Spiegelgrund* was, and what kind of dangers were lurking there. For the others, who were younger upon admission to the *Spiegelgrund*, only a vague sense of anxiety remained, and it was not until adulthood that the connection was made with the terrors of the past.

During the time of our dialogues, at the instigation of some *Spiegelgrund* survivors, proceedings had been commenced to strip Gross of the golden honour medal ("*Ehrenzeichen*") of the Republic of Austria awarded to him some 25 years earlier. It is very easy to understand the significance of this event for his former victims.

The interview with Mr. A serves exemplifies the above. The most terrible stations in the life of Mr. A as a child were the *Hyrtl Orphanage* (a Nazi educational facility) in Mödling, about which he says it was managed like a concentration camp; the *Spiegelgrund*; and the psychiatric hospital in Ybbs. In Ybbs, he experienced first-hand the overnight disappearance of some of the inmates with whom he was locked up. At the time, he suspected the significance of their sudden disappearance; all of them were murdered. The children's group returned from Ybbs to *Spiegelgrund* again. Owing to Mr. A's unbelievably good recollection, he is even able to state the exact date: it was the 4th of July 1941.[8]

The choreography of the dialogue shows the development of feelings of transference, and the development of affects about past events, memories and current processes. A situation emerged between the two interlocutors in which despite, or because of, all the terrible subjects that were addressed, they both experienced affective relief when Mr. A spoke about the desires of revenge he had harboured as a child. Feelings of shame about humiliations and mistreatments that Mr. A had experienced at *Spiegelgrund* appeared almost simultaneously with desires for revenge, which he had already felt in that situation when he was a boy. He said:

" . . . that's also what it says in the nurses' report from the *Spiegelgrund*. And that is also what Illing used in his expert opinion for the prosecution. Because he writes in his expert opinion, 'pursuant to the nurses' report." And the nurses' report was that's what it says there word for word . . . ((quoting)) "He showed *schadenfreude* [malicious glee] at the failures of the Reich. /ahm/ He has no respect for victories and successes". This is what the nurse entered. ((quote continued)): "He openly declares that when the Russians come, he would join the partisans. He takes the side of the enemies." You can check that now, if you want to read it. That is a nurses' report. And she did that, normally they should have classified me as a resistance fighter ((laughs)), because I'd really like to see the fourteen-year-old or the adult, who would have said that to them in those days. And now this is also . . . a part of it . . . As I said before, I was in this cell [Editor's note: A cell in the hospital was used for sanctions, which akin to torture] inside yes, . . . and in the case records, yes, that is something I also still have to say, he does, that Illing /ahm/ does further extend on that with the words ((quoting)) "He also does not hesitate to use threats".

He repeated this several times, and read it aloud from the report, after describing the humiliations he went into more detail:

. . . Today I can't for the life of me say it exactly, it was for, well for military and technical reasons the Eastern Front had to be moved back by 120 kilometres, well and then I just put down my, my, my cup [claps his hands four times], and then in front of all those people I gave them a bravo gesture. I was 14 at the time.

INTERVIEWER: "And you understood what that meant?"

MR. A: "Yes I did, but the nursing staff was listening to me, weren't they? And then there was the, the . . . good nurse Schiener, and she also wrote this nurses' report which also still exists. And that's also what Illing used in his expert opinion for the prosecution. Because he writes in his expert opinion, 'pursuant to the nurses' report."

The dialogue had already gone on for nearly four hours, and the revenge fantasies surfaced towards the end of the dialogue. These fantasies served as relief for both interlocutors. When the dialogue reached the nurse's description of Mr. A's and he reached the part about wanting to be a partisan, they continued with delight and satisfaction: Mr. A: "He stands on the . . . si . . . "

INTERVIEWER: "Side of the enemy"

MR. A: "On the enemy side ((reading from the report)) 'When the Bolsheviks arrive, I will join the partisans.'"

INTERVIEWER: "((in unison with Mr. A)) Partisans ((both are laughing))"

It appears that the transference situation that developed during the dialogue probably also had an oedipal implication for Mr. A. This becomes evident not only during the course of the dialogue with the psychoanalyst, but also in Mr. A's descriptions of his few encounters with his father, who visited him at the *Spiegelgrund*. His father spoke with him about the Red Army and Stalin, whom Mr. A fantasised about as being his avengers, as becomes evident during the course of the dialogue. In the interrogation situation with Illing, Chief Physician at the *Spiegelgrund*, who was sentenced to death and executed in 1946 (Klee 2003, p. 278). Mr. A threatened the physician with Stalin and prophesised that he would be hung following the Red Army's victory (which in fact happened). At the time, Mr. A was about 14 years old, and he demonstrated an extraordinary willingness to fight. In his powerless stubbornness, he identified with the Red Army, which he desperately waited for.

In situations of total powerlessness and humiliation, the notion of the triumphant Red Army was consoling and soothing because it was connected with the father, who in his imagination was his avenger. This notion of revenge also included a narcissistic element: Mr. A's narcissistic integrity, so very hurt from all that anguish and humiliation, was supposed to be restored by means of the Red Army. Stalin as an authoritarian, powerful father figure became his personal ally and avenger.

During the dialogue, Mr. A's desire for, and efforts towards obtaining relief became apparent. He did not want to let the dialogue end, and in a way he could really only finish it when speaking about his revenge, victory and triumph. However, this opportunity was only offered to him after 22 years of fighting the post-war bureaucracy for his clinical history and 57 years after liberation. After obtaining his clinical history, he became fully rehabilitated. Today his criminal record is fully cleared and, partly thanks to him, the crimes of Gross were made public. The recognition by the National Fund and finally the burial of the body parts of the murdered children were a late recompense giving him reassurance and solace.

Conclusion

Hillel Klein was a Jewish survivor of the *Shoah*. As an adolescent he was imprisoned in various concentration camps, and subsequently became a psychoanalyst in Israel. He said in a dialogue:

> *. . . These revenge feelings . . . embodied a sort of humane, humanitarian act of reassurance that causality and justice do exist in the world, and that murder may not be trivialised. What is the meaning of these revenge feelings which in those days embodied a strong motif, a leitmotif, to survive Hitler's defeat by at least one day . . . .? As a scientist I know that this manifested an important part of the instinct of self-preservation: To be able to think again that there is a future, that something is happening for the recovery of the reality principle. For there was no reality principle in the inferno.*

As elaborated by Klein (Klein, H., 2003), the survivors' desires for revenge do not so much revolve around the talion principle but around the desire for justice, which is connected with the reality principle. The above dialogue demonstrates what the survivors' recognition as victims means for them today and should be understood in this context. It simultaneously had a soothing effect on the survivor and enabled him to work through the experience with a partial, empathetic and understanding interlocutor. Giving testimony of past ordeals and humiliations lent additional meaning to the survivors' lives and the dialogue reinforced them in their belief that one can stand up to injustice and reject current humiliations. To publicly denounce the crimes of the National Socialists as a contemporary witness could equally be described as a successful attempt to sublimate unconscious desires for retaliation, or preconscious desires for revenge.

Preconscious desires for retaliation are paid insufficient attention in the literature about the effects of persecution. In our view, this appears to be due to the principal difficulty in confronting revenge fantasies and desires for retaliation. The talion principle is in accordance with archaic standards, which conflict with the standards of our society, it is consistent with the superego demand not to call for revenge and retribution (as Sarastro says in the "Magic Flute": 'In these holy halls, revenge is unknown . . . '). Some have a fear of revenge and retaliation, and others almost make them a taboo. In archaic societies, victory and triumph over the enemy were connected with a complicated ritual, in order to obtain protection against the revenge of the vanquished (see Freud, S. 1912–1913). In the dialogues with the survivors, fear of revenge is recognisable in the reactions of the interviewer as a "counter-transference phenomenon." Again and again in the dialogues, the survivors spoke about feelings of having been treated unjustly. It is not difficult to derive desires for revenge from this, and the interviewers were often unable to respond to these feelings in more detail.

Our dialogue with Ms. K further illustrates this point. Immediately after her birth in 1932, Ms. K was alternately living with foster families or in children's homes. Like many other children, she was later briefly returned to her original family. However, in 1940 she was again taken, this time by the Foster Care Service (*Kinderübernahmestelle* or *KÜST*) of Vienna. From there she ended up in a convent children's home, and was sent to the *Spiegelgrund* in 1943. In the interview, Ms. K talked about the court case against Illing and the other physicians from the *Spiegelgrund*. She had heard about it on the radio at the end of the war, and her mother is also said to have been present. The dialogue with her contained the following segment:

Ms. K: " . . . Well thank God, they got that dirty bastard. And then my mum scolded me because you weren't supposed to say something like that . . . ".

INTERVIEWER: "But that means at the convent [authors' note: she had been accommodated in a convent two years prior to that], during those two years, that's when you were well . . . ? . . . Would you have liked to stay there?"

This segment is particularly significant for our deliberations because when Ms. K talked about her anger and also about her satisfaction that Illing got caught at last, the interviewer behaved almost exactly like her mother: he did not ask further questions about the desires for revenge but about the place in Ms. K's childhood in which she was treated better. Not only were the desires for revenge taboo, in most cases they also remained unsatisfied. They thus confronted the interlocutor with feelings of powerlessness, which was another reason for both the interviewer and Ms. K's mother to deflect them.

The feeling of having been subjected to a most enormous injustice remains very strong in all the survivors of *Spiegelgrund*. As reported by the survivors in our dialogues with them and as detailed in previous publications (Lehmann, 2001, Berger 2007), Gross was not only involved in their sufferings and torture at *Spiegelgrund*, he was also responsible for the disproportionate convictions of former

Spiegelgrund inmates after the war. The discontinuation of legal proceedings against Gross meant that he was never convicted: he literally made his career at the expense of his victims. The sense of injustice about the current situation remains. This was also an issue in the counter-transference feelings of the interviewers, who were confronted with injustices that continued after the war, in that not only were the tormentors not convicted, they also remained in a position that gave them further power over their former victims. Outrage over the fact that, after the war, Gross was able to continue his career unimpeded continues to strain all members of the survivor group as well as the researchers until today. They perceive this as a huge injustice, which makes them helpless and which arouses revenge wishes in the survivors and the researchers.

In our view, insufficient attention has been given to the arousal of revenge feelings in psychoanalysts treating severely traumatized persons after the *Shoah*. Research has dealt with feelings of powerlessness and helplessness arising during the treatment of survivors as a narcissistic threat for the therapist, which would impede his or her capacity to listen and to think. As the interview with Mr. A showed, revenge feelings can be a relief for both the therapist and the patient. However, in the interview with Ms. K, we observe how threatened the interviewer was by the survivor's wish to see her former persecutor punished.

It is not only the wish for revenge that can provide strong reasons for counter-transference, but also the wish that the survivors should be officially recognised as victims of Nazi persecution. The feeling of receiving rightful recognition for suffered pain and ordeals, of being treated as a human being who was arbitrarily and unjustly subjected to infinite suffering, brings comfort/consolation and also narcissistic recognition. Until now, compensation authorities and experts had viewed these people as malingerers and pension neurotics trying to appropriate something to themselves that they were not entitled to (Brainin 2001). The Compensation Act requires applicants to provide evidence that they have been harmed. According to Eissler (1963), a hostile attitude towards victims is consistent with an archaic human attitude towards pain and weakness. Under National Socialism it became an ideology enacted by the state, which was continued in the compensation proceedings. In addition, every Austrian Mark and each Schilling is tantamount to an admission of guilt, which physicians felt compelled to reject, perhaps even more so than other segments of the population. No other profession was as closely linked with the National Socialist policy of annihilation as the medical profession (Brainin 2001). Pseudo-medical arguments were used as reasons for the "cleansing and healing" of the "national body" (*Volkskörper*) from the "other," such as racial and ethnic political opponents, from the sick and marginal groups. After the war, similar pseudo-scientific arguments were used on the very same people, making it more difficult or impossible for them to gain recognition for their pain and suffering.

The feeling of the survivors of "*Spiegelgrund*," of having been betrayed of the recognition as victims of the Nazi terror, tinted the empathy of the researchers. The countertransferal reactions of the researchers, however, did not impede them in their scientific approach to their findings. As psychoanalysts, we possess the skill to subject our countertransference to_a scientific examination, and thus, we are able to convert the countertransference into a tool for our scientific findings.

Ilse Grubsich-Simitis concept of "withholding of empathy" (Grubrich-Simits, I., 1981) can be applied also to our present society where the defence and resistance against the feelings of empathy towards victims can be generally observed. This phenomenon affects the emotional reactions of societies also towards immigration and refugees. The fact that perpetrators assume the role of the victims turns the refugees into a threat for our society. Thus this process of turning the tables obstructs the development of compassion and empathy in our society.

Notes

1 https://www.mishpahot-hantzaha.mod.gov.il/mhn/About/Pages/About.aspx
https://de.wikipedia.org/wiki/Aktion_T4

2 Au lendemain de la guerre, une jeune femme revenue de déportation alla consulter une psychanalyste. Dans le premier entretien (mais il n'y en eut point d'autre), elle lui raconta quelques épisodes de son expérience concentrationnaire. L'analyste, qui l'avait écoutée attentivement, sans mot dire jusqu'à la fin de l'heure, lui demanda alors : «Dans quel mauvais roman avez-vous lu tout cela?" (S. 39, in Revue Francaise de Psychanalyse, 2000, LXIV)

3 "L'ironie de la phrase qui clôt la séance et le rejet dont elle témoigne laissent entrevoir le trou percé par une flèche aiguë dans le bouclier qui avait, jusque-là, permis à cette collègue d'éviter certaines pensées peut-être fauteurs de honte, de culpabilité et d'angoisse". S. 40

4 Le "devoir de mémoire" repose, avant tout, sur un travail collectif de déconstruction des dénis. S. 45

5 Prozess Groß: Grobe Schwächen. Der New Yorker Psychiater und Gerichtssachverständige Peter Stastny über den Beginn des Gross-Prozesses. In: Profil, quoted in: Bizeps: https://www.bizeps.or.at/

prozess-gross-grobe-schwaechen/ (July 3, 2016)

6 https://de.wikipedia.org/wiki/Heinrich_Gross

7 ESRA is the name of the psychosocial center of the Jewish community of Vienna. It provide services in medicine, psychiatry, psychotherapy, psychology, care and social work with a view to helping people to deal with the psychological consequences of traumatic events and to provide them with new perspectives.

8 KAUL (1979) dates the end of the T4 action to 24 August 1941. That is, he dates it to three weeks after the speech of Cardinal Graf von Gahlen at the St. Lamberti church on 3 August 1941, in which he publicly denounced the T4 action as murder.

References

Berger, E. & Rieger, E. (Eds.). (2007). Verfolgte Kindheit: Kinder und Jugendliche als Opfer der NS-Sozialverwaltung. Wien/Köln/Weimar: Böhlau.

Brainin, E. (2001). Entschädigung – Wiedergutmachung oder erneute Traumatisierung (Indemnification – compensation or another traumatisation). In S. Horn & P. Malina (Eds.) *Medizin im Nationalsozialismus (Medicine in National Socialism): Wege der Aufbereitung/Wiener Gespräche zur Sozialgeschichte der Medizin.* Vienna: Press and Publications Office of the Austrian Medical Board.

Brainin, E. & Teicher, S. (1997). Time heals no wounds. In L. Hunt, M. Marshall, & C. Rowlings (Eds.) *Past Trauma in Late Life: European perspectives on therapeutic work with older people.* London: Jessica Kingsley Publishers.

Brainin, E. & Teicher, S. (2008). The terror from the outside – child survivors of the *Spiegelgrund* traumatic experiences in childhood and their effects. *Praxis der Kinderpsychologie und Kinderpsychiatrie, 58*(7): 530–552.

Brainin, E., Ligeti, V., & Teicher, S. (1993). *Vom Gedanjken zur Tat. Zur Psychoanalyse des Antisemitismus.* Frankfurt am Main: Brandes & Apsel.

Chasseguet-Smirgel, J. (2000). Trauma ét croyance. *Revue Française de Psychanalyse.* LXIV: 39–46. Paris: Presses Universitaires de France.

Eissler, K. R., (1963): "Die Ermordung von wievielen seiner Kinder muß ein Mensch symptomfrei ertragen können, um eine normale Konstitution zu haben?" (How many murders of his children does a human being have to bear without symptoms in order to be considered of normal constitution?). *Psyche.* 5/17: 241–291. Stuttgart: Klett-Cotta.

Freud, A., & Dann, S. (1980). *Gemeinschaftsleben im frühen Kindesalter, Die Schriften der Anna Freud (Community life in early childhood, the writings of Anna Freud).* Vol. IV. 1161–1228, Munich: Kindler Verlag. (Original work published in 1951).

Freud, S. (1975). *Totem und Tabu (Totem and taboo).* GW IX. Frankfurt am Main: S. Fischer Verlag. (Original work published between 1912–1913).

Greenacre, P. (1987). *Trauma, Growth and Personality.* London: Karnac Books. (Original work published in 1953).

Grubrich-Simitis, I. (1981). Extreme traumatization as cumulative trauma–psychoanalytic investigations of the effects of concentration camp experiences on survivors and their children. *Psychoanalytic Study of the Child.* 36: 415–450.

Häupl, W. (2006). *Die ermordeten Kinder vom Spiegelgrund. Gedenkdokumentation für die Opfer der NS-Kindereuthanasie in Wien.* Wien: Böhlau.

Kaul, F. K. (1979). *Die Psychiatrie im Strudel der Euthanasie.* Frankfurt am Main/ Köln: Europäische Verlagsanstalt.

Keilson, H. (1979). *Sequentielle Traumatisierung bei Kindern (Sequential Traumatisation in Children).* Stuttgart: Enke Verlag.

Klee, E. (2003). *Das Personenlexikion zum Dritten Reich. Wer warwas vor und nach 1945?.* Frankfurt am Main: S. Fischer Verlag.

Klein, H. (2003). Leben, *Shoah*, Sprache und Psychoanalyse. Hillel Klein im Gespräch mit Dörte von Westernhagen. *Psyche.* 12/57, 1203–1213 Stuttgart: Klett-Cotta.

Lehmann, O., & Schmidt, T. (2001). D*en Fängen des Dr. Gross. Das misshandelte Leben des Friedrich Zawrel.* Wien: Czernin Verlag.

Leuzinger-Bohleber, M. (2014). Den Körper in der Seele entdecken Embodiment und die Annäherung an das Nicht-Repräsentierte. *Psyche.* 09–10, 0922–0950, Stuttgart: Klett-Cotta.

Mitscherlich, A., & Mielke, F. (1983). *Medizin ohne Menschlichkeit. Dokumente des Nürnberger Ärzteprozesses.* Frankfurt am Main: S. Fischer Verlag.

CHAPTER
NINE

Countertransference: Transgender Patients

FRIEDEMANN PFÄFFLIN

The author approaches the highly-volatile subject of gender-reassignment with over 45 years of experience working with transsexual people. He first outlines the history of the first "genital conversion" and "sex change" operations, starting from 1912, when the first such operation was performed. Then, beginning in the early 1970s, he details how, as a medical student already in psychoanalytic training, he believed psychoanalysis would be the proper method to help his patients. Since then, he has seen about 2,000 transgender patients, treated many of them and/or written expert opinions for their legal name and gender change and indications for sex reassignment surgery. With some patients, independent of whether their final decision was to undergo sex reassignment surgery or to remain in their primary gender, he had many different countertransference reactions, and met colleagues and discussed with them their counter transference reactions to presentations of transgender persons.

Genital conversion and sex change before Sex Reassignment Surgery (SRS)

The first sex change operation was performed in 1912. At that time, there was neither a specific name, such as sex reassignment surgery (SRS), for this procedure, nor a generally accepted diagnosis for patients that might profit from such treatment. It was only six years later that the German sexologist Magnus Hirschfeld (1918) mentioned this operation in passing. It is my suspicion that the doctors involved in performing the operation maintained silence about it out of a fear of being accused of malpractice. Even today, depriving a healthy person of healthy organs is a crime in many countries. In 1912, a person who would now be referred to as transgender had neither a specific name nor a medical diagnosis justifying an operation.

The term transvestite was coined by Magnus Hirschfeld (1910) in the context of the gay liberation movement (Pfäfflin, 1997; Dose, 2014). Hirschfeld was not a surgeon but a sexologist who, in 1919, founded the first Institute for Sex Research in Berlin and cooperated with specialists from many other fields. In the 1920s and early 1930s, a number of sex change operations were performed in Berlin (Mühsam, 1926; Abraham, 1931) and Prague (Pokorny & Bondy, 1933). Perhaps the most famous of these cases was that of the Danish painter Andreas Sparre, alias Einar Wegener, alias Lili Elbe (1932), who not only had SRS, but also a transplantation of a uterus and ovaries in the hope of being able to give birth to a child (Elbe, 1932; Herrn, 2005). The operation, from which Lili Elbe died, was performed in Dresden, Germany, a city on the river Elbe, hence the pseudonym Elbe. Already in the 1930s, her autobiography was translated into eight languages.

It was again Hirschfeld (1923) who coined the adjective transsexual (or rather the German adjective *transsexuell*). He used it in passing with the intention of pointing out that some phenomena observed in his patients referred to aspects of their experience reaching far beyond specific sexual problems. At that time, the use of the word was similar to the use of words like transatlantic or trans-Siberian.

It was only after World War II that SRS (in those days still called *sex conversion*, cp. Benjamin, 1966) was applied somewhat more frequently, and most of those undergoing it wrote autobiographies and became very famous (e.g., Cowell, 1954; Jorgensen, 1967; Morris, 1974; cp. Pfäfflin 2012). The story of George, later Christine Jorgensen, an American GI, who sought treatment in 1950, became the ground-breaking story of a sex change (Hertoft & Sörensen, 1979; Pfäfflin, 1997, 2012). As Jorgensen initially did not succeed in finding adequate treatment for his suffering in the US – he wanted to get rid of his female feelings and the distress caused by them – he sought treatment at the *Rigshospitalet*, the University Clinic in Copenhagen, Denmark, the country from which his ancestors had come.

The team of doctors at the *Rigshospitalet* diagnosed Jorgensen as an effeminate homosexual and first offered him male hormones (testosterone), which had recently become available in injectable form, to support his maleness. As he did not feel comfortable with this suggestion and rejected it, they then applied female hormones, hoping these would reduce his drive and being quite aware that this was an experimental treatment. As a result, he grew female breasts and felt more and more female; an effect that clearly contrasted with the initially agreed upon goal of the treatment. After intensive discussion, the doctors then offered him surgical castration, an intervention often applied in those days to sex offenders to release them from their sexual drive, again with the intention to reduce his effeminate behavior. After the castration, the patient still living in the male gender role felt even more female and, at the same time, much more content than before. His doctors, however, were not content with this result, even less so as the patient's diagnosis was still effeminate homosexuality, and homosexual acts between adult men were a crime in those days. The patient, however, felt more and more at ease and accustomed at the prospect of going on living as a woman. Again, the doctors involved had long discussions and finally agreed on performing a penectomy and transforming the scrotum into something similar to a vulva, but no vagina (Hamburger *et al.*, 1953).

He/she then returned to the US, travelling by steamship. As was usual in those days, the list of passengers and information about them was telegraphed in advance to the destination. When arriving in New York, the press was carried away with headlines such as "Sex Change Performed", "Ex-GI Turned into a Beauty", etc. Thus, the press created a sex change that neither had been intended by the patient nor by his doctors when starting the treatment and that had only been partially performed. Jorgensen was invited to one college and university in the US after another where she told her story. In addition, the news spread like wildfire around the globe via television, which was then a new technology for spreading news. All of a sudden, Jorgensen was a celebrity and sex change a fascinating new and controversial topic. At that time, Jorgensen had never heard the words transvestite and transsexual. It was only one or two years later that she completed her sex change by consulting doctors who constructed her a neovagina.

The news about the sex change was a sensation and it evoked approval but also much protest voiced in the lay press as well as in the *Journal of the American Medical Association*. Among the protesters there were some psychoanalysts declaring such operations as totally inadequate if not illegal interventions.

It is worth mentioning that there was a similar critical debate in Germany about a parallel case. After fifty sessions of unsuccessful psychoanalysis as regards the alleviation of the patient's suffering from his female feelings, the analyst, Medard Boss, referred him to a surgeon for castration. He then presented the case at a large conference of psychiatrists and neurologists in South Germany. A heated discussion of the pros and cons of his recommendation ensued. A subsequent survey of the opinions of the leading psychiatrists, neurologists, and psychoanalysts of the time was reported in the most important psychoanalytic journal in the country. It showed that the majority evaluated this decision very skeptically, arguing that a doctor is not God and thus cannot overcome the fundamental difference between men and women (Mitscherlich, 1950–1951; Boss 1950–1951; Mitscherlich *et al.*, 1950/1951 a, b).

Returning to the George/Christine Jorgensen's case, the critical comments in the lay press as well as in the *Journal of the American Medical Association* induced the team of doctors in Copenhagen to justify their treatment decisions. They defended their initial diagnosis of severe effeminate homosexuality, but in the heading of their report they now used the diagnosis transvestism (Hamburger *et al.*, 1953).

In reaction to the news about Jorgensen's story, there were, however, also very positive responses. Hamburger and Jorgensen received more than 1,100 enthusiastic letters from people from all over the world who found their own situation reflected in Jorgensen's story and wished to obtain the same treatment. Alfred Kinsey invited Jorgensen to his institute at the University of Bloomington, Indiana. Kinsey had just released a ground-breaking sociological report on human sexual behavior; the first volume had already been published (Kinsey *et al.*, 1948) and the research was well underway for the second volume (Kinsey *et al.*, 1953). Harry Benjamin (Pfäfflin, 2015), a medical practitioner in New York originally of German origin, who experimented with sex hormones in an effort to prolong human life and who had seen a few similar cases, contacted Jorgensen (Jorgensen, 1988). Co-operations were initiated with many scientists and universities to manage the great demand for adequate treatment. Benjamin started to address many of these letters and their authors, and soon published his first short article on the topic (Benjamin, 1953), later followed by a number of further articles (e.g. Benjamin, 1956, 1964 a, b, c) and by a monograph (Benjamin, 1966) that became the standard textbook for everybody confronted with the phenomenon in those days.

Even before the book was published, the first Gender Identity Clinic (GIC) was established at The Johns Hopkins University and Hospital in Baltimore, MD,[1] followed within a decade by approximately forty further such institutions in the US In 1963, at the same time that the GIC was founded in Baltimore, a Swedish team started a treatment program at the Research Centre, St. Jörgen's Hospital, University of Göteborg, Sweden, and four years later published their first results (Walinder, 1967).

However, the first time that I met a transsexual person, I was totally naïve and had not the faintest idea of any of the information reported in this chapter up till now.

My first encounter with a transsexual person

In the early 1970s, I appreciated the opportunity to regularly assist a famous psychiatrist, Eberhard Schorsch, at the Institute of Sex Research at Hamburg University Clinic, Germany, during his consultation hours. He specialized in forensic issues and mainly saw sexual and violent offender patients.[2] His outstanding ability of being reserved and at the same time treading softly, encouraging, and listening attentively diminished the fears of his patients and allowed them to reveal much more about their backgrounds and the motives for their criminal acting out than any interrogation by the police or hearing by a court would ever have brought to the fore. He was admired for his very differentiated expert opinions presented in court.

In the case of the first patient with transsexual symptoms, however, whom I saw with him, his typical engaging reserve gave way to total passivity. The patient talked and talked, demanding a referral for a sex change operation – at that time not available at Hamburg University Clinic – but received no real feedback from the doctor, only a new appointment for one to three months later to which he did not return. Considering the deep voice of the patient, his half-bald head, the shadow of his beard, and the unfashionable and unsuitable skirt he was wearing, it was hard for me to imagine that he would ever be able to become a woman, and the encounter irritated me a great deal.

After repeatedly observing the difference in the behavior of my mentor vis-à-vis patients who were sexual or violent offenders versus those who presented transsexual symptoms, I summoned the courage to ask him about his passivity. I also wondered aloud to him whether the patients with transsexual symptoms failed to return to the second appointment because they were discouraged by the lack of reaction and response they had experienced in the first meeting. I also asked why he did not offer psychotherapy to these patients. He agreed with my observation and said he could only minimally relate to the patients' wish for "sex change" and "not much could be done anyway". Sex change operations were offered in Casablanca, Morocco, however they often produced poor results and the University Clinic Hamburg did not have enough personnel to tackle this difficult problem. If I was interested, I should go to the US to one of the numerous Gender Identity Clinics to learn more about it.

Following his advice, I spent some weeks at the Psycho-hormonal Research Unit at the Johns Hopkins University Hospital in Baltimore, which was part of their Gender Identity Clinic. There, I had the opportunity to speak with a large number of transsexual persons coming for assessment, therapy, and follow-up. I was amazed by the diversity of the patients, but also by the openness with which they were received by the staff, who supported their wishes by means of reflection as well as through practical advice. Some years later, after having obtained a full-time position at the Department of Sex Research at Hamburg University Clinic, working with transsexuals became a major element of my professional life.

Transference and countertransference

Freud's initial evaluation of the function of transference clearly was a rather skeptical one: it was a mode of resistance and one of the major obstacles on the patient's side to remembering repressed biographical material. Later, he distinguished between negative and positive transference and declared that both variants are potent aids in the hand of the analyst and that their role in the process of recovery can hardly be overestimated.

Countertransference is the unconscious reaction of the analyst to the equally unconsciously shaped attitude and behavior of a neurotic patient in analysis (Laplanche & Pontalis, 1967). Such unconscious reactions occur not only within a specific psychoanalytic setting between patient and analyst but also in other circumstances, such as in interactions between schoolchildren and their teachers, students and their mentors, soldiers and their officers, tenants and their landlords. Indeed, unconscious reactions occur in practically all human interactions that include an element of dependency between the partners, and even in accidental encounters between strangers on the bus or in a shop, where there is no dependency between the partners. The unconscious is ubiquitous and exerts its influence whenever and wherever people meet, think, fantasize about, or judge others. It also exerts its influence on scientific or political statements, even if the authors of those statements and their readers are unaware of it.

The difference between unconscious reactions in casual versus psychoanalytic settings is that, in a psychoanalytic interaction, the analyst focuses on understanding the unconscious roots of the actual states of mind and actions of his or her patient (transference) and, at the same time, on understanding the unconscious ingredients of his or her own reactions (countertransference). The psychoanalyst may consider the countertransference dysfunctional and arising out of his or her own unresolved prior conflicts or he or she may evaluate it as an indication of what is going on in the patient without the patient knowing about it. Regardless, the analyst seeks to use transference and countertransference to promote change and enable the patient to reach a more mature level of functioning.

Examples of countertransference reactions

As regards to this chapter, I suppose the reader expects an answer to the question of whether transgender people evoke specific countertransference reactions in others. In one of my previous publications, I gave some examples of medical doctors suggesting there might be such typical reactions. I am quoting them here (Pfäfflin, 2003, pp. 292–294):

A dramatic encounter: A famous sexologist once described his first encounter with a transsexual patient. It occurred during a time when public reports on transsexualism and transgenderism were not yet available and most physicians had never heard of such a phenomenon. According to the information he had received from his receptionist, he was expecting a male patient and was thunderstruck when a beautiful lady entered his office, pulled a gun out of her handbag, aimed at him and said: 'If you don't issue a referral to the surgeon for sex reassignment surgery immediately, I will shoot you.' It is hard to conceive of a more dramatic first encounter between a patient and a doctor. When trying to imagine yourself in such a situation, what do you experience? Fear? Anxiety? Horror? What would you have done? Would you have knocked the gun out of her hand without hesitation, as you are trained in self-defense? Would you have cried for help? Would you have tried to escape? Or would you politely have offered her a seat in a perfect reaction formation? One may think of many different reactions. To calm you down: There is ample evidence that the story is completely fictitious. The colleague is in good health. One might ask even more so what caused him to publish the event and what he wanted to convey through the story. I have no doubt that he was horrified when confronted with the transsexual desire. In addition, it seems remarkable that he exclusively blames the patient for having caused this horror. But what was it that frightened him so much, when the story is but a fantasy? Might it be possible that he was, due to his own unresolved conflicts, deeply afraid of women so that he could conceive of a woman only as an aggressive phallic being, as a *pistolièra*?

An administrative solution: A family doctor saw a male patient with the same request as the fictitious patient just mentioned, the only difference being that this man uttered his request in a very deep voice and pleadingly, not demandingly. She was so touched by this and so affected by the patient's depressive state and obvious suffering that she felt incited to immediately take action. She sent him to me with a letter: 'Dear colleague, the patient wants a sex reassignment. Please let me know if the health insurance will pay for the operation and if I will be liable when recommending such a treatment. I also need information on how much oestrogen material (sic!) has to be injected.' The doctor thus tried to solve the crisis that she experienced when confronted with the patient's desire by means of administrative steps. That the man had come and said: 'I cannot be a man, please help me, I cannot stand it any longer, I cannot live like that', seems to have moved her so much that she threatened to turn depressed herself and counteracted by resorting to an administrative solution. She took his wish at face value without exploring it in more depth and even without asking me to do this. Her irritation and her doubts were expressed only indirectly in her seemingly neutral question, whether or not she might be liable.

Taking time and reflecting on one's irritation: The third example I owe to a psychotherapist who is strongly opposed to sex reassignment and who hoped to get out of the affair by telling his patient after the first encounter that he did not want to refer him to a surgeon but would be willing to find another doctor or institution with more experience in handling transgender problems that might help him. Between the intake and the second interview he busily inquired about alternative treatment centers, discussed the case with many colleagues, and, during that discussion, became increasingly uncertain as to why he wanted to get rid of this patient so quickly. He realized that he was both made uneasy and fascinated by the patient. He opened the second interview explaining that he had used the time to ponder on the first one, and that he had decided that *he* would not help him find a surgeon. Instead, he would like to offer the patient the opportunity to discuss his wish for sex reassignment surgery and any doubts he might have about such a treatment. The patient's expression froze. To prevent the patient from leaving angrily, the therapist continued talking by referring to a remark of the patient during the first interview. 'You said that you made up your mind that you needed sex reassignment surgery to 99.5 percent. I want to know how large the remaining half per cent is.' Hesitantly the patient nodded, thus indicating at least partial agreement. The therapist explained that he thought he was able to help the patient best in his search for certainty by keeping a neutral stance and neither taking the side of encouraging nor discouraging his wish for surgery. Instead, he wanted to support the patient in finding certainty for himself. With this empathic intervention he respected his own limits but, at the same time, opened a wide space that allowed the patient to explore his wishes in great detail and to engage in a very fruitful psychotherapy in which he resolved a deep depression underlying his transsexual symptoms (Pfäfflin, 2003, pp. 292–294).

Reflecting upon these examples and on my reaction the first time I was confronted with a man's wish to undergo a sex change reveals that it is usually the first encounter that causes the most irritation in therapeutic staff. There are quite a number of single case studies and reports with very small samples whose authors generalize their conclusions as regards psychopathology and often also devaluate the patients (for examples cp. Pfäfflin 2006). Typically, these first encounters leave their traces in the therapists, who rationalize their countertransference reactions by writing an article about this first meeting. Consequent meetings with the patients, however, and meetings with many other patients expressing the same wish to be accepted as a member of the other gender, usually evoke the same large spectrum of countertransference reactions experienced with other patients with other complaints.

What might be the most irritating aspect when first meeting somebody who declares that he or she belongs to the sex and/or gender to which he or she was not assigned at birth is the difficulty to identify with this person, when one feels at home in one's own gender. It is a challenge to empathy, and is often experienced as an attack against one's own gender identity. In addition, the countertransference reaction may be heavily influenced by the therapist's sexual orientation. When the Gender Identity Clinic at The Johns Hopkins University Hospital in Baltimore opened its doors, it accepted only so-called asexual transsexuals, i.e., persons not being sexually active and often not even being interested in sexual activities. This may have been due to the widespread anti-homosexual attitude in the US during the McCarthy era and therefore this stipulation may have been a prerequisite to being able to start the treatment program in those days. Nevertheless, the differentiation between primary or true (asexual) transsexuals on the one hand and secondary (in many ways sexually active) transsexuals on the other hand, which was maintained for quite a long time, should also be reflected under aspects of countertransference by the therapeutic staff. Actually, transgender patients show the very same wide spectrum of sexual behaviors as the population at large.

Countertransference in scientific descriptions

We are used to reflecting on countertransference predominantly within the framework of personal encounters. It seems to me, however, that it also influences what is written about transgender people in scientific studies involving larger samples, in standards of care, and in regulations concerning who will be accepted for what kind of treatment. On a more rationalistic level, one might say the countertransferential aspects are not addressed in these papers but that they reveal themselves in what may appear to be mere prejudice.

To give an example: In the 1970s and 1980s it was very common for some treatment centers to diagnose all their transsexual patients as having a borderline personality organization or even a Borderline Personality Disorder (Person & Ovesey, 1974 a, b; Sigusch *et al.*, 1978; Lothstein, 1983). It is very likely that these diagnoses represented the authors' attempts to rationalize their negative countertransference against this group of patients. In their original texts, Person and Ovesey declared, "To know one is to know them all", and I was happy to read Ethel Person later cringed when rereading her old texts (Person, 2001). It was only 19 years later that Sigusch (1997), the first author of the second-mentioned article above, critically renounced some of the twelve major characteristics and stereotypes that he and his co-authors had used to describe the symptoms and personality organization of transsexuals based on the psychopathological terminology of the late ninetieth and the first half of the twentieth century. Similarly, Leslie Lothstein, when I last met him, renounced his former sweeping statements that all female-to-male transsexuals suffered from severe Borderline Personality Disorders (personal communication).

Present situation and perspectives

Transgender people usually present themselves quite differently nowadays when contacting a psychoanalyst or psychotherapist as compared with the 1960s to 1980s (Pfäfflin, 2010). This is due to many factors, of which the following five may be the most important ones.

(1) In 1978, the World Health Organization included *transsexuality* as an official diagnosis into its diagnostic manual, the ICD-9 (302.5). In the following edition, the ICD-10 (1991), the diagnosis *transsexualism* received a more prominent place, including subtypes, as well as detailed symptom description and criteria (ICD-10, F64).

(2) The legal situation of transsexuals changed rapidly in many

countries, starting with Sweden (1972), followed by Germany (1980) and then by many other countries in the following three decades.

(3) Hormonal and surgical treatments improved and became more easily available in many parts of the world.

(4) Media and internet-communication promoted rapid information exchange among consumers as well as legal and medical experts.

(5) The word *transgender* (first introduced by Virginia Prince in the late 1960s or early 1970s) became an umbrella term for all kinds of trans-phenomena (Ekins & King, 2005).

Thus, the diversity of these phenomena became visible with the consequence that many of the previous narrow concepts of transsexualism and its medical and legal treatment had to be thoroughly revised (Ekins & King, 1996, 2006).

Most patients now come to treatment with pride. They have already lived for quite a while in their desired gender role, have succeeded in being accepted in their social contexts (e.g., family, school or workplace), and have established contact with local, national, and international self-help organizations. They usually know their rights and the national legislation as regards name and gender change, and potentially have even read Resolution 2048 of the Parliamentary Assembly of the Council of Europe (PACE, 2015; cp. Pfäfflin, 2015 b). The PACE-Resolution rejects all forms of discrimination against their way of life, their request for legal name and gender change, and their request for hormonal and surgical reassignment. The right to self-determined gender identity is declared a fundamental right and the member states of the Council of Europe are urged to ensure that the necessary treatment will be reimbursed by public health insurance schemes. The extremely divergent political, economic, social and legal situation in the 47 member states of the Council of Europe, combined with the fact that the Parliamentary Assembly, unlike the European Parliament, has no legislative authority, means that the resolution is certainly not much more than a declaration of wishes and intent and is far from being transformed into everyday practice in all member states. Nevertheless, it still points to a direction that results in quite a different social position for transgender persons as compared with the past century.

The individual countertransference reactions of therapists and medical doctors that transsexuals approach for treatment will, of course, continue in similar ways as during the initial phases of medical treatment for transgender persons, shaped by the histories of the patients as well as the biographies of the therapists just as in the treatment of patients with other complaints. According to my observations, these reactions are not more specific than countertransference reactions that occur in interactions with patients with depressed or bulimic symptoms, obsessive-compulsive symptoms, drug addiction, or any other distress that brings them into therapy. It is primarily the task of the therapist to scrutinize his or her own history and unconscious and to identify whether his countertransference is mainly evoked by the patient's presentation of his or her symptoms or by the therapist's own unresolved conflicts.

Notes

1 According to most sources, the Gender Identity Clinic at The Johns Hopkins University and Hospital was founded in 1965, according to other sources, e.g. Edgerton (1973), this occurred two year earlier in 1963.

2 A more detailed description of my first encounter is found in Pfäfflin (2003, p. 291f).

References

Abraham, F. (1931). Genitalumwandlung an zwei männlichen Transvestiten (The transformation of genitals in two male transvestites). *Zeitschrift für Sexualwissenschaft und Sexualpolitik, 18*: 223–226.

Benjamin, H. (1964 a). Nature and management of transsexualism. With a report on thirty-one operated cases. *Western Journal of Surgery, 72*: 105–111.

Benjamin, H. (1964 b). Transsexualismus. Wesen und Behandlung (Transsexualism. Its nature and its treatment). *Nervenarzt, 35*: 499–500.

Benjamin, H. (1964 c). Clinical aspects of transsexualism in the male and female. *American Journal of Psychotherapy, 18*: 458–469.

Benjamin, H. (1966). *The Transsexual Phenomenon: A scientific report on transsexualism and sex conversion in the human male and female.* New York, NY: Julian Press.

Benjamin, H. (1953). Transvestism and transsexuals. *International Journal of Sexology* 7: 12–14.

Benjamin, H. (1956). Trans-sexualism and transvestism. In D. Cauldwell (Ed.) *Transvestism: Men in female dress.* 15–22. New York (NY): Sexology Corporation.

Boss, M. (1950–1951). Erwiderung zum Bericht über mein Referat auf der 66. Wanderversammlung der süddeutschen Psychiater und Neurologen in Badenweiler. (Reply to the report on my presentation at the 66th Conference of the South German Psychiatrists and Neurologists in Badenweiler). *Psyche – Zeitschrift für Psychoanalyse und ihre Anwendungen, 4*: 394–400.

Cowell, R. (1954). *Roberta Cowell's Story.* New York, NY: British Book Centre, Inc.

Dose, R. (2014). *Magnus Hirschfeld: The origins of the gay liberation movement.* New York, NY: Monthly Review Press.

Edgerton, M. (1973). Introduction. In D. Laub & P. Gandy (Eds.).

Proceedings of the Second Interdisciplinary Symposium on Gender Dysphoria Syndrome. 1–14. Stanford, CA: University of California Press.

Ekins, R., & King, D. (Eds.) (2005). *Virginia Prince: Pioneer of transgendering*. Binghamton, NY: Haworth Press. Simultaneously publishes as special issue *of the International Journal of Transgenderism*, vol. 8, nr. 4, 2005.

Ekins, R., & King, D. (1996). *Blending Genders: Social aspects of cross-dressing and sex-changing*. London, New York: Routledge.

Ekins, R., & King, D. (2006). *The Transgender Phenomenon*. Thousand Oaks, CA: Sage.

Elbe, L. (2004). *Ein Mensch wechselt sein Geschlecht. Eine Lebensgeschichte. Aus hinterlassenen Papieren herausgegeben von Niels Hoyer. Dresden: Carl Reissner-Verlag. (Man into Woman. The first sex change. A portrait of Lili Elbe. The true and remarkable transformation of the painter Einar Wegener.* N. Hoyer (Ed.). London: Blue Boat Books. (Original work was published in 1932; original English edition was published in1933).

Hamburger, C., Stürüp, G., Dahl-Iversen, E. (1953). Transvestism. Hormonal, psychiatric and surgical treatment. *Journal of the American Medical Association, 152*: 391–396.

Herrn, R. (2005). *Schnittmuster des Geschlechts. Transvestitismus und Transsexualität in der frühen Sexualwissenschaft.* (Patterns of sex. Transvestism and transsexuality in early sex research). Giessen: Psychosozial-Verlag.

Hertoft, P., & Sörensen, T. (1979). Transsexuality. Some remarks based on clinical experience. In Ciba Foundation Symposium 62: *Sex, Hormones and Behavior*, pp. 165–181. Amsterdam, Oxford, New York: Ciba Foundation.

Jorgensen, C. (1967). *A Personal Autobiography*. With an introduction by Harry Benjamin, M.D. New York, NY: Paul S. Eriksson, Inc.

Kinsey, A., Pomeroy, W., Martin, C. (1948). *Sexual Behavior in the Human Male*. Philadelphia, PA: W. B. Saunders Company.

Kinsey, A., Pommeroy, W., Martin, C., Gebhard, P. (1953). *Sexual Behavior in the Human Female*. Philadelphia, PA: W. B. Saunders Company.

Laplanche, J., & Pontalis, J. B. (1967/2007). *Vocabulaire de la Psychanalyse*. Paris: Presses Universitaires de France.

Lothstein L (1983). *Female-to-Male Transsexualism: Historical, clinical and theoretical issues*. Boston, London, Melbourne and Henly: Routledge & Kegan Paul.

Mitscherlich, A. (1950–1951). 66. Wanderversammlung der Süddeutschen Psychiater und Neurologen, Badenweiler, 2./3. Juni 1950. Erstes Leitthema: Daseinsanalyse (66th Conference of the South German Psychiatrists and Neurologists, June 2–3, 1950, in Badenweiler. First major topic: Daseinsanalyse). *Psyche – Zeitschrift für Psychoanalyse und ihre Anwendungen, 4*: 226–234.

Mitscherlich, A., Bally, G., Binder, H., Binswanger, L., Bleuler, M., Brun, R., Dührssen, A., Gollner, W. E., Jores, A., Jung, C. G., Kranz, H., Kemper,

W., Meng,, H., Mohr, F., Müller, M., Schultz-Hencke, H., Seitz, W., Staechelin, J. E., Seck, H., Weizäcker, V. V. (1950–1951 a). Rundfrage über ein Referat auf der 66. Wanderversammlung der Süddeutschen Psychiater und Neurologen in Badenweiler (Comments on a presentation at the 66th Conference of the South German Psychiatrists and Neurologists in Badenweiler). *Psyche – Zeitschrift für Psychoanalyse und ihre Anwendungen. 4*: 448–477.

Mitscherlich, A., Georgi, F., Göppert, H., Gundert, H., Mauz, F., Zutt, J., Boss, M. (1950–1951 b). Rundfrage über ein Refereat auf der 66. Wanderversammlung der Süddeutschen Psychiater und Neurologen in Badenweiler (Comments on a presentation at the 66th Conference of South German Psychiatrists and Neurologists in Badenweiler). *Psyche – Zeitschrift für Psychoanalyse und ihre Anwendungen, 4*: 626–640.

Morris, J. (1974). *Conundrum*. London: Faber & Faber.

Mühsam, R. (1926). Chirurgische Eingriffe bei Anomalien des Sexuallebens (Surgical Interventions in Cases of Sexual Anomalities). *Therapie der Gegenwart, 67*: 451–455.

PACE = Parliamentary Assembly of the Council of Europe (2015). *Discrimination against transgender people in Europe.* (http://tgeu.org/pace-resolution-discrimination-against-transgender-people-in-europe/).

Person, E (2001). Response to Juliet Mitchell's reflections. *Studies in Gender and Sexuality, 2*: 261–175.

Person, E., & Ovesey, L. (1974 a). The transsexual syndrome in males. I. Primary transsexualism. *American Journal of Psychotherapy*, 28: 4–20.

Person, E., & Ovesey, L. (1974 b). The transsexual syndrome in males. II. Secondary transsexualism. *American Journal of Psychotherapy*, 28: 174–193.

Pfäfflin, F. (2015 a). Benjamin, Harry (1885–1986). *International Encyclopedia of Human Sexuality*, 113–196. Hoboken, NJ: John Wiley & Sons.

Pfäfflin, F. (2015 b). Zur Resolution der Parlamentarischen Versammlung des Europarats über Maßnahmen gegen die Diskriminierung von Transgender People (Discrimination against transgender people in Europe. Comments on Resolution 2048 [2015] of the Parliamentary Assembly of the Council of Europe [PACE]). *Recht & Psychiatrie, 33*: 140–144.

Pfäfflin, F. (1997). Sex reassignment, Harry Benjamin, and some European roots. *International Journal of Transgenderism 1 (2)* (http:web-archive.org/web/20070505034642/http://symposion.com/ijt/index.htm).

Pfäfflin, F. (2003). Understanding transgendred phenomena. In S. Levine, C. B. Risen, & S. E. Althof (Eds.). *Handbook of Clinical Sexuality for Mental Health Professionals*, First Edition. New York, Hove: Brunner-Routledge. pp. 291–310.

Pfäfflin, F. (2006). Research, research, politics and clinical experience with transsexual patients. In P. Fonagy, R. Krause, & M. Leuzinger-Bohleber

(Eds.). *Identity, Gender and Sexuality 150 Years after Freud*, pp. 139–156. London: International Psychoanalytic Association.

Pfäfflin, F. (2010). Understanding transgendered phenomena. In: S. Levine, C. B. Risen, & S. E. Althof (Eds.). *Handbook of Clinical Sexuality for Mental Health Professionals*. pp. 425–447. Second Edition. New York, Hove: Brunner-Routledge.

Pfäfflin, F. (2012). Autobiografien, Biografien und Filme über Geschlechtswechsel. In Lessenich, L. *Die transzendierte Frau. Eine Autobiografie* (Autobiographies, biographies and movies about sex change). pp. 199–219. Giessen: Psychosozial-Verlag.

Pokorny, M. H., & Bondy, M. H. (1933). Rapport sur un transvestite qui demandait une opération cosmétique. *Revue Neurologique*, 40: 701– 701.

Sigusch, V. (1997). Transsexualismus. Forschungsstand und klinische Praxis (Transsexuality. Research update and clinical practice). *Nervenarzt, 68*: 870– 877.

Sigusch, V., Meyenburg, B., Reiche, R. (1978). Transsexualität (Transsexuality). *Sexualmedizin*, 7: 15–22, 107–116, 191–192.

Walinder, J. (1967). *Transsexualism: A study of forty-three cases*. Göteborg: Akademieförlaget.

CHAPTER
TEN

No Memory But Much Desire

AVIVA EDELMAN

This is a story about the journey of Jonathan, a patient with severe brain injuries, whom the author treated for three years. The author demonstrates how countertransference issues may interfere with the capacity to treat such patients using psychodynamically-oriented psychotherapy. In fact, at times, countertransference can pose an even greater obstacle than the neurological impairments as such.

Case background

Jonathan was 25 when he was injured, while travelling with his parents and younger brother in their car. His parents were killed instantly, whereas his brother survived. Jonathan's consciousness index at the time of the accident (Glasgow Coma Scale; Teasdale & Jennett, 1974) reflected very low chances of survival (4/15). He suffered a brain injury in addition to a severe spinal cord injury. His motor deficiencies were on the surface, and, externally, he resembled a cerebral palsy patient. Otherwise he was a handsome and tall young man. He used a wheelchair and was able, by the time he arrived in our care, to maneuver the chair independently using his one intact hand together with his other, weaker arm.

He was born and raised in Eastern Europe. His parents were well educated, with a high socio-economic status. Jonathan was a fourth-year economics student at the time of the accident, and his brother was studying law. One year after the accident, Jonathan and his brother came to live in Israel for the purpose of rehabilitation, as sufficient resources were unavailable in their country of origin.

On arrival Jonathan was admitted to the Loewenstein Hospital, a leading rehabilitation center in Israel. He was diagnosed as quadriplegic (all four limbs paralyzed) at the time; over time, the diagnosis was updated to paresis (weakness) of his four limbs. He was confined to a wheelchair and needed assistance with all basic functions. He also suffered from language impairment due to difficulties in the mechanical production of speech, for which he was treated by a speech therapist. Even though memory problems prevented him from practicing between the speech therapy sessions, his speech improved gradually and became more understandable in all three languages he spoke: his native tongue, English and Hebrew. In addition to receiving medical care in the hospital's out-patient clinic, Jonathan attended an occupational daycare center for the handicapped and participated in therapeutic horseback riding.

Jonathan was severely cognitively disabled. He was very rigid, his visual-motor coordination was lacking, and he suffered from dysexecutive impairments such as difficulties in initiating action, planning, control and working memory. In addition, he suffered from integration- and inference problems, which impaired higher-order thinking. He learned through trial and error, and when he was confronted with clear and concrete guidelines, his functioning improved. His orientation in time and space was partially impaired; he knew where he was but suffered from deficiencies in chronesthesia, defined as awareness of one's (near and distant) future and past, or capacity to engage in mental time travel (Tulving, 2002). Jonathan did not remember his past; it was largely a blur. He suffered from an inability to access memories preceding the accident (retrograde amnesia; Goldberg & Bilder, 1986) and was also impaired in his ability to create new memories (anterograde amnesia; Sohlberg & Mateer, 1989). He did not address the subject of the car accident, nor did he talk or ask about his parents, and it was unclear if he knew that they had been killed. His knowledge of common facts (semantic memory; Tulving, 1985) was intact, but it was challenging for him to acquire new information. Topics of conversation faded after a few minutes. He could acknowledge having met someone before, or having done something, but could not tell where and when.

Jonathan's autonoetic knowledge (knowledge about the self) was very limited, both in a general sense, and concerning his behavioral and cognitive deficits. This is also termed anosognosia (literally, "to not know a disease", lack of awareness or insight; Anderson & Tranel, 1989). He could bear very little frustration, and his behavior was mostly dis-inhibited. As time passed during his therapy, he became more communicative and more socially adjusted, but his memory deficit stayed more or less the same.

First stage of psychotherapy

Jonathan was referred to me two years after his injury. We evaluated his ability to benefit from psychotherapy as very limited (indeed, it was once customary to assume that patients with severe neuropsychological deficits, such as brain injury and stroke, cannot profit at all from psycho-dynamically oriented psychotherapy, although this ultimately proved not to be the case (Kaplan-Solms & Solms, 2001; Langer, Laatsch & Lewis, 1999; and Stern, 1985). Nonetheless, his brother insisted that we give it a try. His brother was the only person taking care of Jonathan at the time. He completely devoted himself to Jonathan and made every effort to provide the best care available. He was part of Jonathan's therapy, we had consultation meetings whenever necessary, and he was the ideal partner to support Jonathan in the rehabilitation process.

Jonathan impressed me as being a nice and intelligent young man. He had European manners (as opposed to the more straightforward and often impolite attitude typical to Israelis) and relatively broad general knowledge. In the beginning we spoke English only.

The most striking feature of Jonathan's therapy was that there existed only the "here and now", in the narrowest sense. In fact, many theories about psychotherapy regard the present moment as the only time window bearing potential for the creation of real change, the only time in which we experience ourselves subjectively and with raw awareness (Stern, 2004). For Jonathan the present moment was all there was. He could not access the past, and he had no perspective on the future, in part because his integrative abilities could not encompass the amount of information necessary to plan future actions (i.e., insufficient prospective memory; Groot, Wilson, Evans, & Watson, 2002), and in part because, as is common among people who have undergone extreme psychic trauma, he was probably functioning mainly in a survival mode.

"The present" lasted fifteen minutes, at most. One quarter of an hour was our window of opportunity. He could not remember at the end of the half-hour session what had been said in the beginning. By the next meeting, three or four days away, he would forget altogether what we had talked about before. While conducting a conversation, he frequently lost his train of thought and was usually not able to return to a subject by himself, sometimes losing it forever. This was partly due to a very limited working memory, or "working attention" (Baddeley & Hitch, 1974; Miller, E.K., 2013). A functional working memory is necessary in order for an individual to be able to bind disparate events together into a story, a narrative. Jonathan could not do that. His experience seemed completely fragmented. I often took offense when patients did not remember our conversations and any of the "pearls of wisdom" I had been trying to impart to them – Jonathan's case was no exception to the rule.

In the beginning phase, therapy was impersonal, detached and seemed meaningless. There was no clear vector to it, and it felt close to an autistic experience. The purpose of therapy unfolded as we went along. He did not really want to come. And neither did I, at first. Within a relatively short time he was able to remember my name and that he was coming for therapy. This indicated that his implicit memory, i.e., knowledge that a subject expresses in performance without being phenomenally aware that he or she possesses that knowledge (Schacter, McAndrews, & Moscovitch, 1988), was intact. Yet Jonathan did not understand the essence of this particular therapy, and regarded it as something he had to do in order to improve his skills.

Jonathan had sustained frontal lobe damage (Lezak, 1995), which caused him to be very passive. He did not initiate any talk or action; he usually only answered questions, in a laconic and telegraphic manner. His passivity also severely influenced his cognitive abilities, including his memory. Specifically, he "forgot to remember," a memory deficit known as frontal amnesia (Stuss & Benson, 1984, Shimamura, 1995 and others). Frontal amnesia is distinct from temporal lobe amnesia, which relates much more to memory per se (Lezak, 1995). Frontal lobe damage and frontal amnesia are associated with dysexecutive syndrome, from which, as noted above, Jonathan also suffered; this syndrome refers to the impairment of executive functions, characterized as behaviors that are purposeful and self-directed (Lezak, 1982), such as initiation, planning, decision making, judgment, self-perception and self-monitoring (Moscovitch, 1994). Damage to the frontal lobe may cause flatness of affect as well (Damasio & Van Hoesen, 1983).

When asked how he was doing or what he would like to talk about, he usually replied that he did whatever normal people do, and that "everything was normal". As for his wishes, he said he had none. He claimed that he did not come to fulfill his wishes; he came to do what "had to be done". He would add that his feelings were a private matter. It seems that a desire to keep his feelings private had been a personality trait prior to his injury, but it may also have been his way of relating to his absent memory and his inability to reflect on his feelings and thoughts. This made the task of therapy very challenging. The outlook of a person who does not want to look into his feelings was not very promising for therapy, not really what I would have wished for. Yet this is a common feature of brain-injured patients who, because of their injuries, are not able to access their feelings, or suffer from flatness or absence of feeling altogether. In fact, more generally, many rehab patients are reluctant to engage in psychotherapy, and would never have done so of their own initiative: Some are naturally passive with little drive of their own, and others are simply unused to solving problems in this way, e.g., because of social background or a mentality that rejects this approach. Nevertheless, such individuals may be in need of therapy.

Although there was no possibility to "talk about it," one could notice that Jonathan's facial expressions and demonstration of feelings were somehow different from his verbal (non)account of them. His opposition to authority was very vivid, as were his devaluating gestures towards me, such as waving his hand in a dismissive way whenever there were questions or issues he did not want to address. His actions also clearly reflected a desire to do things his way. If an object fell on the ground, he insisted on picking it up himself. This could sometimes take up the whole session, as fine-motor coordination problems made it complicated for him to grasp objects – yet he could not be persuaded to accept any help. I sometimes mirrored his need for independence, but he did not think there was anything unusual about that, for he had always been independent, an individualist. It seemed that although he could not remember the facts about his past, there were nevertheless traces, like impressions, reflecting the ambiance of past moments.

Indeed, Jonathan's brother described Jonathan as a self-sufficient and private person before the accident, and not very socially involved. He did have a girlfriend for two years but lost her after his injury. These character features may have made communication with Jonathan even more limited. Relating to more personal matters would have held some therapeutic potential when practically all other functions were missing, but this was merely a complication, to be added to the whole picture of what seemed an impossible endeavor. I used to reiterate to myself the misfortune of having accepted this challenge, as an unwise and idealistic effort that would end in disappointment for all parties concerned.

Because of Jonathan's communication difficulties and the hardships of conducting conventional therapy practices, I introduced expressive tools and play materials into our sessions. Some of Winnicott's play therapy principles, originally designed for children, have proven to be applicable to adults as well (Winnicott, 1971), as long as they are adapted to adult-appropriate topics and content. Specifically, I incorporated art therapy techniques during the beginning phase of therapy.

These techniques included sculpting with clay, drawing, squiggling (Winnicott, 1971), and chocolate play. Chocolate play was developed especially for the treatment of head-injured patients in our hospital (Edelman & Tadir, 2007). This is a type of expressive play therapy for adults, which has proven to overcome many of the obstacles and resistances associated with conducting psychotherapy with rehab patients. Chocolate therapy does not require any special talent, but nevertheless addresses fundamental psychodynamic issues of oral and anal character, enabling participants to process loss, comfort, repair and healing, and modulating the often impulsive and disorganized behavior characteristic of brain injured patients. The enjoyment and fun that accompanies this therapy usually adds a special dimension to the treatment of patients who have to cope with very difficult life changes.

But Jonathan did not enjoy these activities very much. He usually protested and argued that he couldn't engage in childish play or any "female stuff", or as I interpreted, any affective theme. His stance towards women was very rigid and stereotypical: a man had no business in the kitchen or doing any housework. When he talked to me in Hebrew (where male and female verbs are distinct), he would address me as a man, and would not accept any correction from anyone. This behavior might also have reflected twinship and mirroring needs (Kohut, 1971). Working with clay was more productive compared with other materials, but still, very inconsistent: After one very fruitful session, when he made use of clay to express his anger, and even enjoyed himself, I suggested we do it again – but he refused, and when I tried to persuade him to do it anyway, he wheeled himself out of the room and did not come back. I was hysterical from worry and troubled by his behavior. I ran after him, but he disappeared quickly into the elevator. On checking with his brother, I was reassured that he was safe.

With this episode, I was strongly reminded of Winnicott's writings about hate in the countertransference, which resembles some of the mother's feelings towards her child (1949) for making her look bad, among other reasons. I was overwhelmed by a similar reaction, as well as by feelings of helplessness. I realized my feelings were partly echoing Jonathan's experience of helplessness and anger about it all. And at the same time, Jonathan's need to resist, however inconvenient, was encouraging. He was now able to make use of his limited physical autonomy in order to express his rage and to distance himself from unpleasantness and aversive situations, in contrast to his previous state of complete dependence on other people, with all the infantile feelings stemming from that position. This gave hope, and gave therapy a new turn.

Second stage of psychotherapy

As Jonathan's rage began to take on more concrete forms, we entered a second period of therapy. During this period, his general condition worsened. He skipped many therapy sessions, and sometimes it was not clear if he would come back at all. This was a difficult time. I found myself hating him for leaving therapy and also realized I felt disappointment regarding what may have partially been my fantasy to be the first therapist to ever heal organic amnesia through psychotherapy! Omnipotence and impotence interplayed in this process of restructuring a new and different self, one that was capable of enduring the troubled existence forced upon him.

During this time his brother started to work away from home and hired a caregiver during the day. Jonathan was attached to his brother like a baby to his mother, and his separation anxiety took on catastrophic dimensions. He was doing badly – living in a strange country, far away from his family and culture of origin, without a language, lacking any close support system, and lacking adult coping mechanisms. He could not understand his brother's needs and was not interested in knowing about practical matters such as breadwinning. This was one of the manifestations of his Theory of Mind (TOM) deficiency, an impaired ability to make inferences about others' mental states, and one of the characteristics of frontal lobe damage (Baron-Cohen, 2001). His attitude reflected a lack of empathy towards his brother, although one could tell from his way of behaving to others that he must have been a very gentle and considerate person before his injury. We were informed of violent outbursts at home. He refused to eat unless it was in the presence of his brother, and consequently lost a great deal of weight. Antidepressant medication did not help.

My empathy towards Jonathan deteriorated fast and was overtaken by strong empathy towards his brother – a more complementary empathic stance, as Racker would define it (1957). His brother's experience must have been laden with guilt, whether realistic guilt (we never knew the circumstances of the accident and who was driving the car, and his brother was not a communicative person himself to disclose such problematic material) or perceived survivor guilt. All that he did was "go through hell" to satisfy his brother's rehabilitation needs.

The caregiver went away, and another one came along, this time a man from Jonathan's home country. As a part of his struggle against his brother, he missed many therapeutic appointments, including our meetings. I sometimes felt relief for not having to deal with his anger, which filled the room but could never be addressed directly. His caregiver seemed to be only a very poor substitute for the "real thing", being his brother, and Jonathan did not accept his presence. It also seemed that anyone or anything that reminded Jonathan of his disability was unacceptable. No doubt this must have included myself as well.

Given Jonathan's obvious chaotic response to his situation, it seemed there was a need for more structured work. After some time I introduced some games, such as therapeutic cards, dominos, tangrams. Looking at cards featuring drawings of human figures, Jonathan experienced difficulty because of what he called the unrealistic features of these people. His concrete attitude was a barrier to our work together. However, he agreed to play and was willing to participate in the games most of the time. These games were a way of spending time together, and their rules had to be bent many times so they would be compatible with his cognitive setup and emotional needs. Yet Jonathan's needs were not always clear, as he never expressed them in a direct manner. This forced me to engage in a lot of guesswork.

I felt challenged by this state of working in what sometimes seemed like a complete limbo, as well as by the need for increased capacity to cope with uncertainty, as with no other patient before Jonathan. Frustration was my close companion. And countertransference, which echoed many of Jonathan's feelings in me, was perhaps my dearest friend altogether, and a powerful tool to work with. Countertransference is, after all, a reaction to patients' transference. Acting in and out and projective identification, I believe, do not have to be obstacles, but can all be powerful and effective tools for understanding the patient's inner states and for communicating within the therapeutic relationship. As Langs (1976) put it, the therapeutic potential of such processes is attributable to the effort of inducing in the other aspects of one's own inner state, in order to externally manage them and thereby evoke adaptive responses. Thus, although these interactional processes primarily function as defensive operations, they also reflect object relatedness and communication, which, in turn, serve as vehicles of psychological change (Ogden, 1985).

One incident led me to realize that positive transference might be developing gradually, and that we were heading in the right direction after all. Specifically, Jonathan chose one card of an attractive woman and explained that she had "interesting ideas". Sometime later he chose a card displaying an elderly woman, whom he said resembled his mother's friend. This was the first time Jonathan had ever mentioned his mother, in or outside therapy. My subsequent attempts to encourage Jonathan to talk about his mother were, however, met with harsh resistance. This resistance may have indicated motivational factors behind Jonathan's memory problems. The close interaction between cognitive and emotional factors made this therapy a Sisyphean endeavor, which I sometimes experienced as an unbearable one. There was at times a touch of madness in my experience of the whole situation. A pain one would gladly disengage from. And I would have had the legitimation to do so, as many of my colleagues would agree. This is another example of how countertransference issues may interfere with the psychotherapy of severely brain-injured people.

We continued playing games of all kinds, but Jonathan's cognitive difficulties sabotaged his ability to extrapolate ideas and to engage in reasoning. He eventually demanded to do more interesting things, though he never took any initiative, or made any concrete suggestions. His passivity, another one of the characteristics of frontal lobe damage, made my efforts to conduct this work very one-sided and caused me heavy doubts regarding the efficacy and the need for the continuation of this therapy. We tried listening to music, including music originating from his home country, but music may have been too sensitive a trigger, and he refused to hear any of it.

Jonathan and I got to know each other on more than one level, and I found myself learning from him about the many vicissitudes of memory, about therapy and about myself. The fact that I "used" his problems to learn triggered some feelings of guilt on my part, but also gave me a deep sense of gratitude. I believe this gratitude must have left some imprint on our encounters, and thus might have been something for Jonathan to cherish, perhaps lessening his sense of being a burden. This intersubjective aspect of the therapeutic process has added a significant dimension to it all.

Another episode added some more depth to the therapeutic experience and announced an important development in Jonathan's re-building of a sense of self. Before one of our sessions, I welcomed him in our lobby, and he approached me to shake hands, as usual. The handshake had become a significant part of our contact and a ritual not to be missed. Yet on this particular day, for one second I failed to notice his intentions. He turned away, refused to talk, ignored me altogether, and wheeled himself away to the other side of the lobby. I then found myself experiencing a unique form of countertransference, namely, hoping that Jonathan's memory problems would cover up for my mistakes. In fact, however, they never did: as suggested in the classical and ground breaking work with patient HM (Squire, L.R., 2009), who had been tested many times for his various memory deficits, material of high emotional valence may be, although not consciously, processed on another level (implicit memory, discussed above), such that the patient remembers it despite his deficits.

After a few minutes, Jonathan returned, and started to move towards my room. After we entered the room, I asked him what had happened, but he did not remember anything. No doubt, his memory problems interacted with and perhaps served emotional needs as well: Forgetting/denial would enable him to defend against any narcissistic hurt, or negative feelings, such as rejection, which he may have projected onto me as his therapist instead; correspondingly, projective identification dynamics might have accounted for the feelings of anger I subsequently experienced. However, this experience of anger towards Jonathan was not characteristic of my countertransference towards Jonathan in general, although it may have reflected some truths about his premorbid personality, and may have also interacted with my own doubt about not knowing how to distinguish between the pure organic and the psychological factors behind his memory problems.

On the whole, my countertransference was dominated by extreme helplessness. I often felt unable to fathom how to help Jonathan without there being a chance of processing with him what was going on, especially what was happening in the intersubjective and transitional space, as described by Winnicott in his book *Playing and reality* (1971). But Winnicott has also repeatedly stressed the need to refrain from making comments or interpreting, allowing the process to unfold and let natural mental growth do the work. I also knew that my inner feelings were partly echoing Jonathan's inner world, and particularly his despair. This was a manifestation of powerful defenses being at work, projective identification being one of them, and causing me to lose faith very often. As time passed, however, I was also reminded of the power of implicit memory, which functions without self-awareness or any deliberate action or the need for verbalization. I took comfort in knowing-anticipating-hoping that one of the roads would eventually lead to Rome.

Becoming aware of these interpersonal dynamics and potential healing processes, and re-acknowledging their potential, made me regain my energy and motivation again and again in order to continue Jonathan's therapy. It seems that my "surviving" the extreme and basic emotions he projected onto me made it possible to go one step further in the process of integrating his experience of self.

My motivation to treat Jonathan was challenged many times during the three years in which we worked together. This was especially evident when questions arose regarding the funding of his therapy, forcing me to define the purpose of it all – despite my frequent sense, discussed above, that there was no real purpose, and the powerful temptation to give up and move towards closure. My manager, who took an extraordinary stance towards the problem, often needed to encourage me to go on, and succeeded in persuading me that the work with Jonathan could be done. It seems that it was necessary to have several people involved in order to maintain a holding and hoping environment for Jonathan, hope that often collapsed under the pressure of being engaged in his chaotic experience, and the huge void that had to be filled.

When writing to the funder of Jonathan's therapy, I defined the purpose of therapy as "improving Jonathan's self-awareness to acknowledge his impairment so that he would agree to accept help from the outside as well as improve his mental functioning". I decided to continue working with him in order to attenuate his refusal to look into what was apparently reflected to him in this "broken mirror"—reflecting his complicated situation; every attempt to help him only emphasized for him his devastating situation, which he was only partly aware of, but which led to catastrophic reactions. Although I was still doubtful as to my true ability to achieve these aims with Jonathan in psychotherapy, I was nevertheless overjoyed to receive the funder's letter of confirmation for another set of meetings.

This indicated that the tides were turning. To my understanding, the incident with the "handshake" and my subsequent attempts to repair the relationship (Winnicott, 2009) were significant and laid the groundwork for my becoming Jonathan's self-object (Winnicott, 1969). My impression that the therapeutic alliance was tightening was confirmed when, before leaving the room at the end of one of our sessions, I asked Jonathan if he knew something about his plans for the weekend, and he replied: "I don't plan, I react". I counted my blessings, and whether I truly believed it or not, I told myself that Jonathan had started to be more self-aware and willing to internalize *my* therapeutic goals. Perhaps we had achieved an "odd sympathy", a term coined by Dutch physicist Christiaan Huygens in 1665 – long before the discovery of mirror neurons (Gallese, 2001, Rizzolati & Craighero, 2004), and Freud's work on countertransference before that – to refer to the phenomenon in which two swinging pendulums mounted together, out of sync, will over time begin to swing in synchrony (in Doidge, 2015).

Gradually, Jonathan's behavior became more flexible and less defensive. He started acknowledging that he had difficulties with his memory and other problems, and he also became willing to ask for assistance from time to time "because my hand doesn't work so well". His sense of humor began to recover, facilitating a more fruitful dialogue. In contrast to our interactions earlier in the process, when he asked me for help now, we could laugh together about my becoming his "faithful slave", and that he could enjoy instructing me what to do. It seems that this new way of relating boosted his sense of competence.

Third stage of psychotherapy

The third and last period of Jonathan's therapy paralleled his brother's taking a leave of absence from work prior to an important examination. The brother had once again become Jonathan's full-time caregiver, and Jonathan looked very healthy and well groomed. He looked quite attractive and when entering the room made me aware of my own appearance, something that was very new in our relationship. He had gained weight and rarely skipped any therapeutic sessions. On the day before I presented his case to my study group, he arrived wearing a t-shirt with the text: "I promise you a rose garden". From our conversation it was evident that he was well aware of the contents of the phrase and that it was meant for a woman. After that, we exchanged our thoughts about the weather. Jonathan had suffered from the heat during the Israeli summer, and now that autumn had stepped in, we both agreed that it had become pleasantly cool. Later in the session he followed up on the subject and asked me whether by "cool" I had meant "cold" or "good looking". It was striking how the subject was still alive in his memory, even after the passing of time within the session, more than fifteen minutes. It seemed as if it might be possible to expand the memory span, when dealing with subjects relevant to the self. This was the first time Jonathan, even indirectly, had addressed the subject of his appearance or any questions about manhood. This was an embarrassing phase for me in therapy, as there may have developed a sort of transference love, which obviously was non-discussable. Being a middle-aged woman "courted" by a young man, though unexpected, was a lively experience. Jonathan had moved one phase up from expressing only very basic egocentric needs to a more dyadic form of relating.

When we met again after the presentation of his case to the study group, I noticed he did not take the opportunity to beat me in one of our games. When I tried to find out about Jonathan's intentions, it became quite obvious that he was aware of his behavior, and that he actually wanted to lengthen the time of our game. It seems that the experience of our relatedness added another dimension to his emotional wellbeing. I recall being eager to meet Jonathan during this period in therapy, and other staff members passing by the door of my consulting room later told me about the laughter they heard coming from the room, which sounded like a happy encounter.

Therapy ended due to technical reasons. But, five years after his injury, which included three years of psychotherapy, Jonathan's rehabilitation process was more or less complete, as complete as can be expected under these circumstances.

We renewed our contact for a short while when Jonathan returned to therapy after having had surgery, two years later. His mood stabilized and he spoke basic Hebrew, including slang. He now lived separately from his brother, who had married in the meantime and become a father. Jonathan had moved to live with his grandmother, his mother's mother, with whom he had previously had a conflicted relationship due to profound generation gaps. Now, however, after moving to Israel herself, she devoted herself to his care. He remembered me well, noticed that I had moved to a different room, and when I asked him how he had been, he smilingly replied: "You know that I can't remember". I was told he had a good relationship with his new niece, and whenever he was reminded of her he smiled. Before he was dismissed from our care again, he proudly shared with us his home-made chocolate candy, which he had prepared together with his female tutor, who spent time with him once every week. Jonathan had travelled a long and winding journey to arrive at this point. It seemed to me like a triumph.

Discussion

The case of Jonathan illustrates both the potential and the complexity of treating a totally amnestic patient following severe brain injury, who was nevertheless able to benefit from dynamically-oriented psychotherapy. Although his capacities may have been limited, and he was lacking explicit self-awareness or psychological insight, therapy still enabled profound and durable changes. As outlined by Damasio and others, there are several kinds of experiences of self, besides those of autobiographical and reflective self, which develop later in infancy. One important example is the core self, which is a sense of self in the here and now (Damasio, 2000); one of the main components of this type of self is a feeling of knowing. Another example is the pre-reflective self (consciousness), as described by Dorothee LeGrand, which refers to being bodily in the world (2007). This issue is convincingly elaborated by Damasio in his book *Self comes to mind* (2010), in which he presents an in-depth investigation of the mind-body equation and its complexity. Damasio concludes that emotions are grounded in a near-fusion of body and brain networks, and first emerge from the evolutionarily older regions of the brain, even going as low as the brain stem, rather than from the cerebral cortex, which evolved more recently.

Thus, emotions are at the very basis of the human experience. Even when the cortex is damaged, and perhaps especially in such a case, feelings remain, and vulnerability does, too. This is why treatment of brain-injured patients requires optimal awareness and attunement to the patient's inner world and emotional needs, even if these needs sometimes exceed the therapist's limits of understanding or his or her personal boundaries. When the therapist is forced to deal with extreme chaos and with exposure to powerful and overwhelming transference –countertransference tension, hopelessness can be the predominant and most destructive obstacle to therapy.

Another necessity or even pre-condition for conducting therapy with severely brain-injured patients, as in the case of treatment of people suffering from profound psychiatric illness, is the willingness of the therapist to take a deep look into himself (Langer, Laatsch & Lewis, 1999; Searles, 1979). Specifically, the therapist must become aware of the potential and strength, but also of the many pitfalls of countertransference, especially those concerning expectations, as he may have to let go of nearly all of them. Treatment of brain-injured patients entails dealing with their compromised verbalization capacities and insight, which are the cornerstones of what we – psychologists or anyone else belonging to the helping professions – have come to regard as the essence of psychotherapy. In acknowledging the issues of countertransference that may arise in conjunction with these challenges, the therapist may be able to genuinely meet the patient, whether he is without memory, lacks a narrative self, or owns very little of what reminds us of personal identity, which usually relies extensively on self-awareness and knowledge about the sequence and passing of time (Gallagher & Zahavi, 2008).

It often seems to me that the concepts and norms of psychotherapy are not always valid or applicable when it comes to our expectations with neurological patients, or other groups of patients who do not have access to their history or a good grasp of sequences of events. Rather, much can be learned from the experience of the now-moment, an experience that is encouraged, for instance, in the practice of meditation, which is known to require mental or physical capacities that differ from those that are typically engaged in Western culture. In a meditation state, time does not move but passes out of existence into a homogeneous, continuous now (Stern, 2004). The present instant is always moving and is very short, observable only after it is gone. And perhaps most interesting are the present moments that arise in the context of two (or more) people interacting. The sharing of these moments creates a new intersubjective field between the participants, a sharing that alters their relationship and creates something new. Is it, then, so frustrating to live in the present moment, as we may believe? Is it necessarily an empty, poor experience, as opposed to a rich one? And if we make such assumptions, are we not projecting our own feelings and beliefs onto the other?

In fact, the narrative view of time is potentially problematic. In constructing a narrative, the individual selects episodes of life, even if he or she does not explicitly remember them, and marks them in time: before, after, again, etc. These episodes are re-arranged, not necessarily in historical order, but are meant to tell the most coherent story about what life felt like. Yet Freud's psychic time is what Andre Green (2002) refers to as fragmented time; it disregards linear succession, shifts speed of passage, and doubles back and folds forward on itself. Narratives give us the feeling of continuity in life, but they do not necessarily reflect the essence of life itself.

Present moments are mentally grasped as they are still unfolding, and our awareness of them cannot be verbal, symbolic or explicit. Considerable work has examined nonverbal communication in infants, showing how the nonverbal knowledge gained during the first 18 months of life is vastly important for future stages of development (Stern, 2004). Such knowledge is implicit (i.e., non-symbolic, nonverbal, procedural and unconscious, in the sense of not being reflectively and consciously available) and tells the infant what to expect from people, how to deal with them, how to feel about them and how to be with them. This seems to be a trick of nature that enables babies to learn the "important stuff" before they get distracted and complicated by words. This quality of very early development resides mainly in sub-cortical regions, to be integrated into more advanced ways of operating as the nervous system gradually matures, the frontal lobes being the last phase of the brain's development. The parent-child/therapeutic dyad enhances those processes, helps modulate affect and anxiety, ensures that the processes are attended to and enables the child/patient to integrate them into mental existence, and even create the healthy building blocks of the brain and human mental life itself (Schore, 1994).

We cannot say exactly which regions of Jonathan's brain were lesioned. Medical diagnosis pointed to the frontal lobes, but in reality it did not seem so clear cut. But according to the clinical picture we can hypothesize that his brain and in particular the cortex was extensively damaged, rendering Jonathan with problems of higher-order thinking, executive function and memory. These impairments made integrative and normative adult thinking and conduct very difficult. And still, it seems that the therapeutic experience and the creation of important intersubjective moments contributed to Jonathan's re-growth. And where there was no explicit or declarative memory, and no possibility to relate to or reflect on what has happened as well as no explicit self-awareness, implicit memory came to our rescue and enabled registration of experience on some level, thereby promoting a meaningful therapeutic relationship and process, which in turn contributed to better self-regulation, towards a more complete integration of the self.

We have seen Jonathan move from an infant-like functioning to a better and more integrated and adjusted way of being in the world, particularly in his relation to the immediate and close environment. And we have seen him find some peace of mind. It follows that a person like Jonathan, although suffering from such a shattered and fragmented existence, still possesses a self, and desires an object, which will hold and contain him, function as a self object, thereby helping him to regulate his affect and modify behavior. An auxiliary other who will have more than occasionally to "lend" her own frontal lobes to Jonathan, in order to keep track of memory and hold the sequence of time passing, and most of all, preserve a stance of hope.

Another factor contributing to the relative success of this therapy may have been what is referred to as cognitive reserve, based on efficient utilization of brain networks or of the enhanced ability to recruit alternative networks as needed (Stern, 2002). And there is plasticity, the brain's capacity to heal itself, the property of the brain that enables it to change its own structure and functioning in response to activity and mental experience. This assumption about the healing capacity of the brain is relatively new and opposed to what has until recently been common belief. Thought itself can alter brain circuits, so that mental activity is not only the product of the brain but also the shaper of it (Doidge, 2015). These qualities have probably facilitated Jonathan's optimal use of the brain's previous resources, as well as the maximization of reparative processes.

To conclude on a personal note, this therapeutic experience helped me to appreciate **present** moments as precious '**presents**' given to me, to attend to and cherish before they pass by. The present moment involves a strong sense of self. Although such moments are essentially discontinuous, made up of incidents and events separated in time, they seem also, somehow, connected.

My experience with Jonathan, as well as with others with similar problems, has led me to develop an even more optimistic stance towards psychotherapy. However, I have grown to believe that such therapy should depend on experientiality to a much greater extent than we have previously assumed, and presumably less on cognitive insight and the patient's rational-logical understanding of the situation, all processes that rely on later stages of mind/brain development. This deepened insight has encouraged me to turn to a variety of alternative techniques, some of them soma-related, all enabling now-moment experiences to unfold and to be integrated into the psychotherapy of the more severely neurologically handicapped as well as patients who are profoundly psychically traumatized and who have regressed to earlier stages of psychological development.

Acknowledgement

I would like to thank Dr. Yermi Harel for his support and sharing of knowledge and Kobi Tiberg for his valuable contribution to this chapter.

References

Anderson, S. W., & Tranel, D. (1989). Awareness of disease states following cerebral infarction, dementia, and head trauma: Standardized assessment. *The Clinical Neuropsychologist, 3*, 327–339.

Baddeley, A. D., & Hitch, G. J. (1974). Working memory. In G. H. Bower (Ed.). *The Psychology of Learning and Motivation: Advances in research and theory. Vol. 8* (pp. 47–89). New York, NY: Academic Press.

Baron-Cohen, S. (2001). Theory of mind in normal development and autism. *Prisme, 34*, 174–183.

Damasio, A. (2000). *The Feeling of what Happens: Body, emotion and the making of consciousness*. London: Vintage Press.

Damasio, A. (2010). *Self Comes to Mind: Constructing the conscious brain*. London: William Heinemann.

Damasio, A. R., & Van Hoesen, G. W. (1983). Emotional disturbances associated with focal lesions of the limbic frontal lobe. In K. Heilman & P. Satz (Eds.). *Neuropsychology of Human Emotion*. New York, NY: Guilford Press.

Doidge, N. (2015). *The Brain's Way of Healing*. New York, NY: Penguin Random House.

Edelman, A., & Tadir, M. (2007). The chocolate experience: A new therapeutic workshop. *Psychoactualia*. (In Hebrew).

Gallagher, S., & Zahavi, D. (2008). *The Phenomenological Mind: An introduction to philosophy of mind and cognitive science*. New York, NY: Routledge.

Gallese, V. (2001). The shared manifold hypothesis. *Journal of Neuroscience Studies, 8*, 33–50.

Goldberg, E., & Bilder, R. M. (1986). Neuropsychological perspectives: Retrograde amnesia and executive deficits. In L. W. Poon (Ed.). *Handbook for Clinical Memory Assessment of Older Adults*. Washington, DC: American Psychological Association.

Green, A. (2002). *Le Temps Eclate* (Fragmented Time). Paris: Les Editions de Minuit.

Groot, Y. C. T., Wilson, B. A., Evans, J., & Watson, P. (2002). Prospective memory functioning in people with and without brain injury. *Journal of the International Neuropsychological Society, 8*, 645–654.

Kaplan-Solms, K., & Solms, M. (2001). *Clinical Studies in Neuro-psychoanalysis*. London: H. Karnac Books.

Kohut, H. (1971). *The Analysis of the Self*. New York, NY: International Universities Press.

Langer, K. G., Laatsch, C., & Lewis, L. (Eds.). *Psychotherapeutic Interventions for Adults with Brain Injury or Stroke: A clinician's treatment resource*. Madison, CT: Psychosocial Press.

Langs, R. (1976). *The Therapeutic Interaction: Volume II*. New York, NY: Aronson.

LeGrand, D. (2007). Pre-reflective self-consciousness: On being bodily in the world. *Janus Head, 9*, 493–519.

Lezak, M.D. (1982). The problem of assessing frontal lobe executive functions. *International Journal of Psychology*, 17, 281–297.

Lezak, M.D. (1995). *Neuropsychological Assessment (3rd ed.)*. New York, NY: Oxford University Press.

Miller. E. K. (2013). The "working" of working memory. *Dialogues in Clinical Neuroscience*, Vol. 15, No. 4.

Moscovitch, M. (1994). Memory and working with memory: Evaluation of a component process model and comparisons with other models. In D. L. Schacter & E. Tulving (Eds.). *Memory Systems*. Cambridge, MA: MIT Press.

Ogden, T.G. (1985). On potential space. *International Journal of Psychoanalysis, 66*, 129–141.

Racker, H. (1957). The meanings and uses of countertransference. *Psychoanalytic Quarterly, 26*, 303–357.

Rizzolati, G., & Craighero, L. (2004). The mirror-neuron system. *Annual Review of Neuroscience, 27*, 169–92.

Schacter, D. L., McAndrews, M. P., & Moscovitch, M. (1988). Access to consciousness: Dissociations between implicit and explicit knowledge in neuropsychological syndromes. In L. Weiskrantz (Ed.). *Thought without Language. A Fyssen Foundation symposium* (pp. 242–278). New York, NY: Clarendon Press/Oxford University Press.

Schore, A. N. (1994). *Affect Regulation and the Origin of the Self*. London: Lawrence Erlbaum Associates.

Searles, H. F. (1979). *Countertransference and Related Subjects*. Madison, CT: International Universities Press.

Shimamura, A. P. (1995). Memory and the prefrontal cortex. In J. Grafman, K. J. Holyoak, & F. Boller (Eds.). *Structure and Functions of the Human*

Prefrontal Cortex (pp. 151–159). New York, NY: Annals of the New York Academy of Sciences.

Sohlberg, M. M., & Mateer, C. A. (1989). *Introduction to Cognitive Rehabilitation*. New York, NY: Guilford Press.

Squire, L.R., The legacy of Patient HM for neuroscience, *Neuron*, 2009, 61(1) 6–9.

Stern, D. (2004). *The Present Moment in Psychotherapy and Everyday Life*. New York/London: W. W. Norton & Company.

Stern, J.M. (1985). The psychotherapeutic process with brain injured patients: A dynamic approach. *Israel Journal of Psychiatry and Related Sciences*, 22(1–2), 83–87.

Stern, Y. (2002). What is cognitive reserve? Theory and research application of the reserve concept. *Journal of the International Neuropsychological Society, 8*, 448–460.

Stuss, D. T., & Benson, D. F. (1984). Neuropsychological studies of the frontal lobes. *Psychological Bulletin, 95*, 3–28.

Teasdale, G., & Jennett, B. (1974). Assessment of coma and impaired consciousness. *Lancet, II*, 81–84.

Tulving, E. (2002). Chronesthesia. In D. Stuss & R. T. Knight (Eds.). *Principles of Frontal Lobe Function* (pp. 311–325). New York, NY: Oxford University Press.

Tulving, E. (1985). Memory and consciousness. *Canadian Psychology*, 26:1.

Winnicott, D. W. (1949). Hate in the countertransference. *International Journal of Psychoanalysis*. 30: 69–74.

Winnicott, D. W. (1969). On the use of an object. *International Journal of Psychoanalysis, 50*, 711–716.

Winnicott, D. W. (1971). *Playing and Reality*. London: Routledge.

Winnicott, D. W. (2009). *True Self, False Self: Essays, 1935–1963*. E. Berman (Ed.). Tel Aviv: Am Oved.

Part III

The Biological Routes of Countertransference

Part III of the book explores some of the implication of the scientific studies of the last part of the previous century and the early years of the present one, on the understanding of the emotional processes involved in therapy.

One fertile area of such investigation is the study of infant development, including observations and in-depth studies of parent-infant interaction

Another important area is the study of animal behavior, especially that of non-human mammals, and specifically the study of rat empathy.

Finally, the turn-of-the-century revolution in the study of the living brain (such as fMRI, PET, SPECT, and optogenetics) has opened new perspectives for the study of emotions.

CHAPTER

ELEVEN

Compassion, Parenting Response and the "Social Brain": Implications for Psychoanalysis

Dov R. Aleksandrowicz

Compassion for the patient is a powerful motivating force of therapy and a cardinal component of countertransference. It is also a "double edged tool" that can hinder therapy if injudiciously applied. The author traces the roots of compassion (and its main instrument, empathy) to the "parental response" of mammals. This parental response is derived from the unique mammalian reproductive process, which means that it is a drive that is derived from the sexual instinct.

Those conclusions, supported by ample evidence, clinical as well as experimental, have implications for psychoanalytic theory, clinical practice and supervision. The author presents clinical illustrations of such implications, as well as animal studies, to corroborate his thesis.

The double-edged tool

Relief of suffering is the declared preeminent goal of the healing professions. It is highly valued by all societies and modern society bestows unique privileges and duties on the practitioners of healing arts. Each profession follows its own specific guidelines, however it is generally recognized that dedication to the patient and compassion for his or her suffering are necessary components of the process of healing – "*Salus populi suprema lex esto*" "(the health of the people should be the supreme law) – is a motto adopted by the field of medicine[1]). Indeed, sometimes they may be the decisive factor in achieving that aim, particularly when the therapeutic process is primarily or exclusively psychological. Psychoanalytic literature often deals with empathy, but rarely focuses on the untoward effects of its excess.

Zweig's novel *Impatience of the Heart* (published in English under the title *Beware of Pity*[2]) is a novel set in the days preceding World War I. It tells the story of a relationship between an Austrian cavalry officer and a paraplegic Hungarian girl. The two protagonists meet at a party at the girl's home, where the officer invites the girl to a dance, unaware of her physical limitation. Shaken by the unintended painful embarrassment he caused, the young man returns to apologize, and a friendship between the two develops. The kind-hearted, but naïve, cavalryman continues to visit the invalid girl to cheer her up, acting out of compassion for her condition and remorse for having caused her pain. The situation gets out of hand, however, when the cavalryman, ignoring the warning of his friend, the wise doctor, about potential "untowards effects" of compassion, succumbs to the success of his efforts, becomes carried away by the dramatic effects of his comforting, and the girl falls passionately in love with him. The officer's blundering attempts to deal with the situation lead to a tragic ending. Zweig's cavalryman not only drove the girl to despair; he also scarred himself for life. He, a most highly decorated war-hero, saw himself as a contemptible coward and belittled his exploits. "Whenever my name was mentioned in dispatches for 'outstanding courage in face of the enemy', I felt that I was a fraud", he tells Zweig, a casual companion (Zweig 2011, p. 452).

Compassion, one realizes, is truly a "double edged weapon" that can hurt the patient, the healer, or both. Nor is Zweig's novel a story of some extraordinary, "freak" events. Those of us that practice psychotherapy (especially psychoanalysis) and in particular clinical supervision, do know well that intense compassion, not tempered by clinical judgment, may do harm, while attempting to heal. Psychotherapists far better prepared to deal with suffering than the hapless cavalryman, have at times become entangled in counterproductive compassionate counter-transference. In some extreme cases such a situation may lead to tragedy, as described in the novel.

The commitment to relieve distress and pain is a fundamental part of the therapeutic contract and therefore any ill-conceived expression of it has to be seen as "sinning from excess of zeal". Such imprudent compassion is the expression of an inner pressing *urge,* not necessarily conscious, but powerful nevertheless (traditional medicine had a term for such an approach: "*furor terapeuticus*"). This urge is particularly conspicuous when dealing with patients who are victims of gross injustice, victims of abuse or traumatic events, or patients who are particularly helpless and vulnerable, e.g. children. Such feelings are familiar to every experienced analyst or therapist and are usually taken for granted, since they are congruent with the therapeutic contract. Nevertheless, it is useful to analyze those feelings because they may exceed the requirements of the situation and interfere with treatment.

The following description is a clinical example of misguided compassion. Mr. L. was a professional in his late thirties who was referred to psychotherapy because of a stormy and painful divorce process. The process was complicated by a bitter custody battle. Mr. L. claimed, perhaps with justification, that his wife was asking for exclusive custody not so much out of affection for the children, as out of her desire to retain possession of the jointly-owned apartment, once she was appointed the children's custodian (this was the customary policy of divorce courts in Israel at that time).

Mr. L. was a passive, mild-mannered man with a winning smile. He had a history of a gross rejection by his mother, probably compounded by some developmental deficits, which affected his academic performance while in school. He told the therapist that he "could never do anything that pleased his mother, no matter how hard he tried". Mr. L. considered himself "dumb", but he scored very high on abstract cognitive measures in an I.Q. test. Moreover, he graduated with high grades from a prestigious university.

The psychotherapist felt justifiably empathic about Mr. L's sad childhood, more so since the wife (judging by his description) seemed to share some of the unpleasant characteristics of Mr. L's mother. The wife went as far as to accuse him of sexually molesting their two little daughters, as part of her request for exclusive custody. The therapist was indignant: it was a blatant slur and a malicious manipulation to gain an advantage in the court. She wrote a clinical report and testified in the family court, including undergoing a hostile cross-examination by the wife's attorney. As a result of the proceedings, the charges were dropped and a compromise reached.

As the therapy progressed, however, the therapist realized that she had failed to perceive, and to interpret, that Mr. L's passivity and seeming helplessness (the effects of his unhappy experiences with his mother) also served to manipulate the environment and, occasionally, to express his suppressed aggression. Moreover, once the dust of the legal battle dispersed, it transpired that Mr. L., although far from deliberately harming his daughters was at times unaware of their sensitivities and he needed guidance. No great harm was done to the treatment, (yes, I do) but the therapist learned to "beware of pity" before becoming too entangled in fighting a patient's battles.

The roots of compassion

To understand how compassion, an essential element of therapy, both ego-syntonic and congruent with the therapeutic contract, can also derail it, we have to better understand the nature of compassion and its cardinal constituent, empathy. The two concepts are sometimes used synonymously ("compassion" in Latin means "feeling together", while "empathy" in Greek means "feeling into"), but there is a subtle difference: "empathy" refers to emotional identification, sharing the affect of the other ("*einfuehlung*" in German) and may be used not only in the sense of sharing pain or sorrow, but also sharing other feelings, like joy. "Compassion" ("*Mitleid*" in German) means not only identifying with another's suffering but also wishing to relieve their pain. There is also a difference in how the two conditions can be observed. Affects, like empathy, are expressed by facial expression, posture and behavior and therefore can be observed in humans or non-human animals in a clinical or experimental setting with some degree of reliability The wish to help is a purely subjective experience, which can only be reported, unless it is expressed by helping or comforting behavior.

Psychoanalytic literature shows understandable interest in compassion. Freud first referred to compassion in his paper "Three Essays on the Theory of Sexuality" (Freud, 1905[3]). Freud included it among inhibitions of sexuality ("shame, disgust, pity, etc.".) (p. 219), "a barrier" (against cruelty) which "is developed relatively late" (p. 193). In a later work, "Instincts and their Vicissitudes" (Freud, 1915), Freud referred to compassion as a "reaction formation" against sadism (p. 129), i.e., as a defense mechanism. In that paper, Freud did not address the question of how much of this development was a result of intrinsic maturation and how much a result of environmental pressure. Freud considered all defense mechanisms (including reaction formation) as components of the Ego, developed under the pressure of external reality upon the drives, including the pressure of pro-social values, shaped by parental and other injunctions, i.e., the Super-Ego. In this view, compassion would be a relatively late-development entity, a part of the resolution of the oedipal complex and an internalization of the parental representation .Nevertheless, Freud did suggest a "phylogenetic" origin of morality, that is, a biological substrate (Freud, 1912–1913).

The assumption of a social, rather than biological origin of compassion seems to be explicitly or implicitly shared by most analysts, with the exception of the Kleinian school which assumes the existence of "reparatory" defenses (aroused by the threat of object loss) from late infancy on (Klein, 1975).From the Kleinian point of view, therefore, compassion would result largely from an innate (today we would say genetically-determined), psychic process, subsequently influenced by the environment. Is there any empiric evidence to support the hypothesis of a genetic, innate origin of compassion? The answer is unambiguously positive.

We cannot ascertain empirically the *wish* to help nor observe comforting behavior in newborns, as the Kleinian viewpoint would imply, but we can observe signs of an essential component of compassion, namely empathy. Infants cry when hearing the cry of another one, barely hours after birth (Sagi & Hoffman, 1976) I have seen a highly sensitive infant who would cry when people in a television show were quarrelling. Slightly older infants may occasionally be seen embracing a sibling in distress (personal observation, 2014).

Investigations of brain functioning identified regions apparently involved in empathy (Ben-Ami Bartal & Perry, 2016) Such findings indicate a general, rather than an individual neural mechanism, and, therefore, also support the assumption of a genetically-determined phenomenon.

Are empathy and compassion, the urge to help the suffering and care for the weak, a unique product of the human evolution, reinforced by social relationships? Common language seems to assume so; terms such as "humane" and "humanitarian" imply that these noble qualities are the product of a civilized society. Indeed, a civilized society takes pride in its concern for the weak and the suffering, and promotes and rewards helping behavior. We may conclude, therefore, that it is generally assumed that empathy and compassion are unique qualities of the human species.

We learn from biology, however, that nothing can be further from the truth. "Contagious" empathy can easily be observed in other species, notably birds and mammals. It is common to see a flock of birds taking off simultaneously when one of them is alarmed. Similarly, aggressive impulse can be shared: I was taking photographs of a herd of bison grazing, when I suddenly saw a cow trotting quickly towards a calf that was grazing at some distance from the herd, while the rest of the herd, led by a hulking bull with blood-shot eyes, walked briskly towards me in a well-coordinated manner. There could be no doubt that they were acting upon a shared affect. Additionally, empathy in mammals has been demonstrated experimentally: mice became sensitized to pain when observing another mouse showing signs of it (Langford, *et al.*, 2006).Thus empathy is present in animals, at least in birds and mammals.

Helping behavior and tenderness are not exclusively human either; instead, they are products of the unique reproductive strategy of mammals. Most, and perhaps all, living organisms devise methods, sometimes ingenuous ones, to promote the survival of their offspring. Many invertebrate species assure the nutrition of the offspring (e.g., by laying eggs on a nurturing medium) and their protection. Only female mammals, however, feed their young with their own bodies. This method of nurturing in mammals requires a prolonged and intimate contact between the mother and her offspring, a time during which the mother must protect the newborn and meet its other needs, such as warmth, body contact, or stimulation to promote hormone and brain development (for a review of "maternal regulators" in rats, see Hofer, 2006). Such a maternal role requires exquisite sensitivity to the newborn's needs, sensitivity that only mammals have developed. The instrument for the perception of the newborn's needs is the "social brain", that is the brain's ability to resonate with the emotional state of the other (Schorre, 1994). The mammalian newborn, in turn, has developed a set of cues (such as crying, gazing, smiling or babbling) that evoke a proper response on the part of the caregiver. This intuitive "parenting response" has been the subject of study by investigators of infant development. Papoušek, for example, came to the conclusion that the response to infants is an innate and initially unconscious one and becomes conscious only after a brief lapse of time (Papoušek, 2007). Schorre demonstrated that affect-sharing in mother-child interaction is mediated by a "dialogue between two right hemispheres" (Schorre, 1994).

The urge to relieve suffering, born out of the parenting response, extends beyond the caregiver-infant situation. "Altruistic" behavior has been well documented through naturalistic animal observations, for example, of baboons (Strum, 2001). Other examples include satiated vampire bats that share food with less fortunate companions (Wilkinson, 1984). In horses, elephants, hyenas, dolphins, monkeys and chimpanzees, some individuals form friendships that last for years (Seyfarth & Cheney, 2012). Experiments in rodents likewise demonstrate "selfless" helping behavior (Ben-Ami, *et al.*, 2011; Ben-Ami & Perry, Chapter Twelve in this volume).

The evolutionary benefit of mother-to-infant parenting response in mammals is self-explanatory, but the evolutionary benefit of similar comforting behavior in adult-to-adult relationships is less obvious. Such behavior not only goes counter to the natural individual competitiveness of the animal, it also represents some loss of resources. That, however, seems to be outweighed by the evolutionary gain of consolidating the animal's society and thus benefiting the individual in the long run. For instance, Chalyan and colleagues claim that affectionate behavior (grooming) in baboons contributes to the consolidation of their society's structure (Chalyan, *et al.*, 2012). It appears, therefore, that we can reverse the equation and say thatcompassion and helping behavior are not the *product* of society but its *foundation*.

The understanding that compasssion derives from an innate, genetically determined urge, shaped during its development by the environment (especially by object-relationships) requires a reexamination of its place in the context of psychoanalytic drive theory. The innate origin of compassion does not contradict its important role as a reaction-formation against aggressive impulses, but it does demand an examination of compassion's relationship to the basic two drives. The answer, is provided, once again, by biology: Panksepp reports evidence that the "social bond" (including parental response and adult frienship) in mammals is regulated by the neuroptides oxytocin and vasopressin, the same peptides that regulate reproductive behavior (Panksepp, 1998). [Author's note: The discovery that lust, parental love and friendship share a common biochemical foundation, gives credence to Freud's assertion that all of these are derivatives of the sexual drive, an assertion that provoked fierce attacks by critics.] Compassion, therefore, is just one more manifestation of the sexual drive.

Countertransference issues and supervision

The understanding of the biological foundation of empathy and compassion bolsters the relational approach to psychoanalysis described by Marron (Chapter Two of this volume). A close encounter of two people, especially if it is emotionally charged, protracted, or both, inevitably activates the "social brain" of both and creates a bond, which may be attractive, aversive or ambivalent. Therefore, seen from this perspective, countertransference is a natural, unavoidable product, as much as a facilitator of the therapeutic process. Freud's classic recommendation for the analyst to "model himself after the surgeon who puts aside all of his feelings, *even his human sympathy* (italics are mine) and concentrates his mental forces on the single aim of performing the operation as skillfully as possible") (Freud, 1912), requires a reassessment. Such suppression of empathy, even if it were compatible with the therapeutic commitment, (which most analysts today would agree it would not be) is impossible to implement. The inborn "caring" drive, whose neurophysiology has been described by Panksepp means that commitment and emotional detachment are incompatible (Panksepp 1998). Freud himself provides an explanation for this incompatibility, albeit unintentionally; in the following paragraph he writes: " . . . (the analyst) must turn his unconscious like a receptive organ towards the transmitting unconscious of the patient" (Freud, 1912, p. 115). At that stage, Freud did not yet realize that the "receptive organ" absorbs and *resonates* with the deeply emotional content that such "transmissions" include, and that this process is beyond the analyst's control. All the therapist can do is to be aware of it and turn it into a valuable source of knowledge.

The therapist and the patient share the experience of their encounters and, in a sense, grow together psychologically, as they gain insight into their own personality, as well as that of the other. The relationship, however, is not symmetrical. The shared insight into the patient's psyche is the *goal* of the treatment; the insight into the therapist's unconscious is a (hopefully) beneficial by-product (an "added value" in today's vernacular), part of which may or may not be shared with the patient (according to some therapist).The therapeutic contract also places a very different set of commitments and constraints on the two. That understanding, of sharing the experience but not the responsibilities, is, in my mind, the gist of clinical supervision. Providing insight into the delicate balance between countertransference and the therapeutic contract is particularly relevant when the supervisor must deal with issues of misguided compassion in the supervisee.

Compassion can lead to two kinds of difficulties in psychoanalysis: over-identification and frustration. The therapist who over-identifies with the suffering of the patient may fail to maintain limits or to deal with hostile transference (Searles, 1967). He or she may assume an over-protective attitude or identify with the patient's grudges and unwittingly incite the patient against his environment, not necessarily in the patient's best interests. This is particularly relevant in the case of children or adolescents demonizing their parents as part of their own unconscious conflicts. A conscious or unconscious hostile countertransference towards the patient's parents will inevitably lead them to undermine or terminate the treatment. Over-identification, induced by the patient's suffering, may also lead to falsification of the important process of therapeutic reconstruction of a patient's early relationships. An example may be found in the spate of supposed recovery of "repressed memories" of childhood incest that surfaced during the 1970s only to fade a few years later (a fraction of those allegedly true recollections were found to be reliably truthful, but many others were apparently "implanted" by over-zealous therapists; Loftus, 1993).

Countertransference difficulties also arise when the patient's affect, echoed by the therapist's empathy, is difficult to contain. That happens, for instance, when dealing with severely traumatized patients, such as victims of gross abuse or Holocaust survivors (Daniel, 1980; Brainin & Teicher, 2016).The following case may serve as an example. Years ago, as a beginning supervisor, I supervised a young psychologist who was seeing her first patient. The patient, Ms. H. was a mother of two in her early thirties, who survived the Holocaust as a teenager. She asked for help because of a general dissatisfaction with life, depressive spells and an unsatisfactory marital relationship. Fortunately for the patient, she sought treatment before effective anti-depressants came into use. Today she might have been treated by a variety of drugs, with scarce results, instead of a "talking cure" which she badly needed. The therapy dealt with the patient's resent difficulties and some progress was made; however, the patient often returned to the Holocaust memories, which she blamed for her present unhappiness. The therapist listened, but most of the time she gently steered the topic to the patient's painful childhood memories, which, according to the prevailing understanding, were the root of the personality disorder from which the patient was unquestionably suffering. Neither the therapist nor I were aware that we both were avoiding sharing empathically the horrors, pain, and humiliation of the nightmarish world of the Holocaust. The patient derived some relief, especially in regard to her family situation, but her main difficulties remained, as could be expected. An in-depth study of the mental health professions' coping with the problem of treating Holocaust survivors is presented by Brainin and Teicher in this volume (Chapter Eight). Such an avoidant counter-transference response can be understood as a defense against the threat of being flooded by anxiety impossible to contain, a threat more comprehensible if we consider the involuntary, drive-activated nature of "contagion" empathy.

Another set of difficulties arises when the therapist confronts his or her failure to relieve the patient's suffering. The empathic therapist has to "contain" or to work through the progressively accumulating pain he or she "absorbs" from the patient. The unfulfilled urge to relieve brings about a sense of tension and restlessness, aptly described by Zweig as the "impatience of the heart" (Zweig, 2011). Main provides a vivid account of this feeling: "We know . . . that the practice of medicine has abiding unconscious determinants. We also know that if human needs are not satisfied, they tend to become more passionate . . . and then deteriorate in maturity, with sadism invading the situation, together with its concomitants of anxiety, guilt, depression and compulsive reparative wishes" (Main, 1957).The intensity that such reactions to failure may occasionally reach is less surprising in view of the drive origin of the urge to relieve suffering, since frustration of a drive inevitably generates aggression. Narcissism naturally plays a role in reaction to failure, but the intensity of the rage of the frustrated therapist is more comprehensible in light of the joint pressure of both needs: narcissism and the urge to help.

A dramatic example of the perversion of the therapeutic contract is presented in Ken Kesey's 1962 novel "One Flew over the Cuckoo's Nest", in which "Mac" McMurphy (Jack Nicholson), a rebellious small-time criminal, feigns mental illness in order to be admitted to a mental hospital and avoid incarceration. He soon runs into a conflict with the authoritarian chief nurse, raises havoc on the ward, and incites the patients to have fun at the expense of hospital orderliness. All measures to influence his behavior through "therapeutic" means, including electroconvulsive therapy (ECT), fail, and the staff finally resorts to performing a lobotomy that leaves McMurphy a lifeless zombie.

There is a suggestive similarity between the reaction of a frustrated therapist and that of the desperate parents of a "difficult" child, especially of an infant who fails to respond to comforting (Aleksandrowicz & Aleksandrowicz, 1975). Some parents blame anyone that is available, e.g., the other parent or his or her family; some become "instrumental", going through the motions of soothing the infant while emotionally dissociating themselves from the child's distress; and some become subtly or even overtly aggressive towards the child. An experienced therapist will have no difficulty in recognizing "shadows" of those reactions in him or herself, when dealing with "difficult" or "resistant" patients.

A therapist's remarkably powerful urge to help has been ascribed to different factors: over-compensation of inadequately neutralized aggression (Money-Kyrle, 1956) a projective identification with the helpless victim; a competitive wish to be a better parent than the child's parents have been or are (a wish that may be an extension of a common but usually unconscious desire to be a better parent than our own parents have been); or an unconscious feelings of guilt for having been spared the patient's cruel fate, akin to the "survivor's guilt" of combat veterans or of people who have lost their loved ones in the Holocaust. All of these explanations have merit and apply to many cases of "parenting" countertransference that may have reached undesirable levels; however, the biological source of compassion necessitates the consideration of other factors and, sometimes, a different supervisory counselling. The common practice for a supervising analyst encountering a countertransference difficulty that cannot be resolved by supervision is to advise the supervisee to bring the issue up in his or her own analysis; at times even to return to a terminated training analysis. Excessive compassion, however, may be related not to an unresolved and unconscious conflict, but to personality features less amenable to a psychoanalytic interpretation.

The supervisee may have a low (psychic) pain level, frustration intolerance (such as people affected by attention deficit hyperactivity disorder (ADHD) or unusually imperative "parenting response". A less understood factor is the threshold of the presumed "empathy receptors" (analogous presumably to the motor "mirror neurons"). Such personality features usually remain unnoticed, unless reported by an unusually keen observer. For instance, I have known a supervisee who described herself as a child who had an unusual insight into her parents' minds, and would immediately respond to their emotions, especially the negative ones (she also had some unusual sensory sensitivities). It may also be relevant in some cases to examine whether the supervisee has a "parenting opportunity" in his or her personal life and how he or she deals with it.

Such embodied factors can be better dealt with in supervision than in analysis. Becoming aware of presumably innate personality factors does not "resolve" them as insight into unconscious conflict does, but it can lead to better impulse control and will help the supervisee to keep her or his "parenting response" in check and not to exceed the therapeutic needs.

The biological nature of "parenting" countertransference puts it on par with other drive-activated, namely erotic and aggressive countertransferences. There is a basic difference, however, relevant for the process of clinical supervision. Acting upon erotic or aggressive countertransference is unambiguously a breach of the therapeutic contract, while "parenting response" is congruent with the contract and therefore its excess may be more difficult to diagnose and to control.

Conclusions

Compassion and the desire to relieve suffering are a hallmark of the healing professions, following the injunction: "Let the wellbeing of the sick be the supreme law". They are a critical factor in psychotherapy and psychoanalysis. Yet, injudicious expressions of compassion can hinder or derail therapy. Moreover, the frustration resulting from the desire to relieve suffering may also lead to a harmful countertransference reaction.

The reason for compassion's ability to distort clinical judgment lies in its drive-impelled nature. It is a part of our biological heritage, a derivative of the mammalian "parenting response", a fact amply demonstrated by naturalistic observation as well as experimental studies.

These findings require a revision of the analytic theory of compassion, which (with the exception of the Kleinian school of psychoanalysis) generally assumes that compassion, like other pro-social attitudes, is exclusively a product of the internalization of social values transmitted by the parents and other "significant others".

The biological, drive-motivated nature of compassion also has implications for clinical supervision. The assumption that an inappropriate expression of compassion is always evidence of an unresolved unconscious conflict may not be justified, as demonstrated in this chapter and the clinical chapters in Part II of this book. Given these findings, supervisors should consider incorporating a biological perspective of compassion and empathy as part of their clinical process, affording an in-depth understanding of countertransference with clinical as well as theoretical implications. This additional perspective will also provide the supervisee therapist with a better understanding of his or her patients, and will enhance the therapeutic process.

Notes

1 Cicero, "Let the wellbeing of the Republic be the supreme law," *De Legibus,* book III, part III, sub. VII.
2 Zweig, S. (2011), *Impatience of the Heart*, London, UK, Pushkin, p. 241; The translator used the word "pity", but I believe the term "compassion" better renders the German "*Mitleid*" (literally: "suffering together"). The term "pity" has an unintended belittling connotation, of being "pitiful".
3 Freud used the term "*Mitleid,*" which was translated in the Standard Edition as "pity" rather than compassion; see note 3 for a discussion of this translation.

References

Aleksandrowicz, M. K., & Aleksandrowicz, D. R. (1975). The molding of personality: A newborn's innate characteristics in interaction with parents' personalities, *Child Psychiatry & Human Development,* 5/4: 231–241.

Ben-Ami, B. I., Decety, J., Mason, P. (2011). Empathy and pro-social behavior in rats. *Science,* Vol. 334/6061:1427–1430.

Chalyan, V. G., Pachuliya, I. G., Meishvili, N. V., Rozhkova, Y. Y. (2012). The structure-forming function of grooming in Hamadryas baboons. *Neuroscience and Behavioral Physiology,* Vol. 42, Issue 2, 200–204.

Danieli, Y. (1980). Counter-transference in the treatment and study of Nazi Holocaust survivors and their children. *Victimology: An International Journal*, 5/2-4, 355–367.

Freud, S. (1918). *Totem and Taboo: Resemblances between the psychic lives of savages and neurotics.* A. A. Brill (Trans). New York, NY: Moffat, Yard & Co. (Original work published between 1912–1913).

Freud, S. (1953). Infantile sexuality. In *Three Essays on the Theory of Sexuality.* Standard Edition, Vol. VII, Part II. London: Hogarth. (Original work published in 1905).

Freud. S. (1957). *Instincts and their Vicissitudes.* Standard Edition, Vol. XIV, London: Hogarth. (Original work published in 1915).

Hofer, M. A. (2006). Psychobiological roots of early attachment . *Current Directions in Psychological Science*, 15(2):84–88.

Kesey, K. (1962). *One Flew over the Cuckoo's Nest.* New York, NY: Viking Press.

Klein, M. (1975). *Love, Guilt and Reparation.* New York, N.Y; The Free Press, Simon and Schuster.

Langford, D. J., Crager, S. E., Shehzad, Z., Smith, B., Sotocinal, S. G., Levenstadt, J. S., Chanda, M. L., Levitin, D. J., Mogil, J. S. (2006). Social modulation of pain as evidence for empathy in mice. *Science*, 312(5782):1967–1970.

Loftus, E. F. (1993). The reality of repressed memories, *American Psychologist*, 48/5: 518–537.

Main, T. F. (1957). The ailment. *The British Journal of Medical Psychology*, 30/3:129–145.

Money-Kyrle, R. E. (1956). Normal counter-transference and some of its derivations. *The International Journal of Psychoanalysis*, 37, 360.

Panksepp, J. (1998). Love and the social bond. In *Affective Neuroscience.* Oxford, NY: Oxford University Press.

Papoušek, M. (2007). Communication in early infancy: An arena of intersubjective learning. *Infant Behavior and Development*, 30: 258–266.

Sagi, A., & Hoffman, M. L. (1976). Empathic distress in the newborn. *Developmental Psychology*, Vol. 12(2), 175–176.

Schorre, A. (1994). *Affect Regulation and the Origin of the Self: The neurobiology of emotional development*, Hillside, NJ: L. Erlbaum.

Searles, H.F. (1967). The "dedicated physician" in psychotherapy and psychoanalysis. In R. W. Gibson. (Ed.). *Crosscurrents in Psychiatry and Psychoanalysis.* Philadelphia: J. B. Lippincott Company.

Seyfarth, R. M., & Cheney, D. L. (2012). The evolutionary origins of friendship. *Annual Review of Psychology*, Vol. 63, pp. 153–177.

Strum, S. C. (2001). *Almost Human: A journey into the world of baboons*, Chicago, IL: The University of Chicago Press.

Wilkinson, G. S. (1984). Reciprocal food sharing in the vampire bat. *Nature*, 30:181–184.

Zweig, S. (1946). *Beware of Pity*, Berlin: S. Fischer Verlag. (Original work published in 1939).

CHAPTER
TWELVE

The Evolution of Pro-social Behaviour

INBAL BEN-AMI BARTAL AND ANAT PERRY

Pro-social behavior refers to acts meant to benefit another individual or group of individuals. The imperative to help others is biologically rooted, and evolutionarily ancient. Pro-sociality is part of the natural behavioral repertoire of many animals, including humans. It is thought to have originated with maternal care, later evolving o include the broader social group. Simply, it can be adaptive to act either aggressively or pro-socially, depending on the social context.

In humans, pro-social behavior is often motivated by empathy. Recent evidence suggests that some non-human animals are able to share the distress of others, and can be motivated to act to end that distress. This chapter will present a rat helping behavior paradigm developed by the authors, which demonstrates that rats are motivated by the distress of a trapped cage-mate to help release it from a restrainer. Rats find helping rewarding, and choose to help even when given a choice of accessing chocolates. Moreover, helping is dependent on the social context, as rats do not help strangers of an unfamiliar strain. Importantly, pro-social motivation is flexible, and two weeks of co-housing with a rat of the other strain are sufficient to induce helping towards strangers of that strain. This and other findings from animal studies will be discussed, as well as what lessons we can learn about the mechanisms of pro-sociality in humans.

Red in tooth and claw?

In her book, "Regarding the Pain of Others," philosopher Susan Sontag wrote these discouraging words: "Who believes today that war can be abolished? No one, not even pacifists. We hope only to stop genocide and to bring to justice those who commit gross violations of the laws of war . . . and to be able to stop specific wars by imposing negotiated alternatives to armed conflict" (Sontag, 2003). Truly, when observing the history of humanity, conflict seems to reign. Bloody struggles over territory, resources, and power dictate the actions of individuals and nations. Perhaps this is why Western society has been inclined to view man as primarily aggressive. It is easy to conceive that aggression evolved because it promotes survival and success in a world of limited resources. Aggression was defined by Lorenz as "the fighting instinct in beast and man which is directed against members of the same species" (Lorenz, 1966). It is viewed as an *instinct;* a drive that we do not control. With this view in mind, pro-social behaviors, or actions meant to benefit others, such as helping and sharing, seem almost unnatural. Pro-social behavior was, and in many circles still is, believed to go against our nature, and needs to be drilled and instilled with much effort, to override our "animalistic nature". It is natural only in divine beings, whereas in humans it emerges slowly, with culture and civilization. The common perception has been that humans must overcome their basic nature in order to be good.

In recent decades, however, it has become increasingly apparent that this perception is false. Ethologists and evolutionary biologists have observed that pro-social behavior, defined as any action performed by one organism to alleviate another's need or improve their welfare (Cronin, 2012), is common across multiple species and taxa, from ants and rodents to primates. These observations began with anecdotes and were formalized through planned field studies and laboratory paradigms that follow the rigorous rules of the scientific method. The mass of data points towards a single realization: pro-sociality, just as much as aggression, is a major component of the natural behavior repertoire of many species. It is a basic building block of life in animal societies, and just as deeply ingrained into our nature as is aggression. The context determines which will be chosen. If we wish to promote pro-social choices in humans it is important for us to understand the evolutionary roots and biological mechanisms of this behavior.

The evolutionary advantage of pro-social behavior

The evolutionary advantage of pro-social behavior becomes evident from its pervasiveness across taxa and species. Researchers have documented communal nesting, allomothering, consolation and food-sharing in mammals, birds, and insects (Dugatkin, 1997). From ants helping others escape a trap (Nowbahari *et al.*, 2009), to primates helping a human researcher reach an object (Warneken & Tomasello, 2006), animals appear to go against the Darwinian imperative for self-preservation at the expense of others.

Natural selection, inclusive fitness, group selection, and epigenetic explanations have all emerged to explain why an individual would act "selflessly" rather than "selfishly" (Simpson, 2010; Krebs, 2008). Many animals are dependent on social support from others of their group for survival. Social support ensures that animals can be safe, eat, mate and care for their offspring (Carter, 1998). This dependence renders it important to support the group. Moreover, aiding the survival of others in the group may ensure the continuation of the helper's gene-pool (however, see Allen *et al.*, 2013). Behaviorally, helping displays the helper's fitness, and promotes their desirability as a reproductive partner (Lamb & Jablonka, 2005). Darwin himself recognized that animals that depend on their society for survival would be motivated to seek the company of others and feel empathy for members of their species, and that groups whose members help each other are more likely to prosper, survive and reproduce (Darwin, 1871). Recent work provides strong evidence for multi-level selection models of social behavior in mammals (Fu *et al.*, 2012; Zhang & Perc, 2016).

Explanations for pro-sociality such as group selection focus on the ultimate evolutionary advantage of the behavior for the species, but do not provide a proximate explanation of the biological mechanism driving animals to act in specific situations (Preston & de Waal, 2002). Since it is logical that pro-social behavior is adaptive, promoting survival and thriving of the group, multiple proximate mechanisms must have evolved to promote this analogous behavior in organisms as diverse as ants and apes.

Empathy as a driver of pro-social behavior

In humans, a core mechanism driving pro-social behavior is the affective response evoked by another's need or distress. Empathy, the ability to recognize and share the emotions of others, comprises a powerful causal force for acts that are meant to improve the wellbeing of others. In society, empathy inhibits in-group aggression, promotes cooperation and social learning, and serves as emotional "glue" for social groups (Decety & Jackson, 2004). A failure of this mechanism leads to anti-social behavior seen for instance in psychopathy or autism (see for example, Decety *et al.*, 2009).

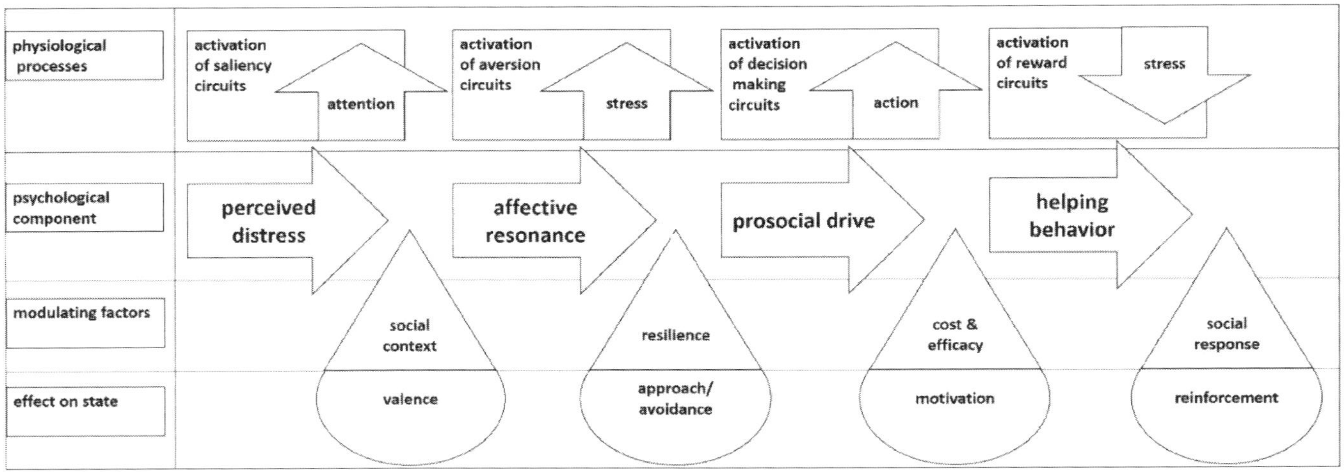

Figure 12.1 (from Decety *et al.*, 2015).

The mechanisms that give rise to social communication of affective information are rooted in the evolution of the central and autonomic nervous systems (Carter *et al.*, 2009; Porges, 1998). The ability to recognize and share the emotional state of others is primal to life in social groups, and does not require complex cognitive functions such as perspective taking (Decety & Svetlova, 2012). The coupling of this ability with care for another's wellbeing is the basic empathic response that underlies pro-social behavior in the wider social context (Decety *et al.*, 2015). For an in-depth review of the biological roots and neural mechanisms of empathy see our chapter on empathy, Chapter Thirteen in this volume.

The route by which witnessing another's distress can lead to helping is described in Figure 12.1 (previous page; taken from Decety *et al.*, 2015). This salient social stimulus leads to an aversive affective arousal combined with a physiological stress response in the observer. In certain social contexts, this experience triggers a pro-social drive which, depending on the context, can lead to pro-social behavior. While eliminating another's distress certainly reduces the observer's distress as well, it is our view that helping is also inherently rewarding, and is not only initiated to reduce tension in the observer, as has been previously suggested (Hull, 1943).

Whether empathy leads to pro-social motivation, or results in action, depends on many variables including the social context, personality traits, the severity of the need, the ease of escape, feelings of efficacy and cost of helping (Decety *et al.*, 2015).

The path from observing another's distress to helping behavior involves the activation of neural circuits involved in orienting attention to the source of distress and initiating a stress response in the observer and behavioral circuits involved in approach. Helping in turns reduces stress and engages reward circuits. Many parameters modulate this response including the relationship with the victim, trait stress reactivity, perceived agency and cost of helping.

Autonomic, endocrine and central mechanisms interact to promote pro-sociality

The perception of distress in an affiliated other initiates a cascade of neural activity, endocrine and autonomic responses that give rise to approach behaviors (Preston, 2004). These processes have much in common with other affiliative social behaviors such as nurturing or pair-bonding (McGraw & Young, 2010; Numan, 2015). It is important to note that social contact is, in and of itself, highly rewarding.

The presence of others activates the "seeking system" (Panksepp, 1998). Regardless of the affective state of others, the neural response shows activity in areas considered to be part of the reward pathway. For instance, mothers who saw images of their babies showed activity in dopamine-associated reward-processing regions, regardless of whether the baby's face was neutral, smiling, or crying (Strathearn *et al.*, 2008).

The response to social events is highly modulated by the neuropeptides oxytocin and vasopressin, which evolved from a common molecule, vasotocin, and are common to a myriad of organisms, both vertebrate and non-vertebrate (Acher *et al.*, 1995). These molecules are involved in various bodily functions, and in recent years there is growing evidence for their role in pro-social behavior (Carter *et al.*, 2016). Apart from its well-recognized role in lactation and contractions, oxytocin has been shown to increase empathy and attachment in humans (Carter *et al.*, 2009) and rodents (Burkett *et al.*, 2016; Marlin *et al.*, 2015; Ferris *et al.*, 2015). Oxytocin interacts with the hypothalamic-pituitary-adrenal (HPA) axis as an anxiolytic. It is both regulated by the stress hormone glucocorticoid and acts as a modulator of glucocorticoid signaling (Beery & Kaufer, 2015). Thus, stress-induced alterations in oxytocin likely play a key role in modulating pro-social motivation, via their effects on regions of the brain involved in motivation and reward (Feldman *et al.*, 2015; Anacker & Beery, 2013).

Vasopressin regulates water balance, blood pressure and autonomic functions. It interacts with the HPA axis as an anxiogenic, and its role in social behavior appears to be opposite to that of oxytocin, with involvement in aggression and defense (Buffone & Poulin, 2014). The view of oxytocin as an affiliative hormone and vasopressin as an aggressive hormone is oversimplified (Shamay-Tsoory & Abu-Akel, 2016). More likely, their interaction produces different results depending on the social context (Febo & Ferris, 2014). Oxytocin and vasopressin work in conjunction, and although the spotlight has been focused mainly on oxytocin, studying their joint function will be important for understanding the neuroendocrine mechanisms of social behavior (Carter *et al.*, 2016).

A moderate stress response is best for helping behavior to occur

Empathy is based on understanding the affective state of others, and emotional contagion appears to be a crucial component of this ability

(Decety *et al.*, 2015). Activity in the stress system, specifically the HPA axis, is a crucial player in empathically motivated pro-social behavior. However, the relationship between stress and successful helping is complex; recent studies with rodents have demonstrated that social reward requires the combined activity of dopamine and oxytocine in areas that process saliency and reward (Dolen *et al.*, 2013; Gunaydin *et al.*, 2014).

Stress has an enormous influence on performance. As early as 1908, the inverted u-shaped relationship between stress and performance was delineated. Yerkes and Dodson posited that while a little bit of stress is correlated with high performance, too much *or* too little stress is actually detrimental (Yerkes & Dodson, 1908). Since then, a similar effect of stress has been demonstrated for various learning and memory tasks (Strathearn *et al.*, 2008; Schilling *et al.*, 2013; Sapolsky, 2015; Salehi *et al.*, 2010; Joels, 2006). When vicarious distress is overwhelming, people, instead of approaching to help, prefer to avoid the situation and escape (Batson *et al.*, 1987). Others also found that too much distress is inversely correlated with helping. Individuals with the short allele polymorphism of the serotonin transporter gene regulatory region (5-HTTLPR) have higher HPA reactivity (Gotlib *et al.*, 2008) and lower pro-social tendencies (Stoltenberg *et al.*, 2013). Rats also demonstrate that high HPA reactivity is detrimental for prosociality. Rats who were subjected to moderate stress were more pro-social in water-sharing behavior following the stressor, than those who were exposed to an intense stressor (Muroy *et al.*, 2016). Martin and colleagues found that administration of a glucocorticoid synthesis inhibitor extends empathic responses to strangers in mice and humans (Martin *et al.*, 2014). Moreover, animals who showed high corticosterone response when exposed to a trapped rat were the least likely to release a trapped cage-mate (Ben-Ami *et al.*, 2016). In summary, HPA activity has a complex influence on social behavior and strongly interacts with trait anxiety in rodents (Beery *et al.*, 2016).

Pro-social behavior in non-human animals

A growing body of evidence points to shared biological elements for affective resonance in humans and rodents, including homologous brain regions and autonomic and endocrine mechanisms (Panksepp & Panksepp, 2013) . For instance, the anterior cingulate cortex (ACC) and amygdala are critical for empathic processing in humans as well as rodents. In mice, the ACC has been implicated in observational fear learning (Jeon *et al.*, 2010), and the amygdala has been shown to play a critical role for pro-social food choice in rats (Hernandez-Lallement *et al.*, 2016). Furthermore, hyperalgesia induced by the observed distress of a cage-mate depends on the medial prefrontal cortex (mPFC) (Li *et al.*, 2014).

While humans are indeed unique in their ability to respond to situations they do not witness directly, the basic response to observed distress is largely shared with other species. Consolation behavior has been demonstrated in birds, rodents and primates. Rooks perform affiliation behaviors with a bonded mate following conflict (Seed *et al.*, 2007). Chimpanzee bystanders console others after a conflict, a behavior that reduces the stress response of the victim (Clay & de Waal, 2013). Prairie voles show increased contact with a fear-conditioned female exposed to a fearful context compared to a neutral context (Burkett *et al.*, 2016). Targeted helping has been demonstrated in chimpanzees that helped a human experimenter by handing them an object that was out of reach (Warneken & Tomasello, 2006). Monkeys refrained from pulling a chain that provided food if that action would also cause another monkey to receive a shock (Masserman *et al.*, 1964). In 1959, Church found that rats that learned to press a lever to obtain food stop doing so if the lever press was paired with a foot-shock to another rat (Church, 1959). Others found that rats press a lever in order to lower a distressed rat that is dangling in the air (Rice & Gainer, 1962).

Another type of pro-social behavior that has been repeatedly demonstrated in animals is a paradigm termed the pro-social choice test. In this task, animals can access a treat. The animal can make a behavioral choice (e.g., go left or right) that will determine whether another animal present will also be given a treat or not. This task presents the animal with an opportunity to benefit another individual at no cost to the self. A preference for making the pro-social choice was first demonstrated in chimpanzees (Horner *et al.*, 2011), and has recently been demonstrated in rats as well (Hernandez-Lallement *et al.*, 2014; Marquez *et al.*, 2015).

Rats lend a helping paw: The helping behavior test

The manifestation of affective resonance in rodents paired with the findings of pro-social behavior presented above suggest that rats, like humans, may be motivated to act pro-socially by a simple form of empathy. The work of one of the authors (Ben-Ami Bartal) has focused on this question. To this order, a novel paradigm was established. In the rat helping behavior test, rats are exposed to a conspecific that is trapped inside a small restrainer. The trapped rat can be released from the restrainer if the observer rat, who is free to roam in the arena (termed "free rat"), opens the restrainer door. It was found that rats are highly motivated to help cage-mates by releasing them from the restrainer (Ben-Ami *et al.*, 2011).

Being trapped inside a small restrainer constitutes a form of mild psychological stress for the trapped rat (Pare &, Glavin, 1986). Rats attempt to escape the restrainer and will do so if given the chance. In the helping behavior test, the door of the restrainer can only be opened from the outside, by the free rat. The rats tested in this paradigm were albino laboratory rats with very poor vision and reduced motor abilities. Moreover, they had no concept of a door being what it is, or of being able to push it up with their snout, so learning to release a trapped cage-mate was not an easy task for them. Over 12 days of testing, the rats had one hour a day in the arena with the trapped cage-mate. From the beginning it was apparent that the rats experienced something salient when exposed to a trapped cage-mate. They began circling the restrainer, poking at it, biting, making digging movements, probing and obviously attempting to reach the trapped rat. At first nothing much happened. A rat would trip the door over a couple of times haphazardly. But after about five sessions, the rats started 'getting it' and began to open the door intentionally. Within a couple of minutes of being placed in the arena, they would push the door up with their snout, and the trapped rat, hesitant at first, would quickly back out into the large arena space. Within 12 days, most rats tested became expert helpers. The persistence that the free rats displayed was noteworthy. During the long sessions, before knowing how to open the restrainer, the rats kept circling around it and attempted to get it to open. Their activity levels remained much higher throughout the entire session than those of rats tested with an empty restrainer or a toy (Ben-Ami *et al.*, 2011). Another crucial point is that the free rats experienced the situation as a stressful one. They treaded very carefully at first, defecated, and were startled at every sound. When the restrainer door fell over, the sound of it hitting the arena floor made rats freeze for many seconds or even minutes. They demonstrated elevations in corticosterone levels. However, all that distress dissipated when rats were finally successful at releasing the trapped cage-mate. When rats first learned to open the restrainer they demonstrated a burst of activity, ran around, and jumped on the other rat with a lot of licking and grooming. They often urinated on the door, a sign of mastery. On the final day of testing, there was no elevation in corticosterone levels in successful helpers, although rats who had not managed to learn how to open the restrainer continued to show elevated levels in response to testing (unpublished data).

Recently, a modified version of the helping behavior test involved presenting rats to a cage-mate trapped in a chamber full of water (Sato *et al.*, 2015) and the findings were similar. Rats helped a conspecific escape from the pool of water by opening a door to allow it access to a dry chamber. They even prioritized this over accessing chocolate chips, hinting at the level of value rats placed on this behavior.

Rat helping is motivated by affective arousal

Pro-social action can be motivated by many factors. In humans, helping others is motivated by empathy only part of the time. As has been previously pointed out, ants also help trapped others, and yet we do not conclude that ants feel empathy for others (Nowbahari *et al.*, 2009). And yet, in humans empathy is often a precursor for helping. In order to be convinced that other mammals are similarly motivated to pro-social behavior by the distress of conspecifics, it is important to show that the system for affective processing and stress is involved. While it is unlikely that animals can take the perspective of others, it is becoming clear that they experience some form of emotional empathy, and their capacity to share the distress of others is coupled with pro-social motivation. For instance, rats tested with a trapped cage-mate are motivated by affective arousal, caused by the conspecific's distress. Administration of the anxiolytic benzodiazepine, Midazolam, to the free rat, significantly reduced door-opening for a trapped cage-mate but not for a restrainer containing chocolate chips (Ben-Ami *et al.*, 2016). However, while the stress response plays an important role in motivating helping, the relationship between stress and empathy is complex. The same study found that a high stress response in the observer rat, indexed by the stress hormone corticosterone, was correlated with reduced helping behavior. Moreover, a study combining mice and human subjects demonstrated that empathy for strangers is blunted by social stress, and that blocking glutocorticoid synthesis, or GR or MR receptors, enhances empathy in the same situation (Martin *et al.*, 2014). Thus, it is likely that moderate stress arousal sets the optimal conditions for helping, and low or elevated stress reduces empathic responses and pro-social behaviors.

In summary, rats as well as primates demonstrate pro-social behavior across different experimental modalities, supporting the idea that the inherent motivation to act for the benefit of others is shared across mammalian species.

The social modulation of pro-social motivation

The selectivity of the empathic response for affiliated conspecifics is observed across species. As such, it is more adaptive for empathy to be selectively expressed towards affiliated others. In humans, empathy and helping are influenced by group membership (Fu *et al.*, 2012; Levine *et al.*, 2005; Cikara *et al.*, 2011). Helping behavior is greater towards members of one's own group (in-group) than for another group (out-group) (Echols & Correll, 2012; Madsen *et al.*, 2007). Moreover, neural responses to others' pain are reduced for out-group members relative to the response to in-group members (Xu *et al.*, 2009). Similar effects have been demonstrated in other animals. Primates demonstrate affective resonance as well, and yawning, which is a contagious behavior sensitive to social context, is demonstrated in chimpanzees to be preferentially transferred between in-group members (Campbell & de Waal, 2011). Geese demonstrate increased heart rate after witnessing a conflict involving their partner or family member (Wascher *et al.*, 2008). Thus, the in-group empathy bias observed in humans (Avenanti *et al.*, 2010) is based on biologically evolved mechanisms.

Darwin intuited that an individual would "extend his social instincts and sympathies to all the members of the same nation, though personally unknown to him" (Darwin, 1871). In support of that, rats tested for helping behavior demonstrated helping behavior towards strangers of their own strain. Yet, in this behavior rats were still biased towards in-group members: while motivated to release trapped rats of their own strain, they did not help rats of an unfamiliar strain. The other strain, with a black-caped fur pattern and black eyes, is strikingly different from the albino rats that were used as the free rats. Albino rats that were presented with a trapped black-caped rat were simply not motivated to help. However, cage-mates, rats who had been housed together with a rat of the other strain, treated that rat as they did their own strain. Importantly, rats then generalized this behavior, releasing *strangers* of the other strain. This shows that pro-social motivation is flexible in rats and can be modified by social experience.

The last experiment in this study tested whether rats had *any* innate mechanism for motivating help for others who are genetically related to themselves. Rats of the albino strain were cross-fostered at birth with litters of the black-caped strain. They were raised with others of that strain and never met another of their own kind. Never, that is, until the day when they were tested for helping behavior with a stranger of their own strain. The results were striking. Rats were absolutely unhelpful towards their own strain. Fostered rats did, however, release rats of the adoptive strain (Ben-Ami *et al.*, 2014). These findings suggest that pro-social motivation for rats in this task is determined primarily by social experience, rather than genetic similarity to the trapped rat. This result supports recent theoretical work by Nowak and colleagues, who demonstrated the limitations of inclusive fitness as a driver of pro-social behavior. According to these researchers, the structure of the social group, rather than degree of kinship, can lead to pro-sociality (Nowak *et al.*, 2010).

While the ultimate mechanism for helping another may very well be inclusive fitness, rats do not possess an internal device for recognizing the genetic makeup of others. Instead, nature has capitalized on existing mechanisms of attachment and affective social behavior to prime pro-social motivation for those in their extended social milieu. The flexibility of the mechanism that guides social behavior, as evidenced in these experiments, makes sense in a world of rapidly changing context. While animals are most likely to be around those who are similar to them in genetic makeup, this might not always be the case. Perhaps this mechanism helped pave the way for different types of animal societies, such as the fission-fusion structures observed in chimpanzees and macaques. In these primates, adult males leave their troop and join other troops. In order for animals in the other troops to accept and integrate them, the social context rather than genetic relatedness must be the crucial parameter to influence their behavior.

Biological mechanisms of social selectivity of pro-social behavior

Evidence is surfacing for the biological mechanisms underlying the display of pro-social behavior in response to affiliation with a conspecific in distress.

One such mechanism is perceptive tuning to the signals of distress from affiliated others. This is a process by which the brain increases the signal and reduces the noise of distress signals from important individuals. For instance, a dam responds differently to her pups' alarm calls than a virgin rat. The mother, but not a virgin rat, will immediately engage in pup-retrieval behavior, fetching the pups back to the nest. This behavior is crucial for pup survival and mothers will cross electric floors, receiving painful shocks, to carry out their task. Interestingly, virgin rats can acquire this behavior pattern, and they do so after 18 hours of housing with the dam and her litter. It has been demonstrated that changes in firing patterns of neurons in the auditory cortex underlie this behavior. Via an oxytocine-mediated mechanism, the noise is reduced and signal is increased in neurons responding to the pup's alarm calls (Marlin *et al.*, 2015). Thus, bottom-up processing that depends on the experience of the observer can change the way the very same signal is perceived in different individuals. In a different situation, processing signals from a mouse of the opposite sex can lead to mating behavior by an adult observer but not a juvenile. This difference is due to specialization that occurs in puberty in response to neurons in the medial amygdala to olfactory signals from conspecifics of the same and opposite sex. Again, the same signal is then processed differently by subcortical areas depending on the age of the animal (Bergan *et al.*, 2014).

The "warm glow" of helping

Pro-social behavior can be initiated by a myriad of motivations. Here we focused mainly on situations in which empathy for other's pain leads to pro-social behavior. The emotionally negative experience of another's pain may be coupled with a strong motivation to help, but sometimes this is not enough. The social response to helping, such as gratitude and recognition, also serve as an important reinforcer of pro-social acts (Gordon *et al.*, 2012; Joel *et al.*, 2013). Gratitude increases the likelihood of costly helping and assistance to strangers (Bartlett & DeSteno, 2006). It is clear that for humans, helping is more than reducing stress and returning to homeostasis. Although helping others in distress helps by reducing the helper's own vicarious distress, it has been well acknowledged that helping others through direct actions or charitable contributions also produces a positive affect. This "warm glow" effect has been related to marked activation in the nucleus accumbens (NAcc), a critical brain area in the reward pathway.

Conclusion

Thanks to our well-developed capacity for theory of mind, we humans have the unique ability to engage in complex perspective-taking tasks, empathizing with people we have never met, imagining the state of mind of people who are very different from us and even responding to imaginary people. In order to uncover the biological mechanisms at the root of these complex behaviors, it is crucial to understand that empathy stems from a simple neural mechanism with ancient evolutionary roots. Thus humans' incredible abilities are imposed on a much simpler phenomenon, the desire to help others, a motivational drive that is prompted by a visceral sharing of their pain. Empathically motivated pro-social behavior is actually part of our animalistic nature, not an opposing force. Human animals are on an evolutionary continuum with other creatures on this planet, and the same mechanisms have been observed across species for functions ranging from breathing and digestion, to emotional processing and social behavior. The evolution of pro-social motivation has favored the development of a psychological system that responds to the distress of others with whom our fate is tied, and directly enhances behavior that is meant to alleviate their distress, even at a cost to the self. We have learned from research with humans and other animals that this system is flexible, and can adapt quickly to new social situations. There may be a lesson in this for all of us: Creating meaningful social bonds with members of other groups may enable us to more instinctively empathize with others, and become more inclusively pro-social.

References

Acher, R., Chauvet, J., Chauvet, M. T. (1995). Man and the chimaera. Selective versus neutral oxytocin evolution. *Advances in Experimental Medicine and Biology*, 395:615–627.

Allen, B., Nowak, M. A., Wilson, E. O. (2013). Limitations of inclusive fitness. *Proceedings of the National Academy of Sciences* (U.S.A.), 110(50):20135–20139.

Anacker, A. M., & Beery, A. K. (2013). Life in groups: The roles of oxytocin in mammalian sociality. *Frontiers in Behavioral Neuroscience*, 7:185.

Avenanti, A., Sirigu, A., Aglioti, S. M. (2010). Racial bias reduces empathic sensorimotor resonance with other-race pain. *Current Biology*, 20(11):1018–1022.

Bartlett, M. Y., & DeSteno, D. (2006). Gratitude and pro-social behavior: Helping when it costs you. *Psychological Science*,17(4):319–325.

Batson, C. D., Fultz, J., Schoenrade, P. A. (1987). Distress and empathy: Two qualitatively distinct vicarious emotions with different motivational consequences. *Journal of Personality*, 55(1):19–39.

Beery, A. K., McEwen, L. M., MacIsaac, J. L., Francis, D. D., Kobor, M. S. (2016). Natural variation in maternal care and cross-tissue patterns of oxytocin receptor gene methylation in rats. *Hormones and Behavior*, 77:42–52.

Beery, A.K,, & Kaufer, D. (2015). Stress, social behavior, and resilience: Insights from rodents. *Neurobiology of Stress*, 1:116–127.

Ben-Ami, B. I., Decety, J., Mason, P. (2011). Empathy and pro-social behavior in rats. *Science*, 334(6061):1427–1430.

Ben-Ami, B. I., Haozhe, S., Molasky, N., *et al.* (2016). Anxiolytic treatment impairs helping behavior in rats. *Frontiers in Psychology*, http://dx.doi.org/10.3389/fpsyg.2016.00850.

Ben-Ami, B. I., Rodgers, D. A., Bernardez-Sarria, M. S., Decety, J., Mason, P. (2014). Pro-social behavior in rats is modulated by social experience. *Elife*, 3:e01385.

Bergan, J. F., Ben-Shaul, Y., Dulac, C. (2014). Sex-specific processing of social cues in the medial amygdala. *Elife*, 3:e02743.

Buffone, A. E., & Poulin, M. J. (2014). Empathy, target distress, and neurohormone genes interact to predict aggression for others-even without provocation. *Personality and Social Psychology Bulletin*, 40(11):1406–1422.

Burkett, J. P., Andari, E., Johnson, Z. V., Curry, D. C., de Waal, F. B. M., Young, L. J. (2016). Oxytocin-dependent consolation behavior in rodents. *Science*, 351(6271):375–378.

Campbell, M. W., & de Waal, F. B. M. (2011). Ingroup-outgroup bias in contagious yawning by chimpanzees supports link to empathy. *PLoS One*, 6(4):e18283.

Carter, C.S. (1998). Neuroendocrine perspectives on social attachment and love. *Psychoneuroendocrinology*, 23(8):779–818.

Carter, S. C., Harri, J., and Porges, S.W. (2009). Neural and evolutionary perspectives on empathy. In W. Ickes & J. Decety (Eds.). *The Social Neuroscience of Empathy*. Cambridge, MA: The MIT Press.169–182.

Carter, S., Ben-Ami, B. I., Porges, E. (2016). The roots of compassion: An evolutionary and neurobiological perspective. In E. M. Seppela, E. Simon-Thomas, S. L. Brown, M. C. Worline, C. D. Cameron, & J. R. Daly (Eds.) *The Oxford Handbook of Compassion*. New York, NY: Oxford University Press.

Church, R. M. (1959). Emotional reactions of rats to the pain of others. *Journal of Comparative and Physiological Psychology*, 52:132–134.

Cikara, M., Botvinick, M. M., Fiske, S. T. (2011). Us versus them: Social identity shapes neural responses to intergroup competition and harm. *Psychological Science*, 22(3):306–313.

Clay, Z., & de Waal, F. B. M. (2013). Development of socio-emotional competence in bonobos. *Proceedings of the National Academy of Sciences* (USA), 110(45):18121–18126.

Cronin, K. A. (2012). Pro-social behavior in animals: The influence of social relationships, communication and rewards. *Animal Behaviour*, 84, 1085–1093.

Darwin, C. (1871). *The Descent of Man, and Selection in Relation to Sex*. Princeton, NJ: Princeton University Press.

Decety, J., & Jackson, P. L. (2004).The functional architecture of human empathy. *Behavioral and Cognitive Neuroscience Reviews*, 3(2):71–100.

Decety, J., & Svetlova, M. (2012). Putting together phylogenetic and ontogenetic perspectives on empathy. *Developmental Cognitive Neuroscience*, 2(1)(Jan):1–24.

Decety, J., Bartal, I. B., Uzefovsky, F., Knafo-Noam, A. (2015). Empathy as a

driver of pro-social behaviour: Highly conserved neurobehavioural mechanisms across species. *Philosophical transactions of the Royal Society of London*, 371(1686).
Decety, J., Michalska, K. J., Akitsuki, Y., Lahey, B. B. (2009). Atypical empathic responses in adolescents with aggressive conduct disorder: A functional MRI investigation. *Biological Psychology*, 80(2):203–211.
Dolen, G., Darvishzadeh, A., Huang, K.W., Malenka, R. C. (2013). Social reward requires coordinated activity of nucleus accumbens oxytocin and serotonin. *Nature*, 501(7466):179–184.
Dugatkin, L. A. (1997). *Animal cooperation among animals: An evolutionary perspective*. New York, NY: Oxford University Press.
Echols, S., & Correll, J. (2012). It's more than skin deep: Empathy and helping behavior across social groups. In J. Decety (Ed.). *Empathy: From bench to bedside*. Cambridge, MA: MIT Press, 55–71.
Febo, M., & Ferris, C. F. (2014). Oxytocin and vasopressin modulation of the neural correlates of motivation and emotion: Results from functional MRI studies in awake rats. *Brain Research*, 1580:8–21.
Feldman, R., Monakhov, M., Pratt, M., Ebstein, R. P. (2016). Oxytocin pathway genes: Evolutionary ancient system impacting on human affiliation, sociality, and psychopathology. *Biological Psychiatry*, 79(3):174–184.
Ferris, C. F., Yee, J. R., Kenkel, W. M., *et al.* (2015). Distinct BOLD activation profiles following central and peripheral oxytocin administration in awake rats. *Frontiers in Behavioral Neuroscience*, 9:245.
Fu, F., Tarnita, C.E., Christakis, N.A., Wang, L., Rand, D. G., Nowak, M. A. (2012). Evolution of in-group favoritism. *Scientific Reports*, 2:460.
Gordon, A. M., Impett, E. A., Kogan, A., Oveis, C., Keltner, D. (2012). To have and to hold: Gratitude promotes relationship maintenance in intimate bonds. *Journal of Personality and Social Psychology*, 103(2):257–274.
Gotlib, I. H., Joormann, J., Minor, K.L., Hallmayer, J. (2008). HPA axis reactivity: A mechanism underlying the associations among 5-HTTLPR, stress, and depression. *Biological Psychiatry*, 63(9):847–851.
Gunaydin, L.A., Grosenick, L., Finkelstein, J. C., *et al.* (2014). Natural neural projection dynamics underlying social behavior. *Cell*, 157(7):1535–1551.
Hernandez-Lallement, J., van Wingerden, M., Marx, C., Srejic, M., Kalenscher, T. (2014). Rats prefer mutual rewards in a prosocial choice task. *Frontiers in Neuroscience*, 8:443.
Hernandez-Lallement, J., van Wingerden, M., Schable, S., Kalenscher, T. (2016). Basolateral amygdala lesions abolish mutual reward preferences in rats. *Neurobiology of Learning and Memory*, 127:1–9.
Horner, V., Carter, J. D., Suchak, M., de Waal, F. B. M. (2011). Spontaneous pro-social choice by chimpanzees. *Proceedings of the National Academy of Sciences* (USA), 108(33):13847–13851.
Hull, C. (1943). *Principles of Behavior*. Englewood Cliffs, NJ: Prentice Hall.
Jeon, D., Kim, S., Chetana, M., *et al.* (2010). Observational fear learning

involves affective pain system and Cav1.2 Ca2+ channels in ACC. *Nature Neuroscience*, 13(4):482–488.

Joel, S., & Gordon, A. M., Impett, E. A,, Macdonald, G., Keltner, D. (2013). The things you do for me: Perceptions of a romantic partner's investments promote gratitude and commitment. *Personality and Social Psychology Bulletin*, 39(10):1333–1345.

Joels, M. (2006). Corticosteroid effects in the brain: U-shape it. *Trends Pharmacology* Science, 27(5):244–250.

Krebs, D. L. (2008). *How Selfish by Nature? Foundations of evolutionary psychology*. Oxford: Routledge. (Original publication: Psycology Press).

Lamb, M., & Jablonka, E. (2005). *Evolution in Four Dimensions: Genetic, epigenetic, behavioral, and symbolic variation in the history of life*. Cambridge, MA: MIT Press.

Levine, M., Prosser, A., Evans, D., Reicher, S. (2005). Identity and emergency intervention: How social group membership and inclusiveness of group boundaries shape helping behavior. *Personality and Social Psychology Bulletin*, 31(4):443–453.

Li, Z., Lu, Y. F., Li, C. L., *et al.* (2014), Social interaction with a cagemate in pain facilitates subsequent spinal nociception via activation of the medial prefrontal cortex in rats. *Pain*, 155(7):1253–1261.

Lorenz, K. (1966). *On Aggression*. (M. Latzke, Trans.). London: Methuen. (Original work published in 1963).

Madsen, E. A., Tunney, R. J., Fieldman, G., *et al.* (2007). Kinship and altruism: A cross-cultural experimental study. *British Journal of Psychology,* 98(Pt 2):339–359.

Marlin, B. J., Mitre, M., D'amour, J.A., Chao, M. V., Froemke, R. C. (2015). Oxytocin enables maternal behaviour by balancing cortical inhibition. *Nature*, 520(7548):499–504.

Marquez, C., Rennie, S. M., Costa, D. F., Moita, M. A. (2015). Pro-social Choice in Rats Depends on Food-Seeking Behavior Displayed by Recipients. *Current Biology*, 25(13):1736–1745.

Martin, L. J., Tuttle, A. H., Mogil, J. S. (2014). The interaction between pain and social behavior in humans and rodents. *Current Topics in Behavioral Neuroscience,* 20:233–250.

Masserman, J. H., Wechkin, S., Terris, W. (1964). "Altruistic behavior in Rhesus monkeys. *American Journal of Psychiatry*, 121:584–585.

McGraw, L. A., & Young, L. J. (2010). The prairie vole: An emerging model organism for understanding the social brain. *Trends in Neuroscience*, 33(2):103–109.

Muroy, S.E., Long, K. L., Kaufer, D., Kirby, E. D. (2016). Moderate stress-induced social bonding and oxytocin signaling are disrupted by predator odor in male rats. *Neuropsychopharmacology*. 41(8):2160–70.

Nowak, M. A. (2006). Five rules for the evolution of cooperation. *Science*, 314(5805):1560–1563.

Nowak, M.A., Tarnita, C. E., Wilson, E. O. (2010). The evolution of eusociality. *Nature*. 466(7310):1057–1062.

Nowbahari, E., Scohier, A., Durand, J. L., Hollis, K. L. (2009). Ants, Cataglyphis cursor, use precisely directed rescue behavior to free entrapped relatives. *PLoS One*, 4(8):e6573.

Numan, M. (2015). *Neurobiology of Social Behavior: Towards an understanding of the pro-social and antisocial brain*. London: Elsevier.

Panksepp, J. (1998). *Affective Neuroscience: The foundations of human and animal emotion*. New York, NY: Oxford University Press.

Panksepp, J., & Panksepp, J, B., (2013). Towards a cross-species understanding of empathy. *Trends in Neuroscience*, 36(8):489–496.

Pare, W. P., & Glavin, G. B. (1986). Restraint stress in biomedical research: A review. *Neuroscience & Biobehavioral Reviews*, 10(3):339–370.

Porges, S. W. (1998). Love: An emergent property of the mammalian autonomic nervous system. *Psychoneuroendocrinology*, 23(8):837–861.

Preston, S. D., & de Waal, F. B. M. (2002). Empathy: Its ultimate and proximate bases. *Behavioral and Brain Sciences*, 25(1):1–20.

Preston, S. D. (2004). Empathy. In M. Bekoff, M., (Ed). *Encyclopedia of Animal Behavior*. Vol 2 D-P. Westport, CT, London: Greenwood Press.

Rice, G. E., & Gainer, P. (1962). "Altruism" in the albino rat. *Journal of Comparative and Physiological Psychology*, 55:123–125.

Salehi, B., Cordero, M. I., Sandi, C. (2010). Learning under stress: The inverted-U-shape function revisited. *Learning & Memory*, 17(10):522–530.

Sapolsky, R. M. (2015). Stress and the brain: Individual variability and the inverted-U. *Nature Neuroscience*, 18(10):1344–1346.

Sato, N,, Tan, L., Tate, K., Okada, M. (2015). Rats demonstrate helping behavior towards a soaked conspecific. *Animal Cognition*, 18(5):1039–1047.

Schilling, T. M., Kolsch, M., Larra, M. F., *et al.* (2013). For whom the bell (curve) tolls: Cortisol rapidly affects memory retrieval by an inverted u-shaped dose-response relationship. *Psychoneuroendocrinology*, 38(9):1565–1572.

Seed, A. M., Clayton, N. S., Emery, N. J. (2007). Postconflict third-party affiliation in rooks, Corvus frugilegus. *Current Biology*, 17(2):152–158.

Shamay-Tsoory, S. G., & Abu-Akel, A. (2016). The social salience hypothesis of oxytocin. *Biological Psychiatry*, 79(3):194–202.

Simpson, J.A., & Beckes, L. (2010). Evolutionary perspectives on pro-social behavior. In M. Mikulincer & P. R. Shaver (Eds.). *Pro-social Motives, Emotions, and Behavior: The better angels of our nature*. Washington, DC: American Psychological Association. 35–53.

Sontag, S., (2003). *Regarding the Pain of Others*, New York, NY: Picador/Farrar, Straus and Giroux.

Stoltenberg, S. F., Christ, C. C., Carlo, G. (2013). Afraid to help:Ssocial anxiety partially mediates the association between 5-HTTLPR triallelic genotype and pro-social behavior. *Society Neuroscience*, 8(5):400–406.

Strathearn, L., Li, J., Fonagy, P., Montague, P. R. (2008). What's in a smile? Maternal brain responses to infant facial cues. *Pediatrics*, 122(1):40–51.

Warneken, F., & Tomasello, M. (2006). Altruistic helping in human infants and young chimpanzees. *Science*, 311(5765):1301–1303.
Wascher, C. A., Arnold, W., Kotrschal, K. (2008). Heart rate modulation by social contexts in greylag geese (Anser anser). *Journal of Comparative Psychology*, 122(1):100–107.
Xu, X., Zuo, X., Wang, X., Han, S. (2009). Do you feel my pain? Racial group membership modulates empathic neural responses. *Journal of Neuroscience*, 29(26):8525–8529.
Yerkes, R.M., and Dodson, J.D. (1908). The relation of strength of stimulus to rapidity of habit-formation. *Journal of Comparative Neurology and Psychology*, Volume 18, Issue 5, pages 459–482, November.
Zhang, H., & Perc, M. (2016). Evolution of conditional cooperation under multilevel selection. *Scientific Reports*, 6:23006.

CHAPTER
THIRTEEN

The Neurobiology of Empathy

Anat Perry and Inbal Ben-Ami Bartal

Empathy is a complex term, which can be used to refer to varying experiences. A simple form of empathy can be defined as the recognition and sharing of an emotional state between individuals. More complex forms of empathy, such as perspective taking, utilize high-level cognitive processes, and underlie humans' unique ability to feel for others who are very different from, or geographically distant than themselves.

Empathy can motivate caring, and lead to actions meant for the benefit of an individual in need. In some instances, empathy serves to promote self-interest, as is observed in psychopathy and narcissism. This chapter will cover findings from neuroscience, developmental and social psychology, which reveal the neural architecture, neuropeptides and systemic activity involved in the empathic response, as well as the biological mechanisms by which social context, personality traits, or pre-existing knowledge interact with empathy.

Empathy and its evolutionary origins

It is widely believed that empathy shapes our social lives by motivating pro-social, caregiving and even altruistic behaviors, facilitating cooperation between members of a social group while inhibiting aggression. However, definitions of empathy vary widely and in the literature, the term is used in different contexts to mean different things (Batson *et al.*, 1987; Cuff, *et al.*, 2016). For some, 'empathy' involves sharing the affective states of another, whereas for others, 'empathy' refers to a higher level cognitive capacity such as intentionally adopting the subjective perspective of another individual in order to understand her feelings, thoughts or intentions. Here we will define empathy as *our understanding of another person's affective state, while knowing that this state is theirs and not our own.* This understanding can be achieved by an automatic bodily sensation, in which we share the affective state of the other, often referred to as *emotional empathy* (cringing or wincing when seeing someone in pain, or smiling when you see someone happy). It can also be achieved by a more cognitive response, sometimes referred to as *cognitive empathy* or mentalizing, in which the affective state is not shared but comprehended (I see that he is crying so I understand that he is sad). The ability to attribute mental states such as beliefs, intentions, desires, and emotions to oneself and others, and the understanding that others have mental states that may differ from one's own, has also been labeled "theory of mind" (ToM) (Premack & Woodruff, 1978; Frith & Frith, 1999). Note that these definitions differ from *emotional contagion* in which one "catches" the emotions of the other, but without awareness of the fact that they are not one's own. The classic example for emotional contagion given in psychology textbooks is that of babies in a nursery that start crying when hearing another baby cry (Simner, 1971). A similar phenomenon is well known to psychotherapy practitioners who constantly need to differentiate between their own affective states and those that may be a consequence of countertransference (Holmes, 2014).

Developmental studies indicate that emotional contagion is evident very early in young babies (e.g., Simner, 1971), while the cognitive ability to consider perspectives, to ascribe agency and intentions, and apply joint attention skills are acquired during a later cognitive development stage (e.g., Carpenter *et al.*, 1998; Johnson, 2003) . A recent study found that babies between 12–24 months are sensitive to videos of pro-social (helping) versus anti-social (interfering) actions (Cowell & Decety, 2015). The famous "contagious yawning effect", i.e., that yawning is often triggered by others yawning (for example, seeing a person yawning, hearing someone yawn on the phone), has been suggested by some to be part of this automatic emotional contagion system as well (Norscia & Palagi, 2011). Although the role of contagious yawning in empathy is still under debate, it is interesting to note that this effect has been observed in other social species such as chimpanzees, (Norscia & Palagi, 2011; Campbell & de Waal, 2011; Campbell *et al.*, 2009), monkeys (Paukner & Anderson, 2006), dogs (Joly-Mascheroni, 2008), and rats (Moyaho *et al.*, 2015), but not in species that do not show social behavior (e.g., tortoises; Wilkinson *et al.*, 2011).

Lastly, empathy differs from *compassion*, where not only do you understand what the other is feeling, but also feel concern for the other and wish to improve their welfare; and from *pro-social behavior*, the action that one might take in order to reduce the other's pain or suffering (see Ben-Ami Bartal & Perry, Chapter Twelve in this volume). While empathy often leads to compassion and pro-social behavior–helping a friend in need, running to a child who just fell, donating money to a deprived society–this is not always the case. In fact, empathy with another's pain might cause overwhelming distress, and result in the empathizer avoiding the other person (Batson *et al.*, 1987; Eisenberg *et al.*, 1989). Another example is psychopathy and antisocial behavior, pathologies in which one might take advantage of their understanding of the other's affective state in order to increase rather than decrease the other's pain (Singer & Lamm, 2009).

Current evolutionary evidence supports the existence of several systems mediating empathy. Darwin (Darwin, 1871) already noted that "many animals certainly sympathize with each other's distress or danger," The selection pressure to develop emotional connectedness between parents and their offspring likely evolved in the context of parental care long before our species (MacLean, 1985). Human and other animal infants, whose survival depended on feeding, cleaning, or maintaining warmth, urged their caregiver to act by signaling their affective state through smiling or crying (Acebo & Thoman, 1995; de Waal, 2008; Bowlby, 1958). Once such an empathic capacity existed, it could be applied outside the rearing context, playing a role in the wider network of social relationships. The fact that mammals retain distress vocalizations into adulthood hints at the continued survival value of these empathy-inducing signals (de Waal, 2008).

De Waal (2008) suggests that the earliest phylogenetically system is the emotional contagion system, in which one is affected by another's emotional or arousal state. Indeed, many animals demonstrate emotional contagion. The cognitive empathic perspective-taking system is a more advanced system and involves higher cognitive functions including mental state attribution. Emotional empathy is probably in between these in terms of evolution, and may have arisen from emotional contagion once the animal could differentiate between its own affective states and those of the other. Emotional contagion and even emotional empathy have been reported in rodents (Panksepp & Lahvis, 2011) and in birds (Wascher *et al.*, 2008). However, although still under debate, it seems that only apes possess the basic traits of cognitive aspects of empathy including some forms of theory of mind and perspective taking (de Waal, 2008; Bowlby, 1958; Panksepp & Lahvis, 2011; Wascher *et al.*, 2008; Call & Tomasello, 2008).

The transfer of distress in animals

Many animals share the distress of others. Affective resonance is expressed through behavioral manifestations of fear such as freezing, as well as through physiological markers of stress including increased stress hormones levels, heart rate, temperature, and pupil dilation. This basic empathic response has been demonstrated in birds (Edgar *et al.*, 2011), pigs (Reimert & Bolhuis, 2015), dogs (Silva *et al.*, 2012) and primates (Norscia & Palagi, 2011).

Rodents have been emerging as an important model organism for studying the biological basis of pro-empathy and social behavior (Keysers & Gazzola, 2016; Mogil, 2015). It has been observed by several researchers that rodents exposed to a demonstrator who is afraid demonstrate fear responses themselves (Panksepp & Panksepp, 2013). In these studies, one animal is subjected to classical fear conditioning in a situation with an imminent or remote threat and the following effect of its presence on a naïve animal are measured. In the observational fear learning paradigms, rodents observe others directly receiving shock. These animals display freezing behaviors, as well as conditioned fear learning of the experimental context (Chen *et al.*, 2009; Jeon *et al.*, 2010; Atsak *et al.*, 2011). In the fear conditioning by-proxy model (Bruchey *et al.*, 2010; Jones *et al.*, 2014), rats encounter conspecifics who are not in immediate pain, but have learned to fear a certain context. Naive animals (observers) are exposed to a novel tone in the presence of a cagemate who was previously fear-conditioned to that same tone (victim). It was demonstrated that the naive observers, for whom the tone is innocuous and has a neutral valence, acquire a fear response to the tone if a victim is present while the tone is sounded. On the next day of testing, observers demonstrate increased freezing in response to the tone compared to their baseline response. This situation demonstrates that rodents can learn to fear neutral stimuli by observing the response of others. This test causes increased measures of emotional arousal in the naïve rat, such as exploratory behavior and acoustic startle response (Knapska *et al.*, 2006; Meyza *et al.*, 2015). Furthermore, exposure to a cagemate that has undergone an aversive learning experience promotes aversive learning and memory (Knapska & Maren, 2009). These effects depend on sex (Langford *et al.*, 2006; Mikosz *et al.*, 2015; Ben-Ami *et al.*, 2011) and familiarity between the two animals (Jones *et al.*, 2014; Gonzalez-Liencres *et al.*, 2014; Li *et al.*, 2014).

Pain responses in rodents are also modulated by the social environment. Mice who observed a cagemate writhing in abdominal pain demonstrated generalized hyperalgesia, as measured by the response to thermally noxious stimuli (Langford *et al.*, 2006). This effect was not observed for mice tested with strangers and interestingly, the presence of a stranger induced the opposite effect, analgesia, in mice exposed to pain (Langford *et al.*, 2011). Another study demonstrated that restraint induced hyperthermia, a physiological response that is caused by a psychological stressor, is modulated by the presence of conspecifics in mice (Watanabe, 2015).

Despite ongoing efforts, neuroscientists have not been able to find an 'empathy brain region', and one probably does not exist. Instead, neuroimaging, lesion and behavioral studies in humans and animals present a complex picture in which many different brain regions, all of which are also involved in other processes, contribute to the different facets of empathy. Here we will outline the major brain networks that are thought to contribute to our different empathic abilities.

Neural mechanisms of empathy with pain

If emotional contagion and emotional empathy represent shared affect, one hypothesis is that the neural representations of these states in an observed animal would show at least some overlap with the observer's self-generated neural representations of that same affective state (Jackson *et al.*, 2005; Keysers *et al.*, 2004; Wicker *et al.*, 2003. This line of thought emerged from the Perception–Action model, according to which perception of a behavior in another automatically activates one's own representations for the behavior, and output from this shared representation automatically proceeds to motor areas of the brain where responses are prepared and executed (Preston & de Waal, 2002). In support of this idea, data from research on empathy for pain has pointed to a specific type of neuron as well as specialized circuits that are activated both when a person feels pain and when they observe another individual experiencing pain. Thus, biological mechanisms exist both on the cellular and network levels to support the somatic representation of the bodies and mental states of others.

The mirror neuron system

The discovery of mirror neurons provided credence to the idea that shared neural representations for self and other give rise to the experience of empathy. This type of neuron, originally found in the macaque monkey, discharges both when the monkey makes a particular goal-directed action and when it observes another individual (monkey or human) performing a similar action (di Pellegrino *et al.*, 1992; Gallese *et al.*, 1996; Rizzolatti *et al.*, 1996). Such neurons have been discovered primarily in areas F5 of the monkey's premotor cortex, in the rostral part of the inferior parietal lobule (IPL, particularly in area PFG) and in the anterior intraparietal sulci (AIP) (Fogassi *et al.*, 2005; Rozzi *et al.*, 2008). Given its observation-execution properties, it was suggested that the mirror neuron system (MNS) is particularly well suited to provide the appropriate mechanism for emotional contagion, and by extension, to enable empathy. In the past two decades, cognitive neuroscientists studying humans, have demonstrated overlaps between regions representing one's own and others actions, intentions and emotions.

Neuroimaging studies in humans found different brain regions that, similar to the MNS in the monkey, are activated both by direct motor performance and indirectly by observing similar movements made by others. Such activity was found primarily in the inferior parietal lobule (IPL), the lower part of the precentral gyrus and the posterior part of the inferior frontal gyrus (IFG), which is the equivalent of the monkey areas F5 (Buccino *et al.*, 2001; Decety *et al.*, 2002; Grafton *et al.*,1996; Grezes *et al.*, 2003; Iacoboni *et al.*,1999). There is growing evidence for the involvement of the IFG in emotional contagion and emotion recognition. Chakrabarti and collegues (Chakrabarti *et al.*, 2006) found a positive correlation between the Empathy Quotient (EQ), a widely used empathy questionnaire, and IFG activation related to the viewing of video clips depicting basic emotions. Jabbi and colleagues (Jabbi *et al.*, 2007) reported that observing positive and disgust facial expressions activated parts of the IFG and that participants' empathy scores were predictive of their IFG activation while witnessing facial expressions. Other neuroimaging studies, involving emotion recognition and empathizing with others have further emphasized the role of the IFG in understanding others (Nummenmaa *et al.*, 2008; Schulte-Ruther *et al.*, 2007).

While the activation of the IFG in tasks that require understanding others has been clearly demonstrated, it is still unclear whether it plays a crucial role in empathy. If the IFG is important for understanding others, damage to regions in this network should lead to deficits in empathic abilities. Some evidence for this relation exists: Shamay-Tsoory and collegues (Shamay-Tsoory *et al.*, 2009), studied eight patients with IFG damage, and compared their results to with those of ventro-medial (VM) lesion patients, posterior lesion patients and healthy controls. The IFG patients differed from the other groups in the emotional empathy subscales of the Interpersonal Reactivity Index (IRI), an empathy questionnaire that differentiates between cognitive and emotional components of empathy (Davis, 1980). In addition, these patients performed significantly worse in an emotional recognition task, but did not differ from healthy individuals in theory of mind tasks. One member of our team (Perry) has been studying IFG lesioned patients for the past few years, and finds that these patients are less accurate and have longer reaction times in tasks requiring the understanding of others' emotions from biological motion cues. At the same time, they show no deficits in social tasks requiring the understanding of social norms that are not related to biological motion cues (Perry *et al.*, 2016).

A different neural manifestation that has been tentatively associated with the MNS in humans is a modulation of electroencephalographic (EEG) oscillations in the 8–13 Hz frequency range over motor and somatosensory cortices, coined mu rhythms (Pineda, 2005). Mu rhythms are desynchronized and their power attenuates when humans engage in motor activity, and, crucially, also while observing actions executed by someone else (Cochin *et al.*, 1999; Cochin *et al.*,1998; Gastaut & Bert, 1954; Muthukumaraswamy *et al.*, 2004). Several studies have shown that, apart from their involvement in observation of motor actions, modulation of mu suppression over the sensorimotor cortex is also seen in social contexts, such as participating in social interactions (Oberman *et al.*, 2007), deciphering the intentions of others (Perry *et al.*, 2010) and in empathy (Cheng *et al.*, 2008; Cheng *et al.*, 2008(b); Perry *et al.*, 2010). In one such study, we examined how one understands the pain of the other when seeing images of others in pain. Importantly, the demonstrator in the experiment could either experience pain similarly to the participant (i.e., feel pain when pricked by a needle, but not when touched by a Q-tip) or differently (i.e., feel pain when touched by a Q-tip, but not when pricked by a needle). A stronger modulation of the mu rhythms was seen whenever participants saw a hand being pricked by a needle (even in knowing that the demonstrators did not experience this as painful). This corresponded with the participants' self-report of feeling that the other was in some pain, and empathizing with them, even when told that this was not painful for the other at all. Both the behavioral and neural results correspond with the hypothesized automaticity of emotional empathy. However, a similar modulation of mu rhythms was also found for the condition in which a hand was being touched by a Q-tip, with the participants aware if it being painful for the other, even though it was not painful for themselves. Put differently, shared representations are not the whole story. Although this system is in some ways automatic, the social context, prior knowledge or beliefs, attention and other top-down processes can modulate and affect it (e.g., Perry *et al.*, 2010; Lamm *et al.*, 2010).

It is important to note that motor regions are not the only areas which exhibit mirror-like mechanisms. Tactile processing mechanisms have also been shown to have mirror properties. The second and third somatosensory cortices can be vicariously recruited by the sight of other people being touched, performing actions or experiencing somatic pain (see Keysers *et al.*, 2010 for a review). Smelling a foul odor engages the same sub-regions of the anterior insula as does watching another person express smell-induced disgust (Wicker *et al.*, 2003).

The contribution of mirror neurons to the emergence of empathy is still being studied. It remains unclear what role neural firing for self as well as others' pain plays in evoking an emotional response to distress in others (Hickok, 2009). The explanation is likely complicated and involves the activity of several types of coordinated circuits, along with hormones related to social behavior (Lamm & Majdandzic, 2015; Ben-Ami Bartal & Perry, Chapter Twelve in this volume).

The affective pain matrix

Our perception of pain contains sensory components as well as emotional components. To a large extent the negative response we have to pain is an emotional one. The neural network that processes this emotional aversion to pain is sometimes referred to as the "affective pain matrix". It has been demonstrated that empathy for the pain of others involves activation in the same areas of this network as does the reaction to one's own pain (Singer *et al.*, 2006; Decety *et al.*, 2010). As described above, pain is often used in empathy studies, as it is relatively easy to induce in a participant (e.g., by a slight electric shock). It is also easy to induce empathy for another (e.g., by telling the participant that another person in a different room is now experiencing these shocks (e.g., Singer *et al.*, 2004), or showing images of someone's finger being cut by a knife, or pricked with a needle (e.g., Lamm *et al.*, 2010; Decety *et al.*, 2010)). Functional Magnetic Resonance Imaging (fMRI) with human subjects shows activation of the "affective pain matrix" in the brain, similar regions to the ones active when you experience pain, including the anterior cingulate cortex, insula, supplementary motor area, amygdala, orbitofrontal cortex and periaqueductal gray when individuals watch facial expressions of pain (Botvinick et al 2005; Lamm *et al.*, 2007) or body parts being injured (Jackson *et al.*, 2005; Cheng et al 2008), when the participants imagine the pain of others (Jackson et al 2006), or simply observe a signal indicating that someone will be hurt (Singer et al 2004). Activation in the ACC and insula has been also found to correlate with the participants' evaluation of the subjective severity of pain experienced by others on the basis of the other's facial pain expression (Schulte-Ruther *et al.*, 2007). This indicates that empathizing with people in pain is associated with hemodynamic activity in the brain that is similar to the activity that occurs when people feel pain themselves (for reviews, see Lamm *et al.*, 2011; Zaki *et al.*, 2016).

The limbic system, and particularly the amygdala, is crucial for emotional empathy. The amygdala is a structure composed of a complex collection of nuclei, and is known for its substantial role in both experiencing and recognizing emotions (especially fear), and in social behavior and reward learning in general (see Adolphs, 2010 for a review). Adolphs and colleagues examined a group of nine individuals with rare bilateral amygdala damage (Adolphs *et al.*, 1999). The subjects as a group were significantly impaired in recognizing fear as compared with controls. An extensive line of research has been done SM, a patient with bilateral amygdale damage, who does not recognize fear in others nor experiences the feeling of fear or danger in herself (Adolphs *et al.*, 1994). Abnormal amygdala activation has also been linked to impaired emotion recognition in psychiatric disorders in which the behavioral relevance of social stimuli is abnormally evaluated, ranging from phobias (e.g., Larson *et al.*, 2006) to depression (e.g., Pezawas *et al.*, 2005), to schizophrenia (e.g., Das *et al.*, 2007; Gur *et al.*, 2007) and autism (e.g., Spezio *et al.*, 2007). Interestingly, a similar impairment has also been found in first-degree relatives of people with autism and may constitute part of an "endophenotype" for impaired amygdala function in autism (Dalton *et al.*, 2005).

The mentalizing network

Some complex forms of empathy involve the ability to create a theory about the other's mental state and cognitively take the perspective of others, without necessarily sharing their emotions. Studies have identified a set of brain regions that are consistently involved in tasks in which one has to infer the emotions, beliefs or intentions of the other. These include the orbitofrontal or ventromedial frontal cortex (OFC / vmPFC), the superior temporal sulcus (STS), the temporoparietal junction (TPJ) and the temporal poles (TP) (Frith & Singer, 2008; Van Overwalle & Baetens, 2009). Accumulative evidence suggests that this network is generally involved in 'self-projection', thinking about the future, or our or another person's upcoming actions, and mentally projecting ourselves into that alternative situation. These abilities all rely on a common set of processes by which past experiences are used adaptively to imagine perspectives and events beyond the present moment (Buckner & Carroll, 2007).

The vmPFC, which has vast connections to the amygdala, appears to be particularly necessary for cognitive empathy or mentalizing the other's affective state, and differentiating between one's own affective states and those of the other (Mitchell, 2009). The frontal lobes in general, especially regions of the prefrontal cortex (PFC), have been associated with executive aspects of cognition, social and moral behavior ever since the description of frontal lobe syndrome-related changes emerged in the nineteenth century (Eslinger *et al.*, 2004). There is ample evidence that the orbitofrontal cortex (OFC) / ventromedial prefrontal cortex (vmPFC) mediate affective information, emotional states and social behavior. Lesions to the vmPFC result, among other things, in impaired empathy (Eslinger, 1998; Shamay-Tsoory *et al.*, 2004) and deficits in complex ToM abilities (Stone *et al.*, 1998). As a result, patients with such lesions do not conform to social norms, and do not use available cues in the social context to alter their social behavior (Beer *et al.*, 2003; Beer *et al.*, 2006; Rolls *et al.*, 1994). For example, in a study of patients with vmPFC/OFC lesions, subjects were found to be aware of social norms of intimacy in a conversation with a stranger, but were unaware that their performance (earlier that day) violated these norms (Beer *et al.*, 2006). Similarly, Stolk and colleagues (Stolk *et al.*, 2015) demonstrated that patients with vmPFC damage were able to select effective communication behaviors during social interactions (describing to another player where to move their figure on a computer screen, by using movements and gestures on the screen); however, their communicative decisions were not fine-tuned to their knowledge of the social partner (e.g., they did not change their behavior when told that the other player was a child versus an adult).

Interactions between regions and networks

Although research by nature tries to simplify the paradigms and focus on one aspect of empathy over the other, in reality a combination of these brain networks is probably active in any given real life task. Put differently, both emotional and cognitive components of empathy may operate partly autonomously, yet it is likely that every empathic response will evoke both components to some extent, depending on the social context. For example, imagine you are walking down the street and suddenly seeing someone fall and bend their leg. You may feel an automatic cringe (emotional contagion), together with a realization that the pain is not your own but someone else's (emotional empathy). You may also feel bad for the person that fell and realize that they may be embarrassed by the situation (cognitive empathy), and lastly, you might approach them and help them stand up (prosocial behavior).

Similarly, de Waal (de Waal, 2008) describes a recurring interaction between apes and their offspring: A mother ape that hears the whimpering of her youngster first whimpers herself, then returns to the youngster to help it from one tree to the next. She does so by swaying her own tree towards the one on which the youngster is trapped and then draping her body between both trees. Her response likely involves emotional contagion (whimpering), along with assessment of the reason for the other's distress and the other's goals. In both human and ape situations, the other's emotions are '"shared'" through brain areas involved in motor or somatosensory representations, or in regions representing fear. The ability to accurately infer the other's perspective and imagine their state of mind requires a mentalizing network, self-other decoding and ToM abilities.

In a study aiming to bridge the gaps between the different views on empathy and the neural networks enabling it, Zaki and colleagues (Zaki, *et al.*, 2009) elegantly showed that empathically accurate evaluation of others' affective states depended both on the activation of structures within the human mirror neuron system (thought to be involved in emotional empathy) and on the activation of regions implicated in mentalizing (or cognitive empathy) such as the prefrontal cortex. Future studies should further focus on the interactions between the two systems and the different conditions that may affect the activation of each.

Pathology

Autism spectrum disorder

Autism spectrum disorder (ASD) is a neurodevelopmental disorder characterized by impaired social interaction, verbal and non-verbal communication, and restricted and repetitive behavior. Individual with ASD often experience difficulties understanding the intentions, thoughts, and feelings of others, and differentiating between one's own knowledge or affective state and that of the other (Baron-Cohen, 2000). While there is ample evidence that people with ASD exhibit deficits in cognitive empathy (Baron-Cohen, *et al.*,1985; Frith, 2001; Frith *et al.*, 1991; Senju *et al.*, 2009), the neural basis for these deficits is still unknown. In fact, it is highly likely that different people diagnosed with ASD have different underlying abnormalities. There are two main theories regarding the social deficits in ASD: One focuses on a deficit in cognitive empathy / mentalizing abilities (Frith *et al.*, 1991), while the other stresses earlier deficits in shared representations, which later cause deficits in mentalizing (Oberman, 2007).

Neuroimaging support for the first comes from an fMRI study by Lombardo and colleagues (Lombardo *et al.*, 2010) who demonstrated that while typical individuals recruit the ACC and the OFC/vmPFC in response to self and other-referential processing respectively, in individuals with autism, the vmPFC responded equally to self and other. Furthermore, the magnitude of neural self-other distinction in the vmPFC was strongly related to the magnitude of early childhood social impairments in the autistic individuals. Individuals whose vmPFC made little to no distinction between mentalizing about self and other were the most socially impaired. Castelli and colleagues also showed deficits in the mentalizing network in individuals with autism in a positron emission tomography (PET) study of attribution of mental states to animated shapes (Castelli *et al.*, 2002).

Initial support for the second theory comes from imitation studies. When typical adults imitate hand actions, they show activity in MNS regions (Grezes *et al.*, 2003; Buccino *et al.*, 2004) and damage to MNS regions in adults may result in imitation difficulties (Heilman *et al.*, 1982; Frenkel-Toledo *et al.*, 2016). Children with autism often exhibit deficits in imitation as well (for a meta-analysis, see Williams *et al.*, 2004), and some studies report abnormal brain responses in ASD children during imitation (Dapretto *et al.*, 2006). In line with this, studies of EEG mu suppression in individuals with ASD show normal mu suppression while self-performing hand movements, but no suppression when passively viewing someone else performing the same movements (Martineau *et al.*, 2004; Oberman *et al.*, 2008; Oberman *et al.*, 2005; Raymaekers *et al.*, 2009; Hare & Neumann, 2008) .

Psychopathy

Psychopathy is a personality disorder associated with a constellation of traits including lack of empathy, guilt or remorse, lack of attachment to others, narcissism, superficial charm, dishonesty, reckless risk-taking and impulsive antisocial behavior (Hare & Neumann, 2008). In different experimental contexts, it has been shown that psychopaths do not experience distress cues as aversive – an experience that is a critical component in the mechanism underlying empathy (e.g., Hare & Neumann, 2008; Kiehl *et al.*, 2001). In line with these results, studies using both fMRI and EEG have reported that children and adolescents with psychopathic traits and conduct problems, in response to stimuli depicting physical distress, show reduced neural activity in the ACC, anterior insula and amygdala, structures typically activated during empathic responses to others' pain (Cheng *et al.*, 2012; Lockwood *et al.*, 2013; Marsh *et al.*, 2013).

Atypical functional and anatomical connectivity between the amygdala, insula and vmPFC has been reported in individuals with psychopathy, and may account for their decreased sensitivity to the negative affective states of others (Yoder *et al.*, 2015). To assess the empathic abilities in people with psychopathic tendencies, researchers used a task that examines affective versus cognitive ToM processing in separate conditions. The ToM abilities of criminal offenders diagnosed with antisocial personality disorder with high psychopathy features was compared with that of participants with localized lesions in the vmPFC, with participants with non-frontal lesions, and with healthy controls. Individuals with psychopathy and those with vmPFC lesions were impaired in tasks involving inferring others' affective states. The study suggests that mentalizing impairments in psychopathy resembles those seen in participants with lesions of the frontal lobe, particularly with vmPFC damage, and provides support for the suggestion of amygdala-vmPFC dysfunction in psychopathy (Blair, 2007; Finger, *et al.*, 2008). In a series of studies using dynamic stimuli of individuals in physical distress and facial expressions of pain, brain activation patterns were compared between incarcerated psychopaths and incarcerated controls. In line with the previous studies, individuals with psychopathy exhibited significantly less activation in the vmPFC, lateral orbitofrontal cortex and PAG relative to controls.

Frontotemporal dementia

Frontotemporal dementia (FTD) is a neurodegenerative disease that selectively affects the frontal and anterior temporal lobes of the brain, regions that are crucial for proper social and emotional functioning (Rosen *et al.*, 2005; Werner *et al.*, 2007). Dramatic social and emotional changes, including emotional blunting, lack of empathy, disinhibition, and poor insight, are early and striking manifestations of this disease and serve as diagnostic criteria to distinguish it from other forms of dementia (Neary *et al.*,1998; Neary *et al.*, 2005; Boxer & Miller, 2005). Shany-Ur and colleagues (Shany-Ur *et al.*, 2012) investigated whether face-to-face testing of patients' ability to comprehend insincere communication would enable researchers to effectively discriminate among patients with different neurodegenerative disease.

The authors examined the patients' ability to comprehend lies and sarcasm from a third-person perspective, using contextual cues, in patients with either FTD, Alzheimer's disease, progressive supranuclear palsy (PSP) or vascular cognitive impairment. While all subjects understood sincere remarks equally, FTD patients displayed impaired comprehension of lies and sarcasm compared with normal age matched controls. Moreover, performance on the test was correlated with information provided by informants (relatives, friends) about the subjects' empathy, perspective taking and neuropsychiatric symptoms in everyday life. All patient groups exhibited some deficiencies in these complex social communication tasks, which require multiple cognitive and emotional processes. However, FTD patients showed uniquely focal and severe impairments at every level of cognitive empathy skills, showing an inability to identify even obvious examples of deception and sarcasm. These results suggest that FTD may target a specific neural network necessary for perceiving social salience and social outcomes (Shany-Ur *et al.*, 2012). Similarly, Rosen and collegues (Rosen *et al.*, 2002) compared FTD patients with age matched control in an emotion comprehension task. The FTD group was impaired in emotional comprehension, with a more severe impairment for emotions with negative valence, including sadness, anger, and fear, than for happiness. Emotional comprehension was correlated with atrophy in the right amygdala and the right OFC, and not with atrophy in other structures.

Schizophrenia

Schizophrenia constitutes a complex mental disorder, which includes '"positive symptoms'" (delusions, hallucinations, disorganized speech, disorganized, or catatonic behavior), and/or '"negative symptoms'" (affective flattening, alogia, or anhedonia). Patients suffering from schizophrenia tend to show impaired emotional and social behavior, including impaired empathy skills. Shamay-Tsoory and colleagues (Shamay-Tsoory *et al.*, 2007) showed that patients with schizophrenia made significantly more errors in the evaluation of the affective states of others as compared to controls. Furthermore, correlation analysis indicated that impairments in these patients correlated with their level of negative symptoms. The authors noted that the pattern of mentalizing impairments in schizophrenia resembled those seen in patients with frontal lobe lesions, particularly with vmPFC damage, providing support for the suggestion of a disturbance of the fronto-limbic circuits in schizophrenia (Shamay-Tsoory *et al.*, 2007). A different study showed that ToM skills are related to gray matter volume (GMV) in the vmPFC in schizophrenia (Hooker *et al.*, 2011). The authors used voxel-based morphometry and a multi-method behavioral assessment of ToM processing, including performance-based, self-report, and interview-rated ToM assessments, to investigate whether ToM skills were related to vmPFC GMV. Compared with healthy participants, schizophrenia participants had worse ToM performance and lower self-reported ToM processing in daily life. Importantly, schizophrenia participants had less vmPFC GMV than did the healthy participants. Together, these studies suggest a strong correlation between abnormalities in vmPFC and cognitive empathy skills in schizophrenia patients.

Conclusions

Empathy, broadly defined, is a phylogenetically ancient capacity that likely evolved in the context of parental care long before the emergence of our species. Consistent with kin selection, both human and animal studies suggest that empathy favors familiar individuals and previous cooperators. While emotion contagion and emotional empathy appear early in human development, and exist in other social animals, only humans, and perhaps apes, possess cognitive aspects of empathy such as mentalizing, theory of mind, and perspective taking. Brain networks that enable the understanding of others are not specific to empathy and serve other functions as well. These networks include shared representations networks such as the mirror neuron system and the pain matrix, the limbic system, and the mentalizing system. The increasing knowledge from the relatively new field of social neuroscience may enable better understanding of psychopathologies related to empathy, and promote the development of new diagnostic tools and interventions.

References

Acebo, C., Thoman, E. B. (1995). Role of infant crying in the early mother-infant dialogue. *Physiology & Behavior*, 57:541– 547.

Adolphs. R., Tranel, D., Damasio, H., Damasio, A. (1994). Impaired recognition of emotion in facial expressions following bilateral damage to the human amygdala. *Nature*, 372:669– 672.

Adolphs. R., Tranel, D., Hamann, S., *et al.* (1999). Recognition of facial emotion in nine individuals with bilateral amygdala damage. *Neuropsychologia*, 37:1111–1117.

Adolphs. R. (2010). What does the amygdala contribute to social cognition? *Annals of the New York Academy of Sciences*, 1191:42–61.

Atsak, P., Orre, M., Bakker, P., *et al.* (2011). Experience modulates vicarious freezing in rats: A model for empathy. *PLoS One*, 6:e21855.

Baron-Cohen, S., Leslie, A.M., Frith, U. (1985). Does the autistic child have a "theory of mind?" *Cognition*, 21:37–46.

Baron-Cohen, S. (2000). Theory of mind and autism: A fifteen year review. In S. Baron-Cohen, H. Tager-Flusberg, & D. Cohen. (Eds), (2000). *Understanding Other Minds: Perspectives from developmental cognitive neuroscience* (Second Edition.). (pp. 3–20). New York, NY: Oxford University Press, xix, 530 pp.

Baron-Cohen, E., Tager-Flusberg, H., Cohen, D. J. (Eds.). (2000). *Understanding Other Minds: Perspectives from developmental cognitive neuroscience* (Second Edition.). (pp. 3–20). New York, NY: Oxford University Press, xix, 530 pp.

Batson, C. D., Fultz, J., Schoenrade, P. A. (1987). Distress and empathy: two qualitatively distinct vicarious emotions with different motivational consequences. *Journal of Personality*, 55:19–39.

Beer, J. S., Heerey, E.A., Keltner. D., Scabini, D., Knight, R. T. (2003). The regulatory function of self-conscious emotion: Insights from patients with orbitofrontal damage. *Journal of Personality and Social Psychology,* 85:594–604.

Beer, J. S., John, O. P., Scabini, D., Knight, R. T. (2006). Orbitofrontal cortex and social behavior: Integrating self-monitoring and emotion-cognition interactions. *Journal of Cognitive Neuroscience*, 18:871–879.

Ben-Ami, B. I., Decety, J., Mason, P. (2011). Empathy and pro-social behavior in rats. *Science*, 334:1427–1430.

Blair, R. J. (2007). The amygdala and ventromedial prefrontal cortex in morality and psychopathy. *Trends in Cognitive Science*, 11:387–392.

Bowlby, J. (1958). The nature of the child's tie to his mother. *International Journal of Psychoanalysis*, 39:350–373.

Boxer, A. L., & Miller, B. L. (2005). Clinical features of frontotemporal dementia. *Alzheimer Disease and Associated Disorders*, 19 Suppl. 1:S3–S6.

Bruchey, A. K., Jones, C. E., Monfils, M. H. (2010). Fear conditioning by-proxy: Social transmission of fear during memory retrieval. *Behavioural Brain Research*, 214:80–84.

Buccino, G., Binkofski, F., Fink, G. R., *et al.*, (2001). Action observation activates premotor and parietal areas in a somatotopic manner: An fMRI study. European Journal of Neuroscience, 13:400–404.

Buccino, G., Vogt, S., Ritzl, A., *et al.*, (2004). Neural circuits underlying imitation learning of hand actions: An event-related fMRI study. *Neuron*, 42:323–334.

Buckner, R.L., & Carroll, D. C. (2007). Self-projection and the brain. *Trends in Cognitive Science*, 11:49–57.

Call, J., & Tomasello, M. (2008). Does the chimpanzee have a theory of mind? 30 years later. *Trends in Cognitive Science,*12:187–192.

Campbell, M. W., Carter, J. D., Proctor, D., Eisenberg, M. L., de Waal, F. B.

M. (2009). Computer animations stimulate contagious yawning in chimpanzees. *Proceedings of the Royal Society B: Biological Sciences,* 276:4255–4259.

Campbell, M. W., & de Waal, F. B. M. (2011). Ingroup-outgroup bias in contagious yawning by chimpanzees supports link to empathy. *PLoS One*, 6:e18283.

Carpenter, M., Nagell, K., Tomasello, M. (1998). Social cognition, joint attention, and communicative competence from 9 to 15 months of age. *Monographs of the Society for Research in Child Development*, 63:i–143.

Castelli, F., Frith, C., Happé, F., Frith, U. (2002). Autism, Asperger syndrome and brain mechanisms for the attribution of mental states to animated shapes. *Brain*. 125:1839–1849.

Chakrabarti, B., Bullmore, E., Baron-Cohen, S. (2006). Empathizing with basic emotions: Common and discrete neural substrates. *Society of Neuroscience*,1:364–384.

Chen, Q., Panksepp, J. B., Lahvis, G. P. (2009). Empathy is moderated by genetic background in mice. *PLoS One*, 4:e4387.

Cheng, Y., Hung, A. Y., Decety, J. (2012). Dissociation between affective sharing and emotion understanding in juvenile psychopaths. *Development and Psychopathology*, 24:623–636.

Cheng, Y., Lee, P. L., Yang, C. Y., Lin, C. P., Hung, D., Decety, J. (2008). Gender differences in the mu rhythm of the human mirror-neuron system. *PLoS One*, 3:e2113.

Cheng, Y., Yang, C. Y., Lin, C. P., Lee, P. L., Decety, J. (2008). The perception of pain in others suppresses somatosensory oscillations: a magnetoencephalography study. *Neuroimage*, 40:1833–1840.

Cochin, S., Barthelemy, C., Lejeune, B., Roux, S., Martineau, J. (1998). Perception of motion and qEEG activity in human adults. *Electroencephalography and Clinical Neurophysiolog*, 107:287–295.

Cochin, S., Barthelemy, C., Roux, S., Martineau, J. (1999). Observation and execution of movement: Similarities demonstrated by quantified electroencephalography. *European Journal of Neuroscience*, 11:1839–1842.

Cowell, J. M., & Decety, J. (2015). Precursors to morality in development as a complex interplay between neural, socioenvironmental, and behavioral facets. *Proceedings of the National Academy of Sciences* (USA), 112:12657–12662.

Cuff, B. M. P., Brown, S. J., Tayor, L., Howat, D. J. (2016). Empathy: A review of the concept. *Emotion Review*, 8:144–153.

Dalton. K. M., Nacewicz, B. M., Johnstone, T., et al., (2005). Gaze fixation and the neural circuitry of face processing in autism. *Nature Neuroscience*, 8:519–526.

Dapretto, M., Davies, M. S., Pfeifer, J. H., et al., (2006). Understanding emotions in others: Mirror neuron dysfunction in children with autism spectrum disorders. Nature *Neuroscience,* 9:28–30.

Darwin, C. (1871). *The Descent of Man, and Selection in Relation to Sex*. Princeton, NJ: Princeton University Press.

De Waal, F. B. M. (2008). Putting the altruism back into altruism: The evolution of empathy. *Annual Review of Psychology,* 8;59:279–300.

Decety, J., Chaminade, T., Grezes, .J, Meltzoff, A. N. (2002). A PET exploration of the neural mechanisms involved in reciprocal imitation. *Neuroimage,* 15:265–272.

Decety, J., Yang, C. Y., Cheng, Y. (2010). Physicians down-regulate their pain empathy response: an event-related brain potential study. *Neuroimage,* 50:1676–1682.

Di Pellegrino, G. ., Fadiga, L., Fogassi, L., Gallese, V., Rizzolatti, G. (1992). Understanding motor events: A neurophysiological study. *Experimental Brain Research*, 91:176–180.

Edgar, J. L., Lowe, J. C., Paul, E. S., Nicol, C. J. (2011). Avian maternal response to chick distress. *Proceedings of the Royal Society B: Biological Sciences*, 278:3129–3134.

Eisenberg, N., Miller, P. A., Fultz, J., Shell, F., *et al.*, (1989). Relation of sympathy and personal distress to pro-social behavior: A multimethod study. *Journal of Personality and Social Psychology*, 57:55–66.

Eslinger, P. J., Flaherty-Craig, C. V., Benton, A. L. (2004). Developmental outcomes after early prefrontal cortex damage. *Brain and Cognition,* 55:84–103.

Eslinger, P. J. (1998). Neurological and neuropsychological bases of empathy. *European Neurology*, 39:193–199.

Finger, E. C., Marsh, A. A., Mitchell, D. G., *et al.*, (2008). Abnormal ventromedial prefrontal cortex function in children with psychopathic traits during reversal learning. *Archives of General Psychiatry*, 65:586–594.

Fogassi, L., Ferrari, P.F., Gesierich, B., Rozzi, S., Chersi, F., Rizzolatti, G. (2005). Parietal lobe: From action organization to intention understanding. *Science*, 308:662–667.

Frenkel-Toledo, S., Liebermann, D. G., Bentin, S., Soroker, N. (2016). Dysfunction of the human mirror neuron system in Ideomotor Apraxia: evidence from Mu Suppression. *Journal of Cognitive Neuroscience*, 28:775–791.

Frith, C. D., & Frith, U. (1999). Interacting minds – a biological basis. *Science*, 286:1692–1695.

Frith, C. D., & Singer, T. (2008). The role of social cognition in decision making. *Philosophical Transactions of the Royal Society B: Biological Sciences*, 363:3875–3886.

Frith, U., Morton, J., Leslie, A. M. (1991). The cognitive basis of a biological disorder: Autism. *Trends in Neuroscience*, 14:433–438.

Frith, U. (2001). Mind blindness and the brain in autism. *Neuron*, 32:969–979.

Gallese, V., Fadiga, L., Fogassi, L., Rizzolatti, G. (1996). Action recognition in the premotor cortex. *Brain*, 119 (Pt 2):593–609.

Gastaut, H. J., & Bert, J. (1954). EEG changes during cinematographic presentation: Moving picture activation of the EEG. *Electroencephalography and Clinical Neurophysiology*, 6:433–444.

Gonzalez-Liencres, C., Juckel, G., Tas, C., Friebe, A., Brune, M. (2014). Emotional contagion in mice: The role of familiarity. *Behavioural Brain Research*, 263C:16–21.

Grafton, S. T., Arbib, M. A., Fadiga, L., Rizzolatti, G. (1996). Localization of grasp representations in humans by positron emission tomography. 2. Observation compared with imagination. *Experimental Brain Research*, 112:103–111.

Grezes, J., Armony, J. L., Rowe, J., Passingham, R. E. (2003). Activations related to "mirror" and "canonical" neurons in the human brain: An fMRI study. *Neuroimage*, 18:928–937.

Gur, R. E., Loughead, J., Kohler, C. G., *et al.*, (2007). Limbic activation associated with misidentification of fearful faces and flat affect in schizophrenia. *Archives of General Psychiatry*, 64:1356–1366.

Hare, R. D., & Neumann, C. S. (2008). Psychopathy as a clinical and empirical construct. *Annual Review of Clinical Psychology*, 4:217–246.

Heilman, K. M., Rothi, L. J., Valenstein, E. (1982). Two forms of ideomotor apraxia. *Neurology*, 32:342–346.

Hickok, G. (2009). Eight problems for the mirror neuron theory of action understanding in monkeys and humans. *Journal of Cognitive Neuroscience*, 21:1229–1243.

Holmes, J. (2014). Countertransference before Heimann: An historical exploration. *Journal of the American Psychoanalytical Association*, 62:603–629.

Hooker, C. I., Bruce, L., Lincoln, S. H., Fisher, M., Vinogradov, S. (2011). Theory of mind skills are related to gray matter volume in the ventromedial prefrontal cortex in schizophrenia. *Biological Psychiatry*, 70:1169–1178.

Iacoboni, M., Woods, R. P., Brass, M., Bekkering, H., Mazziotta, J. C., Rizzolatti, G. (1999). Cortical mechanisms of human imitation. *Science*, 286:2526–2528.

Jabbi, M., Swart, M., Keysers, C. (2007). Empathy for positive and negative emotions in the gustatory cortex. *Neuroimage*, 34:1744–1753.

Jackson, P. L., Meltzoff, A. N., Decety, J. (2005). How do we perceive the pain of others? A window into the neural processes involved in empathy. *Neuroimage*, 24:771–779.

Jeon, D., Kim, S., Chetana, M., *et al.*, (2010). Observational fear learning involves affective pain system and Cav1.2 Ca2+ channels in ACC. *Nature Neuroscience*, 13:482–488.

Johnson, S. C. (2003). Detecting agents. *Philosophical Transactions of the Royal Society B: Biological Sciences*, 358:549–559.

Joly-Mascheroni, R. M., Senju, A., Shepherd, A, J. (2008). Dogs catch human yawns. *Biology Letters*, 4:446–448.

Jones, C. E., Riha, P. D., Gore, A. C., Monfils, M. H. (2014). Social transmission of Pavlovian fear: Fear-conditioning by-proxy in related female rats. *Animal Cognition*, 17:827–834.

Keysers, C., & Gazzola, V. (2016). A plea for cross-species social neuroscience. *Current Topics in Behavioral Neurosciences.* [Epub ahead of print.]

Keysers, C., Kaas, J, H., Gazzola, V. (2010). Somatosensation in social perception. *Nature Reviews Neuroscience*, 11:417–428.

Keysers, C., Wicker, B., Gazzola, V., Anton, J. L., Fogassi, L., Gallese, V. (2004). A touching sight: SII/PV activation during the observation and experience of touch. *Neuron*, 42:335–346.

Kiehl, K. A., Smith, A. M., Hare, R. D., *et al.*, (2001). Limbic abnormalities in affective processing by criminal psychopaths as revealed by functional magnetic resonance imaging. *Biological Psychiatry*, 50:677–684.

Knapska, E., &Maren, S. (2009). Reciprocal patterns of c-Fos expression in the medial prefrontal cortex and amygdala after extinction and renewal of conditioned fear. *Learning & Memory*, 16:486–493.

Knapska, E., Nikolaev, E., Boguszewski, P., *et al.*, (2006). Between-subject transfer of emotional information evokes specific pattern of amygdala activation. *Proceedings of the National Academy of Sciences* (USA), 103:3858–3862.

Lamm, C., Decety, J., Singer, T. (2011). Meta-analytic evidence for common and distinct neural networks associated with directly experienced pain and empathy for pain. *Neuroimage*, 54:2492–2502.

Lamm, C., & Majdandzic, J. (2015). The role of shared neural activations, mirror neurons, and morality in empathy – a critical comment. *Neuroscience Research*, 90:15–24.

Lamm, C., Meltzoff, A. N., Decety, J. (2010). How do we empathize with someone who is not like us? A functional magnetic resonance imaging study. *Journal of Cognitive Neuroscience*, 22:362–376.

Langford, D. J., Crager, S. E., Shehzad, Z., *et al.*, (2006). Social modulation of pain as evidence for empathy in mice. *Science*, 312:1967–1970.

Langford, D. J., Tuttle, A .H., Briscoe, C., *et al.*, (2011). Varying perceived social threat modulates pain behavior in male mice. *The Journal of Pain*, 12:125–132.

Larson, C. L., Schaefer, H. S., Siegle, G. J., Jackson, C. A., Anderle, M. J., Davidson, R. J. (2006). Fear is fast in phobic individuals: amygdala activation in response to fear-relevant stimuli. *Biological Psychiatry*, 60:410–417.

Li, Z., Lu, Y. F., Li, C. L., *et al.* (2014), Social interaction with a cagemate in pain facilitates subsequent spinal nociception via activation of the medial prefrontal cortex in rats. *Pain*, 155(7):1253–1261.

Lockwood, P. L., Sebastian, C. L., McCrory, E. J., *et al.*, (2013). Association of callous traits with reduced neural response to others' pain in children with conduct problems. *Current Biology*, 23:901–905.

Lombardo, M. V., Chakrabarti, B., Bullmore, E. T., *et al.*, (2010). Atypical neural self-representation in autism. *Brain*, 133:611–624.

MacLean, P. D. (1985). Brain evolution relating to family, play, and the separation call. *Archives of General Psychiatry*, 42:405–417.

Marsh, A. A., Finger, E. C., Fowler, K. A., *et al.*, (2013). Empathic responsiveness in amygdala and anterior cingulate cortex in youths with psychopathic traits. *Journal of Child Psychology and Psychiatry*, 54:900–910.

Martineau, J., Schmitz, C., Assaiante, C., Blanc, R., Barthelemy, C. (2004). Impairment of a cortical event-related desynchronisation during a bimanual load-lifting task in children with autistic disorder. *Neuroscience Letters*, 367:298–303.

Meyza, K., Nikolaev, T., Kondrakiewicz, K., Blanchard, D. C., Blanchard, R. J., Knapska, E. (2015). Neuronal correlates of asocial behavior in a BTBR T (+) Itpr3(tf)/J mouse model of autism. *Frontiers in Behavioral Neuroscience*, 9:199.

Mikosz, M., Nowak, A., Werka, T., Knapska, E. (2015). Sex differences in social modulation of learning in rats. *Scientific Reports*, 5:18114.

Mitchell, J. P. (2009). Inferences about mental states. *Philosophical Transactions of the Royal Society B: Biological Sciences*, 364:1309–1316.

Mogil, J. S. (2015). Social modulation of and by pain in humans and rodents. *Pain*, 156 Suppl 1:S35–S41.

Moyaho, A., Rivas-Zamudio, X., Ugarte, A., Eguibar, J. R., Valencia, J. (2015). Smell facilitates auditory contagious yawning in stranger rats. *Animal Cognition,* 18:279–290.

Muthukumaraswamy, S. D., Johnson, B. W., McNair, N. A. (2004). Mu rhythm modulation during observation of an object-directed grasp. *Brain Research. Cognitive Brain Research*, 19:195–201.

Neary, D., Snowden, J. S., Mann, D. (2005). Frontotemporal dementia. *Lancet Neurology*, 4:771–780.

Neary, D., Snowden, J. S., Gustafson, L., *et al.*, (1998). Frontotemporal lobar degeneration: A consensus on clinical diagnostic criteria. *Neurology*, 51:1546–1554.

Norscia, I., & Palagi, E. (2011).Yawn contagion and empathy in Homo sapiens. *PLoS One*, 6:e28472.

Nummenmaa, L., Hirvonen, J., Parkkola, R., Hietanen, J. K. (2008). Is emotional contagion special? An fMRI study on neural systems for affective and cognitive empathy. *Neuroimage*, 43:571–580.

Oberman, L. M., Hubbard, E. M., McCleery, J. P., Altschuler, E. L., Ramachandran, V. S., Pineda, J. A. (2005). EEG evidence for mirror neuron dysfunction in autism spectrum disorders. *Brain Research. Cognitive Brain Research*, 24:190–198.

Oberman, L. M., Pineda, J. A., Ramachandran, V. S. (2007). The human mirror neuron system: a link between action observation and social skills. *Social Cognitive and Affective Neuroscience*, 2:62–66.

Oberman, L. M., Ramachandran, V. S., Pineda, J. A. (2008). Modulation of mu suppression in children with autism spectrum disorders in response to familiar or unfamiliar stimuli: The mirror neuron hypothesis. *Neuropsychologia,* 46:1558–1565.

Das, P., Kemp, A. H., Flynn, G., *et al.*, (2007). Functional disconnections in the direct and indirect amygdala pathways for fear processing in schizophrenia. *Schizophrenia Research*, 90:284–294.

Panksepp, J. B., & Panksepp, J. B. (2013). Towards a cross-species understanding of empathy. *Trends in Neurosciences*, 36:489–496.

Panksepp, J. B., & Lahvis, G. P. (2011). Rodent empathy and affective neuroscience. *Neuroscience & Biobehavioral Reviews*, 35:1864–1875.

Paukner, A., & Anderson, J. R. (2006). Video-induced yawning in stumptail macaques (Macaca arctoides). *Biology Letters*, 2:36–38.

Perry, A., Bentin, S., Bartal, I. B., Lamm, C., Decety, J. (2010). "Feeling" the pain of those who are different from us: Modulation of EEG in the mu/alpha range. *Cognitive, Affective, & Behavioral Neuroscience*, 10:493–504.

Perry, A., Troje, N. F., Bentin, S. (2010). Exploring motor system contributions to the perception of social information: Evidence from EEG activity in the mu/alpha frequency range. *Society Neuroscience*, 5:272–284.

Perry, A., Solbakk, A. K., Endestad, T., Saunders, S., Stiso, J., Dewar, C., & Knight, R. T. (2016). Understanding others' actions and emotions following lesions to the prefrontal cortex, with or without the inferior frontal gyrus: Evidence from EEG and behavioral studies. (In review).

Pezawas, L., Meyer-Lindenberg, A., Drabant, E. M. *et al.*, (2005). 5-HTTLPR polymorphism impacts human cingulate-amygdala interactions: A genetic susceptibility mechanism for depression. *Nature Neuroscience*, 8:828–834.

Premack, D., & Woodruff, G. (1978). Chimpanzee problem-solving: A test for comprehension. *Science*, 202:532–535.

Preston, S. D., & de Waal, F. B. M. (2002). Empathy: Its ultimate and proximate bases. *Behavioral and Brain Sciences*, 25:1–20.

Raymaekers, R., Wiersema, J. R., Roeyers, H. (2009). EEG study of the mirror neuron system in children with high functioning autism. *Brain Research*, 1304:113–121.

Reimert, I., Bolhuis, J. E., Kemp, B., Rodenburg, T. B. (2015). Emotions on the loose: Emotional contagion and the role of oxytocin in pigs. *Animal Cognition*, 18:517–532.

Rizzolatti, G., Fadiga, L., Gallese, V., Fogassi, L. (1996). Premotor cortex and the recognition of motor actions. *Brain Research. Cognitive Brain Research*, 3:131–141.

Rolls, E. T., Hornak, J., Wade, D., McGrath, J. (1994). Emotion-related learning in patients with social and emotional changes associated with frontal lobe damage. *Journal of Neurology, Neurosurgery & Psychiatry*, 57:1518–1524.

Rosen, H. J., Allison, S. C., Schauer, G. F., Gorno-Tempini, M. L., Weiner, M. W., Miller, B. L. (2005). Neuroanatomical correlates of behavioural disorders in dementia. *Brain*, 128:2612–2625.

Rosen, H. J., Perry, R. J., Murphy, J., *et al.*, (2002). Emotion comprehension in the temporal variant of frontotemporal dementia. *Brain*, 125:2286–2295.

Rozzi. S., Ferrari, P. F., Bonini, L., Rizzolatti, G., Fogassi, L. (2008). Functional organization of inferior parietal lobule convexity in the macaque monkey: Electrophysiological characterization of motor, sensory and mirror responses and their correlation with cytoarchitectonic areas. *European Journal of Neuroscience*, 28:1569–1588.

Schulte-Ruther, M., Markowitsch, H. J., Fink, G. R., Piefke, M. (2007). Mirror neuron and theory of mind mechanisms involved in face-to-face interactions: A functional magnetic resonance imaging approach to empathy. *Journal of Cognitive Neuroscience*, 19:1354–1372.

Senju, A., Southgate, V., White, S., Frith, U. (2009). Mindblind eyes: An absence of spontaneous theory of mind in Asperger syndrome. *Science*, 325:883–885.

Shamay-Tsoory, S. G., Aharon-Peretz, J., Perry, D. (2009). Two systems for empathy: A double dissociation between emotional and cognitive empathy in inferior frontal gyrus versus ventromedial prefrontal lesions. *Brain*, 132:617–627.

Shamay-Tsoory, S. G., Shur, S., Harari, H., Levkovitz, Y. (2007). Neurocognitive basis of impaired empathy in schizophrenia. *Neuropsychology*, 21:431–438.

Shamay-Tsoory, S. G., Tomer, R., Goldsher, D., Berger, B. D., Aharon-Peretz, J. (2004). Impairment in cognitive and affective empathy in patients with brain lesions: Anatomical and cognitive correlates. *Journal of Clinical and Experimental Neuropsychology*, 26:1113–1127.

Shany-Ur, T., Poorzand, P., Grossman, S. N., *et al.*, (2012). Comprehension of insincere communication in neurodegenerative disease: Lies, sarcasm, and theory of mind. *Cortex*, 48:1329–1341.

Silva, K., Bessa, J., de Sousa L. (2012). Auditory contagious yawning in domestic dogs (Canis familiaris): First evidence for social modulation. *Animal Cognition*, 15:721–724.

Simner, M. L. (1971). Newborn's response to the cry of another infant. *Developmental Psychology*, 5:136–150.

Singer, T., & Lamm, C. (2009). The social neuroscience of empathy. *Annals of the New York Academy of Sciences*, 1156:81–96.

Singer, T., Seymour, B., O'Doherty, J., Kaube, H., Dolan, R. J., Frith, C. D. (2004). Empathy for pain involves the affective but not sensory components of pain. *Science*, 303:1157–1162.

Singer, T., Seymour, B., O'Doherty, J. P., Stephan, K. E., Dolan, R. J., Frith, C. D. (2006). Empathic neural responses are modulated by the perceived fairness of others. *Nature*, 439:466–469.

Spezio, M. L., Huang, P. Y., Castelli, F., Adolphs, R. (2007). Amygdala damage impairs eye contact during conversations with real people. *Journal of Neuroscience*, 3994–3997.

Stolk, A., D'Imperio, D., di Pellegrino, G., Toni, I. (2015). Altered communicative decisions following ventromedial prefrontal lesions. *Current Biology*, 25:1469–1474.

Stone, V. E., Baron-Cohen, S., Knight, R. T. (1998). Frontal lobe contributions to theory of mind. *Journal of Cognitive Neuroscience*, 10:640–656.

Van Overwalle, F., & Baetens, K. Understanding others' actions and goals by mirror and mentalizing systems: A meta-analysis. *Neuroimage* , 48:564–584.

Wascher, C. A., Arnold, W., Kotrschal, K. (2008). Heart rate modulation by social contexts in greylag geese (Anser anser). *Journal of Comparative Psychology*, 122:100–107.

Watanabe, S. (2015). Social factors modulate restraint stress induced hyperthermia in mice. *Brain Research*, 1624:134–139.

Werner, K. H., Roberts, N. A., Rosen, H. J., *et al.*, (2007). Emotional reactivity and emotion recognition in frontotemporal lobar degeneration. *Neurology*, 69:148–155.

Wicker, B., Keysers, C., Plailly J, Royet JP, Gallese V, Rizzolatti G. (2003). Both of us disgusted in My insula: The common neural basis of seeing and feeling disgust. *Neuron*, 40:655–664.

Wilkinson, A., Sebanz, N., Mandl, I., Huber, L. (2011). No evidence of contagious yawning in the red-footed tortoise Geochelone carbonaria. *Current Zoology*, 57:477–484.

Williams, J. H., Whiten, A., Singh, T. (2004). A systematic review of action imitation in autistic spectrum disorder. *Journal of Autism and Developmental Disorders*, 34:285–299.

Yoder, K. J., Porges, E. C., Decety, J. (2015). Amygdala subnuclei connectivity in response to violence reveals unique influences of individual differences in psychopathic traits in a nonforensic sample. *Human Brain Mapping*, 36:1417–1428.

Zaki, J., Wager, T. D., Singer, T., Keysers, C., Gazzola, V. (2016). The anatomy of suffering: Understanding the relationship between nociceptive and empathic pain. *Trends in Cognitive Science*, 20:249–259.

Zaki, J., Weber, J., Bolger, N., Ochsner, K. (2009). The neural bases of empathic accuracy. *Proceedings of the National Academy of Sciences* (USA), 106:11382–11387.

PART IV

Conclusion and Summary

Part IV of this book offers the reader a glimpse into how empathy, which Eric Leake cites as the basis of morality and global responsibility, enables the promise and practice of cosmopolitan empathy. This type of empathy, Leake shows, is applicable in everyday interactions, such as conversations, and especially in education in the instruction of how we read, understand, represent, and respond to one another.

Finally, Part IVs part provides a summary of the chapters that amply illustrate the role played by what therapists and supervisors call countertransference.

CHAPTER
FOURTEEN

The Promise and Practice of Cosmopolitan Empathy

Eric Leake

Theories of empathy and cosmopolitanism may help provide information as to how people might best relate to one another personally, affectively, and ethically. Although empathy alone is insufficient for morality, its addition contributes a valuable moral foundation to cosmopolitanism in the consideration of our commitments to others, while cosmopolitanism is useful as a way of describing the world as it is, and as we might hope to make it.

The author thus defines the term "cosmopolitan empathy" as the practice of teaching and relating, which may be best characterized through the metaphor of conversation. This, he explains, is especially critical in educating students to be more aware and responsible in how they consider themselves–and act–as members of extended communities. Teaching cosmopolitanism should not be considered as a subject or content area, but rather as an ideal and a process, which is why empathy is so valuable a component of this definition.

Introduction: The promise and practice of cosmopolitan empathy

The question of how to live with others is an old one. Although it was probably always difficult, our communities now are both larger and more fractured. They extend from our families and friends to include common interest groups, neighborhoods and cities, national and international communities, culminating in the global community of all of us. Relations were once in person, so that we might see one another's face. Now we relate to others through a diverse array of communications that bridge distances even as they possibly augment misunderstandings. We read and write through social networks and digital media, often not with others directly but with second- and third-party representations, raising anew the question of how to live with others.

I turn to theories of empathy and cosmopolitanism to consider how people might best relate to one another personally, affectively, and ethically, recognizing what philosopher Kwame Appiah describes as "universality plus difference" (2007, p. 151). Cosmopolitanism is useful as a way of describing the world as it is and as we might hope to make it. I argue that empathy is a necessary component of cosmopolitanism as an ideal way of foregrounding human-centered and critically reflective modes of understanding one another. Although empathy alone is insufficient for morality, its addition contributes a valuable moral foundation to cosmopolitanism in considering our commitments to others. The practice of cosmopolitan empathy, then, is the practice of trying to encounter the world from another's perspective and situation without losing sight of that other person, for the purpose of potentially fostering greater communities amid differences. Built upon the practice of empathy, cosmopolitanism begins with attending to particular people. This practice is applicable in everyday interactions, such as conversations and the ways that we read, understand, represent, and respond to one another across media. It is especially critical in educating students to be more aware and responsible in how they consider themselves–and act–as members of extended communities.

Shared values in cosmopolitanism and empathy

To establish the mutual interests and complications of cosmopolitanism and empathy, I want to first review their definitions. Cosmopolitanism, derived from the Greek *cosmos* meaning "universe" and *polis* meaning "city" and "citizenship," refers to the idea that one is a citizen of the world, that all of the world is a shared community. Education professor Torill Strand offers a broad definition of cosmopolitanism, writing, "Cosmopolitanism expresses the idea that all human beings–regardless of national, religious, cultural, or political affiliations–should be seen as members of the same community, and that this community should be cultivated" (2010a, p. 103). With this, Strand adds, "the global village becomes the locus of ethical, political, and educational concerns". Cosmopolitanism is a complicated concept, one that sometimes contradicts itself. Appiah identifies two veins of thought in the concept:

> *One is the idea that we have obligations to others, obligations that stretch beyond those to whom we are related by the ties of kith and kind, or even the more formal ties of a shared citizenship. The other is that we take seriously the value not just of human life but of particular human lives, which means taking interest in the practices and beliefs that lend them significance.* (2007, p. xv)

Cosmopolitanism thus pairs the general with the specific in balancing universal responsibilities with particular interests. These can come into conflict, as Appiah notes: "As we'll see, there will be times when these two ideals–universal concern and respect for legitimate differences–clash. There's a sense in which cosmopolitanism is the name not of the solution but of the challenge" (p. xv).

Empathy is a critical addition to cosmopolitanism for the ways that it adds an affective charge, particular concerns, and awareness of imaginative perspective-taking. One of the most succinct definitions of empathy is provided by psychologist Martin Hoffman, who defines empathy as "an affective response more appropriate to another's situation than one's own" (2001, p. 4). Philosopher Amy Coplan's definition is also helpful; she writes that empathy is "a complex imaginative process in which an observer simulates another person's situated psychological states while maintaining a clear self-other differentiation" (2011, p. 5). Both Hoffman and Coplan include affective and cognitive components in their theories of empathy, and both emphasize the complicated questions that empathy raises regarding self- and other-identification. Empathic concern, especially in the theories of Hoffman, leads to the moral regard of others, which forms a foundation for cosmopolitanism.

One shared value of empathy and cosmopolitanism is the emphasis on the human and the particular. This is important because people relate to one another foremost as individuals, and empathy provides a mechanism for that. Appiah, for example, argues against criticism that cosmopolitanism's sense of communities is vague, abstract, and lacking significant power. "Engagement with strangers is always going to be engagement with particular strangers", he writes (2007, p. 98). For Appiah that engagement may start with abstract interests or shared identities, but it becomes more concrete when it is attached to a name, face, set of circumstances, and a body. Appiah stresses attention to the human and the particular when he writes, "Cosmopolitanism, as we've been conceiving it, starts with what is human in humanity" (p. 134). Cosmopolitanism for Appiah thus may be understood as a sense of obligations and communities, working more as a process than a realization, that depend foremost upon attention to not only who others are but how they live their lives and experience their worlds individually and communally.

By focusing on the particular and the human as a way of creating communities and understanding obligations and relations, Appiah puts cosmopolitanism in line with philosopher Arne Vetlesen's evaluation of empathy. For Vetlesen, the particular is the way in which we act upon our capacity for empathy in perceiving the human and the moral. Vetlesen sees an absence of the human dimension of a situation as part of a process of dehumanization and moral neutralization. On the perception of the human and the moral, Vetlesen writes,

> *We perceive the moral dimension of a situation by virtue of perceiving the human reality involved. This is–mutatis mutandis–to argue that processes of dehumanization are likely to lead to moral neutralization and thus to pave the way for immoral acts. I postulate a link between the human and the moral, one bearing on the connection between our being and our doing. The link is such that the perceived human reality of a situation involving the weal and woe of others addresses me, calls upon me, lays a moral obligation on me because I am, see myself as, and wish to be able to continue to see myself as a human being.* (1994, p. 178)

I read this as the same moral obligation that Appiah posits as a necessary quality of empathy. In both instances this obligation is arrived at though an attention to the particulars of human existence, what Vetlesen terms the "human reality" of a situation. Appiah likewise looks to the value of "particular human lives", and Hoffman understands a similar process of empathy to be foundational for moral development. Cosmopolitanism depends upon empathy in responding to the particulars of human existence.

A second shared value between empathy and cosmopolitanism is found in their concern with balancing regard for self and other. This balance is always in flux as it forces questions about identifications and affinities. Those questions are productive because they foreground awareness of the difficulties of empathy and cosmopolitanism. Maintaining that awareness is a crucial part of critical practice. In cosmopolitanism a tenuous balance is evident between the local and the universal. Appiah advocates a "partial cosmopolitanism" in maintaining allegiance both to the local and the universal (2007, p. xvii). Those allegiances may come into conflict with one another, but there is a benefit to recognizing the importance of the local in one's relationship to the global, because the local always informs how one relates to the global. An individual cannot be a citizen of the world without also being a citizen of one of the countries of the world–and, further down the line, a citizen of one of the regions, cities, neighborhoods, and families of the world. Those primary citizenships influence the more expansive ones.

Empathy likewise asks us to maintain a difficult balance between self and other, in terms of identifications and responsibilities. Hoffman (2001) explores this tension as he distinguishes self-focused role-taking and other-focused role-taking and expands upon empathy's biases. (In summary of those biases, we are most likely to empathize with those most like us.) In self-focused role-taking the empathizer focuses upon how she would feel in another's situation. In other-focused role-taking, the empathizer focuses on how the other person feels in a particular situation. Self-focused role-taking is more emotionally powerful but risks a disconnect with the other as it becomes more about the self. Hoffman describes this disconnect as "egoistic drift" (p. 57). The most effective way to empathize then is to manage the tension between self- and other-focused role-taking so as to enable a stronger empathic response but not one that drifts towards attention only to one's own emotions or identification with oneself in the form of another. A similar balance between self and other within empathy is considered by rhetorician Dennis Lynch (1998). Lynch considers the common description of empathy as putting yourself into another's shoes. The problem, he explains, is that in doing so you must remove the other person from the shoes, effectively erasing that individual. He argues for the value of embracing both the invitations and limitations of empathy as a way of better understanding our relations.

For empathy and cosmopolitanism the best available negotiation of this tension is a critical recognition of difference. Indeed, both empathy and cosmopolitanism depend upon difference, because without difference there is no distance to bridge, no need for communication. Empathy without difference is simply self-identification. The same holds for the importance of difference in cosmopolitanism. The balance between the local and the global, between self and other, acquires meaning and relevance precisely because of the differences among diverse communities. If there are no differences, there is only a unitary community and cosmopolitanism becomes a meaningless concept. As Kenneth Burke writes, "Rhetoric is concerned with the state of Babel after the Fall", because if there is no difference, only a common language and common understanding, then there is so need for communication across differences (1950, p. 23).The critical and paradoxical move in empathy and cosmopolitanism is to attempt to bridge differences even while recognizing that differences can never be fully bridged. Recognition of the enduring quality of differences allows for those practicing empathy and cosmopolitanism to question their moves towards understanding and to always remind themselves that the empathizer cannot know the experiences of the empathized, nor can the interests and values of the local be entirely congruent with those of other locales. Appiah places this fact as central to the understanding of the cosmopolitan, writing, "People are different, the cosmopolitan knows, and there is much to learn from our differences" (2007, p. xv). Similar value is found in empathy, where Lynch argues that empathy is meaningful exactly because of the questions it poses. He proposes "rhetorics of proximity" as a way of understanding the invitation and desire to identify with another even as that desire is necessarily frustrated by recognition of differences. As Lynch writes, "Within rhetorics of proximity, then, there are spaces for differing relations, for different kinds of listening, for differing understandings–and for keeping those differences well-lit and clear–but only, I hope I have argued, if we still make the effort to empathize" (1998, p. 20). Differences themselves acquire salience because their recognition is a necessary part of moves towards empathy and cosmopolitanism, which have meaning and purpose only insofar as they acknowledge the relevance of differences. The critical practice of cosmopolitan empathy should recognize that empathy and communities tend to be unequal. It should ask the question that literary scholar Theresa Kulbaga poses: "Empathy [and cosmopolitanism] to what end?" (2008, p. 518). If practiced with an awareness of the liabilities of empathy and the inequalities of cosmopolitanism–for example, who gets to be cosmopolitan?–cosmopolitan empathy might find value in raising the very concerns that keep processes of understanding ongoing, never complete.

Teaching and conversing: where we might begin

Cosmopolitan empathy is the practice of teaching and relating, which may be best characterized through the metaphor of conversation. To teach cosmopolitanism is not to teach it as a subject or content area. Instead it is to teach cosmopolitanism as an ideal and a process, which is why empathy is so valuable a component. Strand writes that one of the ways of understanding cosmopolitanism is as an ideal for how local and global communities might interact. This is part of an outlook in which one sees oneself as a citizen of a locality as well as of the world. In Strand's words, "As an ideal, the term 'cosmopolitanism' expresses the idea that all human beings–regardless of national, religious, cultural or political affiliation–should be seen as members of the same community, and that this community should be cultivated" (2010b, p. 232). Strand adds that "Education–as one of the most important pillars within any welfare-state–is therefore seen as a vital institution for promoting such ideals and for cultivating a cosmopolitan ethos coined with democratic literacy and ideals" (p. 233). She also notes that in an increasingly pluralistic society these ideals are also subject to contestation. One person's cosmopolitanism and valuation thereof is not always the same as another's. Similarly, philosopher Douglas Chismar argues for attention to the empathic, the particular, and the human in cosmopolitan education. This is where empathy adds method to cosmopolitanism. Chismar writes, "This suggests the need for a kind of empathic education which effectively goes beyond the kind of uninspiring memorization of capitals, geographical details and remote historical events presently making up many 'Social Studies' classes" (1988, p. 263). The type of education he and Strand suggest focuses upon individual experiences rather than abstractions, on ways of relating and understanding rather than decontextualized facts.

An educational approach that aims to develop cosmopolitanism with empathy needs to recognize the importance of historical and social context on the lives of others. The necessary evaluations for empathy, as put forth by philosopher Martha Nussbaum (2003) in relation to compassion, align strongly with ideas of cosmopolitanism. For example, for one to empathize with another's suffering, one must see the other's suffering as not the other's fault or beyond the other's control. To read this condition in the plight of another requires attention to the significance of context. Context includes those dynamic global forces that lead to suffering through historical inequities and systematic oppressions. To empathize with somebody in a distinctly different community requires some cosmopolitan work to understand how a particular place, history, and community affects another's life. By empathizing with another, one may better come to enact those cosmopolitan ideals of seeing oneself and another as part of interlocking and overlapping communities with shared human interests and a critical respect for differences.

That cosmopolitan ideal, of seeing oneself and another with shared interests and part of related communities, mirrors one of the appraisal conditions of empathy. Nussbaum refers to this condition as "eudaimonistic judgment", meaning that "this person, or creature, is a significant element in my scheme of goals and projects, an end whose good is to be promoted" (2003, p. 321). She explains,

> *The recognition of one's own related vulnerability is, then, an important and frequently an indispensable epistemological requirement for*

> *compassion in human beings – the thing that makes the difference between viewing hungry peasants as beings whose sufferings matter and viewing them as distant objects whose experiences have nothing to do with one's own life. Such a judgment is psychologically powerful in moving other people into one's own circle of concern.* (319)

Nussbaum's principle of "eudaimonistic judgment" equally applies to cosmopolitanism, as one of the basic elements of cosmopolitanism is that of "moving other people into one's own circle of concern". What empathy adds is a means of developing cosmopolitanism. There is an important pedagogical distinction to be made between telling people that they should move others into their circle of concern versus teaching them to empathize critically and reflectively with others, the act of which may move those others into another's concern. The concern is based not upon the other's use value but upon a common humanity and shared regard. Teaching to not blame victims of social circumstances and to look for shared vulnerabilities helps develop empathy and promotes cosmopolitanism ideals.

The development of cosmopolitan ideals–the hope and work of a cosmopolitanism in the making–is a pedagogical and social enterprise. Cosmopolitanism describes relations as they are as well as how we might hope them to be. It is not enough, however, to expect the adoption of cosmopolitan values simply as a result of an increasingly interconnected world in which people come into greater contact with others from different backgrounds. Cosmopolitan empathy needs to be responsibly practiced; the value is in the practice. Cross-cultural and international education has access to greater technological options today. Digitally-mediated communities have a tendency to move towards homogeneity, however, so those technological options need to be exercised towards cosmopolitan ends. Students can exchange with those in other communities across social media; or they might begin by focusing on their relations in their own class, as any given classroom already has the making of a cosmopolitan community. In communicative exchanges the emphasis should be on recognizing the personal within a historical and cultural context. The international and cross-cultural thus becomes personal through relations to specific individuals. In these relations and attempts at understanding, the limits of cosmopolitanism and the liabilities of empathy should not be minimized but emphasized as a meaningful, critical, and moral part of the process.

As a first step, cosmopolitan empathy as education and practice might begin with conversation. Like Appiah, I am thinking of conversation both as the actual act of conversing and as a metaphor for how we might engage others. Conversation requires listening, not for the purposes of judging or responding, but for understanding and taking in. A teacher preparing students to partake in this conversation, for example, might start by teaching them to listen without the necessity of response, with an ear for quiet voices and what is not said, and with sensitivity to the cultural logics, experiences, and identities that inform what is being said, in written communications as well as oral, visual, and bodily communications. I am working here with rhetorician Krista Ratcliffe's (1999) idea of "rhetorical listening", which includes listening to our own discourses as well as those of others. Conversation is an instrument for people to try to understand one another, create communities, and learn to be in one another's company. It is ongoing as a process and often is enjoyable. Conversation does not conclude with a position or an agreement so much as it promises a continuance; the process of conversing itself becomes sometimes more important than what is said. Shared understanding may result, but the initial goal is simply to engage in conversation for the sake of conversing with another. Appiah says as much in describing conversation as an imaginative process of engagement, much like empathy. "Conversation doesn't have to lead to consensus about anything, especially not values; it's enough that it helps people get used to one another", he writes (2007, p. 85). That offers a fine place to begin, in the classroom and with one another.

References

Appiah, K. A. (2007). *Cosmopolitanism: Ethics in a world of strangers*. New York, NY: W.W. Norton.

Burke, K. (1950). *A Rhetoric of Motives*. Berkeley, CA: University of California Press.

Chismar, D. (1988). Empathy and sympathy: The important difference. *The Journal of Value Inquiry, 22*, 257–266.

Coplan, A. (2011). Understanding empathy: Its features and effects. In A. Coplan & P. Goldie (Eds.). *Empathy: Philosophical and psychological perspectives* (3–18). New York, NY: Oxford University Press.

Hoffman, M. L. (2001). *Empathy and Moral Development: Implications for caring and justice*. New York, NY: Cambridge University Press.

Kulbaga, T. A. (2008). Pleasurable pedagogies: *Reading Lolita in Tehran* and the rhetoric of empathy. *College English*. *70*(5), 506–521.

Lynch, D. A. (1998). Rhetorics of proximity: Empathy in Temple Grandin and Cornel West. *Rhetoric Society Quarterly*. 28(1), 5–23.

Nussbaum, M. (2003). *Upheavals of Thought: The intelligence of emotions*. New York, NY: Cambridge University Press.

Ratcliffe, K. (1999). Rhetorical listening: A trope for rhetorical invention and a 'code of cross-cultural conduct. *College Composition and Communication. 51*(2), 195–224.
Strand, T. (2010). Introduction: Cosmopolitanism in the making. *Studies in Philosophy and Education. 29,* 103–109.
Strand, T. (2010). The making of a new cosmopolitanism. *Studies in Philosophy and Education. 29*, 229–242.
Vetlesen, A. J. (1994). Perception, empathy, and judgment: An inquiry into the preconditions of moral performance. State College, PA: Pennsylvania State University Press.

CHAPTER
FIFTEEN

Conclusions

Dov R. Aleksandrowicz

The chapters presented in this volume amply illustrate the role played by what therapists commonly call "countertransference", which, although taken literally ("reaction to transference",) frame the term as a misnomer. Therapy, especially intensive and prolonged one, as exemplified in psychoanalysis, is a deeply emotional experience, for the therapist no less than for the patient, and the relationship between the two has a critical impact on the course of therapy. Far from being a minor nuisance, a "bug" in the smooth program of the therapy process, countertransference is a principal player. The patient's transference is but a factor of countertransference, important but not exclusive. The same may be said of the therapist's conscious or unconscious needs and unresolved psychic conflicts, important as they may be.

The contributors to this volume illustrate some of these factors; one such factor is the nature of the problem that brings the patient into therapy, a factor that is amply recognized in the literature, such as papers on the treatment of psychotic patients, victims of severe trauma (e.g., childhood sexual abuse or Holocaust survivors). Very little, however, has been written on the role played by social factors, namely the attitudes of the society in which the treatment takes place to the reason the patient sought therapy. The therapist, as well as the patient, is embedded in a social fabric. His or her conscious and unconscious attitudes and values might be congruent with that of their society (for the therapist, more often than not, but in the case of the patient, this is not necessarily true) or alienated or even antagonistic. The therapist treating a Holocaust victim cannot avoid being affected by the fact that the therapy takes place in Israel, Poland, or Austria, nor can they ignore the fact that the therapist may be Jewish or non-Jewish. The same applies to potentially conflictual issues such as race (see Sikora, Chapter Three of this volume) or that of gender identity (Pfäfflin, Chapter Nine of this volume), which describes the evolution of the author's own attitude towards gender identity, paralleling the evolution of Western societies' attitudes. Many of these issues are emotionally highly charged; the therapist cannot avoid feeling strongly about these issues and in such cases, "emotional neutrality" might be more of a myth than a reality. The therapist (and his or her supervisor) may be aware of his or her attitude, and yet not to appreciate its impact on the countertransference.

The colleagues we have invited to contribute to this book do not merely engage in different clinical areas; they also come from different backgrounds and operate in different circumstances. By including this diversity, we hoped to better demonstrate what countertransference tells us about who we are and how it can best tell us how to relate to "the Other" (*autrui*, as coined by the French philosopher Emmanuel Lévinas (Lévinas, 1961). In this we have been richly rewarded; by sharing their experiences with the reader in a frank and unedited discussion, the authors have provided us with a broad perspective of a deceptively simple concept.

The other aspect of countertransference emphasized in this volume is its compelling nature, which is made clear through an understanding of the biology and neuropsychology of the process. Sharing of emotions and building relationships based on emotions is what makes us capable of creating societies, a characteristic of our mammalian heritage. Countertransference, therefore, is one more example of how psychoanalytic theory can expand its perspective by drawing on insight from biology. At the same time, psychoanalysis provides biology and neuropsychology with a rich repertoire of intriguing questions that can lead to fertile research.

There was a time in the last century when it seemed that psychoanalysis had exhausted the scope of insight that could be learned from its method of data collection (Freud, 1914; Kandel, 1999). We hope that this volume will serve as an model, by expanding the scope of this field's study and enriching itself, drawing on knowledge from social and biological sciences, psychoanalysis remains as vital and relevant as ever.

References

Freud, S. (1957). *On Narcissism: An introduction*, Standard Edition. vol. 14. London, Hogarth Press. (Original work published 1914). 67–102.

Kandel, E. R. (1999). Biology and the future of psychoanalysis: A new intellectual framework for psychiatry revisited, *American Journal of Psychiatry*, Volume 156 Issue 4, April. 505–524

Lévinas, E. (1961). *Totalité et Infini: Essai sur l'extériorité,* Paris: Le Livré de Poche.

Consolidated Bibliography

Abraham, F. (1931). Genitalumwandlung an zwei männlichen Transvestiten (The transformation of genitals in two male transvestites). *Zeitschrift für Sexualwissenschaft und Sexualpolitik, 18*: 223–226.

Acebo, C., Thoman, E. B. (1995). Role of infant crying in the early mother-infant dialogue. *Physiology & Behavior*, 57:541– 547.

Acher, R., Chauvet, J., Chauvet, M. T. (1995). Man and the chimaera. Selective versus neutral oxytocin evolution. *Advances in Experimental Medicine and Biology*, 395:615–627.

Ackerl, I. (1999). *Vienna modernism: 1890–1910.* Vienna: Federal Press Service.

Adolphs. R. (2010). What does the amygdala contribute to social cognition? *Annals of the New York Academy of Sciences*, 1191:42–61.

Adolphs. R., Tranel, D., Damasio, H., Damasio, A. (1994). Impaired recognition of emotion in facial expressions following bilateral damage to the human amygdala. *Nature*, 372:669– 672.

Adolphs. R., Tranel, D., Hamann, S., *et al.*, (1999). Recognition of facial emotion in nine individuals with bilateral amygdala damage. *Neuropsychologia*, 37:1111–1117.

Agazarian, I., & Peters, R. (1981). *The Visible and Invisible Group*. London: Routledge & Kegan.

Aleksandrowicz, D. R. (1978). Interminable mourning as a family process. *Israel Annals of Psychiatry & Related Disciplines*, 16(2), 161–169.

Aleksandrowicz, D. R. (1980). Family split as a result of mourning. *Interaction*, 3(2), 85–91.

Aleksandrowicz, M. K., & Aleksandrowicz, D. R. (1975). The molding of personality: A newborn's innate characteristics in interaction with parents' personalities, *Child Psychiatry & Human Development, 5*/4: 231–241.

Alighieri, D. (2009). Inferno. In *The Divine Comedy*, Vol. I, Canto 1. Trans. H.W. Longfellow, Project Gutenberg. (Original work published circ. 1308–21).

Allen, B., Nowak, M. A., Wilson, E. O. (2013). Limitations of inclusive fitness. *Proceedings of the National Academy of Sciences* (U.S.A.), 110(50):20135–20139.

Almodavar, P. (Dir.) (2006). *Volver*. Spain.

Anacker, A. M., & Beery, A. K. (2013). Life in groups: The roles of oxytocin in mammalian sociality. *Frontiers in Behavioral Neuroscience*, 7:185.

Anderson, S. W., & Tranel, D. (1989). Awareness of disease states following cerebral infarction, dementia, and head trauma: Standardized assessment. *The Clinical Neuropsychologist, 3*, 327–339.

Anzieu, D. (1989). Beckett and Bion. *International Review of Psycho-Analysis, 16*, 163–169.

Appiah, K. A. (2007). *Cosmopolitanism: Ethics in a world of strangers*. New York, NY: W.W. Norton.

Apter A., Bleich, A., King, R. A., Kron, S., Fluch, A., Kotler, M., Cohen, D. J. (1993). Death without warning? A clinical postmortem study of suicide in 43 Israeli adolescent males. *Archives of General Psychiatry*, Feb; 50(2), 138–42.

Aron, L. (1991). The patient's experience of the analyst's subjectivity. *Psychoanalytic Dialogues, 1*(1), 29–51.

Aron, L. (1996). *A Meeting of Minds: Mutuality in psychoanalysis*: Hillsdale, NJ: The Analytic Press.

Aron, L. (1998). "Yours, thirsty for honesty, Ferenczi": Some background to Sándor Ferenczi's pursuit of mutuality. *The American Journal of Psychoanalysis, 58*(1), 5–20.

Atsak, P., Orre, M., Bakker, P., *et al.*, (2011). Experience modulates vicarious freezing in rats: A model for empathy. *PLoS One*, 6:e21855.

Avenanti, A., Sirigu, A., Aglioti, S. M. (2010). Racial bias reduces empathic sensorimotor resonance with other-race pain. *Current Biology*, 20(11):1018–1022.

Baddeley, A. D., & Hitch, G. J. (1974). Working memory. In G. H. Bower (Ed.). *The Psychology of Learning and Motivation: Advances in research and theory. Vol. 8* (pp. 47–89). New York, NY: Academic Press.

Balint, M. (1957). *The Doctor, his Patient and the Illness*. Oxford: International Universities Press.

Baron-Cohen, E., Tager-Flusberg, H., Cohen, D. J. (Eds.). (2000). *Understanding Other Minds: Perspectives from developmental cognitive neuroscience* (Second Edition.). (pp. 3–20). New York, NY: Oxford University Press, xix, 530 pp.

Baron-Cohen, S. (2000). Theory of mind and autism: A fifteen year review. In S. Baron-Cohen, H. Tager-Flusberg, & D. Cohen. (Eds), (2000). *Understanding Other Minds: Perspectives from developmental cognitive neuroscience* (Second Edition.). (pp. 3–20). New York, NY: Oxford University Press, xix, 530 pp.

Baron-Cohen, S. (2001). Theory of mind in normal development and autism. *Prisme, 34*, 174–183.

Baron-Cohen, S., Leslie, A.M., Frith, U. (1985). Does the autistic child have a "theory of mind"? *Cognition*, 21:37–46.

Bartlett, M. Y., & DeSteno, D. (2006). Gratitude and pro-social behavior: helping when it costs you. *Psychological Science*,17(4):319–325

Batson, C. D., Fultz, J., Schoenrade, P. A. (1987). Distress and empathy: two qualitatively distinct vicarious emotions with different motivational consequences. *Journal of Personality*, 55(1):19–39.

Batson, C. D., Fultz, J., Schoenrade, P. A. (1987). Distress and empathy: Two qualitatively distinct vicarious emotions with different motivational consequences. *Journal of Personality*, 55:19–39.

Beer, J. S., Heerey, E.A., Keltner. D., Scabini, D., Knight, R. T. (2003). The regulatory function of self-conscious emotion: Insights from patients with orbitofrontal damage. *Journal of Personality and Social Psychology*, 85:594–604.

Beer, J. S., John, O. P., Scabini, D., Knight, R. T. (2006). Orbitofrontal cortex and social behavior: Integrating self-monitoring and emotion-cognition interactions *Journal of Cognitive Neuroscience*, 18:871–879.

Beery, A. K., McEwen, L. M., MacIsaac, J. L., Francis, D. D., Kobor, M. S. (2016). Natural variation in maternal care and cross-tissue patterns of oxytocin receptor gene methylation in rats. *Hormones and Behavior*, 77:42–52.

Beery, A.K,, & Kaufer, D. (2015). *Stress, Social Behavior, and Resilience: Insights from rodents. Neurobiology of Stress*, 1:116–127.

Ben-Ami, B. I., Decety, J., Mason, P. (2011). Empathy and pro-social behavior in rats. *Science,* Vol. 334/6061:1427–1430

Ben-Ami, B. I., Haozhe, S., Molasky, N., *et al.* (2016). Anxiolytic treatment impairs helping behavior in rats. *Frontiers in Psychology*, http://dx.doi.org/10.3389/fpsyg.2016.00850.

Ben-Ami, B. I., Rodgers, D. A., Bernardez-Sarria, M. S., Decety, J., Mason, P. (2014). Pro-social behavior in rats is modulated by social experience. *Elife*, 3:e01385.

Benjamin, H. (1964 a). Nature and management of transsexualism. With a report on thirty-one operated cases. *Western Journal of Surgery, 72*: 105–111.

Benjamin, H. (1964 b). Transsexualismus. Wesen und Behandlung (Transsexualism. Its nature and its treatment). *Nervenarzt, 35*: 499–500.

Benjamin, H. (1964 c). Clinical aspects of transsexualism in the male and female. *American Journal of Psychotherapy, 18*: 458–469.

Benjamin, H. (1966). *The Transsexual Phenomenon: A scientific report on transsexualism and sex conversion in the human male and female.* New York, NY: Julian Press.

Benjamin, H. (1953). Transvestism and transsexuals. *International Journal of Sexology* 7: 12–14.

Benjamin, H. (1956). Trans-sexualism and transvestism. In D. Cauldwell (Ed.) *Transvestism: Men in female dress*. 15–22. New York (NY): Sexology Corporation.

Benjamin, J. (1988). The bonds of love: Psychoanalysis, feminism, and the problem of domination. New York, NY: Pantheon.

Bergan, J. F., Ben-Shaul, Y., Dulac, C. (2014). Sex-specific processing of social cues in the medial amygdala. *Elife*, 3:e02743.

Berger, E. & Rieger, E. (Eds.). (2007). Verfolgte Kindheit: Kinder und Jugendliche als Opfer der NS-Sozialverwaltung. Wien/Köln/Weimar: Böhlau.

Bernstein, J. W. (1999). Countertransference: Our new royal road to the unconscious? *Psychoanalytic Dialogues*, *9*(3), 275–299.

Bettelheim, B. (1979). *Surviving and Other Essays*. London: Thames and Hudson.

Billow, R. M. (2000). Bion's "passion": The analyst's pain. *Contemporary Psychoanalysis*, *36*(3), 411–426.

Bion, W. R. (1954). Notes on the theory of schizophrenia. *The International Journal of Psycho-Analysis*, *35*, 113–118.

Bion, W. R. (1961). *Experiences in Groups and Other papers*. London: Tavistock.

Bion, W. R. (1970). *Attention and Interpretation: A scientific approach to insight in psycho-analysis and groups*. London: Tavistock.

Bion, W. R. (1979). Making the best of a bad job. *Bulletin of the British Psychoanalytic Society*, 10:15.

Bion, W. R. (1984). *Elements of Psychoanalysis*. London: Karnac Books.

Bion, W. R. (1990). *Brazilian Lectures: 1973*, São Paulo; 1974, Rio de Janeiro/São Paulo. London: Karnac Books.

Blair, R. J. (2007). The amygdala and ventromedial prefrontal cortex in morality and psychopathy. *Trends in Cognitive Science*, 11:387–392.

Bloom, S. L. (1998). By the crowd they have been broken, by the crowd they shall be healed: The social transformation of trauma. In R. G. Tedeschi, C. L. Park & L. G. Calhoun (Eds.). *Posttraumatic Growth: Positive changes in the aftermath of crisis* (pp. 179–213). Mahwah (NJ): Lawrence Erlbaum Associates, Publishers.

Bollas, C. (1983). Expressive uses of the countertransference: Notes to the patient from oneself. *Contemporary Psychoanalysis*, *19*(1), 1–34.

Boschan, P. J. (2011). Transference and countertransference in Sándor Ferenczi's clinical diary. *The American Journal of Psychoanalysis*, *71*(4), 309–320.

Boss, M. (1950–1951). Erwiderung zum Bericht über mein Referat auf der 66. Wanderversammlung der süddeutschen Psychiater und Neurologen in Badenweiler. (Reply to the report on my presentation at the 66th Conference of the South German Psychiatrists and Neurologists in Badenweiler). *Psyche – Zeitschrift für Psychoanalyse und ihre Anwendungen, 4*: 394–400.

Boszormenyi-Nagy, I., & Spark, G. M. (1973). *Invisible Loyalties: Reciprocity in intergenerational family therapy*. Hagerstown, MD: Harper & Row.

Bowlby, J. (1951). *Maternal Care and Mental Health*. Geneva: WHO.

Bowlby, J. (1958). The nature of the child's tie to his mother. *International Journal of Psychoanalysis*, 39:350–373.

Boxer, A. L., & Miller, B. L. (2005). Clinical features of frontotemporal dementia. *Alzheimer Disease and Associated Disorders*, 19 Suppl. 1:S3–S6.

Brainin, E. & Teicher, S. (1997). Time heals no wounds. In L. Hunt, M. Marshall, & C. Rowlings (Eds.) *Past Trauma in Late Life: European perspectives on therapeutic work with older people*. London: Jessica Kingsley Publishers.

Brainin, E. & Teicher, S. (2008). The terror from the outside – child survivors of the *Spiegelgrund* traumatic experiences in childhood and their effects. *Praxis der Kinderpsychologie und Kinderpsychiatrie*, *58*(7); 530–552.

Brainin, E. (2001). Entschädigung – Wiedergutmachung oder erneute Traumatisierung (Indemnification – compensation or another traumatisation). In S. Horn & P. Malina (Eds.) *Medizin im Nationalsozialismus (Medicine in National Socialism): Wege der Aufbereitung/Wiener Gespräche zur Sozialgeschichte der Medizin*. Vienna: Press and Publications Office of the Austrian Medical Board.

Brainin, E., Ligeti, V., & Teicher, S. (1993). *Vom Gedanjken zur Tat. Zur Psychoanalyse des Antisemitismus*. Frankfurt am Main: Brandes & Apsel.

Brand, S. R., Schechter, J. C., Hammen, C. L., Brocque, R. L., Brennan, P. A. (2011). Do adolescent offspring of women with PTSD experience higher levels of chronic and episodic stress?. *Journal of Traumatic Stress*, 24(4): 399–404.

Braude, S. E. (2000). Dissociation and latent abilities: The strange case of Patience Worth. *Journal of Trauma & Dissociation*, 1(2), 13–48.

Brenman, E. (2006). The recovery of the good object relationship: The conflict with the superego. In G. Fornari Spoto (Ed.) *Recovery of the Lost Good Object*. London: Routledge.

Brenman-Pick, I. (2012). Working through in the counter transference – second thoughts, *Bulletin of the British Psychoanalytic Society*, 48: 3–9.

Briere, J., & Elliott, D. M. (2003). Prevalence and psychological sequelae of self-reported childhood physical and sexual abuse in a general population sample of men and women. *Child Abuse & Neglect*, *27*(10), 1205–1222.

Britton, R., & Steiner, J. (1994). Interpretation: Selected fact or overvalued idea? *International Journal of Psychoanalysis*, 75: 1069–1078.

Bromberg, P. M. (2011). The shadow of the tsunami: And the growth of the relational mind. New York, NY: Routledge.

Bronstein, C. (2013). Finding unconscious phantasy in the session: Recognizing form. *Bulletin of the British Psychoanalytic Society*, 49, 14–21.

Bruchey, A. K., Jones, C. E., Monfils, M. H. (2010). Fear conditioning by-proxy: Social transmission of fear during memory retrieval. *Behavioural Brain Research*, 214:80–84.

Buccino, G., Binkofski, F., Fink, G. R., *et al.*, (2001). Action observation activates premotor and parietal areas in a somatotopic manner: An fMRI study. European Journal of Neuroscience, 13:400–404.

Buccino, G., Vogt, S., Ritzl, A., *et al.*, (2004). Neural circuits underlying imitation learning of hand actions: An event-related fMRI study. *Neuron*, 42:323–334.

Buckner, R.L., & Carroll, D. C. (2007). Self-projection and the brain. Trends in *Cognitive Science*, 11:49–57.

Buffone, A. E., & Poulin, M. J. (2014). Empathy, target distress, and neurohormone genes interact to predict aggression for others-even without provocation. *Personality and Social Psychology Bulletin*, 40(11):1406–1422.

Burke, K. (1950). *A Rhetoric of Motives*. Berkeley, CA: University of California Press.

Burkett, J. P., Andari, E., Johnson, Z. V., Curry, D. C., de Waal, F. B. M., Young, L. J. (2016). Oxytocin-dependent consolation behavior in rodents. *Science,* 351(6271):375–378.

Burt, M. R., & Katz, B. L. (1987). Dimensions of recovery from rape focus on growth outcomes. *Journal of Interpersonal Violence, 2*(1), 57–81.

Calhoun, L. G., & Tedeschi, R. G. (1989–1990). Positive aspects of critical life problems: Recollections of grief. *Omega – Journal of Death and Dying, 20*(4), 265–272.

Calhoun, L. G., & Tedeschi, R. G. (1990). Positive aspects of critical life problems: Recollections of grief. *Omega – Journal of Death and Dying, 20*(4), 265–272.

Calhoun, L. G., & Tedeschi, R. G. (2006). *Handbook of Posttraumatic Growth: Research and practice*. New York, NY: Routledge.

Calhoun, L. G., Tedeschi, R. G., & Tedeschi, R. G. (1999). *Facilitating Posttraumatic Growth: A clinician's guide*. New York, NY: Routledge.

Call, J., & Tomasello, M. (2008). Does the chimpanzee have a theory of mind? 30 years later. *Trends in Cognitive Science,*12:187–192.

Camp, N. (1993). The Vietnam War and the ethics of combat psychiatry. *The American Journal of Psychiatry,* Vol. 150 (7), 1000–1010.

Campbell, M. W., & de Waal, F. B. M. (2011). Ingroup-outgroup bias in contagious yawning by chimpanzees supports link to empathy. *PLoS One*, 6:e18283.

Campbell, M. W., Carter, J. D., Proctor, D., Eisenberg, M. L., de Waal, F. B. M. (2009). Computer animations stimulate contagious yawning in chimpanzees. *Proceedings of the Royal Society B: Biological Sciences,* 276:4255–4259.

Carpenter, M., Nagell, K., Tomasello, M. (1998). Social cognition, joint attention, and communicative competence from 9 to 15 months of age. *Monographs of the Society for Research in Child Development*, 63:i–143.

Carter, C.S. (1998). Neuroendocrine perspectives on social attachment and love. *Psychoneuroendocrinology*, 23(8):779–818.

Carter, C.S. Harri, J., and Porges, S.W. (2009). Neural and evolutionary perspectives on empathy. In W. Ickes & J. Decety (Eds.). *The Social Neuroscience of Empathy*. Cambridge, MA: The MIT Press.169–182.

Carter, S., Ben-Ami, B. I., Porges, E. (2016). The roots of compassion: An evolutionary and neurobiological perspective. *The Oxford Handbook of Compassion*. New York, NY: Oxford University Press (Manuscript in progress).

Carveth, D.L. (2012). Concordant and complementary countertransference: A clarification. *Canadian Journal of Psychoanalysis*, 20, 70–84.

Castelli, F., Frith, C., Happé, F., Frith, U. (2002). Autism, Asperger syndrome and brain mechanisms for the attribution of mental states to animated shapes. *Brain*. 125:1839–1849.

Chakrabarti, B., Bullmore, E., Baron-Cohen, S. (2006). Empathizing with basic emotions: Common and discrete neural substrates. *Society of Neuroscience*,1:364–384.

Chalyan, V. G., Pachuliya, I. G., Meishvili, N. V., Rozhkova, Y. Y. (2012). The structure-forming function of grooming in Hamadryas baboons. *Neuroscience and Behavioral Physiology*, Volume 42, Issue 2, 200–204.

Chasseguet-Smirgel, J. (2000). Trauma ét croyance. *Revue Française de Psychanalyse*. LXIV: 39–46. Paris: Presses Universitaires de France.

Chen, Q., Panksepp, J. B., Lahvis, G. P. (2009). Empathy is moderated by genetic background in mice. *PLoS One*, 4:e4387.

Cheng, Y., Hung, A. Y., Decety, J. (2012). Dissociation between affective sharing and emotion understanding in juvenile psychopaths. *Development and Psychopathology*, 24:623–636.

Cheng, Y., Lee, P. L., Yang, C. Y., Lin, C. P., Hung, D., Decety, J. (2008). Gender differences in the mu rhythm of the human mirror-neuron system. *PLoS One*, 3:e2113.

Cheng, Y., Yang, C. Y., Lin, C. P., Lee, P. L., Decety, J. (2008). The perception of pain in others suppresses somatosensory oscillations: A magnetoencephalography study. *Neuroimage*, 40:1833–1840.

Chismar, D. (1988). Empathy and sympathy: The important difference. *The Journal of Value Inquiry, 22,* 257–266.

Chu, J. A., & Dill, D. L. (1990). Dissociative symptoms in relation to childhood physical and sexual abuse. *The American Journal of Psychiatry, 147*(7), 887–892.

Church, R. M. (1959). Emotional reactions of rats to the pain of others. *Journal of Comparative and Physiological Psychology*, 52:132–134.

Cikara, M., Botvinick, M. M., Fiske, S. T. (2011). Us versus them: Social identity shapes neural responses to intergroup competition and harm. *Psychological Science*, 22(3):306–313.

Clay, Z., & de Waal, F. B. M. (2013). Development of socio-emotional competence in bonobos. *Proceedings of the National Academy of Sciences* (USA), 110(45):18121–18126.

Cochin, S., Barthelemy, C., Lejeune, B., Roux, S., Martineau, J. (1998). Perception of motion and qEEG activity in human adults. *Electroencephalography and Clinical Neurophysiolog*, 107:287–295.

Cochin, S., Barthelemy, C., Roux, S., Martineau, J. (1999). Observation and execution of movement: Similarities demonstrated by quantified electroencephalography. *European Journal of Neuroscience*, 11:1839–1842.

Coplan, A. (2011). Understanding empathy: Its features and effects. In A. Coplan & P. Goldie (Eds.). *Empathy: Philosophical and psychological perspectives* (3–18). New York, NY: Oxford University Press.

Cowell, J. M., & Decety, J. (2015). Precursors to morality in development as a complex interplay between neural, socioenvironmental, and behavioral facets. *Proceedings of the National Academy of Sciences* (USA), 112:12657–12662.

Cowell, R. (1954). *Roberta Cowell's Story*. New York, NY: British Book Centre, Inc.

Cronin, K. A. (2012). Pro-social behavior in animals: The influence of social relationships, communication and rewards. *Animal Behaviour*, 84, 1085–1093.

Cuff, B. M. P., Brown, S. J., Tayor, L., Howat, D. J. (2016). Empathy: A review of the concept. *Emotion Review*, 8:144–153.

Dalenberg, C. (2000). *Countertransference and the Treatment of Trauma*. Washington, DC: American Psychological Association.

Dalton. K. M., Nacewicz, B. M., Johnstone, T., *et al.*, (2005). Gaze fixation and the neural circuitry of face processing in autism. *Nature Neuroscience*, 8:519–526.

Damasio, A. (2000). *The Feeling of what Happens: Body, emotion and the making of consciousness*. London: Vintage Press.

Damasio, A. (2010). *Self Comes to Mind: Constructing the conscious brain*. London: William Heinemann.

Damasio, A. R., & Van Hoesen, G. W. (1983). Emotional disturbances associated with focal lesions of the limbic frontal lobe. In K. Heilman & P. Satz (Eds.). *Neuropsychology of Human Emotion*. New York, NY: Guilford Press.

Danieli, Y. (1980). Counter-transference in the treatment and study of Nazi Holocaust survivors and their children. *Victimology: An International Journal*, 5/2-4, 355–367.

Danieli, Y. (1981). Differing adaptation styles in families of survivors of the Nazi Holocaust. *Child Today*, 10: 6–10.

Danieli, Y. (1994). Countertransference, trauma and training. In J. P. Wilson & J. D. Lindy (Eds.). *Countertransference in the Treatment of PTSD*. New York, NY: Guilford Press. 368–388.

Danieli, Y. (2015). The Danieli inventory of multigenerational legacies of trauma, Part I: Survivors' posttrauma adaptational styles in their children's eyes. *Journal of Psychiatric Research*, 68:167–175.

Dapretto, M., Davies, M. S., Pfeifer, J. H., *et al.*, (2006). Understanding emotions in others: Mirror neuron dysfunction in children with autism spectrum disorders. Nature *Neuroscience*, 9:28–30.

Darwin, C. (1871). *The Descent of Man, and Selection in Relation to Sex*. Princeton, NJ: Princeton University Press.

Das, P., Kemp, A. H., Flynn, G., *et al.*, (2007). Functional disconnections in the direct and indirect amygdala pathways for fear processing in schizophrenia. *Schizophrenia Research*, 90:284–294.

Dasberg, H. (1993). How psychotherapists cope with their patients' trauma. In S. Robinson (Ed.). *Echoes of the Holocaust: Bulletin of the Jerusalem Center for Research into the Late Effects of the Holocaust*. Jerusalem: Talbieh Mental Health Center. 31–45.

Dasberg, H., Bartura, J., Amit, Y. (2001). Narrative group therapy with ageing child survivors of the Holocaust. *Israel Journal of Psychiatry and Related Sciences,* 38: 27–35.

Davids, F. (2011). *Internal Racism: A psychoanalytic approach to race and difference.* Basingstoke (UK): Palgrave Macmillan.

Davies, J. M. (1994). Love in the afternoon: A relational reconsideration of desire and dread in the countertransference. *Psychoanalytic Dialogues*, *4*(2), 153–170.

Davies, J. M. (2004). Whose bad objects are we anyway? Repetition and our elusive love affair with evil. *Psychoanalytic Dialogues, 14*(6), 711–732.

Davies, J. M., & Frawley, M. G. (1992). Dissociative processes and transference countertransference paradigms in the psychoanalytically oriented treatment of adult survivors of childhood sexual abuse. *Psychoanalytic Dialogues, 2*(1), 5–36.

Davies, J. M., & Frawley, M. G. (1994). Treating the adult survivor of childhood sexual abuse: A psychoanalytic perspective. New York (NY): Basic Books.

Davis, C. G., & McKearney, J. M. (2003). How do people grow from their experience with trauma or loss?. *Journal of Social and Clinical Psychology, 22*(5), 477–492.

De Waal, F. B. M. (2008). Putting the altruism back into altruism: The evolution of empathy. *Annual Review of Psychology,* 8;59:279–300.

Decety, J., & Jackson, P. L. (2004).The functional architecture of human empathy. *Behavioral and Cognitive Neuroscience Reviews*, 3(2):71–100.

Decety, J., & Svetlova, M. (2012). Putting together phylogenetic and ontogenetic perspectives on empathy. *Developmental Cognitive Neuroscience,* 2(1) (Jan.):1–24.

Decety, J., Bartal, I. B., Uzefovsky, F., Knafo-Noam, A. (2015). Empathy as a driver of pro-social behaviour: Highly conserved neurobehavioural mechanisms across species. *Philosophical Transactions of the Royal Society of London*, 371(1686).

Decety, J., Chaminade, T., Grezes, .J, Meltzoff, A. N. (2002). A PET exploration of the neural mechanisms involved in reciprocal imitation. *Neuroimage,* 15:265–272.

Decety, J., Michalska, K. J., Akitsuki, Y., Lahey, B. B. (2009). Atypical empathic responses in adolescents with aggressive conduct disorder: a functional MRI investigation. *Biological Psychology*, 80(2):203–211.

Decety, J., Yang, C. Y., Cheng, Y. (2010). Physicians down-regulate their pain empathy response: An event-related brain potential study. *Neuroimage,* 50:1676–1682.

Dekel, S., Ein-Dor, T., & Solomon, Z. (2012). Posttraumatic growth and posttraumatic distress: A longitudinal study. *Psychological Trauma: Theory, Research, Practice, and Policy, 4*(1), 94–101.

Di Pellegrino, G. ., Fadiga, L., Fogassi, L., Gallese, V., Rizzolatti, G. (1992). Understanding motor events: A neurophysiological study. *Experimental Brain Research*, 91:176–180.

Doidge, N. (2015). *The Brain's Way of Healing*. New York, NY: Penguin Random House.

Dolan, Y. (1991). *Resolving Sexual Abuse: Solution focused therapy and Ericksonian hypnosis for adult survivors*. London: Norton.

Dolen, G., Darvishzadeh, A., Huang, K.W., Malenka, R. C. (2013). Social reward requires coordinated activity of nucleus accumbens oxytocin and serotonin. *Nature*, 501(7466):179–184.

Dose, R. (2014). *Magnus Hirschfeld: The origins of the gay liberation movement*. New York, NY: Monthly Review Press.

Draucker, C. B. (1992). Construing benefit from a negative experience of incest. *Western Journal of Nursing Research, 14*(3), 343–353.

Dugatkin, L. A. (1997). Animal cooperation among animals: An evolutionary perspective. New York, NY: Oxford University Press.

Durst, N. (2003). Child survivors of the Holocaust: Age specific traumatization and the consequences for therapy. *American Journal of Psychotherapy*, 57: 499 – 518.

Eaton, C. (1963). The leaven of democracy: The growth of the democratic spirit in the time of Jackson. New York, NY: G. Braziller.

Echols, S., & Correll, J. (2012). It's more than skin deep: Empathy and helping behavior across social groups. In J. Decety (Ed.). *Empathy: From bench to bedside*. Cambridge, MA: MIT Press, 55–71.

Edelman, A., & Tadir, M. (2007). The chocolate experience: A new therapeutic workshop. *Psychoactualia*. (In Hebrew).

Edgar, J. L., Lowe, J. C., Paul, E. S., Nicol, C. J. (2011). Avian maternal response to chick distress. *Proceedings of the Royal Society B: Biological Sciences*, 278:3129–3134.

Edgerton, M. (1973). Introduction. In D. Laub & P. Gandy (Eds.). *Proceedings of the Second Interdisciplinary Symposium on Gender Dysphoria Syndrome*. 1–14. Stanford, CA: University of California Press.

Eisenberg, N., Miller, P. A., Fultz, J., Shell, F., *et al.*, (1989). Relation of sympathy and personal distress to pro-social behavior: A multimethod study. *Journal of Personality and Social Psychology*, 57:55–66.

Eisler, J. (2006). *Polski rok 1968. (Polish year 1986)*. Warszawa: Instytut Pamięci Narodowej Komisja Ścigania Zbrodni Przeciwko Narodowi Polskiemu.

Eissler, K. R., (1963): "Die Ermordung von wievielen seiner Kinder muß ein Mensch symptomfrei ertragen können, um eine normale Konstitution zu haben?" (How many murders of his children does a human being have to bear without symptoms in order to be considered of normal constitution?). *Psyche*. 5/17: 241–291. Stuttgart: Klett-Cotta.

Ekins, R., & King, D. (Eds.) (2005). *Virginia Prince: Pioneer of transgendering*. Binghamton, NY: Haworth Press. Simultaneously publishes as special issue *of the International Journal of Transgenderism*, vol. 8, nr. 4, 2005.

Ekins, R., & King, D. (1996). *Blending Genders: Social aspects of cross-dressing and sex-changing*. London, New York: Routledge.

Ekins, R., & King, D. (2006). *The Transgender Phenomenon*. Thousand Oaks, CA: Sage.

Elbe, L. (2004). *Ein Mensch wechselt sein Geschlecht. Eine Lebensgeschichte. Aus hinterlassenen Papieren herausgegeben von Niels Hoyer. Dresden: Carl Reissner-Verlag. (Man into Woman. The first sex change. A portrait of Lili Elbe. The true and remarkable transformation of the painter Einar Wegener.* N. Hoyer (Ed.). London: Blue Boat Books. (Original work was published in 1932; original English edition was published in1933).

English, O. S., & Pearson, G. H. J. (1937). *Common Neuroses of Children and Adults*. New York, NY: W. W. Norton & Co.

Erikson, E. H. (1970). Autobiographic notes on the identity crisis. *Daedalus*, *99*(4), 730–759.

Eslinger, P. J. (1998). Neurological and neuropsychological bases of empathy. *European Neurology*, 39:193–199.

Eslinger, P. J., Flaherty-Craig, C. V., Benton, A. L. (2004). Developmental outcomes after early prefrontal cortex damage. *Brain and Cognition*, 55:84–103.

Etchegoyen, R. H. (2005). *The Fundamentals of Psychoanalytic Technique*. London: Karnac Books.

Faye, J. (2014). Copenhagen interpretation of quantum mechanics. In E. Zalta (Ed.), *The Stanford Encyclopedia of Philosophy* (Fall 2014 Edition). Retrieved from http://plato.stanford.edu/archives/fall2014/entries/qm-copenhagen/.

Febo, M., & Ferris, C. F. (2014). Oxytocin and vasopressin modulation of the neural correlates of motivation and emotion: Results from functional MRI studies in awake rats. *Brain Research*, 1580:8–21.

Feder, A., Southwick, S. M., Goetz, R. R., Wang, Y., Alonso, A., Smith, B. W., *et al.*, (2008). Posttraumatic growth in former Vietnam prisoners of war. *Psychiatry, 71*, 359–370.

Feldman, M. (2009). The problem with conviction in the session. In B. Joseph (Ed.), *Doubt, Conviction and the Analytic Process*. London: Routledge.

Feldman, R., Monakhov, M., Pratt, M., Ebstein, R. P. (2016). Oxytocin pathway genes: Evolutionary ancient system impacting on human affiliation, sociality, and psychopathology. *Biological Psychiatry*, 79(3):174–184.

Ferenczi, S. (1931). Child-analysis in the analysis of adults. *International Journal of Psychoanalysis, 12*, 468–482.

Ferenczi, S. (1932). *The Clinical Diary of Sandor Ferenczi* (M. Balint & N. Z. Jackson, Trans.). Cambridge, MA: Harvard University Press.

Ferenczi, S. (1949). Confusion of the tongues between the adults and the child – (the language of tenderness and of passion). *International Journal of Psycho-Analysis, 30*, 225–230.

Ferenczi, S., & Rank, O. (1988). The development of psychoanalysis: A historical critical retrospect. In B. Wolstein (Ed.), *Essential Papers on Countertransference* (pp. 25–35). New York, NY: New York University Press. (Original work published in 1925).

Ferris, C. F., Yee, J. R., Kenkel, W. M., *et al.* (2015). Distinct BOLD activation profiles following central and peripheral oxytocin administration in awake rats. *Frontiers in Behavioral Neuroscience*, 9:245.

Finegold, S. M. (1969). Intestinal bacteria – The role they play in normal physiology, pathologic physiology, and infection. *California Medicine*, *110*(6), 455.

Finger, E. C., Marsh, A. A., Mitchell, D. G., *et al.*, (2008). Abnormal ventromedial prefrontal cortex function in children with psychopathic traits during reversal learning. *Archives of General Psychiatry*, 65:586–594.

Fisher, C. D. (2004). Ethical issues in therapy: Therapist self-disclosure of sexual feelings. *Ethics & Behavior*, *14*(2), 105–121.

Fogassi, L., Ferrari, P.F., Gesierich, B., Rozzi, S., Chersi, F., Rizzolatti, G. (2005). Parietal lobe: from action organization to intention understanding. *Science*, 308:662–667.

Fogelman, E. (1998). Group belonging and mourning as factors in resilience in second generation of Holocaust survivors. *Psychoanalytic Review*, 85; 537–549.

Fogelman, E., & Savran, B. (1979). Therapeutic groups for children of Holocaust survivors. *International Journal of Group Psychotherapy.* 29 (2): 211–235.

Fossion, P., Leys, C., Vandeleur, C., Kempenaers, C., Braun, S., Verbanck, P., Linkowski, P. (2015). Transgenerational transmission of trauma in families of Holocaust survivors: The consequences of extreme family functioning on resilience, sense of coherence, anxiety and depression. *Journal of Affective Disorders*, 171: 48–53.

Frankel, J. B. (1998). Ferenczi's trauma theory. *The American Journal of Psychoanalysis, 58*(1), 41–61.

Frankel, J. B. (2002). Exploring Ferenczi's concept of identification with the aggressor: Its role in trauma, everyday life, and the therapeutic relationship. *Psychoanalytic Dialogues, 12*(1), 101–139.

Frazier, P., Conlon, A., & Glaser, T. (2001). Positive and negative life changes following sexual assault. *Journal of Consulting and Clinical Psychology, 69*, 1048–1055.

Frenkel-Toledo, S., Liebermann, D. G., Bentin, S., Soroker, N. (2016). Dysfunction of the human mirror neuron system in Ideomotor Apraxia: Evidence from Mu Suppression. *Journal of Cognitive Neuroscience*, 28:775–791.

Freud, A. (1992). *The Ego and the Mechanisms of Defence*. London: Karnac Books.

Freud, A., & Dann, S. (1980). *Gemeinschaftsleben im frühen Kindesalter, Die Schriften der Anna Freud (Community life in early childhood, the writings of Anna Freud)*. Vol. IV. 1161–1228, Munich: Kindler Verlag. (Original work published in 1951).

Freud, S. (1918). *Totem and taboo: Resemblances between the psychic lives of savages and neurotics*. A. A. Brill (Trans). New York, NY: Moffat, Yard & Co. (Original work published between 1912–1913).

Freud, S. (1953). Infantile sexuality. In *Three Essays on the Theory of Sexuality*. Standard Edition, Vol. VII, Part II. London: Hogarth. (Original work published in 1905).

Freud, S. (1955a). Recommendations to physicians practising psycho-analysis. In J. Strachey (Ed. and Trans.), *Standard Edition of the Cmplete Psychological Works of Sigmund Freud* (Vol. 12, pp. 1911–1913). London: Hogarth Press. (Original work published in 1912).

Freud, S. (1955b). Beyond the pleasure principle. In J. Strachey (Ed. and Trans.), *Standard Eition of the Complete Psychological Works of Sigmund Freud* (Vol. 18, pp. 7–23). London: Hogarth Press. (Original work published in 1920).

Freud, S. (1957). *On Narcissism: An introduction,* Standard Edition. vol. 14. London, Hogarth Press. (Original work published 1914). 67–102.

Freud, S. (1957). The future prospects of psycho-analytic therapy. In J. Strachey (Ed. and Trans.), *Standard Edition of the Complete Psychological Works of Sigmund Freud* (Vol. 11, pp. 139–151). London: Hogarth Press. (Original work published in 1910).

Freud, S. (1959). *Postscript to: The question of lay analysis (Standard Edition*, vol. 20). London: Hogarth Press. (Original work published in 1927).

Freud, S. (1974). Letter from Sigmund Freud to C. G. Jung, June 7, 1909. In W. McGuire (Ed.) & R. F. C. Hull (Trans.), *The Freud/Jung Letters: The correspondence between Sigmund Freud and C. G. Jung* (pp. 230–232). Princeton, NJ: Princeton University Press.

Freud, S. (1975). *Totem und Tabu (Totem and taboo)*. GW IX. Frankfurt am Main: S. Fischer Verlag. (Original work published between 1912–1913).

Freud. S. (1957). *Instincts and their Vicissitudes*. Standard Edition, Vol. XIV, London: Hogarth. (Original work published in 1915).

Fried, H. (1996). *The Road to Auschwitz: Fragments of a life*. Lincoln, NE, University of Nebraska Press.

Friston, K. (2003). Learning and inference in the brain. *Neural Networks*, 16, 1325–1352.

Frith, C. D., & Frith, U. (1999). Interacting minds – a biological basis. *Science*, 286:1692–1695.

Frith, C. D., & Singer, T. (2008). The role of social cognition in decision making. *Philosophical Transactions of the Royal Society B: Biological Sciences*, 363:3875–3886.

Frith, U. (2001). Mind blindness and the brain in autism. *Neuron*, 32:969–979.

Frith, U., Morton, J., Leslie, A. M. (1991). The cognitive basis of a biological disorder: Autism. *Trends in Neuroscience*, 14:433–438.

Fromm-Reichmann, F. (1950). *Principles of Intensive Psychotherapy.* Chicago, IL: University of Chicago Press.

Fu, F., Tarnita, C.E., Christakis, N.A., Wang, L., Rand, D. G., Nowak, M. A. (2012). Evolution of in-group favoritism. *Scientific Reports*, 2:460.

Gabbard, G.O., & Wilkinson, S.M. (1994). *Management of*

Countertransference with Borderline Patients. Washington, DC: American Psychiatric Press.

Gadamer, H. G. (1996). Philosophy and practical medicine. In *The Enigma of Health*. Stanford, CT: Stanford University Press.

Gallagher, S., & Zahavi, D. (2008). *The Phenomenological Mind: An introduction to philosophy of mind and cognitive science*. New York, NY: Routledge.

Gallese, V. (2001). The shared manifold hypothesis. *Journal of Neuroscience Studies*, *8*, 33–50.

Gallese, V., Fadiga, L., Fogassi, L., Rizzolatti, G. (1996). Action recognition in the premotor cortex. *Brain*, 119 (Pt 2):593–609.

Gampel, Y. (1998). Reflections on countertransference in psychoanalytic work with child survivors of the *Shoah*. *Journal of American Academy of Psychoanalysis*, 26: 343 – 368.

Gastaut, H. J., & Bert, J. (1954). EEG changes during cinematographic presentation: Moving picture activation of the EEG. *Electroencephalography and Clinical Neurophysiology*, 6:433–444.

Gerson, S. (1996). Neutrality, resistance, and self disclosure in an intersubjective psychoanalysis. *Psychoanalytic Dialogues*, 6(5), 623–645.

Ghent, E. (1995). Interaction in the psychoanalytic situation. *Psychoanalytic Dialogues*, *5*(3), 479–491.

Giladi, L., & Bell, T. S. (2013). Protective factors for intergenerational transmission of trauma among second and third generation Holocaust survivors. *Psychological Trauma: Theory, Research, Practice, and Policy*, 5(4):384.

Glover, E. (1927). Lectures on technique in psycho-analysis. *The International Journal of Psycho-Analysis*, *8*, 486.

Goldberg, E., & Bilder, R. M. (1986). Neuropsychological perspectives: Retrograde amnesia and executive deficits. In L. W. Poon (Ed.). *Handbook for clinical memory assessment of older adults*. Washington, DC: American Psychological Association.

Gonzalez-Liencres, C., Juckel, G., Tas, C., Friebe, A., Brune, M. (2014). Emotional contagion in mice: The role of familiarity. *Behavioural Brain Research*, 263C:16–21.

Gordon, A. M., Impett, E. A., Kogan, A., Oveis, C., Keltner, D. (2012). To have and to hold: Gratitude promotes relationship maintenance in intimate bonds. *Journal of Personality and Social Psychology*, 103(2):257–274.

Gotlib, I. H., Joormann, J., Minor, K.L., Hallmayer, J. (2008). HPA axis reactivity: a mechanism underlying the associations among 5-HTTLPR, stress, and depression. *Biological Psychiatry*, 63(9):847–851.

Grafton, S. T., Arbib, M. A., Fadiga, L., Rizzolatti, G. (1996). Localization of grasp representations in humans by positron emission tomography. 2. Observation compared with imagination. *Experimental Brain Research*, 112:103–111.

Green, A. (2002). *Le Temps Eclate* (Fragmented time). Paris: Les Editions de Minuit.

Greenacre, P. (1987). *Trauma, Growth and Personality*. London: Karnac Books. (Original work published in 1953).

Greene, T., Lahav, Y., Kanat-Maymon, Y., & Solomon, Z. (2015). A longitudinal study of secondary posttraumatic growth in wives of ex-POWs. *Psychiatry: Interpersonal and Biological Processes, 78*, 186–197.

Grezes, J., Armony, J. L., Rowe, J., Passingham, R. E. (2003). Activations related to "mirror" and "canonical" neurons in the human brain: An fMRI study. *Neuroimage*, 18:928–937.

Groot, Y. C. T., Wilson, B. A., Evans, J., & Watson, P. (2002). Prospective memory functioning in people with and without brain injury. *Journal of the International Neuropsychological Society, 8*, 645–654.

Grubrich-Simitis, I. (1981). Extreme traumatization as cumulative trauma – psychoanalytic investigations of the effects of concentration camp experiences on survivors and their children. *Psychoanalytic Study of the Child*. 36:415–450.

Gunaydin, L.A., Grosenick, L., Finkelstein, J. C., *et al.* (2014). Natural neural projection dynamics underlying social behavior. *Cell*, 157(7):1535–1551.

Gur, R. E., Loughead, J., Kohler, C. G., *et al.*, (2007). Limbic activation associated with misidentification of fearful faces and flat affect in schizophrenia. *Archives of General Psychiatry*, 64:1356–1366.

Haans, T. (1988). Group psychotherapy with survivors of World War II persecution. *Group Analysis*, 21: 267–280.

Hacker, F. J. (1957). Freud, Marx, and Kierkegaard. In B. Nelson (Ed.), *Freud and the Twentieth Century* (pp. 125–142). Cleveland, OH: World Publishing Company.

Hafkenscheid, A. (2005). Event countertransference and vicarious traumatization: Theoretically valid and clinically useful concepts? *European Journal of Psychotherapy, Counselling and Health*, 7: 159–168.

Hamburger, C., Stürüp, G., Dahl-Iversen, E. (1953). Transvestism: Hormonal, psychiatric and surgical treatment. *Journal of the American Medical Association, 152*: 391–396.

Hardey, M. (1999). Doctor in the house: The Internet as a source of lay health knowledge and the challenge to expertise. *Sociology of Health & Illness, 21*(6), 820–835.

Hare, R. D., & Neumann, C. S. (2008). Psychopathy as a clinical and empirical construct. *Annual Review of Clinical Psychology*, 4:217–246.

Harris, A., & Aron, L. (1997). Ferenczi's semiotic theory: Previews of postmodernism. *Psychoanalytic Inquiry, 17*(4), 522–534.

Hass, A. (1990). In the shadow of the Holocaust. New York, NY: Cornell University Press.

Häupl, W. (2006). *Die ermordeten Kinder vom Spiegelgrund. Gedenkdokumentation für die Opfer der NS-Kindereuthanasie in Wien.* Wien: Böhlau.

Heilman, K. M., Rothi, L. J., Valenstein, E. (1982). Two forms of ideomotor apraxia. *Neurology*, 32:342–346.

Heimann, P. (1950). On counter-transference. *International Journal of Psycho-Analysis*, *31*, 81–84.

Heisenberg, W. (1973). Development of concepts in the history of quantum theory. In J. Mehra (Ed.), *The Physicist's Conception of Nature* (pp. 264–275). Dordrecht: Springer Netherlands.

Helgeson, V. S., Reynolds, K. A., & Tomich, P. L. (2006). A meta-analytic review of benefit finding and growth. *Journal of Consulting and Clinical Psychology, 74*, 797–816

Helmreich, W. B. (1996). *Against all Odds: Holocaust survivors and the successful lives they made in America*. New York, NY: Transaction.

Herman, J. (1997). *Trauma and Recovery*. New York, NY: Basic Books.

Herman, J. L. (1992). *Trauma and Recovery*. New York, NY: Basic Books.

Herman, J. L., & van der Kolk, B. A. (1987). Traumatic antecedents of borderline personality disorder. In B. A. van der Kolk (Ed.), *Psychological Trauma* (pp. 111–126). Washington, DC: American Psychiatric Publishing, Inc.

Hernandez-Lallement, J., van Wingerden, M., Marx, C., Srejic, M., Kalenscher, T. (2014). Rats prefer mutual rewards in a prosocial choice task. *Frontiers in Neuroscience*, 8:443.

Hernandez-Lallement, J., van Wingerden, M., Schable, S., Kalenscher, T. (2016). Basolateral amygdala lesions abolish mutual reward preferences in rats. *Neurobiology of Learning and Memory*, 127:1–9.

Herrn, R. (2005). *Schnittmuster des Geschlechts. Transvestitismus und Transsexualität in der frühen Sexualwissenschaft*. (Patterns of sex. Transvestism and transsexuality in early sex research). Giessen: Psychosozial-Verlag.

Hertoft, P., & Sörensen, T. (1979). Transsexuality. Some remarks based on clinical experience. In Ciba Foundation Symposium 62: *Sex, Hormones and Behavior*, pp. 165–181. Amsterdam, Oxford, New York: Ciba Foundation.

Herzog, J. (1982). World beyond metaphor. Thoughts of the transmission of trauma. In M. S. Bergmann & M. E. Jucovy (Eds.). *Generations of the Holocaust*, New York, NY: Basic Books. pp. 103–119.

Hickok, G. (2009). Eight problems for the mirror neuron theory of action understanding in monkeys and humans. *Journal of Cognitive Neuroscience*, 21:1229–1243.

Hinshelwood, R. D. (1989). *A Dictionary of Kleinian Thought*. London: Free Association Books.

Hinshelwood, R. D. (1999). Countertransference. *The International Journal of Psycho-analysis*, *80*(4), 797.

Hobfoll, S. E., Hall, B. J., Canetti Nisim, D., Galea, S., Johnson, R. J., & Palmieri, P. A. (2007). Refining our understanding of traumatic growth in the face of terrorism: Moving from meaning cognitions to doing what is meaningful. *Applied Psychology, 56*, 345–366.

Hofer, M. A. (2006). Psychobiological roots of early attachment . *Current Directions in Psychological Science,* 15(2):84–88.

Hoffman, M. L. (2001). *Empathy and Moral Development: Implications for caring and justice.* New York, NY: Cambridge University Press.

Holmes, J. (2014). Countertransference before Heimann: An historical exploration. *Journal of the American Psychoanalytical Association,* 62:603–629.

Hooker, C. I., Bruce, L., Lincoln, S. H., Fisher, M., Vinogradov, S. (2011). Theory of mind skills are related to gray matter volume in the ventromedial prefrontal cortex in schizophrenia. *Biological Psychiatry,* 70:1169–1178.

Hopkins. J. (2012). Psychoanalysis, representation, and neuroscience. In A. Fotopoulu, D. Pfaff, & M. Conway (Eds.). *From the Couch to the Lab.* Oxford, UK: Oxford University Press.

Hoppe, K. D. (1984). Severed ties. In S. A. Luel & P. Marcus (Eds.). *Psychoanalytic Reflections on the Holocaust: Selected essays.* New York, NY: KATV Pulishing House. 94–111.

Horner, V., Carter, J. D., Suchak, M., de Waal, F. B. M. (2011). Spontaneous pro-social choice by chimpanzees. *Proceedings of the National Academy of Sciences* (USA), 108(33):13847–13851.

Horney, K. (1939). *New Ways in Psychoanalysis.* New York, NY: Norton.

Hull, C. (1943). *Principles of Behavior.* Englewood Cliffs, NJ: Prentice Hall.

Iacoboni, M., Woods, R. P., Brass, M., Bekkering, H., Mazziotta, J. C., Rizzolatti, G. (1999). Cortical mechanisms of human imitation. *Science,* 286:2526–2528.

Israel Ministry of Defense, Department of Family and Commemoration publication, https://www.mishpahot-hantzaha.mod.gov.il.

J.C.L.: unpublished lecture.

Jabbi, M., Swart, M., Keysers, C. (2007). Empathy for positive and negative emotions in the gustatory cortex. *Neuroimage,* 34:1744–1753.

Jackson, P. L., Meltzoff, A. N., Decety, J. (2005). How do we perceive the pain of others? A window into the neural processes involved in empathy. *Neuroimage,* 24:771–779.

Jacobs, T. J. (1999). Countertransference past and present: A review of the concept. *The International Journal of Psycho-analysis, 80*(3), 575.

Jankoski, J. A. (2010). Is vicarious trauma the culprit? A study of child welfare professionals. *Child Welfare,* 89: 105–120.

Jeon, D., Kim, S., Chetana, M., *et al.* (2010). Observational fear learning involves affective pain system and Cav1.2 Ca2+ channels in ACC. *Nature Neuroscience,* 13(4):482–488.

Joel, S., & Gordon, A. M., Impett, E. A,, Macdonald, G., Keltner, D. (2013). The things you do for me: Perceptions of a romantic partner's investments promote gratitude and commitment. *Personality and Social Psychology Bulletin,* 39(10):1333–1345.

Joels, M. (2006). Corticosteroid effects in the brain: U-shape it. *Trends Pharmacology* Science, 27(5):244–250.

Johannesen, N., & Zucman, G. (2014). The end of bank secrecy? An evaluation of the G20 tax haven crackdown. *American Economic Journal: Economic Policy*, 6(1), 65–91.

Johnson, S. C. (2003). Detecting agents. *Philosophical Transactions of the Royal Society B: Biological Sciences*, 358:549–559.

Joly-Mascheroni, R. M., Senju, A., Shepherd, A, J. (2008). Dogs catch human yawns. *Biology Letters*, 4:446–448.

Jones, C. E., Riha, P. D., Gore, A. C., Monfils, M. H. (2014). Social transmission of Pavlovian fear: Fear-conditioning by-proxy in related female rats. *Animal Cognition*, 17:827–834.

Jorgensen, C. (1967). *A Personal Autobiography*. With an introduction by Harry Benjamin, M.D. New York, NY: Paul S. Eriksson, Inc.

Jung, C. (1966). Problems of modern psychotherapy. In G. Adler (Ed.) & R. F. C. Hull (Trans.), *The Collected Works of C. J. Jung, Bollingen series XX* (Original work published in 1929).

Kaba, R., & Sooriakumaran, P. (2007). The evolution of the doctor–patient relationship. *International Journal of Surgery*, 5(1), 57–65.

Kandel, E. R. (1999). Biology and the future of psychoanalysis: A new intellectual framework for psychiatry revisited, *American Journal of Psychiatry*, Volume 156 Issue 4, April. 505–524.

Kaplan-Solms, K., & Solms, M. (2001). *Clinical Studies in Neuro-psychoanalysis*. London: H. Karnac Books.

Kardiner, A. (1957). Freud – The man I knew, the scientist, and his influence. In B. Nelson (Ed.), *Freud and the Twentieth Century* (pp. 46–58). Cleveland, OH: World Publishing Company.

Kaul, F. K. (1979). *Die Psychiatrie im Strudel der Euthanasie*. Frankfurt am Main/ Köln: Europäische Verlagsanstalt.

Keff, B. (2008). *Utwór o Matce i Ojczyżnie. (A song about mother and motherland)*. Kraków: Korporacja Halart.

Keilson, H. (1979). *Sequentielle Traumatisierung bei Kindern (Sequential traumatisation in children)*. Stuttgart: Enke Verlag.

Kellerman, N. P. (2001). Psychopathology in children of Holocaust survivors: a review of research literature. *The Israel Journal of Psychiatry and Related Sciences*, 38(1):36–45.

Kellerman, N. P. (2008). Transmitted Holocaust trauma: Curse or legacy? The aggravating and mitigating factors of Holocaust transmission. *The Israel Journal of Psychiatry and Related Sciences*. 45(4): 263–70.

Kellermann, N. P. (2009). *Holocaust Trauma: Psychological effects and treatment*. New York, Bloomington: iUniverse.

Kernberg, O. (1965). Notes on countertransference. *Journal of the American Psychoanalytic Association*, *13*(1), 38–56.

Kesey, K. (1962) *One Flew over the Cuckoo's Nest*. New York, NY: Viking Press.

Kestenberg, J. (1982). A metapsychological assessment based on an analysis of a survivor's child. In M. S. Bergmann & M. E. Jucovy (Eds.). *Generations of the Holocaust*. New York, NY: Basic Books.

Kestenberg, J. S. (1989). Transposition revisited: Clinical, therapeutic and developmental consideration. In P. Marcus & I. A. Rosenberg (Eds.). *Healing their Wounds: Psychotherapy with Holocaust survivors and their families.*Westport, CT: Praeger. pp. 67–82.

Kestenberg, J., & Gampel, Y. (1983). Growing up in the Holocaust culture. *The Israel Journal of Psychiatry and Related Sciences*, 20:129–146.

Keysers, C. (2011). *The Empathic Brain.* Amsterdam: Social Brain Press (Independent Publisher).

Keysers, C., & Gazzola, V. (2016). A plea for cross-species social neuroscience. *Current Topics in Behavioral Neurosciences.* [Epub ahead of print.]

Keysers, C., Kaas, J, H., Gazzola, V. (2010). Somatosensation in social perception. *Nature Reviews Neuroscience*, 11:417–428.

Keysers, C., Wicker, B., Gazzola, V., Anton, J. L., Fogassi, L., Gallese, V. (2004). A touching sight: SII/PV activation during the observation and experience of touch. *Neuron*, 42:335–346.

Kiehl, K. A., Smith, A. M., Hare, R. D., *et al.*, (2001). Limbic abnormalities in affective processing by criminal psychopaths as revealed by functional magnetic resonance imaging. *Biological Psychiatry*, 50:677–684.

Kinsey, A., Pomeroy, W., Martin, C. (1948). *Sexual Behavior in the Human Male.* Philadelphia, PA: W. B. Saunders Company.

Kinsey, A., Pommeroy, W., Martin, C., Gebhard, P. (1953). *Sexual Behavior in the Human Female.* Philadelphia, PA: W. B. Saunders Company.

Klee, E. (2003). *Das Personenlexikion zum Dritten Reich. Wer warwas vor und nach 1945?.* Frankfurt am Main: S. Fischer Verlag.

Klein, H. (1968). Problems in the psychotherapeutic treatment of Israeli survivors of the Holocaust. In H. Krystal (Ed.). *Massive Psychic Trauma.* New York, NY: International Universities Press, Inc. pp. 233–248.

Klein, H. (2003). Leben, *Shoah*, Sprache und Psychoanalyse. Hillel Klein im Gespräch mit Dörte von Westernhagen. *Psyche.* 12/57, 1203–1213 Stuttgart: Klett-Cotta.

Klein, M. (1946). Notes on some schizoid mechanisms. *International Journal of Psycho-analysis*, 27: 99–110.

Klein, M. (1975). *Love, Guilt and Reparation.* New York, N.Y; The Free Press, Simon and Schuster.

Knapska, E., & Maren, S. (2009). Reciprocal patterns of c-Fos expression in the medial prefrontal cortex and amygdala after extinction and renewal of conditioned fear. *Learning & Memory*, 16:486–493.

Knapska, E., Nikolaev, E., Boguszewski, P., *et al.*, (2006). Between-subject transfer of emotional information evokes specific pattern of amygdala activation. *Proceedings of the National Academy of Sciences* (USA), 103:3858–3862.

Knobler, H. Y., Haber, L., Brutin, B., Zemishlany, Z. (2015). Myth and reality: on "future generations" of the Holocaust. In N. Davidovitch & D. Soen (Eds.) *Shoa and Experience – a Journey in Time.* Boston, MA: Academic Studies Press.

Kohut, H. (1971). *The Analysis of the Self.* New York, NY: International Universities Press.

Krebs, D. L. (2008). *How Selfish by Nature? Foundations of Evolutionary Psychology.* Oxford: Routledge. (Original publication: Psycology Press).

Kulbaga, T. A. (2008). Pleasurable pedagogies: *Reading Lolita in Tehran* and the rhetoric of empathy. *College English. 70*(5), 506–521.

Kuryluk, E. (2004). *Goldi.* Warszawa: Wydawnictwo Twój Styl.

Lahav, Y., Bellin, E., & Solomon, Z. (In Press). Posttraumatic growth and shattered world assumptions among ex-POWs: The role of dissociation. *Psychiatry: Interpersonal and Biological Processes.*

Lamb, M., & Jablonka, E. (2005). *Evolution in Four Dimensions: Genetic, epigenetic, behavioral, and symbolic variation in the history of life.* Cambridge, MA: MIT Press.

Lamm, C., & Majdandzic, J. (2015). The role of shared neural activations, mirror neurons, and morality in empathy – a critical comment. *Neuroscience Research*, 90:15–24.

Lamm, C., Decety, J., Singer, T. (2011). Meta-analytic evidence for common and distinct neural networks associated with directly experienced pain and empathy for pain. *Neuroimage*, 54:2492–2502.

Lamm, C., Meltzoff, A. N., Decety, J. (2010). How do we empathize with someone who is not like us? A functional magnetic resonance imaging study. *Journal of Cognitive Neuroscience*, 22:362–376.

Langer, K. G., Laatsch, C., & Lewis, L. (Eds.). Psychotherapeutic interventions for adults with brain injury or stroke: A clinician's treatment resource. Madison, CT: Psychosocial Press.

Langford, D. J., Crager, S. E., Shehzad, Z., *et al.*, (2006). Social modulation of pain as evidence for empathy in mice. *Science*, 312:1967–1970.

Langford, D. J., Tuttle, A .H., Briscoe, C., *et al.*, (2011). Varying perceived social threat modulates pain behavior in male mice. *The Journal of Pain*, 12:125–132.

Langs, R. (1976). *The Therapeutic Interaction: Volume II.* New York, NY: Aronson.

Laplanche, J., & Pontalis, J. B. (1967/2007). *Vocabulaire de la Psychanalyse.* Paris: Presses Universitaires de France.

Laplanche, J., & Pontalis, J. B. (1973). *The Language of Psycho-analysis.* (D. Nicholson-Smith, Trans.). London: Hogarth Press.

Larson, C. L., Schaefer, H. S., Siegle, G. J., Jackson, C. A., Anderle, M. J., Davidson, R. J. (2006). Fear is fast in phobic individuals: Amygdala activation in response to fear-relevant stimuli. *Biological Psychiatry*, 60:410–417.

Laub, D. (1992). Bearing witness, or the vicissitudes of listening. In S. Felman & D. Laub (Eds.). *Testimony: Crisis of witnessing in literature, psychoanalysis, and history* (pp. 57–74). New York, NY: Routledge.

LeGrand, D. (2007). Pre-reflective self-consciousness: On being bodily in the world. *Janus Head, 9*, 493–519.

Lehmann, O., & Schmidt, T. (2001). *Den Fängen des Dr. Gross. Das misshandelte Leben des Friedrich Zawrel.* Wien: Czernin Verlag.

Leśniak, R. (1964). Zmiany osobowości u byłych więźniów obozu koncentracyjnego Oświęcim-Brzezinka. Doniesienie wstępne. (Changes of personality in former prisoners of the concentration camp Oświęcim-Birkenau. Preliminary report). *Przegląd Lekarski,* 1: 29–30.

Leśniak, R., Mitarski, J., Orwid, M., Szymusik, S., Teutsch, A. (1961). Niektóre zagadnienia psychiatryczne obozu w Oświęcimiu w świetle własnych badań. II doniesienie wstępne. (Some issues in the psychiatric camp in Oświęcim in light of their own research. II preliminary report). *Przegląd Lekarski,* 1: 64–73.

Leuzinger-Bohleber, M. (2014). Den Körper in der Seele entdecken Embodiment und die Annäherung an das Nicht-Repräsentierte. *Psyche.* 09– 10, 0922– 0950, Stuttgart: Klett-Cotta.

Levav, I., Levinson, D., Radomislensky, I., Shemesh, A., Kohn, R. (2007). Psychopathology and other health dimensions among the offspring of Holocaust survivors: results from the Israel National Health Survey. *The Israel Journal of Psychiatry and Related Sciences.* 44.2:144–51.

Lévinas, E. (1961). *Totalité et Infini: Essai sur l'extériorité,* Paris: Le Livré de Poche.

Levine, M., Prosser, A., Evans, D., Reicher, S. (2005). Identity and emergency intervention: How social group membership and inclusiveness of group boundaries shape helping behavior. *Personality and Social Psychology Bulletin,* 31(4):443–453.

Levine, S. Z., Laufer, A., Hamama Raz, Y., Stein, E., & Solomon, Z. (2008). Posttraumatic growth in adolescence: Examining its components and relationship with PTSD. *Journal of Traumatic Stress, 21,* 492–496.

Lezak, M.D. (1982). The problem of assessing frontal lobe executive functions. *International Journal of Psychology,* 17, 281–297.

Lezak, M.D. (1995). *Neuropsychological Assessment (3rd ed.).* New York, NY: Oxford University Press.

Li, Z., Lu, Y. F., Li, C. L., *et al.* (2014), Social interaction with a cagemate in pain facilitates subsequent spinal nociception via activation of the medial prefrontal cortex in rats. *Pain,* 155(7):1253–1261.

Linley, P. A., & Joseph, S. (2004). Positive change following trauma and adversity: A review. *Journal of Traumatic Stress, 17*(1), 11–21.

Little, M. (1951). Counter-transference and the patient's response to it. *The International Journal of Psychoanalysis, 32,* 32–40.

Lockwood, P. L., Sebastian, C. L., McCrory, E. J., *et al.*, (2013). Association of callous traits with reduced neural response to others' pain in children with conduct problems. *Current Biology,* 23:901–905.

Loftus, E. F. (1993). The reality of repressed memories, *American Psychologist,* 48/5: 518–537.

Lombardo, M. V., Chakrabarti, B., Bullmore, E. T., *et al.*, (2010). Atypical neural self-representation in autism. *Brain,* 133:611–624.

Lorenz, K. (1966). *On Aggression.* (M. Latzke, Trans.). London: Methuen. (Original work published in 1963)

Lothstein L (1983). *Female-to-Male Transsexualism. Historical, clinical and theoretical issues.* Boston, London, Melbourne and Henly: Routledge & Kegan Paul.

Lubin, G., Werbeloff, N., Halperin, D., Shmushkevitch, M., Weiser, M., Knobler, H. Y. (2010). Decrease in suicide rates after a change of policy reducing access to firearms in adolescents: a naturalistic epidemiological study. *Suicide and Life-Threatening Behavior*, 40, 421–424.

Lynch, D. A. (1998). Rhetorics of proximity: Empathy in Temple Grandin and Cornel West. *Rhetoric Society Quarterly.* 28(1), 5–23.

MacLean, P. D. (1985). Brain evolution relating to family, play, and the separation call. *Archives of General Psychiatry*, 42:405–417.

Madsen, E. A., Tunney, R. J., Fieldman, G., *et al.* (2007). Kinship and altruism: A cross-cultural experimental study. *British Journal of Psychology,* 98(Pt 2):339–359.

Maercker, A., & Zoellner, T. (2004). The Janus face of self-perceived growth: Towards a two-component model of posttraumatic growth. *Psychological Inquiry, 15*, 41–48.

Magner, L. N. (2005). *A History of Medicine.* New York, NY: Informa Healthcare.

Main, T. F. (1957). The Ailment. *The British Journal of Medical Psychology,* 30/3:129–145.

Marcus, D. M. (1998). Self disclosure: The wrong issue. *Psychoanalytic Inquiry*, *18*(4), 566–579.

Marcus, P. (1984). Jewish consciousness after the Holocaust. In S. A. Luel & P. Marcus (Eds.). *Psychoanalytic Reflections on the Holocaust: Selected essays.* New York, NY: KATV Publishing House. 179–195.

Marlin, B. J., Mitre, M., D'amour, J.A., Chao, M. V., Froemke, R. C. (2015). Oxytocin enables maternal behaviour by balancing cortical inhibition. *Nature*, 520(7548):499–504.

Marquez, C., Rennie, S. M., Costa, D. F., Moita, M. A. (2015). Pro-social Choice in Rats Depends on Food-Seeking Behavior Displayed by Recipients. *Current Biology*, 25(13):1736–1745.

Marsh, A. A., Finger, E. C., Fowler, K. A., *et al.*, (2013). Empathic responsiveness in amygdala and anterior cingulate cortex in youths with psychopathic traits. *Journal of Child Psychology and Psychiatry*, 54:900–910.

Martin, L. J., Tuttle, A. H., Mogil, J. S. (2014). The interaction between pain and social behavior in humans and rodents. *Current Topics in Behavioral Neuroscience,* 20:233–250.

Martineau, J., Schmitz, C., Assaiante, C., Blanc, R., Barthelemy, C. (2004). Impairment of a cortical event-related desynchronisation during a bimanual load-lifting task in children with autistic disorder. *Neuroscience Letters*, 367:298–303.

Masserman, J. H., Wechkin, S., Terris, W. (1964). "Altruistic behavior in Rhesus monkeys. *American Journal of Psychiatry*, 121:584–585.

Mayer, E. L. (1996). Changes in science and changing ideas about knowledge and authority in psychoanalysis. *The Psychoanalytic Quarterly*, *65*, 158–200.

McCann, L., & Coletti, I. (1994). The dance of empathy. In J. P. Wilson & J. D. Lindy (Eds.). *Countertransference in the Treatment of PTSD*. New York, NY: Guilford Press. 87–121.

McCann, L., & Pearlman, L.A. (1990). Vicarious traumatization: a framework for understanding the psychological effects of working with victims. *Journal of Traumatic Stress,* 1:131–149.

McFarland, C., & Alvaro, C. (2000). The impact of motivation on temporal comparisons: Coping with traumatic events by perceiving personal growth. *Journal of Personality and Social Psychology, 79*, 327–343.

McGraw, L. A., & Young, L. J. (2010). The prairie vole: An emerging model organism for understanding the social brain. *Trends in Neuroscience*, 33(2):103–109.

McLaughlin, J. T. (1981). Transference, psychic reality, and countertransference. *The Psychoanalytic Quarterly*, *50*(4), 639–664.

McMillen, C., Zuravin, S., & Rideout, G. (1995). Perceived benefit from child sexual abuse. *Journal of Consulting and Clinical Psychology, 63*(6), 1037–1043.

Meissner, W. W. (2002). The problem of self-disclosure in psychoanalysis. *Journal of the American Psychoanalytic Association*, *50*(3), 827–867.

Meyza, K., Nikolaev, T., Kondrakiewicz, K., Blanchard, D. C., Blanchard, R. J., Knapska, E. (2015). Neuronal correlates of asocial behavior in a BTBR T (+) Itpr3(tf)/J mouse model of autism. *Frontiers in Behavioral Neuroscience*, 9:199.

Mikosz, M., Nowak, A., Werka, T., Knapska, E. (2015). Sex differences in social modulation of learning in rats. *Scientific Reports*, 5:18114.

Miller. E. K. (2013). The "working" of working memory. *Dialogues in Clinical Neuroscience*, Vol. 15, No. 4.

Mitchell, J. P. (2009). Inferences about mental states. *Philosophical Transactions of the Royal Society B: Biological Sciences*, 364:1309–1316.

Mitscherlich, A. (1950–1951). 66. Wanderversammlung der Süddeutschen Psychiater und Neurologen, Badenweiler, 2./3. Juni 1950. Erstes Leitthema: Daseinsanalyse (66th Conference of the South German Psychiatrists and Neurologists, June 2–3, 1950, in Badenweiler. First major topic: Daseinsanalyse). *Psyche – Zeitschrift für Psychoanalyse und ihre Anwendungen, 4*: 226–234.

Mitscherlich, A., & Mielke, F. (1983). *Medizin ohne Menschlichkeit. Dokumente des Nürnberger Ärzteprozesses*. Frankfurt am Main: S. Fischer Verlag.

Mitscherlich, A., Bally, G., Binder, H., Binswanger, L., Bleuler, M., Brun, R., Dührssen, A., Gollner, W. E., Jores, A., Jung, C. G., Kranz, H., Kemper, W., Meng,, H., Mohr, F., Müller, M., Schultz-Hencke, H., Seitz, W.,

Staechelin, J. E., Seck, H., Weizäcker, V. V. (1950–1951 a). Rundfrage über ein Referat auf der 66. Wanderversammlung der Süddeutschen Psychiater und Neurologen in Badenweiler (Comments on a presentation at the 66th Conference of the South German Psychiatrists and Neurologists in Badenweiler). *Psyche – Zeitschrift für Psychoanalyse und ihre Anwendungen. 4*: 448–477.

Mitscherlich, A., Georgi, F., Göppert, H., Gundert, H., Mauz, F., Zutt, J., Boss, M. (1950–1951 b). Rundfrage über ein Refereat auf der 66. Wanderversammlung der Süddeutschen Psychiater und Neurologen in Badenweiler (Comments on a presentation at the 66th Conference of South German Psychiatrists and Neurologists in Badenweiler). *Psyche – Zeitschrift für Psychoanalyse und ihre Anwendungen, 4*: 626–640.

Mogil, J. S. (2015). Social modulation of and by pain in humans and rodents. *Pain*, 156 Suppl. 1:S35–S41.

Moi, T. (1981). Representation of patriarchy: Sexuality and epistemology in Freud's "Dora." *Feminist Review*, *9*(1), 60–74.

Money-Kyrle, R. E. (1956). Normal counter-transference and some of its derivations. *The International Journal of Psycho-analysis*, *37*, 360.

Money-Kyrle, R. E. (1978). Normal countertransference and of its deviation. In D. Meltzer & E. O'Shaughnessy (Eds.). *Collected Papers of Money-Kyrle*. Starthtay, Pertshire (UK): Clunie Press. (Original work published in 1956).

Morris, J. (1974). *Conundrum*. London: Faber & Faber.

Moscovitch, M. (1994). Memory and working with memory. Evaluation of a component process model and comparisons with other models. In D. L. Schacter & E. Tulving (Eds.). *Memory Systems*. Cambridge, MA: MIT Press.

Moss, E., & Raz, A. (2001). The ones left behind: A siblings' bereavement group. *Group Analysis,* 34, 395–407.

Moyaho, A., Rivas-Zamudio, X., Ugarte, A., Eguibar, J. R., Valencia, J. (2015). Smell facilitates auditory contagious yawning in stranger rats. *Animal Cognition,* 18:279–290.

Mühsam, R. (1926). Chirurgische Eingriffe bei Anomalien des Sexuallebens (Surgical interventions in cases of sexual anomalities). *Therapie der Gegenwart, 67*: 451–455.

Muroy, S.E., Long, K. L., Kaufer, D., Kirby, E. D. (2016). Moderate stress-induced social bonding and oxytocin signaling are disrupted by predator odor in male rats. *Neuropsychopharmacology*. 41(8):2160–70.

Muthukumaraswamy, S. D., Johnson, B. W., McNair, N. A. (2004). Mu rhythm modulation during observation of an object-directed grasp. *Brain Research. Cognitive Brain Research,* 19:195–201.

Neary, D., Snowden, J. S., Gustafson, L., *et al.*, (1998). Frontotemporal lobar degeneration: A consensus on clinical diagnostic criteria. *Neurology*, 51:1546–1554.

Neary, D., Snowden, J. S., Mann, D. (2005). Frontotemporal dementia. *Lancet Neurology*, 4:771–780.

Neumann, D. A., & Gamble, S. J. (1995). Issues in the professional development of psychotherapists: Countertransference and vicarious traumatization in the new trauma therapist. *Psychotherapy: Theory, Research, Practice, Training, 32*(2), 341–347.

Newell, J. M., Nelson-Gardell, D., MacNeil, G. (2016). Clinician responses to client traumas: a chronological review of constructs and terminology. *Trauma, Violence & Abuse (Trauma Violence Abuse)*, 17:306–313.

Nietzsche, F. (1954). On truth and lie in an extra-moral sense. In W. Kaufmann (Ed. and Trans.), *The Portable Nietzsche* (pp. 46–47). New York, NY: Penguin.

Norscia, I., & Palagi, E. (2011). Yawn contagion and empathy in Homo sapiens. *PLoS One*, 6:e28472.

Nowak, M. A. (2006). Five rules for the evolution of cooperation. *Science*, 314(5805):1560–1563.

Nowak, M.A., Tarnita, C. E., Wilson, E. O. (2010). The evolution of eusociality. *Nature*. 466(7310):1057–1062.

Nowbahari, E., Scohier, A., Durand, J. L., Hollis, K. L. (2009). Ants, Cataglyphis cursor, use precisely directed rescue behavior to free entrapped relatives. *PLoS One*, 4(8):e6573.

Numan, M. (2015). *Neurobiology of Social Behavior: Towards an understanding of the pro-social and antisocial brain*. London: Elsevier.

Nummenmaa, L., Hirvonen, J., Parkkola, R., Hietanen, J. K. (2008). Is emotional contagion special? An fMRI study on neural systems for affective and cognitive empathy. *Neuroimage*, 43:571–580.

Nussbaum, M. (2003). *Upheavals of Thought: The intelligence of emotions*. New York, NY: Cambridge University Press.

Oberman, L. M., Hubbard, E. M., McCleery, J. P., Altschuler, E. L., Ramachandran, V. S., Pineda, J. A. (2005). EEG evidence for mirror neuron dysfunction in autism spectrum disorders. *Brain Research. Cognitive Brain Research*, 24:190–198.

Oberman, L. M., Pineda, J. A., Ramachandran, V. S. (2007). The human mirror neuron system: A link between action observation and social skills. *Social Cognitive and Affective Neuroscience*, 2:62–66.

Oberman, L. M., Ramachandran, V. S., Pineda, J. A. (2008). Modulation of mu suppression in children with autism spectrum disorders in response to familiar or unfamiliar stimuli: The mirror neuron hypothesis. *Neuropsychologia*, 46:1558–1565.

Ogden, T. H. (1977). *Subjects of Analysis*. Lanham, MD: Jason Aronson.

Ogden, T. H. (1998). *Reverie and Interpretation*. Lanham, MD: Jason Aronson.

Ogden, T. H. (2005). *This Art of Psychoanalysis: Dreaming undreamt dreams and interrupted cries*. London: Routledge.

Ogden, T. H. (2009). Bion's four principles of mental functioning. In *Rediscovering Psychoanalysis: Thinking and dreaming, learning and forgetting* (pp. 90–113). East Sussex: Routledge.

Ogden, T.G. (1985). On potential space. *International Journal of Psychoanalysis, 66*, 129–141.

Organization, W. H. (1992). *The ICD-10 Classification of Mental and Behavioural Disorders: Clinical descriptions and diagnostic guidelines.* Geneva: World Health Organization. 208–210.

Organization, W. H. (1999). Report of the consultation on child abuse prevention, 29–31 March 1999, WHO, Geneva. Geneva: Author.

Orr, D. W. (1954). Transference and countertransference: A historical survey. *Journal of the American Psychoanalytic Association, 2*(4), 621–670.

Orwid, M. (1962). Uwagi o przystosowaniu do życia poobozowego u byłych więźniów obozu koncentracyjnego w Oświęcimiu. (Remarks on adapting to life after the camp of former prisoners of the Auschwitz concentration camp). *Przegląd Lekarski*, 1:94–97.

Orwid, M. (1964). Socjopsychiatryczne następstwa pobytu w obozie koncentracyjnym Oświęcim-Brzezinka. (Social and psychiatric consequences of staying in the concentration camp of Auschwitz-Birkenau). *Przegląd Lekarski*, 1:17–22.

Orwid, M., Domagalska-Kurdziel, E., Pietruszewski, K. (1994a). Psychospołeczne następstwa Holocaustu u osób ocalonych i żyjących w Polsce (The psychosocial consequences of the Holocaust on survivors and people living in Poland). *Psychiatria Polska*, 1: 91–112.

Orwid, M., Domagalska-Kurdziel, E., Pietruszewski, K., Czaplak, E., Izdebski, R., Kamińska, M. (1995). Psychosocial effects of the Holocaust on survivors and the second generation in Poland: Preliminary report. In J. Lemberger (Ed.). *A Global Perspective on Working with Holocaust Survivors and the Second Generation*. Jerusalem: JDC. 205–242.

Orwid, M., Domagalska-Kurdziel, E., Pietruszewski, K., Czaplak, E., Izdebski, R., Kamińska, M. (1995a). The psychosocial effects of the holocaust on Jewish survivors living in Poland. *Psychiatria Polska*, 293(suppl.): 29–48. http://www.holocaustechoes.com/5orwid.html (b).

Orwid, M., Domagalska-Kurdziel, E., Pietruszewski, K., Czaplak, E., Izdebski, R. (1994), Kamińska M. Psychospołeczne następstwa Holocaustu w drugim pokoleniu ofiar Holocaustu ocalonych w Polsce. (Psychosocial consequences of the Holocaust in the second generation of Holocaust survivors in Poland). *Psychiatria Polska*, 1:113–130.

Orwid, M., Domagalska-Kurdziel, E., Pietruszewski, K., Czaplak, E., Izdebski, R., Kamińska, M. (1997). The psychosocial effects of the Holocaust on Jewish survivors living in Poland. *Psychiatria Polska*. 5: 3–13.

O'Shaughnessy, E. (1994). What is clinical fact? *International Journal of Psychoanalysis*, 75, 939–947.

PACE = Parliamentary Assembly of the Council of Europe (2015). *Discrimination against Transgender People in Europe*. (http://tgeu.org/pace-resolution-discrimination-against-transgender-people-in-europe/).

Panksepp, J. (1998). *Affective Neuroscience: The foundations of human and animal emotion*. New York, NY: Oxford University Press.

Panksepp, J. (1998). Love and the social bond. In *Affective Neuroscience*. Oxford, NY: Oxford University Press.

Panksepp, J. B., & Lahvis, G. P. (2011). Rodent empathy and affective neuroscience. *Neuroscience & Biobehavioral Reviews*, 35:1864–1875.

Panksepp, J. B., & Panksepp, J. B. (2013). Towards a cross-species understanding of empathy. *Trends in Neurosciences*, 36:489–496.

Paolucci, E. O., Genuis, M. L., & Violato, C. (2001). A meta-analysis of the published research on the effects of child sexual abuse. *The Journal of Psychology, 135*(1), 17–36.

Papoušek, M. (2007). Communication in early infancy: An arena of intersubjective learning. *Infant Behavior and Development*, 30: 258–266.

Pare, W. P., & Glavin, G. B. (1986). Restraint stress in biomedical research: a review. *Neuroscience & Biobehavioral Reviews*, 10(3):339–370.

Paukner, A., & Anderson, J. R. (2006). Video-induced yawning in stumptail macaques (Macaca arctoides). *Biology Letters*, 2:36–38.

Perel, E., & Saul, J. (1989). A family therapy approach to Holocaust survivor families. In P. Marcus & A. Rosenberg (Eds.). *Healing their Wounds: Psychotherapy with Holocaust survivors and their families*. New York, NY: Praeger.135–152.

Perry, A., Bentin, S., Bartal, I. B., Lamm, C., Decety, J. (2010). "Feeling" the pain of those who are different from us: Modulation of EEG in the mu/alpha range. *Cognitive, Affective, & Behavioral Neuroscience*, 10:493–504.

Perry, A., Solbakk, A. K., Endestad, T., Saunders, S., Stiso, J., Dewar, C., & Knight, R. T. (2016). Understanding others' actions and emotions following lesions to the prefrontal cortex, with or without the inferior frontal gyrus: Evidence from EEG and behavioral studies. (In review).

Perry, A., Troje, N. F., Bentin, S. (2010). Exploring motor system contributions to the perception of social information: Evidence from EEG activity in the mu/alpha frequency range. *Society Neuroscience*, 5:272–284.

Person, E (2001). Response to Juliet Mitchell's reflections. *Studies in Gender and Sexuality*, 2: 261–175.

Person, E., & Ovesey, L. (1974 a). The transsexual syndrome in males. I. Primary transsexualism. *American Journal of Psychotherapy*, 28: 4–20.

Person, E., & Ovesey, L. (1974 b). The transsexual syndrome in males. II. Secondary transsexualism. *American Journal of Psychotherapy*, 28: 174–193.

Pezawas, L., Meyer-Lindenberg, A., Drabant, E. M. *et al.*, (2005). 5-HTTLPR polymorphism impacts human cingulate-amygdala interactions: A genetic susceptibility mechanism for depression. *Nature Neuroscience*, 8:828–834.

Pfäfflin, F. (1997). Sex reassignment, Harry Benjamin, and some European roots. *International Journal of Transgenderism 1 (2)* (http:web-archive.org/web/20070505034642/http://symposion.com/ijt/index.htm).

Pfäfflin, F. (2003). Understanding transgendred phenomena. In S. Levine, C. B. Risen, & S. E. Althof (Eds.). *Handbook of Clinical Sexuality for Mental Health Professionals*, First Edition. New York, Hove: Brunner-Routledge. pp. 291–310.

Pfäfflin, F. (2006). Research, research, politics and clinical experience with transsexual patients. In P. Fonagy, R. Krause, & M. Leuzinger-Bohleber (Eds.). *Identity, Gender and Sexuality 150 Years after Freud*, pp. 139–156. London: International Psychoanalytic Association.

Pfäfflin, F. (2010). Understanding transgendered phenomena. In: S. Levine, C. B. Risen, & S. E. Althof (Eds.). *Handbook of Clinical Sexuality for Mental Health Professionals*. pp. 425–447. Second Edition. New York, Hove: Brunner-Routledge.

Pfäfflin, F. (2012). Autobiografien, Biografien und Filme über Geschlechtswechsel. In Lessenich, L. *Die transzendierte Frau. Eine Autobiografie* (Autobiographies, biographies and movies about sex change). pp. 199–219. Giessen: Psychosozial-Verlag.

Pfäfflin, F. (2015 a). Benjamin, Harry (1885–1986). *International Encyclopedia of Human Sexuality*, 113–196. Hoboken, NJ: John Wiley & Sons.

Pfäfflin, F. (2015 b). Zur Resolution der Parlamentarischen Versammlung des Europarats über Maßnahmen gegen die Diskriminierung von Transgender People (Discrimination against transgender people in Europe. Comments on Resolution 2048 [2015] of the Parliamentary Assembly of the Council of Europe [PACE]). *Recht & Psychiatrie, 33*: 140–144.

Pick, I. B. (1985). Working through in the countertransference. *International Journal of Psychoanalysis*, *66*, 157–166.

Pokorny, M. H., & Bondy, M. H. (1933). Rapport sur un transvestite qui demandait une opération cosmétique. *Revue Neurologique*, 40: 701– 701.

Porges, S. W. (1998). Love: An emergent property of the mammalian autonomic nervous system. *Psychoneuroendocrinology*, 23(8):837–861.

Potel, J. Y. (2010). *Koniec Niewinności. (End of Innocence)*. Kraków: Znak. 275–297.

Premack, D., & Woodruff, G. (1978). Chimpanzee problem-solving: A test for comprehension. *Science*, 202:532–535.

Preston, S. D., & de Waal, F. B. M. (2002). Empathy: Its ultimate and proximate bases. *Behavioral and Brain Sciences*, 25(1):1–20.

Preston, S. D. (2004). Empathy. In M. Bekoff, M., (Ed). *Encyclopedia of Animal Behavior*. Vol. 2 D-P. Westport, CT, London: Greenwood Press.

Prot, K. (2011). Le sentiment de culpabilité et de honte chez les survivants de l'Holocauste (Guilt and shame in Holocaust survivors). *L'évolution psychiatrique*, 76: 201–217.

Prot, K., (2009). *Życie po Zagładzie: Skutki traumy u ocalałych z Holocaustu: świadectwa z Polski i Rumunii (Life after Holocaust: effects of trauma among the survivors. Testimony documentation from Poland and Romania)*. Warsaw: Institute of Psychiatry and Neurology.

Prot, K., Szwajca, K., Biedka, Ł., Bierzyński, K., Domagalska, E., Izdebski, R.

(2011). Psychotherapy of Holocaust survivors – group process analysis. *Archives of Psychiatry and Psychotherapy*, 1:21–33.

Psillos, S. (2008). Philosophy of science. In D. Moran (Ed.), *The Routledge Companion to Twentieth-Century Philosophy* (pp. 618–658). London: Routledge.

Putnam, F. W. (1993). Dissociative disorders in children: Behavioral profiles and problems. *Child Abuse & Neglect,* 17(1), 39–45.

Racker, H. (1953). A contribution to the problem of counter-transference. *The International Journal of Psycho-analysis*, *34*, 313.

Racker, H. (1957). The meanings and uses of countertransference. *Psychoanalytic Quarterly, 26*, 303–357.

Racker, H. (1968). *Transference and Countertransference*. London: The Hogarth Press.

Rapoport, E. R. (2011). Growing up in the shadow of the Holocaust: A psychoanalyst addresses intergenerational transmission of trauma in her family. *Isssues In Psychoanalytic Psychology,* 33: 43–50.

Ratcliffe, K. (1999). Rhetorical listening: A trope for rhetorical invention and a 'code of cross-cultural conduct. *College Composition and Communication. 51*(2), 195–224.

Raymaekers, R., Wiersema, J. R., Roeyers, H. (2009). EEG study of the mirror neuron system in children with high functioning autism. *Brain Research*, 1304:113–121.

Reich, A. (1951). On counter-transference. In R. Langs (Ed.), *Classics in Psychoanalytic Technique* (pp. 153–159). Lanham, MD: Jason Aronson.

Reimert, I., Bolhuis, J. E., Kemp, B., Rodenburg, T. B. (2015). Emotions on the loose: Emotional contagion and the role of oxytocin in pigs. *Animal Cognition*, 18:517–532.

Renik, O. (1993). Analytic interaction: Conceptualizing technique in light of the analyst's irreducible subjectivity. *Psychoanalytic Quarterly*, *62*(4), 553–571.

Rice, G. E., & Gainer, P. (1962). "Altruism" in the albino rat. *Journal of Comparative and Physiological Psychology*, 55:123–125.

Rizzolati, G., & Craighero, L. (2004).The mirror-neuron system. *Annual Review of Neuroscience, 27*, 169–92.

Rizzolatti, G., Fadiga, L., Gallese, V., Fogassi, L. (1996). Premotor cortex and the recognition of motor actions. *Brain Research. Cognitive Brain Research*, 3:131–141.

Rolls, E. T., Hornak, J., Wade, D., McGrath, J. (1994). Emotion-related learning in patients with social and emotional changes associated with frontal lobe damage. *Journal of Neurology, Neurosurgery & Psychiatry*, 57:1518–1524.

Rosen, H. J., Allison, S. C., Schauer, G. F., Gorno-Tempini, M. L., Weiner, M. W., Miller, B. L. (2005). Neuroanatomical correlates of behavioural disorders in dementia. *Brain*, 128:2612–2625.

Rosen, H. J., Perry, R. J., Murphy, J., *et al.*, (2002). Emotion comprehension in the temporal variant of frontotemporal dementia. *Brain*, 125:2286–2295.

Rozzi. S., Ferrari, P. F., Bonini, L., Rizzolatti, G., Fogassi, L. (2008). Functional organization of inferior parietal lobule convexity in the macaque monkey: Electrophysiological characterization of motor, sensory and mirror responses and their correlation with cytoarchitectonic areas. *European Journal of Neuroscience*, 28:1569–1588.

Rubenfeld, S. (2005). Relational perspectives regarding countertransference in groups and trauma. *International Journal of Group Psychotherapy*, 55:115–135.

Rubin, S. (1990). Death of the future? An outcome study of bereaved parents in Israel. *Journal of Death and Dying*, 20, 323–339.

Ryn, Z. (2005). Auschwitz survivors: clinical-psychiatric studies. In *Medical Review – Auschwitz*. Kraków: *Przegląd Lekarski* (Medical Review), in cooperation with the Auschwitz-Birkenau State Museum in Oświęcim.

Saakvitne, K. W. (1990). *Psychoanalytic Psychotherapy with Incest Survivors: Transference and countertransference paradigms*. Paper presented at the Annual Convention of the American Psychological Association Boston, MA.

Sagi, A., & Hoffman, M. L. (1976). Empathic distress in the newborn. *Developmental Psychology,* Vol. 12(2), 175–176.

Salehi, B., Cordero, M. I., Sandi, C. (2010). Learning under stress: The inverted-U-shape function revisited. *Learning & Memory*, 17(10):522–530.

Sandler, J. (1976). Countertransference and role-responsiveness. *International Review of Psychoanalysis*, *3*, 43–47.

Sandler, J. (1976). Countertransference and role-responsiveness. *International Review of Psychoanalysis*, *3*, 43–47.

Sapolsky, R. M. (2015). Stress and the brain: Individual variability and the inverted-U. *Nature Neuroscience*, 18(10):1344–1346.

Sato, N,, Tan, L., Tate, K., Okada, M. (2015). Rats demonstrate helping behavior towards a soaked conspecific. *Animal Cognition*, 18(5):1039–1047.

Schacter, D. L., McAndrews, M. P., & Moscovitch, M. (1988). Access to consciousness: Dissociations between implicit and explicit knowledge in neuropsychological syndromes. In L. Weiskrantz (Ed.). *Thought without Language. A Fyssen Foundation symposium* (pp. 242–278). New York, NY: Clarendon Press/Oxford University Press.

Schaefer, J. A., & Moos, R. H. (1998). The context for posttraumatic growth: life crises, individual and social resources, and coping. In R. G. Tedeschi, C. L. Park, & L. G. Calhoun (Eds.). *Posttraumatic Growth: Positive changes in the aftermath of crisis* (pp. 99–125). New Jersey: Lawrence Erlbaum Associates.

Schafer, R. (2003). *Insight and Interpretation*. London: Karnac.

Schilling, T. M., Kolsch, M., Larra, M. F., *et al.* (2013). For whom the bell (curve) tolls: Cortisol rapidly affects memory retrieval by an inverted u-shaped dose-response relationship. *Psychoneuroendocrinology*, 38(9):1565–1572.

Schneiderman, G., & Budziszewska, M. (2012). Sixty-five years after World War II: a family secret. *Psychiatric Times*. http://www. psychiatrictimes.com/ptsd/sixty-five-years-after-world-war-ii-family-secret.

Schore, A. (1994). *Affect Regulation and the Origin of the Self: The neurobiology of emotional development*, Hillside, NJ: L. Erlbaum.

Schulte-Ruther, M., Markowitsch, H. J., Fink, G. R., Piefke, M. (2007). Mirror neuron and theory of mind mechanisms involved in face-to-face interactions: A functional magnetic resonance imaging approach to empathy. *Journal of Cognitive Neuroscience*, 19:1354–1372.

Searles, H. F. (1979). *Countertransference and Related Subjects*. Madison, CT: International Universities Press.

Searles, H. F. (1979). *Countertransference and Related Subjects: Selected papers*. New York, NY: International Universities Press.

Searles, H.F. (1967). The "dedicated physician" in psychotherapy and psychoanalysis. In R. W. Gibson. (Ed.). *Crosscurrents in Psychiatry and Psychoanalysis*. Philadelphia: J. B. Lippincott Company.

Sedlak, V. (2015). The development of the psychoanalyst – the role of the superego. *Bulletin of the British Psychoanalytic Society*, 51:3–14.

Seed, A. M., Clayton, N. S., Emery, N. J. (2007). Postconflict third-party affiliation in rooks, Corvus frugilegus. *Current Biology*, 17(2):152–158.

Segal, H. (1964). Symposium on phantasy–fantazy and other mental processes. *International Journal of Psychoanalysis*, 45, 191–194.

Segal, H. (1981). Countertransference. In *The Work of Hanna Segal*. London: Jason Aronson.

Segal, H. (1986). Countertransference. In H. Segal (Ed.). *The Work of Hanna Segal*. London: Free Association Books & Maresfield Library. 81–87.

Segal, H., Private communication.

Seligman, Z. (2004). Introduction to incest. In Z. Seligman & Z. Solomon (Eds.). *Critical and Clinical Perspectives on Incest*. Tel Aviv: Tel Aviv University & Hakibbutz Hameuchad.

Senju, A., Southgate, V., White, S., Frith, U. (2009). Mindblind eyes: An absence of spontaneous theory of mind in Asperger syndrome. *Science*, 325:883–885.

Seritan, A. L., Gabbard, G. O., Benjamin, L. (2006). War and peace: Psychotherapy with a Holocaust survivor. *American Journal of Psychiatry*, 163: 1705–1709.

Seyfarth, R. M., & Cheney, D. L. (2012). The evolutionary origins of friendship. *Annual Review of Psychology*, Vol. 63, pp. 153–177.

Shamay-Tsoory, S. G., & Abu-Akel, A. (2016). The social salience hypothesis of oxytocin. *Biological Psychiatry*, 79(3):194–202.

Shamay-Tsoory, S. G., Aharon-Peretz, J., Perry, D. (2009). Two systems for empathy: A double dissociation between emotional and cognitive empathy in inferior frontal gyrus versus ventromedial prefrontal lesions. *Brain*, 132:617–627.

Shamay-Tsoory, S. G., Shur, S., Harari, H., Levkovitz, Y. (2007). Neurocognitive basis of impaired empathy in schizophrenia. *Neuropsychology*, 21:431–438.

Shamay-Tsoory, S. G., Tomer, R., Goldsher, D., Berger, B. D., Aharon-Peretz, J. (2004). Impairment in cognitive and affective empathy in patients with brain lesions: Anatomical and cognitive correlates. *Journal of Clinical and Experimental Neuropsychology*, 26:1113–1127.

Shany-Ur, T., Poorzand, P., Grossman, S. N., *et al.*, (2012). Comprehension of insincere communication in neurodegenerative disease: Lies, sarcasm, and theory of mind. *Cortex*, 48:1329–1341.

Shimamura, A. P. (1995). Memory and the prefrontal cortex. In J. Grafman, K. J. Holyoak, & F. Boller (Eds.). *Structure and Functions of the Human Prefrontal Cortex* (pp. 151–159). New York, NY: Annals of the New York Academy of Sciences.

Shoshan, T. (1989). Mourning and longing from generation to generation. *American Journal of Psychotherapy*, 43: 193–207.

Sigusch, V. (1997). Transsexualismus. Forschungsstand und klinische Praxis (Transsexuality. Research update and clinical practice). *Nervenarzt, 68*: 870–877.

Sigusch, V., Meyenburg, B., Reiche, R. (1978). Transsexualität (Transsexuality). *Sexualmedizin*, 7: 15–22, 107–116, 191–192.

Silva, K., Bessa, J., de Sousa L. (2012). Auditory contagious yawning in domestic dogs (Canis familiaris): First evidence for social modulation. *Animal Cognition*, 15:721–724.

Silver, R. L., Boon, C., & Stones, M. H. (1983). Searching for meaning in misfortune: Making sense of incest. *Journal of Social Issues, 39*(2), 81–101.

Simner, M. L. (1971). Newborn's response to the cry of another infant. *Developmental Psychology*, 5:136–150.

Simpson, J.A., & Beckes, L. (2010). Evolutionary perspectives on pro-social behavior. In M. Mikulincer & P. R. Shaver (Eds.). *Pro-social Motives, Emotions, and Behavior: The better angels of our nature*. Washington, DC: American Psychological Association. 35–53.

Singer, T., & Lamm, C. (2009). The social neuroscience of empathy. *Annals of the New York Academy of Sciences*, 1156:81–96.

Singer, T., Seymour, B., O'Doherty, J. P., Stephan, K. E., Dolan, R. J., Frith, C. D. (2006). Empathic neural responses are modulated by the perceived fairness of others. *Nature*, 439:466–469.

Singer, T., Seymour, B., O'Doherty, J., Kaube, H., Dolan, R. J., Frith, C. D. (2004). Empathy for pain involves the affective but not sensory components of pain. *Science*, 303:1157–1162.

Sledge, W. H., Boydstun, J. A., & Rabe, A. J. (1980). Self-concept changes related to war captivity. *Archives of General Psychiatry, 37*, 430–443.

Smith, A. J., Kleijn, W. C., Trijsburg, R. W., Hutschemaekers, G. J. (2007).

How therapists cope with clients' traumatic experiences. *Torture*, 17: 203–15.

Sohlberg, M. M., & Mateer, C. A. (1989). *Introduction to Cognitive Rehabilitation*. New York, NY: Guilford Press.

Sontag, S., (2003). *Regarding the Pain of Others*, New York, NY: Picador/Farrar, Straus and Giroux.

Spezio, M. L., Huang, P. Y., Castelli, F., Adolphs, R. (2007). Amygdala damage impairs eye contact during conversations with real people. *Journal of Neuroscience*, 3994–3997.

Spillius, E. (1992). Clinical experiences of projective identification. In R. Anderson (Ed.), *Clinical Lectures on Klein and Bion* (pp. 59–73). London: Routledge.

Spillius, E., Milton, J., Garvey, P., Couve, C., & Steiner D. (2011). Unconscious phantasy. In *The New Dictionary of Kleinian Thoughts*. London: Routledge.

Squire, L.R., The legacy of Patient HM for neuroscience, *Neuron*, 2009, 61(1) 6–9.

Steiner, J. (2006). Interpretative enactments and analytic setting. *International Journal of Psychoanalysis*, 87, 315–320.

Stern, D. (2004). *The Present Moment in Psychotherapy and Everyday Life*. New York/London: W. W. Norton & Company.

Stern, J.M. (1985). The psychotherapeutic process with brain injured patients: A dynamic approach. *Israel Journal of Psychiatry and Related Sciences*, 22(1–2), 83–87.

Stern, Y. (2002). What is cognitive reserve? Theory and research application of the reserve concept. *Journal of the International Neuropsychological Society, 8*, 448–460.

Stola, D. (2000). *Kampania antysyjonistyczna w Polsce 1967–1968. (Anti-Zionist campaign in Poland 1967–1968)*. Warszwa: ISP PAN.

Stolk, A., D'Imperio, D., di Pellegrino, G., Toni, I. (2015). Altered communicative decisions following ventromedial prefrontal lesions. *Current Biology*, 25:1469–1474.

Stolorow, R. D., Brandchaft, B., & Atwood, G. E. (1983). Intersubjectivity in psychoanalytic treatment: With special reference to archaic states. *Bulletin of the Menninger Clinic*, 47(2), 117.

Stoltenberg, S. F., Christ, C. C., Carlo, G. (2013). Afraid to help: Social anxiety partially mediates the association between 5-HTTLPR triallelic genotype and pro-social behavior. *Society Neuroscience*, 8(5):400–406.

Stone, V. E., Baron-Cohen, S., Knight, R. T. (1998). Frontal lobe contributions to theory of mind. *Journal of Cognitive Neuroscience*, 10:640–656.

Strand, T. (2010). Introduction: Cosmopolitanism in the making. *Studies in Philosophy and Education. 29*, 103–109.

Strand, T. (2010). The making of a new cosmopolitanism. *Studies in Philosophy and Education. 29*, 229–242.

Strathearn, L., Li, J., Fonagy, P., Montague, P. R. (2008). What's in a smile? Maternal brain responses to infant facial cues. *Pediatrics*, 122(1):40–51.

Strum, S. C. (2001). *Almost Human: A journey into the world of baboons*, Chicago, IL: The University of Chicago Press.

Stuss, D. T., & Benson, D. F. (1984). Neuropsychological studies of the frontal lobes. *Psychological Bulletin, 95*, 3–28.

Sullivan, H. S. (1953). *The Interpersonal Theory of Psychiatry.* New York, NY: Norton.

Szecsödy, I. (2007). Sándor Ferenczi – The first intersubjectivist. *The Scandinavian Psychoanalytic Review, 30*(1), 31–41.

Szwajca, K. (2009). *Uwarunkowania Transgeneracyjnego Przekazu Traumy u Potomstwa Osób Ocalałych z Holocaustu. (The Conditionings of Transgenerational Transmission of Trauma in Offspring of Holocaust Survivors).* (Doctoral dissertation, Jagiellonian University Medical College).

Szymusik, A. (1964). Astenia poobozowa u byłych więźniów obozu koncentracyjnego w Oświęcimiu. (Asthenia after the camp among the former concentration camp prisoners in Oświęcim). *Przegląd Lekarski,* 1:23–29.

Tauber, Y. (1998). *In the Other Chair: Holocaust survivors and the second generation as therapists and clients.* Hewlett, NY: Gefen Publishing House.

Tauber, Y. (2003). We're listening, but can we hear? Psychotherapy with Holocaust survivors and the second generation in Israel, under (threat of) conditions of armed conflict. *Journal of Trauma Practice*, 2:17–46.

Tauber, Y., & van der Hal, E. (1998). Countertransference and life-and-death issues in group psychotherapy with child Holocaust survivors. *American Journal of Psychotherapy,* 52: 301–312.

Taylor, S. E. (1989). Positive illusions: Creative self-deception and the healthy mind. New York, NY: Basic Books.

Teasdale, G., & Jennett, B. (1974). Assessment of coma and impaired consciousness. *Lancet, II*, 81–84.

Tedeschi, R. G., & Calhoun, L. G. (1988). *Perceived Benefits in Coping with Physical Handicaps.* Paper presented at the Annual meeting of the American Psychological Association Atlanta, GA.

Tedeschi, R. G., & Calhoun, L. G. (1995). *Trauma and Transformation: Growing in the aftermath of suffering.* Thousand Oaks, CA: Sage Publications.

Tedeschi, R. G., & Calhoun, L. G. (2004). Posttraumatic growth: Conceptual foundations and empirical evidence. *Psychological Inquiry, 15*(1), 1–18.

Tennen, H., Affleck, G., Urrows, S., Higgins, P., & Mendola, R. (1992). Perceiving control, construing benefits, and daily processes in rheumatoid arthritis. *Canadian Journal of Behavioural Science/Revue Canadienne des Sciences du Comportement, 24*(2), 186–203.

Teutsch, A. (1962). Próba analizy procesu przystosowania do warunków obozowych osób osadzonych w czasie II wojny światowej w hitlerowskich obozach koncentracyjnych. Doniesienie wstępne. (An attempt to analyze the process of adapting to the conditions of the camp of prisoners during World War II in Nazi concentration camps. Preliminary report). *Przegląd Lekarski*, 1:90–94.

Thompson, C. (1964). *Interpersonal Psychoanalysis: The selected papers of Clara M. Thompson*. M. Green (Ed.). New York, NY: Basic Books.

Ticho, E. A., & Ticho, G. R. (1972). Freud and the Viennese. *The International Journal of Psycho-analysis*, *53*, 301.

Tulli, M. (2011). *Włoskie Szpilki. (Italian high heels)*. Warszawa: Wydawnictwo Nisza.

Tulving, E. (1985). Memory and consciousness. *Canadian Psychology*, 26:1.

Tulving, E. (2002). Chronesthesia. In D. Stuss & R. T. Knight (Eds.). *Principles of Frontal Lobe Function* (pp. 311–325). New York, NY: Oxford University Press.

Tuszyńska, A. (2005). *Rodzinna Historia Lęku. (Family History of Anxiety)*. Kraków: Wydawnictwo Literackie.

van der Kolk, B. A., Roth, S., Pelcovitz, D., Sunday, S., & Spinazzola, J. (2005). Disorders of extreme stress: the empirical foundation of a complex adaptation to trauma. *Journal of Traumatic Stress, 18*(5), 389–399.

Van Overwalle, F., & Baetens, K. Understanding others' actions and goals by mirror and mentalizing systems: A meta-analysis. *Neuroimage*, 48:564–584.

Veronen, L. J., & Kilpatrick, D. G. (1983). Rape: A precursor of change. In E. J. Callahan & K. A. McCluskey (Eds.). *Life Span Development Psychology: Non-normative events* (pp. 167–191). New York, NY: Academic Press.

Vetlesen, A. J. (1994). Perception, empathy, and judgment: An inquiry into the preconditions of moral performance. State College, PA: Pennsylvania State University Press.

Walinder, J. (1967). *Transsexualism: A study of forty-three cases*. Göteborg: Akademieförlaget.

Walters, D. A. (2009). Transference and countertransference as existential themes in the psychoanalytic theory of W. R. Bion. *Psychodynamic Practice*, *15*(2), 161–172.

Wardi, D. (1999). Therapists' responses in Holocaust survivors and second generation psychotherapy. *Croatian Medical Journal*, 40: 479–485.

Warneken, F., & Tomasello, M. (2006). Altruistic helping in human infants and young chimpanzees. *Science*, 311(5765):1301–1303.

Wascher, C. A., Arnold, W., Kotrschal, K. (2008). Heart rate modulation by social contexts in greylag geese (Anser anser). *Journal of Comparative Psychology*, 122(1):100–107.

Watanabe, S. (2015). Social factors modulate restraint stress induced hyperthermia in mice. *Brain Research*, 1624:134–139.

Weinberg, M. K., & Cummins, R. A. (2013). Intergenerational effects of the Holocaust: Subjective well-being in the offspring of survivors. *Journal of Intergenerational Relationships*, 11(2):148–161.

Werner, K. H., Roberts, N. A., Rosen, H. J., *et al.*, (2007). Emotional reactivity and emotion recognition in frontotemporal lobar degeneration. *Neurology*, 69:148–155.

Wicker, B., Keysers, C., Plailly J, Royet JP, Gallese V, Rizzolatti G. (2003).

Both of us disgusted in My insula: The common neural basis of seeing and feeling disgust. *Neuron*, 40:655–664.

Wilkinson, A., Sebanz, N., Mandl, I., Huber, L. (2011). No evidence of contagious yawning in the red-footed tortoise Geochelone carbonaria. *Current Zoology*, 57:477–484.

Wilkinson, G. S. (1984). Reciprocal food sharing in the vampire bat. *Nature*, 30:181–184.

Williams, J. H., Whiten, A., Singh, T. (2004). A systematic review of action imitation in autistic spectrum disorder. *Journal of Autism and Developmental Disorders*, 34:285–299.

Wilson, J. P., & Lindy, J. D. (1994). Empathic strain and countertransference. In J. P. Wilson & J. D. Lindy (Eds.). *Countertransference in the Treatment of PTSD*. New York, NY: Guilford Press. 5–30.

Winnicott, D. W. (1949). Hate in the countertransference. *International Journal of Psychoanalysis*. 30: 69–74.

Winnicott, D. W. (1965). *The Maturational Process and the Facilitating Environment*. London: Hogarth Press.

Winnicott, D. W. (1969). On the use of an object. *International Journal of Psychoanalysis*, *50*, 711–716.

Winnicott, D. W. (1971). *Playing and Reality*. London: Routledge.

Winnicott, D. W. (2009). *True Self, False Self: Essays, 1935–1963*. E. Berman (Ed.). Tel Aviv: Am Oved.

Witztum, E., Malkinson, R., Rubin, S. (2001). Death, bereavement and traumatic loss in Israel: a historical and cultural perspective. *Israel Journal of Psychiatry and Related Sciences*, 38,157–170.

Xu, X., Zuo, X., Wang, X., Han, S. (2009). Do you feel my pain? Racial group membership modulates empathic neural responses. *Journal of Neuroscience*, 29(26):8525–8529.

Yehuda, R., Bell, A., Bierer, L. M., Schmeidler, J. (2008). Maternal, not paternal, PTSD is related to increased risk for PTSD in offspring of Holocaust survivors. *Journal of Psychiatric Research*, 42(13):1104–1111.

Yehuda, R., Halligan. S. L., Grossman, R. (2001). Childhood trauma and risk for PTSD: Relationship to intergenerational effects of trauma, parental PTSD, and cortisol excretion. *Development and Psychopathology*, 13:733–753.

Yerkes, R.M., and Dodson, J.D. (1908). The relation of strength of stimulus to rapidity of habit-formation. *Journal of Comparative Neurology and Psychology*, Volume 18, Issue 5, pages 459–482, November.

Yoder, K. J., Porges, E. C., Decety, J. (2015). Amygdala subnuclei connectivity in response to violence reveals unique influences of individual differences in psychopathic traits in a nonforensic sample. *Human Brain Mapping*, 36:1417–1428.

Young, R. M. (1994). *Mental Space*. London: Process Press.

Zaki, J., Wager, T. D., Singer, T., Keysers, C., Gazzola, V. (2016). The anatomy of suffering: Understanding the relationship between nociceptive and empathic pain. *Trends in Cognitive Science*, 20:249–259.

Zaki, J., Weber, J., Bolger, N., Ochsner, K. (2009). The neural bases of empathic accuracy. *Proceedings of the National Academy of Sciences* (USA), 106:11382–11387.

Zhang, H., & Perc, M. (2016). Evolution of conditional cooperation under multilevel selection. *Scientific Reports,* 6:23006.

Zheleva, E., & Getoor, L. (2009). To join or not to join: The illusion of privacy in social networks with mixed public and private user profiles. In *Proceedings of the 18th international conference on world wide web* (pp. 531–540). New York, NY: ACM.

Zoellner, T., & Maercker, A. (2006). Posttraumatic growth in clinical psychology – a critical review and introduction of a two component model. *Clinical Psychology Review,* 26(5), 626–653.

Zweig, S. (1946). *Beware of Pity*, Berlin: S. Fischer Verlag. (Original work published in 1939).

Index